Historians have long ignored the military aspect of the Wars of Religion which raged in France during the late sixteenth century, dismissing the conflicts as aimless or hopelessly confused. In contrast, *The king's army* – a meticulously researched analysis of the royal army and its operations during the early civil wars – brings warfare back to the centre of the picture. James B. Wood explains the reasons for the initial failure of the monarchy to defeat the Huguenots, a   amines how that failure prolonged the conflict. He argues that the nature and outcome   civil wars can only be explained by the fusion of religious rebellion and incomplete m   revolution. *The king's army* makes an important contribution to the history of mil   ces, warfare and society, and will be of great interest to those engaged in the debate   "Military Revolution" in early modern Europe.

Mai
Tel:

To be returned on or before the day .

D1425482

CAMBRIDGE STUDIES IN EARLY MODERN HISTORY

The king's army

CAMBRIDGE STUDIES IN EARLY MODERN HISTORY

Edited by Professor Sir John Elliott, University of Oxford
Professor Olwen Hufton, European University Institute, Florence
Professor H. G. Koenigsberger, University of London
Dr H. M. Scott, University of St Andrews

The idea of an "early modern" period of European history from the fifteenth to the late eighteenth century is now widely accepted among historians. The purpose of Cambridge Studies in Early Modern History is to publish monographs and studies which illuminate the character of the period as a whole, and in particular focus attention on a dominant theme within it, the interplay of continuity and change as they are presented by the continuity of medieval ideas, political and social organization, and by the impact of new ideas, new methods and new demands on the traditional structure.

For a list of titles published in the series, please see end of book

The king's army

Warfare, soldiers, and society during the
Wars of Religion in France, 1562–1576

JAMES B. WOOD

Williams College, Massachusetts

 **CAMBRIDGE**
UNIVERSITY PRESS

PUBLISHED BY THE PRESS SYNDICATE OF THE UNIVERSITY OF CAMBRIDGE
The Pitt Building, Trumpington Street, Cambridge, United Kingdom

CAMBRIDGE UNIVERSITY PRESS
The Edinburgh Building, Cambridge CB2 2RU, UK
40 West 20th Street, New York NY 10011–4211, USA
477 Williamstown Road, Port Melbourne, VIC 3207, Australia
Ruiz de Alarcón 13, 28014 Madrid, Spain
Dock House, The Waterfront, Cape Town 8001, South Africa

http://www.cambridge.org

First published 1996
First paperback edition 2002

A catalogue record for this book is available from the British Library

Library of Congress Cataloguing in Publication data
Wood, James B., 1946–
The king's army: warfare, soldiers, and society during the Wars
of Religion in France, 1562–1576 / James B. Wood.
p.   cm. – (Cambridge studies in early modern history)
Includes bibliographical references and index.
ISBN 0 521 55003 3 (hc)
1. France – History – Wars of the Huguenots, 1562–1598.   2. Charles
IX, King of France, 1550–1574 – Military leadership.   3. Henry III,
King of France, 1551–1589 – Military leadership.   4. France. Armée –
History – 16th century.   I. Title.   II. Series.
DC116.5.W66   1996
944'.029–dc20   95-40713   CIP

ISBN 0 521 55003 3 hardback
ISBN 0 521 52513 6 paperback

To Margi and Daniel

Contents

Contents

Figures

List of figures

Preface

This book was long in gestation and marks a complete change in focus from my previous work on the nobility of Bayeux. From the beginning I had three primary goals. The first was to write a social history of warfare during the French civil wars that made comprehensible what always seemed from existing accounts a hopelessly confused mess, a kind of latter-day Lebanon. A second goal was to write on the military affairs and institutions of the time in a way that was accessible not only to the interested early modernist or specialist military historian but to all students of European and French history, and to the general reader as well. This goal carried the special obligation of making understandable a way of warfare which in its technical, social, and cultural aspects is decidedly foreign today, though to those familiar with American military operations in the Vietnam war much of the royal army's wearying and ultimately unsuccessful pursuit of the Huguenot "main force" will have a familiar ring. My third goal was never to lose sight of the human dimensions of the wars.

The reader will of course be the final judge of my success in fulfilling these goals, but even to attempt to implement them required the assistance and encouragement of many people and institutions. First, to the NEH and Williams College for generous provisions of leave-time during which the research for the book took place, and especially for a critical semester sabbatical at the Oakley Center for the Humanities and Social Sciences, an ideal place to work, where the bulk of the writing took place. Thanks also are due to the archives and libraries in France, Great Britain, and the USA, without whose services this book could never have been attempted, and especially to the Williams College Sawyer Library whose purchases and interlibrary loan services have served me as well as any first-rate university library could have.

A number of my colleagues at Williams read drafts or listened to my musings, including Bob Dalzell, Michael Brown, Gordon Winston, and the scholars-in-residence at the Oakley Center during my stay there. I owe a special debt to my friend and colleague Tom Kohut, without whose advice I could never have made it through multiple rewrites of the Introduction and Conclusion. Two people outside Williams also played crucially supportive roles: Professors J. Russell Major of Emory University and Mack Holt of George Mason University.

Thanks also to Georgia Swift, the history department secretary, who was helpful in typing some early stages of the manuscript and to Lois Cooper, who was an indispensable aid in the many translations which crowd the book. Dean of the Faculty John Reichert also provided timely encouragement and advice as well as real financial help through the instrument of the Division II Research Fund. The one person in an official capacity to whom I owe the greatest debt, however, is Frank Oakley, Dean of the Faculty and President of Williams for almost two decades. Frank combined an uplifting vision of the importance of original scholarship in the liberal arts setting with a generous propensity to provide resources and time to those who shared that vision. Scores of Williams faculty can attest to the important role his help and encouragement played in their scholarship. In my case his supportive intervention at a delicate moment in my own career was indispensable to the completion of this book.

Finally, to my wife Margi and my son Daniel I owe the greatest debt of all – for their love, encouragement, and patience as well as many hard-nosed readings of drafts. They now know more about early modern warfare than they ever imagined existed. I owe them so much and to them I dedicate this book.

Abbreviations

Biron, *AHG*	Biron, Armand de Gontaut, baron de. "Correspondence inédite du maréchal Armand de Gontaut-Biron." *Archives historiques du département de la Gironde*, 14 (1873), 1–271.
Biron, *LD*	Biron, Armand de Gontaut, baron de. *The Letters and Documents of Armand de Gontaut, Baron de Biron, Marshal of France (1524–1592)*, eds. Sidney H. E. Ehrman and James W. Thompson (2 vols., Berkeley, 1936).
BN Mss. Fr.	Bibliothèque nationale. *Fonds français.*
Brantôme, *Discours*	*Discours sur les colonels de l'infanterie de France*, ed. Etienne Vaucheret (Paris, 1973).
Brantôme, *Oeuvres*	*Oeuvres complètes de Pierre de Bourdeille, seigneur de Brantôme*, ed. Ludovic Lalanne (11 vols., Paris, 1864–82).
CDM	Medici, Catherine de. *Lettres de Catherine de Médicis*, eds. Hector de la Ferrière-Percy and Gustave Baguenault de Puchesse (11 vols., Paris, 1880–1909).
CSPF/E	*Calendar of State Papers, Foreign Series, of the Reign of Elizabeth. Preserved in the Public Record Office* (23 vols., London, 1901–50).
EDC	Merlet, Lucien, ed. "Etat des dépenses faites par la ville de Chartres, pendant les troubles et pendant le siège de ladite ville (1er Octobre 1567 – 18 Avril 1568)." *Bulletin historique et philologique du comité des travaux historiques et scientifiques* (1840), 394–438.
Gigon	Gigon, S.-C. *La troisième guerre de religion. Jarnac–Moncontour (1568–69)* (Paris, 1909).
Henri III	Henry III. *Lettres de Henri III, roy de France*, ed. Michel François (6 vols., Paris, 1959).
HM	Contamine, Philippe, ed. *Histoire militaire de la France*, vol. 1, *Des origines à 1715* (Paris, 1992).
Monluc, *Commentaires*	Monluc, Blaise de. *Commentaires de Blaise de Monluc, Maréchal de France*, ed. Paul Courteault (3 vols., Paris, 1911).

List of abbreviations

O.M.	*Dépôt de la Guerre (Service Historique de l'Armée de Terre, Château de Vincennes). Ordonnances militaires*, vol. 10 (1558–77).
Paschal, *1562*	Paschal, Pierre de. *Journal de ce qui s'est passé en France durant l'année 1562 principalement dans Paris et à la cour*, ed. Michel François (Paris, 1950).
PRO/SP	Public Record Office. State Papers (Foreign).

Introduction

Le secret des finances de France, published in 1581 under the pseudonym Nicolas Froumenteau, estimated that well over one million people had lost their lives in the religious strife that raged almost continuously in France between 1560 and 1580. Included in this total were some twenty thousand Catholic clergy, thirty thousand nobles, eighty thousand victims of massacres and executions, and hundreds of thousands of common soldiers. The material costs of warfare had also been high: since 1550 war-related taxes alone had exceeded 300 million *livres* while the depredations of armies had cost more than ten times that amount. Over 100,000 individual dwellings and some 600 villages had been destroyed.[1]

Whatever the precise accuracy of these grim figures, Froumenteau's contemporaries could have had few illusions about the tremendous financial, material, and human costs of the wars of religion, costs that were the direct result of their militarily indecisive nature: by 1581 they had been grinding on remorselessly for almost two decades, and no end was in sight. Civil war had become the defining experience for the French people and would remain so until the end of the sixteenth century.[2]

---

[1] For an analysis of Froumenteau's work see James B. Wood, "The Impact of the Wars of Religion: A View of France in 1581," *Sixteenth Century Journal*, 15, no. 2 (1984), 131–68.

[2] The best general history of France during the sixteenth century remains J. H. M. Salmon, *Society in Crisis: France in the Sixteenth Century* (New York, 1975). On the era of the wars of religion James Westfall Thompson, *The Wars of Religion in France, 1559–1576* (New York, 1909), remains useful, though it is very outdated. Among more recent work see Michel Pernot, *Les guerres de religion en France, 1559–1598* (Paris, 1987); Henry Heller, *Iron and Blood: Civil Wars in Sixteenth-Century France* (Montreal, 1991); and Mack Holt, *The French Wars of Religion* (Cambridge, 1995). The most convincing summary of developments during the period of the first five wars is the conclusion to Philip Benedict, *Rouen During the Wars of Religion* (New York, 1981), 233–50. Robert R. Harding, *Anatomy of a Power Elite: The Provincial Governors of Early Modern France* (New Haven, 1978) and Mack Holt, *The Duke of Anjou and the Politique Struggle During the Wars of Religion* (Cambridge, 1986) are also very useful, especially on the transition to the later wars. The most illuminating and convincing studies of religious violence, besides Benedict's work on Rouen, are Natalie Z. Davis, "The Rites of Violence," chapter 6 in her *Society and Culture in Early Modern France: Eight Essays* (Stanford, 1975), 152–187, and Barbara B. Diefendorf, *Beneath the Cross. Catholics and Huguenots in Sixteenth Century Paris* (Oxford, 1991). But see also Denis Crouzet, *Les guerriers de Dieu: La violence au temps des troubles de religion, vers 1525–vers 1610* (Seyssel, 1990), 2 vols. For the socioeconomic impact of the wars during this period see Jean Jacquart, *La crise rurale en Ile-de-France, 1550–1670* (Paris, 1974), and E. Le Roy Ladurie, *Les paysans de Languedoc* (Paris, 1966), 2 vols.

Introduction

During the reign of Charles IX (1560–74) there were five successive general civil wars marked by extensive formal military operations. During those early wars, the last of which continued into the beginning of Henry III's reign, the monarchy always enjoyed substantial advantages in military resources and its army won most of the battles and sieges it fought. But a decisive military victory over the Huguenots eluded the royal forces, preventing the suppression or destruction of their enemy and leading to temporizing and sometimes humiliating peace treaties at the end of every war that compromised royal authority while doing little to prevent the renewal of fighting.[3] This enabled the Huguenots to survive and recover between wars and in some places to strengthen their position, which in turn prolonged the warfare and the suffering, and prevented France from playing a very significant role in international affairs during most of the second half of the sixteenth century.

Given the direct and frequently catastrophic impact of the civil wars in France, it would seem critically important to focus scholarly attention on their course and conduct. Many other aspects of French history during the wars of religion have been extensively studied, but social, political, and religious historians have long been content to ignore the military side of the civil wars. Even among military historians the period remains little understood and largely ignored. For decades there was only the posthumous work of Ferdinand Lot devoted to the royal army during the Hapsburg–Valois wars, which, though not concerned with the events after 1562, at least provided a brief sketch of the royal army near the beginning of the religious wars.[4] Besides Lot, the only significant recent contribution in French to the military history of the wars is a single general chapter by André Corvisier in

---

[3] For the peace treaties see N. M. Sutherland, *The Huguenot Struggle for Recognition* (New Haven, 1980).

[4] Ferdinand Lot, *Recherches sur les effectifs des armées françaises des Guerres d'Italie aux Guerres de Religion, 1494–1562* (Paris, 1962). See also Hélène Michaud, "Les institutions militaires des guerres d'Italie aux guerres de religion," *Revue historique*, 258, no. 1 (1977), 29–43; the very useful article by Philippe Contamine, "Les industries de guerre dans la France de la Renaissance: L'exemple de l'artillerie," *Revue historique*, 172 (1984), 249–80, and David Potter's excellent operational study, "The duc de Guise and the fall of Calais, 1557–1558," *The English Historical Review*, 388 (July, 1983), 481–512. Howell Lloyd, *The Rouen Campaign, 1590–1592. Politics, Warfare, and the Early Modern State* (Oxford, 1973), is an in-depth analysis of an important episode near the end of the sixteenth-century wars. See also Jean de Pablo, "Contribution à l'étude de l'histoire des institutions militaires huguenotes, ii, L'armée huguenote entre 1562 et 1573," *Archiv für Reformationsgeschichte*, 48, no. 2 (1957), 192–216, and the appropriate chapters in the old, but still stimulating, Sir Charles Oman, *A History of the Art of War in the Sixteenth Century*, reprint of 1937 ed. (New York, 1979). John A. Lynn's "Tactical Evolution in the French Army, 1560–1660," *French Historical Studies*, 14 (1985), 176–91, while an interesting attempt at an overview, is based too narrowly on secondary sources. James B. Wood, "The Royal Army During the Early Wars of Religion, 1559–1576," in Mack P. Holt, ed., *Society and Institutions in Early Modern France. Essays presented to J. Russell Major* (Athens, 1991), 1–35, represents my initial attempt to identify the most important military problems confronted by the royal army during the civil wars. I thank the University of Georgia Press for permission to use material that first appeared in chapter 1 of this publication.

2

the first volume of the projected four-volume *Histoire militaire de la France*.[5] This lack of work by French scholars has recently been somewhat offset by David Potter's study of warfare and the organization of French military power in Picardy between 1470 and 1560. But though Potter's work greatly expands our knowledge of the impact of the Hapsburg–Valois wars on the most militarily exposed province in France, it, like Lot's study, ends before the beginning of the wars of religion.[6]

It is surprising, then, how little historical attention has been devoted to the period's military events and the people involved in them – surprising and distressing. For how profound can our understanding of the period of the wars of religion be if we know so little about how its wars were fought and why their course was so indecisive, prolonged, and destructive? This study of the royal army is intended to put warfare back at the center of the French wars of religion. It explores in detail a form of warfare that in its technical, social, and cultural aspects can seem quite foreign today, and it contextualizes that warfare in a way that connects it to and sheds light on the social and political history of the period. In direct contrast to traditional portrayals of the military aspects of the civil wars as hopelessly confused, aimless, and meaningless, the book seeks to make the overall conduct and outcome of the warfare of the period understandable without at all losing sight of the wars' human dimensions. In particular it brings into sharp focus the reasons for the failure of the monarchy to deal a knock-out blow to the Huguenots in the critical opening phases of the civil war and traces how that failure led to the prolongation of the conflict for over three decades.

As the only comprehensive account of the organization and operations of the forces under royal control during the French civil wars, the book bridges the gap between comparable studies dealing with the periods before and after the wars of religion.[7] It therefore completes a survey, decades in the making, of the history of the relationship between military forces, warfare, society, and the state in France from late medieval times to the death of Louis XIV. Thus it should make a timely contribution to the ongoing debate about the origin and nature of the so-called Military Revolution, the transformation of feudal hosts into the standing armies and navies, and the bureaucracies that supported them, which enabled early modern European states to consolidate power, fight one another on an unparalleled scale, and dominate much of the rest of the world.[8]

Since a study of this kind involves a combination of military, political, social, economic, and cultural history, I have cast a much wider net for evidence than traditional military historians usually do. Thus it makes systematic use of long

---

[5] André Corvisier, "Les guerres de religion, 1559–1598," chapter XIII, in *HM*, 304–30.

[6] David Potter, *War and Government in the French Provinces. Picardy, 1470–1560* (Cambridge, 1993).

[7] Principally Potter, *Picardy*; Philippe Contamine, *Guerre, état et société à la fin du moyen âge. Études sur les armées des rois de France, 1337–1494* (Paris, 1972), and André Corvisier, *L'armée française de la fin du XVIIe siècle au ministère de Choiseul: Le soldat* (Paris, 1964), 2 vols. *HM* is also generally good for the earlier and later periods.

[8] Geoffrey Parker, *The Army of Flanders and the Spanish Road, 1567–1659* (Cambridge, 1972) and *The*

3

neglected materials in French archives, including: war plans; headquarter log-books; military correspondence; tables of organization; muster, ration, and pay records; casualty lists; state budgets; arsenal inventories; technical memoranda; disciplinary codes; and illustrations of soldiers and armies in action. As a result it rests on a comprehensive and extensive documentary – rather than simply a memorialistic – base.

In terms of organization, the book begins with a narrative of the principal military campaigns of the crown during the first five civil wars. It then examines the prewar and peacetime armies as well as the forces mobilized by the crown during the civil war period itself. Analyses of the three principal and distinctive military and social components of the royal army – the infantry, cavalry, and artillery – and the effects on them of chronic campaigning in an unprecedented civil war situation follow. Four detailed case studies of the royal army on campaign and in action – the battle of Dreux in 1562, the defense of Chartres in 1567–68, the Jarnac–Moncontour campaign in 1568–69, and the siege of La Rochelle in 1573 – illustrate the actual conduct of operations, illuminate the human dimensions of camp, march, and combat, and identify the principal determinants of military success or failure. The last chapter investigates the cost of mounting military campaigns and the reasons for the crown's increasing inability to pay for them. The book concludes with an assessment of the limits imposed on the crown's ability to act by the fragility of its instrument of war and the consequences this had for society and government during the remainder of the civil war years. A discussion of the sources used in writing this account will be found in the Appendix.

My principal argument is that the ultimate failure of the royal army to achieve a decisive victory over the Huguenots grew out of a deep and intractable set of military problems which from 1562 on manifested themselves as a repeating cycle of military insufficiency. As we shall see, this cycle provided the civil wars with a perverse kind of continuity and made it virtually impossible for the crown to achieve clear and decisive military outcomes. The obstacles to victory were further compounded after 1567 when the army's major operations had to shift south of the Loire river, into increasingly difficult country, far from the monarchy's most secure political and resource base, and against ever more effectively fortified, inaccessible, and fanatically defended places. By 1576 the chronic and unrelenting warfare (the army was in the field in nine of the ten years between 1567 and 1576) had exhausted the army, debased its behavior, and produced a

Military Revolution. Military Innovation and the Rise of the West, 1500–1800; William H. McNeill, *The Pursuit of Power. Technology, Armed Force, and Society, since A.D. 1000* (Chicago, 1982); J. R. Hale, *War and Society in Renaissance Europe, 1450–1620* (New York, 1985). John F. Guilmartin, *Gunpowder and Galleys: Changing Technology and Mediterranean Warfare at Sea in the Sixteenth Century* (New York, 1974); Simon Pepper and Nicholas Adams, *Firearms and Fortifications. Military Architecture and Siege Warfare in Sixteenth Century Siena* (Chicago, 1986). See also Fred Anderson, *A People's Army. Massachusetts Soldiers and Society in the Seven Years' War* (New York, 1985); John Keegan, *The Face of Battle* (New York, 1976); Christopher R. Friedrichs, *Urban Society in an Age of*

profound and quasi-permanent failure of royal finances that essentially paralyzed the crown's ability to exert effective military force against its disobedient subjects.

The nature and ultimate outcome of the civil wars in France, then, were determined not by their religious origins but by the combination of religious rebellion and an incomplete Military Revolution. Fully mobilized, the royal army was a formidable instrument of war. But the material and technical means of waging war had yet to be totally monopolized by the state, and the integration of firearms and artillery with more effective fortifications made sieges of even poorly defended towns and cities a formidable and time-consuming task. Moreover the financial and administrative apparatus of the French state was not yet capable of sustaining the expanded forces needed to fight extensive campaigns over long periods of time, and the peacetime army was too small and dispersed to overawe the opposition or prevent the outbreak or renewal of civil war. What presented problems for the state, however, offered opportunity for the Protestant minority in France, since all that was needed to exploit these vulnerabilities was a cause capable of mobilizing widespread support.

When religion fused with rebellion, the Huguenots were able with their own resources or the aid of foreign powers to sustain military resistance long enough to exhaust both the royal army and the royal treasury. Easy to begin, the civil wars were too difficult and expensive to fight to any clear conclusion. The result was military stalemate; it was also widespread devastation and misery, and postponement to the seventeenth century of any serious attempt by the French monarchy to solve the problems that the still incomplete Military Revolution posed for all governments of the time.

War: Nördlingen, 1580–1720 (Princeton, 1979); Myron P. Gutmann, *War and Rural Life in the Early Modern Low Countries* (Princeton, 1980); and J. R. Hale, *Artists and Warfare in Renaissance Europe* (New Haven, 1990). And though it by no means exhausts the literature on these subjects the interested reader can also consult with profit: Fernand Braudel, *The Mediterranean and the Mediterranean World in the Age of Philip II*, trans. Sian Reynolds (New York, 1972), 2 vols.; André Corvisier, *Armies and Societies in Europe, 1494–1789*, trans. Abigail T. Siddall (Bloomington, 1979); M. E. Mallet and J. R. Hale, *The Military Organization of a Renaissance State: Venice, c. 1400 to 1617* (New Haven, 1984); John A. Lynn, ed., *Tools of War. Instruments, Ideas, and Institutions of Warfare, 1445–1871* (Urbana, 1990), "The *trace italienne* and the Growth of Armies: The French Case," *The Journal of Military History*, 55, no. 3 (1991), 297–330, and "How War Fed War: The Tax of Violence and Contributions During the *Grand Siècle*," *The Journal of Modern History*, 65 (June, 1993), 286–310, as well as *Feeding Wars. Logistics in Western Warfare from the Middle Ages to the Present* (Boulder, 1993); Clifford J. Rogers, *The Military Revolution. Readings on the Military Transformation of Early Modern Europe* (Boulder, 1995); Brian M. Downing, *The Military Revolution and Political Change. Origins of Democracy and Autocracy in Early Modern Europe* (Princeton, 1992); Russell F. Weigley, *The Age of Battles. The Quest for Decisive Warfare from Breitenfeld to Waterloo* (Bloomington, 1991); Richard Bonney, *The European Dynastic States, 1494–1660* (New York, 1991); Jeremy Black, *European Warfare 1660–1815* (New Haven, 1994); David Kaiser, *Politics and War. European Conflict from Philip II to Hitler* (Harvard, 1990); Paul Kennedy, *The Rise and Fall of the Great Powers. Economic Change and Military Conflict from 1500 to 2000* (New York, 1987); and John Keegan, *A History of Warfare* (New York, 1993).

The campaigns of the army, 1562–76

THE DIMENSIONS OF CIVIL WAR

At first glance, the convulsions of violence that move across France during the Wars of Religion seem to deny the historian's compulsive need to impose patterns of order and meaning. Notwithstanding the title usually given to this period, much of its religious and civil conflict did not take the form of wars waged between conventionally operating military forces, nor were the wars fought exclusively over religious issues. The popular violence associated with persecution, repression, and massacres often did not wait for official declarations of war nor necessarily depend upon the presence or absence of formally organized armies. Even that most spectacular outbreak of violence, the 1572 Saint-Bartholomew's Day massacre, owed almost nothing to the formal military apparatus of the crown beyond the involvement of the king's French and Swiss guards in the killing in Paris.

This said, however, the fact remains that during these years of religious conflict formal warfare did come to dominate, both directly and indirectly, much of French life. During Charles IX's reign alone there were five openly declared periods of civil war in which the royal army fought a series of conventional military campaigns against the Huguenots. During those years much of the crown's attention and most of its resources were devoted to waging war. On the military outcome of the campaigns of the royal army hinged most of its hopes for eliminating or at least containing religious and political rebellion.

The timeline presented in Figure 1 illustrates the chronological extent of the open and declared wars begun during Charles IX's reign. From the beginning of the first war in March, 1562, to the end of the fifth war in May, 1576, there was civil war in 85 out of a possible 171 months, or half the time. During that same period there were only two intervals of peace which lasted longer than six months: the slightly more than four years between the first and second wars and two years between the third and fourth wars. These two peaceful intervals separated three outbursts of warfare: the first civil war, in 1562–63, the second and third wars, from 1567 to 1570, and the fourth and fifth wars, from 1572 to 1576.[1]

---

[1] Inclusive dates for the first five wars are: first, March 1562–March 1563; second, September 1567–March 1568; third, August 1568–August 1570; fourth, August 1572–June 1573; and fifth, February 1574–May 1576. These represent "official" months of war, i.e., from the public outbreak of hostilities and the call to arms to the proclamation of the peace treaties. Even if formal hostilities took

The actions of the royal army during each of these outbursts of warfare had some distinctive features and consequences. In the first war, in 1562–63, the army had to adapt itself, like most of French society, to the concept and actuality of fighting an intensely contested civil war, a task for which it was, in some respects, ill-suited. Nevertheless, the main army actually adapted itself quite well to the task of neutralizing the main Huguenot field army and to recapturing the major cities of north central France, around Paris, and along the Seine and Loire valleys. In the second and third wars, from 1567 to 1570, the principal objective of the army was the pursuit and defeat of the main Huguenot forces and their German mercenary allies. At the battle of Moncontour, in 1569, this objective was finally, in fact, almost entirely realized. But the crown's ability to follow up its near destruction of the enemy army foundered under the tremendous financial strain of maintaining its forces in the field and a decision to revert to a policy of recapturing places, which gave the Huguenots time to recover from their disaster. In the fourth war, in 1572–73, having eliminated much of the Protestant nobility in the Saint-Bartholomew's Day massacre, the crown had a genuine opportunity to deal French Protestantism a mortal blow by eliminating its major base at La Rochelle. But despite a long, bitter, exhausting, and ultimately dispiriting siege, the army failed to reduce the town. Another series of debilitating sieges of Protestant-held towns was pursued by the weakened royal army during the fifth war, 1574–76. To the continued erosion of the monarchy's military resources caused by those operations was then added the political defection of important nobles like Marshal Damville and King Henry III's younger brother, Alençon. By 1576 the crown's authority and military power had so disintegrated that peace was virtually dictated to it by a Huguenot-led German mercenary army camped unopposed in the center of the kingdom.[2]

Clearly, by the mid-1570s civil war was becoming a chronic rather than a merely episodic factor in French life. From Charles' accession in December, 1560, to the beginning of the second war in September, 1567, for example, there were only 13 months of civil war, covering about 14 percent of roughly the first half of his reign. By contrast, 48 out of the next 81 months (from the beginning of the second war to Charles' death in May, 1574) were war months, or 60 percent of the second half of his reign. And from the beginning of the second war to the end of the fifth war in May, 1576, 72 out of a possible 105 months, or 69 percent, were months of war. The increased prevalence of war reflected significant changes in the nature of the armed

up only part of a month, Figure 1 identifies it as a war month. This inflates slightly the number of months shown devoted to war in Figure 1, but it is more than counterbalanced by the fact that at the national level demobilizations tended to drag on for weeks or even months beyond the formal end of hostilities and that in some areas, especially after 1573, hostilities continued virtually unabated even between wars.

[2] For a general discussion of the principal sources from which a narrative of the wars can be constructed, see Appendix, Part A, and then the initial note for each individual war in the following narrative sections.

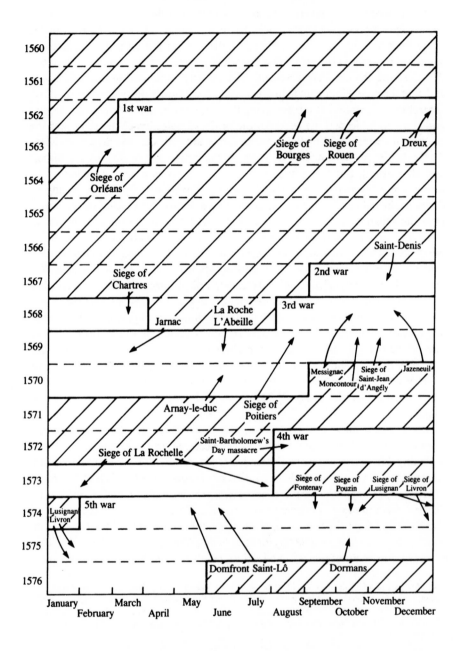

Fig. 1. Timeline of the early wars, 1560–76

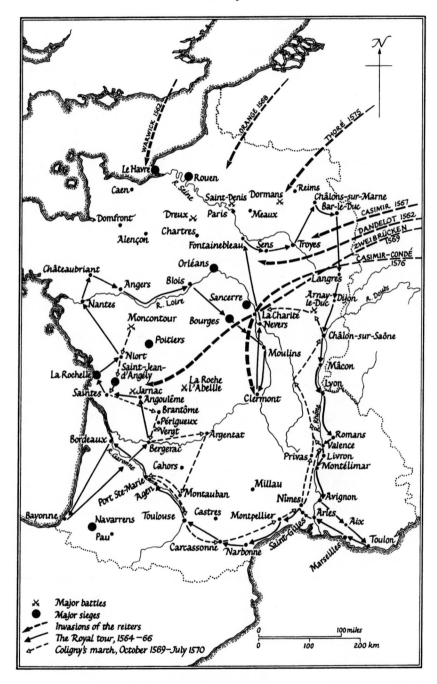

Fig. 2. France during the early wars of religion, 1562–76 (after J. H. M. Salmon, *Society in Crisis*, N.Y., 1975). © J. H. M. Salmon; reproduced with permission of St Martin's Press, Incorporated)

struggle faced by the royal army due to the cumulative impact of the military outcomes and peace settlements of the early wars. By 1576 the religious division of the kingdom had hardened along broadly geographical and militarily irreducible fault lines, and military operations had ceased to hold their earlier promise of decisive or significant results.

Historians have often characterized the period from the outbreak of the civil wars in 1562 to the Saint-Bartholomew's Day massacre in 1572 as the "golden age of religious riot," a period of religious disturbance and struggle fought out within bitterly divided individual communities. In the aftermath of Saint-Bartholomew's Day these struggles had essentially resolved themselves at the local level all over France in favor of one confessional group or another. In areas controlled by the Catholics the Protestant presence had been eliminated or reduced to insignificance. In those places where the Huguenots had seized control and managed to maintain it in the face of all attempts to dislodge them, an opposite evolution took place and religious domination became institutionalized at the expense of local Catholics. As a result of this mutual consolidation of territorial and religio-political control, there were after the mid-1570s fewer opportunities for popular confessional strife to develop. The civil wars seem from then on to have been fought at the local level without the religious passion of earlier years, and at the national level to have become primarily a product of the intrigues of the greater nobility, Catholic and Protestant alike. Even the Catholic League uprisings of 1588–89, which reintroduced an element of religious passion at the local and provincial level, took on less the aspect of a crusade against Protestantism than of a struggle between ultra-Catholic France and the crown for control of the royal succession.[3]

In attempting to understand French life and history during the civil wars the role played by the royal army has often been overlooked. Yet its military operations during the first five wars constituted a reasonably coherent and distinctive whole which mirrored remarkably well at the national level the process and historical outcome of the popular religious struggle at the local level. The main role of the royal army during this period, as we will see, was first to contain the Protestant revolt and then to eliminate it by destroying its armies and recapturing those places and areas it had seized. The army several times came close to defeating the Huguenots militarily and in the process succeeded in providing Catholic France with the opportunity to defend itself and to launch the counterattack which rolled back the Huguenots from many of their early successes. But over time the cost of this massive military effort exhausted the crown's resources and the religious partition which had developed at the level of individual communities during those years also hardened into a regional and national military partition of the country which the technology and organization of the increasingly ill-supported royal army was simply not adequate to overcome.

[3] Benedict, *Rouen*, 233–50.

To understand the military reasons for this outcome, we need to subject the royal army to the kind of detailed institutional, operational, and social analysis which can illuminate its actions and limitations as the direct product of a distinctive kind of military and human organization. As we will see, the operations of the royal army exhibited both impressive continuities and some clear general developments which are sometimes obscured by the daunting confusion and complexities of the period. The rest of this chapter is therefore designed to provide for the reader a unified and integrated overview of the army's role in the complicated events of the first five civil wars, as well as a coherent account of the changing contexts of the crown's main military efforts over their course.[4]

THE DEFENSE OF THE REALM, 1562–63

Though the coming of civil war to France in 1562 was not surprising, the fact of war did catch most contemporaries unprepared. Confessional confrontation and violence had been increasing since Henry II's untimely accidental death in 1559, and the government's attempt to relieve the situation by granting limited religious tolerance in the January, 1562, Edict of Saint-Germain served more to encourage Protestant aggressiveness and to outrage Catholics than to soothe religious passions. Long before the beginning of open warfare in late March and April of 1562, local conflicts in many areas had turned into armed confrontations. But the actual situation over which general war broke out was the struggle at the heart of royal government to control the young king and his mother, Catherine de Medici. In an atmosphere of mutual suspicions, Condé's failure to prevent the crown's principal military commanders, the duke of Guise, Constable Montmorency, Marshal Saint-André, and the lieutenant general of the realm, Antoine, king of Navarre, from conducting the royal family back to Paris led, at the beginning of April, to the Huguenot seizure of Orléans and the raising of the standard of religious revolt.[5]

Proclamations and appeals for assistance poured out of both Paris and Orléans as both sides engaged in a war of words while beginning to assemble their forces. Reports poured into Paris of widespread revolt around the country as scores of the principal towns and cities of France, including Rouen, Lyon, Bourges, Poitiers, and

---

[4] Though there are some useful older histories of individual episodes and wars, there is no integrated and coherent narrative of the military operations of the royal army during the reign of Charles IX and the first years of Henry III's rule (to the end of the fifth civil war). A list of the main printed primary and secondary sources upon which the general narrative developed in this chapter rests can be found in the Appendix, Part A. Sources, both printed and original, which were particularly useful in the construction of the narrative of individual wars are cited in Appendix, Part B, under the subheading for each war. Part C of the Appendix details at some length, under the subheadings for the individual wars, the sources used to reconstruct the composition and strength of the army.

[5] Though it was an object of intense interest and prolific writing by contemporaries, the first civil war left relatively few traces in the central administrative archives. Most of the surviving documents on the army's operations during the first war are to be found in BN Mss. Fr. 15,876 and 15,877. Other important sources are listed in Parts B and C of the Appendix.

Tours, fell to the Protestants or, like Toulouse, became the site of intense street fighting. There were defections to the enemy camp of veteran soldiers and captains, including a significant number of nobles from the heavy cavalry companies. The situation was further confused by a clever claim made by the rebels that they were acting in the name and with the approval of the king, whom they declared to be a prisoner of the actual legitimate authorities. While the queen mother attempted to negotiate, the Catholic leadership used traditional mobilization routines to build up an army at Paris. In June, 1562, with its leaders secure in the knowledge that they enjoyed superior numbers in infantry and artillery and that Swiss and German reinforcements were on their way, the royal army, numbering about 16,000 men, began its advance on the Huguenot army's stronghold at Orléans.[6]

The strategic problem faced by the army's leadership was, at bottom, one of determining the most efficient use of the forces they had or could expect to collect. From the beginning, local commanders in the more distant provinces, such as Monluc in Guyenne or Tavannes in Burgundy and the Lyonnais, were given authorization to raise sizeable forces, but they were left to their own devices in terms of resources. Only one large field army could be supported from central resources, and the question was whether to strike directly at Orléans or to break up into columns in order to restore order in the provinces surrounding Paris. In the event, the royal army adopted an effective double strategy: a direct advance on Orléans in June and July threatened to pin the main Huguenot army there, allowing provincial Catholic commanders to begin the reconquest of local places. The Huguenot leaders, who had missed an opportunity to surprise the royal army at Talcy, in early July, and whose large cavalry forces would have only been a hindrance in defending Orléans in a siege, decided to disperse much of their army. Freed from the need to cover Paris, the royal army, having recaptured Blois and established its main camp there, sent out flying columns under Saint-André and the duke of Montpensier to liberate the cities of the Loire and Poitou while another force under the duke of Aumale engaged in an attempt to retake Rouen and clear the Seine.

From Blois, strengthened by sizeable German and Swiss contingents, and accompanied by the young king, the royal army advanced in mid-August to Bourges, which rendered by composition after a short siege. Having cut Orléans off from help to the south and the west, the decision was then taken by the royal council to bypass the Huguenot headquarters in Orléans and to march directly on Rouen, the second richest city in the kingdom. Sizeable blocking forces were left around Orléans and the rest of the army arrived before Rouen in late September, quickly beginning formal siege operations against the city. The correctness of the decision to bypass Orléans was reinforced by news early in October that the Huguenots had betrayed Le Havre to a sizeable force of English soldiers. The taking of Rouen,

---

[6] This statement and all those which follow in this chapter about the size and composition of the royal army at different times during the civil wars are derived from, in chapter 2, Table 2.9 and note 50, and, in chapter 3, Figure 10, Table 3.1 and note 3.

however, was delayed by the queen mother, who, hopeful of a negotiated settlement, tried in vain to persuade the defenders to compose. After a number of assaults, royal troops penetrated into the city on October 26, where, despite promises of double pay and the best efforts of the leadership to restore discipline, they indulged in uncontrolled looting of the city for several days.

The Rouen campaign had been complicated by several developments. First, the lieutenant general, Navarre, had been mortally wounded while visiting the trenches, setting in train a process of elimination of the top leadership of the army that would lead finally to the complete ascendancy of the duke of Guise in military matters. Second, to the consternation of the leadership, the Huguenots had managed to procure a sizeable force of German mercenaries which began to enter France in late October. The screening forces around Orléans and much of the army's cavalry were diverted eastward of Paris under the command of Saint-André in an unsuccessful attempt to block the Germans who, guided by Andelot, arrived near Orléans at the beginning of November. The arrival of the Germans changed the face of the campaign. The Huguenots, led by Condé and Coligny, and also rejoined by some of the forces they had earlier dispatched to their home provinces, now struck for Paris at the head of an army of about 20,000 men. Only an ill-advised attack on the town of Corbeil delayed the Huguenots long enough to allow the constable and Guise with the leading elements of the Rouen army, as well as Saint-André's force, to throw themselves in mid-November into the previously prepared defenses of the capital's suburbs.

The stress and strain of the campaign, now some seven months old, had begun to weaken the royal army. Finding funds to pay the troops was a serious problem, and there had been substantial infantry casualties and attrition. Many soldiers, moreover, had disbanded with their booty after the sack of Rouen and much of the cavalry had to be furloughed to prevent its desertion. But since mid-October the royal council had been calling on the western and southwestern provinces to send reinforcements, and by early December, in addition to an additional draft of Swiss troops, contingents from Brittany and the southwest, including a sizeable band of Spanish infantry sent by Philip II, had arrived at Paris.

The Huguenot army, having lost its race to Paris, mounted some probing attacks of the defenses and harassed the villages around the suburbs. But realizing its impotence in the face of that vast city and aware of the danger of attack from the rapidly increasing royal forces, it began a forced march in the direction of Chartres on the way to Normandy, where it expected to link up with English forces from Le Havre and to pay the Germans from funds provided by Queen Elizabeth of England. Hoping to prevent this juncture, the royal army, now stronger than the Huguenots in total numbers though inferior in cavalry, marched in pursuit from Paris on December 11.

To this point in the campaign there had been little contact between the main Huguenot and royal armies. Blois, Bourges, and Rouen had been defended by

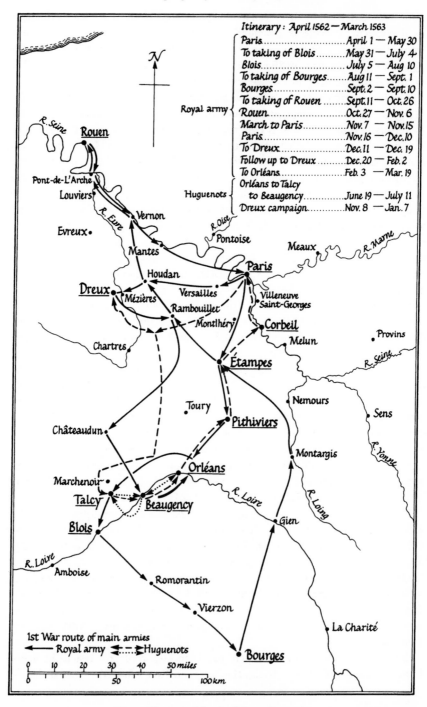

Itinerary : April 1562 — March 1563

Royal army
Paris . . . . April 1 — May 30
To taking of Blois . . . . May 31 — July 4
Blois . . . . July 5 — Aug 10
To taking of Bourges . . . . . . Aug 11 — Sept. 1
Bourges . . . . Sept. 2 — Sept. 10
To taking of Rouen . . . . Sept. 11 — Oct. 26
Rouen . . . . Oct. 27 — Nov. 6
March to Paris . . . . Nov. 7 — Nov. 15
Paris . . . . Nov. 16 — Dec. 10
To Dreux . . . . Dec. 11 — Dec. 19
Follow up to Dreux . . . . . . Dec. 20 — Feb. 2
To Orléans . . . . Feb. 3 — Mar. 19

Huguenots
Orléans to Talcy
to Beaugency . . . . June 19 — July 11
Dreux campaign . . . . Nov. 8 — Jan. 7

1st War route of main armies
◄——— Royal army ◄·—·—·► Huguenots

0 10 20 30 40 50 miles
0   50   100 km

Fig. 3. First war. March of the main armies

detachments of infantry, and, in the last case, townspeople and a few English troops. Neither the nobility who made up the bulk of the heavy cavalry forces nor the major infantry formations on both sides had yet faced one another. The Catholic leadership was reluctant to risk a pitched battle before receiving explicit authorization from the king's council, which came on the march in the form of deferring responsibility for any decision to give battle to the military commanders on the spot. Armed with this ambiguous authority, and by dint of a night march and river crossing, the constable and Guise on the morning of December 19 drew up the army in battle formation on an open plain just south of the town of Dreux from which they could easily threaten the right flank of the Huguenot army as it marched along. Alerted to this danger, Condé and Coligny also deployed in battle formation and fighting began. Five hours later, as night fell, the first major battle between the main field armies during the civil wars was over. Perhaps as many as 8,000 dead and wounded littered the ground. The Catholic army held the field, had won many battle flags, and captured most of the Huguenots' small artillery train, all conventional signs of victory. Most of the Huguenot infantry had been destroyed or captured, but their cavalry, though much harassed, managed to withdraw safely and begin a retreat to Orléans. The royal army, though victorious, was quite beaten up. Much of its cavalry, including a number of prominent noble captains, had been killed or wounded and there were heavy casualties among the Swiss infantry whose heroic holding of ground against repeated attacks had greatly contributed to the victory. Just as importantly, the old constable, nominal leader of the army, had been captured, and Marshal Saint-André killed, leaving the duke of Guise, who had decided the day with a charge of reserve forces under his command, in undisputed control of the royal forces.[7]

In the aftermath of the battle, Guise, who understood the importance of quick exploitation of the victory, moved to reconstitute his battered forces for a march on Orléans, just about the only important place in northern France (besides Le Havre) still held for the Huguenots. New captains were appointed and fresh companies of heavy cavalry ordered raised. But the greatest effort by the newly appointed lieutenant general was directed at raising money for pay, which was seriously in arrears, and beginning to lead to disorders. In early February, 1563, the army, absent its heavy siege train, delayed by terrible weather, advanced against Orléans. Operations proceeded swiftly under Guise's energetic direction, and the city would have surely fallen, if the duke himself had not died early in March from the wounds of an assassination attempt. The loss of this great soldier, last of the original top leadership, thoroughly dispirited the army. But Catherine, who had long chafed under the yoke of the great noblemen who dominated army leadership and the royal council, and who had feared Guise's growing influence as generalissimo, took the opportunity to

---

[7] The Dreux campaign, battle, and aftermath are analyzed in depth in chapter 7. Also see chapter 5 for a discussion of the political and military importance of the casualties inflicted on the royal army's heavy cavalry at the battle.

swiftly conclude a negotiated peace, the Edict of Amboise, with the captive prince of Condé on March 19, 1563, a peace granting limited religious toleration on terms favorable to the Protestant nobility. The queen then worked energetically to pay off many of the foreign mercenaries, who were hurried across the frontiers, and to direct French energies against the English at Le Havre. After a short siege its disease ravaged garrison surrendered on July 28, 1563. Demobilization then proceeded in earnest while the court turned to the difficult task of restoring peace and enforcing the Edict of Amboise throughout the kingdom.

The first civil war had proven the royal army to be a powerful military instrument to use against the Huguenots. In an active campaign lasting about nine months, the army had successfully conducted three formal sieges, defended Paris, and crippled the Huguenot army at the bloody pitched battle of Dreux. The main armed Huguenot threat had first been contained and then practically eliminated from the northern half of the country. Yet despite this happy military outcome, a compromise peace had to be concluded and the war had also revealed a number of potential problems associated with the deployment and use of the army.

First of all, there was a limit to how large an area the main army could operate in and how many of the multiple missions posed by civil war – the defense of Paris, general garrisoning and defense of the frontiers, besieging, fighting pitched battles, and intercepting enemy forces entering the country from abroad – it could reasonably be expected to accomplish. To organize a fully equipped army for the field was also a very slow process. The Valois army in peacetime was oriented towards garrisoning the frontier and when mobilized for war was heavily dependent upon foreign contingents. Once the army was mobilized, to maintain it in the field was a tremendously expensive undertaking, both in human and monetary terms. Weaknesses in the financial apparatus of the state, in particular, had made the campaign a desperate race against time. Clearly, in this first test of arms with the Huguenots, the monarchy and Catholic France owed their survival to the actions of the royal army. But despite its successes, the royal army, slow to organize, fantastically expensive, limited in its operations, even politically threatening, given the crown's fear and distrust of the great subjects who commanded it, had proven to be a somewhat problematic instrument of policy.[8]

CHASING THE HUGUENOTS, 1567–70

Four years after the end of the first civil war, despite the best efforts of the queen mother, the rival confessional groups remained unreconciled. There were frequent disturbances and murders and on both sides of the religious divide many simply waited for an opportunity to avenge real or imagined wrongs. Added to popular unrest were the maneuvering and rivalries of the great noble houses, heightened by

[8] For the mobilization of the army see chapter 2, and for its organization and composition in the field, chapter 3.

passions raised during the first war, especially the enmity of the Guise clan for Coligny, whom they held responsible for the 1563 assassination of the duke of Guise. Into this tense situation came news in 1566–67 of the revolt of the Low Countries and of Philip II's plans to send the duke of Alva with a large army to Flanders by way of the Spanish Road. Huguenot leaders urged that forces be raised to flank Alva's march. But once Alva had passed without incident, and the crown showed little inclination to dismiss the newly raised forces, including 6,000 Swiss, the suspicious Huguenots concluded that those forces were going to be turned against them. Secretly mobilizing hundreds of cavalry, they attempted to seize the king in a surprise attack on the virtually unarmed royal court at Meaux, northeast of Paris, in late September, 1567. Only the fortuitous intervention of the Swiss troops, who happened to be encamped at nearby Château-Thierry, enabled the king to escape under escort to Paris.

The Protestants, foiled in their main design, but strengthened by some late-arriving forces, began a blockade of the major approaches to Paris, hoping both to punish the most rabid anti-Huguenot inhabitants in the kingdom as well as to force the government to redress their grievances on favorable terms. The attempt to kidnap the king, however, had backfired badly. Royal summons for help promptly went out and within six weeks the crown had collected a force of some 25,000 men, including the Swiss and a large but militarily dubious Parisian militia. It was this army that Constable Montmorency, under intense pressure from the Parisians, who were beginning to suffer the effects of the blockade, led to battle against the Protestants (who were outnumbered seven to one) outside the gates of Saint-Denis on November 10, 1567.[9]

The short but sharp battle of Saint-Denis, nominally a Catholic victory, had two major consequences. The first was to decide the Huguenots, increasingly outnumbered around Paris, to begin a long retreat towards the eastern frontier where they hoped to link up with a large force of German mercenaries they had hired. The second consequence was an important change in leadership for the royal army. The elderly constable, in overall command of crown forces, had been mortally wounded by an assassin while temporarily captured during the battle, and this permanently removed the last member of the Catholic military leadership who had led the army into the first civil war. Catherine de Medici, unwilling to favor a candidate for overall military command she could not control, persuaded the king to name his

---

[9] Almost all the contemporary histories and memoirs cited in the Appendix contain detailed accounts of the army's operations during the second civil war. The campaign can also be followed in some detail through the daybook of the duke of Anjou's council, which notes important events and decisions and contains summaries of dispatches sent and received by Anjou. The daybook begins in late November, 1567, when the main army left Paris, and ends in early March, 1568, when it regained Paris. The daily summaries, which are interspersed with copies of correspondence, are in BN Mss. Fr. 15,543, 15,544, and 15,545. The nearest thing to a collection of administrative and financial documents for the army's operations are BN Mss. Fr. 4,553 and 4,554, while BN Mss. Fr. 15,608 contains a wealth of documents on the German reiters of both sides. For other sources see the Appendix,

younger brother, the duke of Anjou (later Henry III), as lieutenant general of the realm and commander of the royal army. A council of military advisors was appointed to assist him in making decisions, beginning an unhappy experiment in collective leadership.

The royal army now slowly began to organize itself for a pursuit. The Paris militia was of little value, and it took time to assemble sufficient troops for a main field army as well as provide for garrisons around Paris and along the route of the army's march. Some fifty new companies of cavalry were ordered raised and a Breton contingent under the count of Martigues and a force of Flemish gendarmes sent by the duke of Alva were hurried to Paris. Royal forces under the duke of Aumale were also sent to Champagne to block the eastern passages into the kingdom while the duke of Nevers, the military commander of French Piedmont, was ordered to march north through Burgundy with a sizeable force he was assembling near Lyon, including more Swiss and a contingent of Italian troops.

It was only in late November that the royal army, numbering close to 40,000 men, left Paris and established its camp at Nemours.[10] There it remained in early December for almost two more weeks while it finished organizing its artillery train and waited for the arrival of a large Gascon reinforcement, all the while keeping watch on the Huguenot army, which hovered around Montereau, on the Seine, hoping itself to collect detachments approaching from south of the Loire. But when it was reported that the Huguenots had deserted their positions on the Seine and were rapidly moving eastward, the advance began and after a hot nine-day pursuit the army caught up with the enemy on November 22–23 at Notre-Dame-de-L'Epine near Châlons-sur-Marne. The chance to crush the enemy, however, who were heavily outnumbered and suffering from the march and the season, was lost when a delay in bringing up the main body of the army allowed the Huguenots to slip away during the night and flee, in disarray, to Pont-à-Mousson, on the Moselle, where they were joined by John Casimir's German forces, on January 11, 1568.

Anjou's army, which was itself beginning to suffer from the rough passage and the weather, abandoned its pursuit and established a camp at Vitry-le-François, on the Marne, where it was joined in early January by the columns commanded by Aumale and Nevers. The queen mother arrived and dismissed Marshal Cossé, blamed for the lost chance at a decisive battle and suspected of Protestant sympathies, from the military council, in which Gaspard de Tavannes now began to function as the chief military advisor to Anjou. The commanders, having let the enemy escape, now had to devise an alternate strategy. Despite the fact that the combined forces under Anjou's command, including garrisons, now numbered almost 60,000 men, it was decided that the newly gained Protestant strength in German cavalry made it too dangerous to hazard the kingdom on the outcome of a single battle. So while waiting for the arrival of 8,500 German cavalry of their own, the leadership decided to adopt

---

[10] For a detailed description of Anjou's army see the beginning of chapter 3.

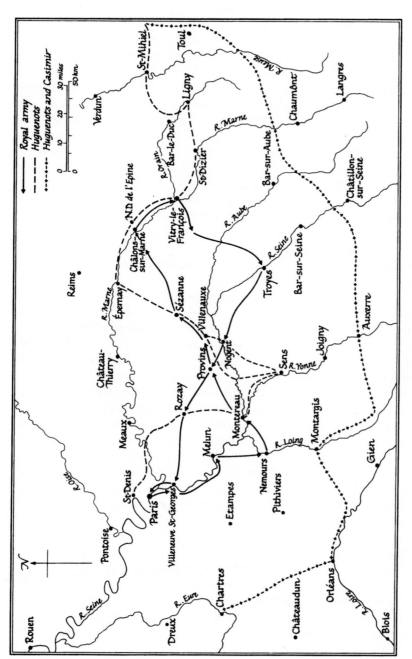

Fig. 4. Second war. Army routes

a Fabian policy, hoping that the stress of the season and lack of money would lead the Huguenots' Germans to mutiny and their French forces to fade away.

Unfortunately for the crown, none of its Germans were to arrive in Champagne before late February, 1568, and the enemy army had already in mid-January begun a rapid advance back into the heart of the kingdom through Champagne and upper Burgundy. The huge royal army camped around Vitry, instead of fighting, split up: Nevers with a detachment to harass the enemy south of their path and Anjou with the rest of the army to shadow them on the north. The Huguenots, virtually unmolested, quickly pressed on into the interior of France, attacking and looting the villages and small towns in their path which refused to open their gates or be ransomed. By mid-February they had linked up with an infantry reinforcement coming from the south and were crossing the Loing at Montargis on their way to Orléans, which had again been in their possession since the beginning of the war. The bulk of the royal army under Anjou's command, racked by illness and exhaustion, and with pay arrears mounting rapidly, stumbled back into Paris in late February and early March.

The Huguenots, perhaps 30,000 strong, and increasingly desperate for the means to pay their German mercenaries, rapidly mounted a siege of the rich cathedral town of Chartres at the end of February. The townspeople and some 4,000 royal troops who had entered the city just before the arrival of the enemy mounted a determined defense.[11] Unable financially to continue to support what may have been the largest royal field army ever raised during the civil wars, desperate to avoid the loss of Chartres, yet afraid to use the main army at Paris to bring the Protestants to battle or relieve the siege, the crown on March 23, 1568 concluded the Peace of Longjumeau.

From beginning to end the second civil war lasted about six months. For the massive effort involved – huge sums of money had been spent or pledged and very large numbers of soldiers raised – the army had proven much less effective than in the first civil war.[12] Though the army had relieved the blockade of Paris by its attack on the outnumbered Huguenots at Saint-Denis, it had been unable to bring the enemy forces to battle during the march to the frontier or to prevent them from reentering the kingdom with their German auxiliaries, and the siege of Chartres was lifted by the conclusion of the peace rather than effective action by the crown's main military forces.

Caught by surprise by the attempted kidnapping of the king, the crown and the army had relinquished the initiative to the enemy from the beginning of the war. With the exception of the two-week pursuit of the main enemy force in December, 1567, most of its time had been spent waiting in camps for more reinforcements or providing increasingly disorderly garrisons for detached duty in vulnerable towns around Paris and in Champagne. Some of the army's lack of aggressiveness can be attributed to the appointment of a quarrelsome and divided military council,

[11] For a detailed description and analysis of the siege of Chartres, see chapter 8.
[12] For the expense of Anjou's army during the second civil war see chapter 11, 284–86.

headed by a boy of sixteen. But on both sides there was a reluctance to engage without advantages of place or numbers, and under ordinary circumstances it was difficult to bring the opposing army to battle if it wanted to avoid one. Caution also arose from an understandably prudent desire not to risk the fortunes of the royal cause on the outcome of a single battle, in the presence of untrustworthy foreign troops, so near to the capital and to the vulnerable heart of the kingdom. In a war with few fixed geographical boundaries, no mutually accepted military calendar, and little opportunity to predict or control the course of events, the rhythm of the campaign had been dictated by attempts to exploit the temporary advantages provided by ponderous mobilization routines and the unpredictable arrival of reinforcements from the periphery or abroad.

After the signing of the peace in March, 1568, the French elements of the Protestant army had quickly disbanded. Many units of the royal army were also dismissed, but the Swiss and a considerable number of French troops continued to be maintained around Paris while others, including some Italian troops, were sent to garrison critical towns. As part of the peace terms the crown committed itself to advancing payment for the Protestants' German allies. The king's own late-arriving Germans also had to be paid. An intense and only partly successful effort was mounted to raise the enormous sums that were needed, and it was several months before the mercenaries were persuaded by a combination of cash, promises, and threats, to leave the kingdom. Their departure, however, did little to lessen suspicions on both sides: the crown believed that the Huguenots were trying to renege on the repayment of the money it had advanced to their mercenaries while the Huguenots in turn did not accept the crown's explanations for its maintenance of strong forces under arms. In August, 1568, in real or imagined fear for their personal safety, Condé and Coligny fled to La Rochelle, where they once again raised the banner of revolt. Thus, only four months after the peace, the crown was forced to begin the recall and reassembly of its forces.

The short interval between the second and third wars, however, had changed the strategic situation in favor of the Catholic cause. The German auxiliaries who had provided a considerable amount of the Huguenot army's punch were gone, and precautions had been taken in the interwar period to garrison strongpoints in the interior of the country. As a result, for the first time in the civil wars the capital and most of France above the Loire was secure and there was an opportunity to take the war directly to the heart of Huguenot-dominated territory in the west. There the royal army could pin the enemy army in place, prevent it from breaking out, and destroy it, breaking the back of Huguenot military power and ending the rebellion.[13]

---

[13] The campaign from October, 1568, to June, 1569, can be followed in detail in the logbook kept by Nicolas de Neufville, seigneur de Villeroy, the *secrétaire d'état*: BN Mss. Fr. 17,528. Collections of pertinent correspondence and documents for 1569 are BN Mss. Fr. 15,549 and 15,550. Other useful

To this purpose various contingents were hurried forward in September to join the duke of Montpensier, who had begun the concentration of forces at Saumur, on the Loire, while the rest of the army began gathering near Orléans for the march south with Anjou, again named lieutenant general. Early in October Montpensier advanced south to Périgueux, near where he intercepted and inflicted heavy losses on a Protestant column coming from Provence and Dauphiny. Anjou, accompanied by many units of cavalry, the Swiss, a lavishly equipped field artillery train, and his chief military advisor, Gaspard de Tavannes, arrived at Châtellerault, on the Vienne, early in November. The Protestant army, which had grown to a formidable size, especially in infantry, abandoned a siege of Pons and began a hot pursuit of Montpensier, who joined Anjou at Châtellerault on November 7.

The royal army now numbered close to 20,000 men, enough for Anjou to pursue his twin strategic goals of preventing the Huguenots from crossing the Loire and defeating them in battle.[14] After giving Montpensier's worn-out men a short rest, the reorganized army advanced past Poitiers. At Jazeneuil on November 17 the rival armies fought a sharp musketry action in difficult country from which the Huguenots withdrew during the night, and then headed north in an attempt to pass the Loire and take the war back into the heart of France. The royal army marched to cut this movement off and in December both armies maneuvered in vain around Loudon in wretched weather trying to gain an advantageous position from which to attack the other. With their numbers rapidly diminishing from illness and the weather, mutual exhaustion finally brought the campaign to an end. The royal army recrossed the Vienne and established its base camp at Chinon, sending strong detachments up and down the Loire to keep watch on the Huguenot army, which, after a failed attempt on Saumur, established its winter camp nearby. While his troops recovered from their hard marching and exposure to the elements, Anjou searched for supplies and awaited reinforcements and the coming of the spring campaign.

By early January, 1569, however, the overall strategic situation was rapidly complicating. In late 1568 the northern frontier had been threatened by the incursion of an army led by the prince of Orange, part of the debris of the war in the Low Countries. A blocking force under Marshal Cossé successfully forced Orange to turn back, but then news came that a large German mercenary force under the duke of Zweibrücken was preparing to enter the kingdom with the aim of joining Condé and Coligny's forces in the west. The specter of a repeat of the second civil war raised its head and the duke of Aumale, given the task of preventing Zweibrücken from entering the kingdom, set about assembling forces, including German cavalry, a contingent of troops sent by the duke of Alva, and forces from the Rhône valley led by the duke of Nemours, to form a second army on the Champagne frontier.

---

documents relating to the army's operations are in BN Mss. Fr. 4,554, 17,870, and 18,587. For a discussion of other sources see Parts B and C of the Appendix.

[14] For a detailed look at the strength and composition of the royal army in the third civil war see chapter 9, Figure 27, and note 5.

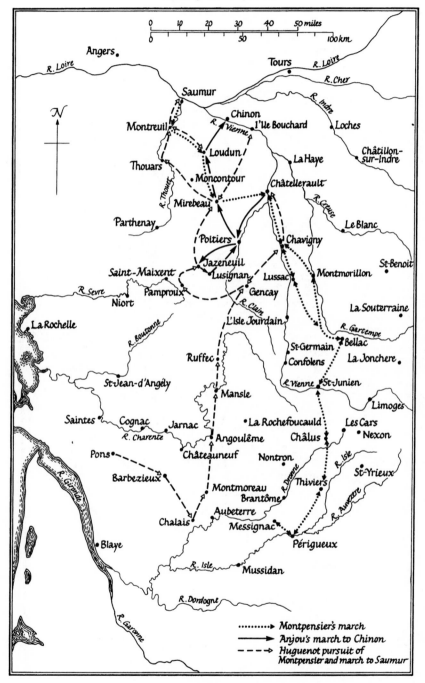

Fig. 5. Third war. Fall campaign of 1568

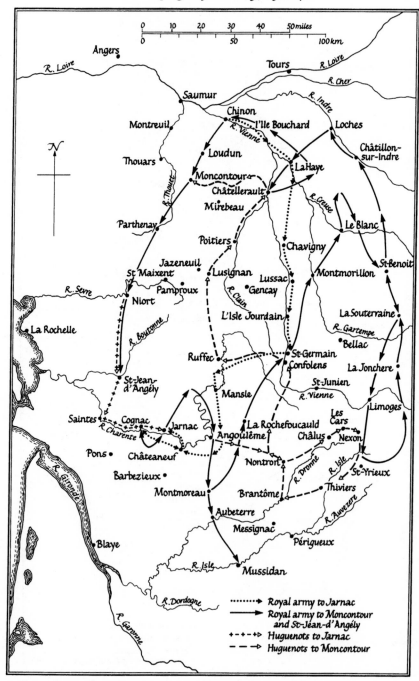

Fig. 6. Third war. Jarnac and Moncontour campaigns of 1569

In late January, 1569, Anjou received word that the Huguenots had left their winter camps and were headed south for the Charente river crossings, apparently searching for an opportunity to break out to the southeast. The army's leadership recalled its scattered forces and, accompanied by a smaller and more mobile artillery train than in the previous campaign, marched southward from Chinon to cut the Protestants off and bring them to battle. Excluding the regional defense forces left under the command of the count of Lude, the army numbered about 27,000 combatants.

After some weeks of maneuvering against the enemy, who wished to avoid combat until reinforced by their Germans, the army took advantage of lax Huguenot security to effect a crossing of the Charente at Châteauneuf during the night of March 12–13. Advancing on the village of Jarnac, the royal forces launched a surprise attack on the rear of the Protestant army, which was strung out westward along the river as far as Cognac. The prince of Condé attempted to rally the rear guard and fight a delaying action until help could come, but he was overwhelmed by numbers, captured, and promptly assassinated. The battle, primarily a rear-guard action, caused only a few hundred casualties and the bulk of the Huguenot forces managed to escape to Cognac or further westward to Saintes. The pursuit of the royal army was brought up short in front of Cognac, which could not be attacked without the heavy artillery pieces which were still on their way from Paris. After some hesitation the pursuit was abandoned and the army headed south of Angoulême where, in April, waiting for the heavy guns to arrive, it mounted short but successful sieges of Mussidan (which cost the life of young Brissac, one of the two colonel generals of the infantry) and Aubterre. The Protestant army, shaken but largely intact, rallied around Saintes, where, swearing allegiance to the young prince of Condé and the king of Navarre, it waited for news of its German allies. Though the battle of Jarnac, including Condé's death, was trumpeted by the crown as a great victory, it was in fact strategically hollow. Delays in the delivery of heavy siege guns from Paris had condemned the army to waiting while the logistical difficulties of operating in such rough country rapidly multiplied. By mid-May the situation was becoming critical and the army, now camped at Le Blanc on the Creuse, had since the battle of Jarnac lost half of its strength to detachments and attrition, particularly illness and desertion.

Meanwhile news had been arriving that the attempt to block Zweibrücken on the frontier was an ignominious failure, crippled by bickering between Aumale and Nemours. In mid-May Zweibrücken stormed the town of La Charité on the Loire, and began moving southwestwardly to link up with Coligny's army, which was now reapproaching Angoulême. At this point (May 24) the queen mother arrived at Le Blanc to help restore order and bolster morale, and with her encouragement the army early in June began advancing to Limoges, joined along the way by the mutinous remains of Aumale's army, reduced to less than a third of its original numbers by its long march from the frontier. At Limoges the combined force under Anjou was poised to prevent the juncture of Coligny and Zweibrücken but on two occasions Anjou's German cavalry, ill-paid, refused to march. On June 11–12 the two enemy forces themselves finally united and the royal army's leadership, feeling too understrength and demoralized to risk the security of the kingdom on a single battle, decided merely to shadow the enemy. This tactic backfired, however, when the army, which had just received a substantial reinforcement of Italians sent by the pope, stumbled on June 25 into an ill-advised and poorly supported skirmish in a driving rainstorm with the Huguenot army near La Roche L'Abeille, south of Limoges. This action cost the royal army hundreds of casualties among its French infantry, including the capture of the other remaining colonel general of the infantry, Strossi. Brought up short by this defeat, the army, without pay or provisions, riven by illness and desertion, began a retirement to the north, reaching Loches on July 27.

Luck now intervened to give the thoroughly demoralized royal army, much of which had been on campaign without significant rest since September of the previous year, a chance to recover. Pressure by Poitvin Huguenots forced Coligny to use his army, now superior in numbers to the royal army, for a siege of Poitiers. This extremely ill-advised move squandered the initiative the Huguenots had recently acquired. Poitiers was defended by forces under the count of Lude, some of the long-awaited and newly arrived heavy artillery from Paris, and a few hundred cavalry from the main army led into the city by the young duke of Guise just before its investment. The Huguenots, very weak in artillery, besieged the city from July 24 to September 7, but were stymied by an active defense by the garrison and townspeople. Their concentration on Poitiers gave the royal army, which at this time consisted almost entirely of foreign troops, time to recuperate while the royal council, which had been moved to Tours, made every effort to raise new forces. By early September, Anjou felt recovered enough to attempt to raise the siege by attacking the nearby Protestant garrison at Châtellerault. An assault on that place on September 7 by the Italians was bloodily repulsed, but it gave Coligny, who could hear the sound of the artillery, the pretext he had been looking for to abandon the increasingly costly operations at Poitiers. When he moved to attack the Catholic army, however, it successfully retreated across the Creuse river and moved on to Chinon, where it established its camp.

The royal army was still in poor shape, but so now were the Protestants, who had suffered many casualties and much sickness during the siege and whose German auxiliaries were increasingly mutinous. Realizing that the enemy was in a weakened and demoralized state, the army leaders and the royal council redoubled their efforts to raise new troops and hasten the arrival of reinforcements. By the end of September their efforts had borne fruit, and the strength of the royal army had grown to about 26,000 combatants. Crossing the Vienne, the army launched a pursuit of the enemy, who, withdrawing slowly westward towards their secure areas, were unable to escape. On October 3, 1569, near the village of Moncontour, the army forced the Huguenots to turn and give battle. The result was a great victory for the royal forces. In exchange for the loss of a few hundred casualties of its own the army inflicted around 10,000 casualties on the enemy, butchering the Huguenots' German and French infantry without mercy, taking more than one hundred standards, and capturing most of the enemy's baggage and all of their artillery. The remnants of the Huguenot army, mostly French and German cavalry, fled for their lives.

As great a victory as Moncontour was, however, it was by no means obvious to the leadership how best to exploit it. From the beginning of the war the army's strength had been maintained only by constant injections of new forces and units.[15] Even victory could not restore those depleted units to their original strengths, nor provide them the many months of pay they were owed. Tavannes, who had ably directed the army during the campaign and at the battle, urged that if the army was not going to concentrate on pursuing the remnants of the enemy army, the crown should take the opportunity to make peace on favorable terms. But there were alternative arguments that the army should use the opportunity to recapture as many places in the west as it could. In the end it was the latter policy which was adopted and the army, under extremely wretched conditions, advanced to besiege the city of Saint-Jean-d'Angély, a key to the reconquest of Saintonge and one of the few Protestant-held places in the west that had not voluntarily opened its gates in the hysteria of the weeks after Moncontour. But, just as the siege of Poitiers had ruined the Huguenot army, so now did a siege precipitate the collapse of the royal army. Ongoing negotiations for the surrender of Saint-Jean were unsuccessful. Though the town was poorly fortified, it was ably and actively defended by its Huguenot garrison. Despite the best efforts of Gontaut de Biron, newly named grand master of artillery, the siege, begun on October 16, proceeded slowly under very difficult conditions. The king, jealous of the glory won by his younger brother, now joined the army to share in this anticipated triumph, but under his eyes several assaults were bloodily repulsed. Attrition skyrocketed, due to casualties (including the count of Martigues, shot dead in the trenches), sickness, and desertion, leaving only a rump of an army, after most of the foreigners were released, to accept the city's surrender, on terms, on December 2, 1569. As the remnants of the army were dispersed to winter quarters the crown found itself, after two years of almost constant campaigning (including the second civil war), virtually without troops and funds.[16]

Meanwhile, Coligny, knowing that the royal army was bogged down before Saint-Jean, mounted the small number of infantrymen he had left and with his Huguenot and German cavalry began a remarkable nine-month perambulation through southern France, looting and burning along the Garonne, through Languedoc from

---

[15] An analysis of the patterns of reinforcement and attrition during 1568–69 can be found in chapter 9, 229–37.

[16] For an analysis of the royal army's patterns of marching, camping, and fighting during the third war see chapter 9, 237–41.

Toulouse to Nîmes, and up the right bank of the Rhône to Chalon-sur-Sâone. The court, bereft of resources, watched impotently for months as local governors and commanders proved unable to halt Coligny's march. Finally enough money was raised by desperate expedients to assemble a force at Orléans under Marshal Cossé, which fought an inconclusive battle with Coligny near Arnay-le-Duc, in Burgundy, in June of 1570.

Negotiations for a peace had been proceeding for months. With Coligny still at large and new rebellions springing up in the west under François de la Noue the Huguenots were in a position to demand significant concessions. The August 8, 1570, Edict of Saint-Germain finally ended the third civil war by granting the Protestants even wider toleration than the 1562 Edict of Amboise, including explicit civil and judicial rights, full rehabilitation for acts committed in the past, and the possession of four *places de sûreté* (La Rochelle, Montauban, Cognac, and La Charité) for two years.

This stunning reversal of fortune less than a year after Moncontour had important military causes and results. During the third civil war the crown had made a supreme effort, sparing no expense, in a determined and unyielding pursuit of the destruction of the Huguenot army. And, with the victory at Moncontour, it had achieved this basic goal. But in the long run, to achieve victory on the battlefield proved as debilitating as defeat, for it had taken over two years of war and had exhausted the military resources of the crown. After Moncontour there were no more reserves and no money left, only an army too weakened to take a poorly fortified town like Saint-Jean-d'Angély without disintegrating. In that sense it was Moncontour rather than the siege of Saint-Jean that had destroyed the royal army and left the crown in a position where it had no choice but to conclude an unfavorable peace.

So, at the very moment of victory the royal army had proven to be not only an expensive, but also a very brittle instrument, with many of the problems and weaknesses which had been evident in the first and second civil wars magnified by the longer effort required by the third war. The frustrating experience of the siege of Saint-Jean-d'Angély, moreover, and the granting of *places de sûreté* to the Protestants, were an ominous portent of the future. The peace facilitated the Huguenot effort to entrench themselves militarily on a territorial basis and to prepare openly for the type of low intensity warfare – the defense of places and the "small wars" of raid and counter raid – for which their forces were well suited. It was to be no accident that the royal army would fight no major, decisive, battles for many years after Moncontour. Instead, siege operations, with all their attritional, immobilizing, and time-consuming aspects, would come to predominate as the royal army was forced to undertake reconquest of the fortified centers of French Protestantism allowed by the peace.

A STALEMATE OF SIEGES, 1572–76

For a time after the end of the third civil war it appeared, to the horror of the ultra-Catholics, that the Huguenots and the crown might be reconciled. Coligny in particular began to play an important role as advisor to the king, urging him to intervene against Spain in the war in the Low Countries. And in August, 1572, the rift was supposed to be symbolically repaired by the public wedding, at Paris, of the young king of Navarre and Margaret of Valois, King Charles' sister. But a botched assassination attempt on Coligny precipitated the probably unpremeditated but nevertheless deadly massacre of Saint-Bartholomew's Day in Paris. The August 24, 1572, massacre and its continuation in the provinces severely injured the Huguenot movement. Thousands of Protestants were killed, including a large number of the nobility who had provided the fighting backbone and military leadership of the Huguenot armies. Tens of thousands, stunned by the turn of events, abjured their faith, or fled the country. La Rochelle, which had served as headquarters of the revolt during the third civil war, now became one of the few places of refuge left for those who had escaped the massacre and its repressive aftermath. The fourth civil war was to be dominated by the crown's attempt to gain the submission of the Rochellais. Though operations were mounted elsewhere – the famous siege of Sancerre, for example, with its episode of cannibalism – by far the major portion of royal troops, treasure, and material was dedicated to the reduction of La Rochelle.[17]

The king would have preferred to receive the submission of the city peacefully. Saint-Jean-d'Angély had demonstrated the difficulty and costs of supplying the munitions and manpower needed to mount a major siege operation far from the main military resources of the crown at Paris and the frontiers, and La Rochelle was a much stronger place, possessing fairly up-to-date fortifications and guarded on all but one side by marshes and the sea. Casualties were sure to be high and the royal treasury was still exhausted from earlier military exertions. Furthermore, though the massacre had been a great success as a punitive measure, it destroyed whatever trust the Protestants might have had left in the king and released them from any obligations they might have felt as subjects. The crown initiated negotiations with the city soon after the massacre but the inhabitants and refugees, including many ministers, consumed with suspicion and religious passion, refused to submit, denying entrance to the city to Biron, who had been named royal governor. Though attempts at negotiations would continue on and off, by November, 1572, it was clear that the only way the city could be returned to obedience was by force.

Anjou was again appointed to lead the army and given orders to besiege the city and to treat it, in defeat, as Rome had treated Carthage. Throughout December and

---

[17] There are some useful original pieces in BN Mss. Fr. 3,240 and 4,554, but the most indispensable primary sources for the siege are in BN Mss. Fr. 4,765: the duke of Nevers' daybook, "Journal du premier siège de la Rochelle," fols. 15r-53r, and the duke of Anjou's after action report, "Discours sur le siège de la Rochelle," fols. 57r-77r. For other useful sources see Parts B and C of the Appendix.

January a stream of men and munitions flowed south to Biron, who was responsible for organizing land and sea blockades of the city as the first stage in the siege. Matters proceeded slowly, hampered by bad weather, a lack of materials, unpaid and mutinous troops, and the vigorous sorties of the Rochellais. When Anjou and his escort arrived on February 11, 1573, the investment on land was complete but no approach trenches had been started and despite the presence of a strong flotilla of galleys and warships the entrance to the harbor had only been partially closed by sunken hulks and uncompleted shore batteries.[18]

Within a few weeks of Anjou's arrival the army had attained a strength of about 25,000 soldiers, artillerymen, and pioneers, not counting the sailors of the flotilla, or a contingent of 6,000 Swiss who would only arrive in May. Anjou vigorously pushed the closing of the harbor to a successful conclusion, reconnoitered the defenses, and conferred with his commanders on the army's council. Establishment of command responsibilities proved, however, to be a contentious business and planning for the attack was hampered by differences of opinion on the best way to approach the city's walls. The council, which contained most of the famous commanders of the day, including Monluc, Aumale, Nevers, and Strossi, was swollen to an unreasonable size by a number of ambitious younger nobles, including the king's youngest brother, Alençon, and the dukes of Guise and Mayenne, as well as the prince of Condé and king of Navarre (the future Henry IV), who had been forcibly converted and were virtual prisoners.

On the night of February 26–27 the approach trenches were finally opened, and for the next three weeks the army devoted itself to advancing the trenches to the town's ditch and to the construction of battery positions, from which the suppression of the defenders' fire and the destruction of the town's fortifications could begin. This work was slowed by a lack of material, bad weather, high casualties among the pioneers, and constant sorties from the town. But on April 20 the approach trenches finally reached the counterscarp and dry moat on the north side of town, near the bastion of the Evangile, which was the chosen point of attack, only to discover in the ditch a number of hidden pillboxes designed to provide flanking fire against any attacker at the base of the walls. New batteries were constructed directly on the shoulder of the ditch to pound a breach in the bastion while the old batteries continued their job of sweeping the parapets of the town's walls with their fire. But the slowness of the approach, for which many blamed Biron, and several postponements of the day of assault because of the pillboxes and rainwater in the ditch, gave the town time to strengthen its defenses by preparing inner works at the by now obvious points of attack.

On April 7, preceded by an intense preparatory barrage, the first assault of French infantry and nobility went into the breach, only to be decimated by showers of deadly anti-personnel incendiaries and the concentrated small-arms fire of the

---

[18] For a detailed analysis of operations at the siege of La Rochelle see chapter 10 and Figure 32.

defenders. Over the next three months, as the attacks on the fortifications continued, prepared by sapping, preceded by the explosion of mines, and supported by cannon fire – eight major assaults in all – the ditch, bastion, and breach took on the aspect of a smoldering cauldron. Casualties steadily mounted as did illness and desertions. Morale plummeted, soldiers refused to go to the assault and officers had to be cashiered for fleeing enemy sorties. Ammunition was exhausted and only a couple of hundred pioneers remained. Anjou was forced to assign the great nobles to guard duty in the trenches. Though an attempt to relieve the city by sea had been driven off in mid-April, in mid-May a single relief ship filled with gunpowder successfully ran the blockade into the harbor, enabling the Rochellais, who were at the end of their supply, to fight on. Only the arrival of the Swiss reinforcement enabled the Catholics to continue to man the trenches. A last assault in June gained part of the wall and two of its towers, only to be confronted by a new set of formidable inner works.

Anjou, increasingly frustrated and bored with the siege, surrounded by potential traitors, squabbling commanders, and dispirited soldiers, by the end of May was only looking for a way to abandon his duties without too thoroughly compromising his honor. His opportunity came with the news that he had been elected king of Poland, and most of June was spent in truces and negotiations with the Rochellais, who stubbornly refused to sign any peace terms that did not include their coreligionists in Montauban and Nîmes. Finally, on June 25, peace terms were accepted, and after approval by the king, published on July 10, when Biron, as governor, made a brief and symbolic entry into the town.

On both sides of the wall, it had been one of the most bitterly and desperately fought sieges of the century. It was also a disastrous defeat for the royal army. Though the total number of casualties will never be known, of the roughly 18,000 French infantry who made up the great majority of the army, at least five or six thousand were killed or wounded in the assaults and many more than that total succumbed to illness or deserted. There were also critical losses among the leaders of the army: more than two hundred officers and gentlemen, including most of the regimental and company commanders, were killed or wounded.[19]

But the bitterest pill to swallow was the knowledge that the failure to take La Rochelle had cost the army and the crown an opportunity to deal the Protestants a blow from which they probably could not have recovered. The massacre and its aftermath had completely thrown the Huguenots on the defensive. They had been unable to field an army or to import large numbers of German auxiliaries. So, for the first time in the civil wars, it was not necessary to deal with the Protestant field army, the most troublesome military problem always initially faced by the royal army in the first three civil wars. The treasury, however, and the country as a whole were so exhausted from previous military exertions that the crown hesitated and at

---

[19] For a discussion of casualties see chapter 10, 269–72.

first tried negotiations. Then, once the decision to take the city was made, it took months to prepare enough munitions and material and transport them from all over France to La Rochelle and to assemble the minimal number of troops necessary for the siege.[20] In the end, because of delays and shortages, the Rochellais were given almost six months to prepare for the siege, time they used wisely. During the siege itself operations were hampered and security often breached by a contentious and divided leadership. It also proved almost impossible to keep the army properly supplied with food, forage, munitions, and laborers. By the end, more than two-thirds of the army may have been casualties of one kind or another and the officer corps had been decimated. The strength of the city's situation and relatively modern fortifications could not be overcome by even the most desperate of assaults, and over time the besieging army had simply melted away.

Cities and towns, of course, had always constituted important military objectives from the beginning of the civil wars, and the sieges of Rouen, Chartres, Poitiers, and Saint-Jean-d'Angély, as we have seen, played crucial roles in the outcome of the first three civil wars. At the beginning of the wars the royal army had been able to take or retake urban places with relative ease. After decades of internal peace the weak, antiquated, and run-down fortifications of most towns and cities in France presented few obstacles to experienced commanders and veteran troops accompanied by an adequate artillery train. But as the wars went on some cities, like La Rochelle, began to add more sophisticated defenses and even smaller towns began to adopt cruder and less expensive, yet nevertheless effective, self-defense measures. The sieges of Saint-Jean-d'Angély and La Rochelle demonstrated how much conditions had changed and how immobilizing, time-consuming, and costly such operations could be for the royal army. La Rochelle, in particular, showed that it was more likely to destroy the royal army than to defeat the Huguenots if extended, large-scale operations had to be mounted to take well-defended cities far from the heart of the kingdom.

It should be pointed out that during the first four civil wars the main royal army had campaigned little, if at all, in Languedoc, Gascony, the Rhône valley, Dauphiny, or Provence, though it had frequently drawn the military resources of those areas to itself for operations in the north and west: the forces raised around Lyon by Nevers in 1567 and Nemours in 1568, and the Gascon contingents sent by Monluc in each of the first three wars, are good examples. The south of the country had, of course, seen some of the most bitter religious disturbances of the times, and military operations had often been mounted there on a fairly large scale. But the responsibility for those operations had been left for the most part entirely to the local military governors – like the duke of Nemours, who tried to take Lyon during the first civil war, or Marshal Damville, who had led the Catholic cause in Languedoc since the second civil war – and had been financed primarily from local resources provided

---

[20] Chapter 6 analyzes the growing logistical strain placed on the artillery by sieges in general, and La Rochelle in particular.

by municipalities and provincial estates. Perhaps partly as a result of this relative neglect by the crown, and also of the advantage given to the defense by the roughness of much of the country, the Protestants had managed slowly to consolidate their control of selected areas in the south: near the kingdom of Navarre, in Languedoc around Montauban and Nîmes, and at scattered towns in the hills and mountains of the Vivarais, Dauphiny, and Provence.

The events of the fourth civil war and the temporary eclipse of the great nobles who had previously dominated their party pushed the Huguenot towns of the Midi and the west to work to perfect their regional organization, with its own hierarchy of command, taxation systems, and garrisoned *places de sûreté*. It had proved impossible in the fourth civil war to reconquer the most important of these urban communities, and they and the areas they controlled now represented the most formidable military problem the royal army faced.

For despite the peace, the Protestants remained unreconciled to Charles IX, and a virtual state of war continued in the south and southeast of the country. In late February, 1574, around Mardi Gras, Huguenot horsemen attempted to attack the court, which was at Saint-Germain, and launched a well-planned insurrection in many parts of the country, seizing towns in Lower Normandy, Poitou, and the Rhône valley. So, despite the military exertions of the past, the crown suddenly found itself faced once again with widespread rebellion and though there was little money, the king had no choice but to issue the call to arms. Anjou, of course, was now king of Poland, and Charles was unwilling to give the post of lieutenant general to his brother Alençon, who was suspected of plotting against him. So, to put down the rebellion, rather than assemble a single army under unified command, the crown planned to organize three smaller armies: in Lower Normandy, under Matignon, in Poitou under Montpensier, and in Dauphiny under Montpensier's son, the prince Dauphine. None of these armies were confronted by large or especially formidable Huguenot forces. Their problem was rather how to retake a series of towns of medium strategic significance: Saint-Lô and Carentan in Normandy, Fontenay and Lusignan in Poitou, and Pouzin and Livron in Dauphiny.[21]

The queen mother threw herself enthusiastically into the war, determined to avenge herself at last on the count of Montgommery, the Protestant commander in Normandy, who had been involved in the jousting accident which had killed her husband Henry II in 1559. Montgommery had landed in Normandy in March, seized Saint-Lô and Carentan, and then was trapped with a few companions in the fortress of Domfront by Matignon in mid-May. Matignon's army at Domfront, constantly reinforced by units from Paris and the frontier, despite several unsuc-

---

[21] Because of its length and complexity, the royal army's operations during the fifth civil war are the hardest to reconstruct. Primary sources are quite scarce and, unlike the first four wars, there are no good unified secondary treatments of events. So, even more than for the earlier civil wars, the history of the fifth war has to be pieced together from a wide range of materials. For primary sources, there are useful army documents in BN Mss. Fr. 3,256 and especially 4,555, which also includes many documents on the army in the sixth civil war. For other sources see Parts B and C of the Appendix.

cessful assaults, compelled Montgommery to yield and promptly sent him off to Paris to be executed. Reversing its direction, Matignon's army, numbering about 7,500 men, then took Saint-Lô by assault on June 10. Carentan soon after opened its gates and this force, which was unpaid and disorderly, was promptly disbanded, its infantry (including many prisoners who had been recruited to replace the casualties of the assaults) and artillery hurried south across the Loire, into Poitou, creating a number of disturbances on the way.

Montpensier had been forced to lift a premature siege of Fontenay in May, but with the arrival of the reinforcements from Normandy his force was brought to a strength of about 8,600 men, and he retook the field. Fontenay surrendered after a three-week siege on September 22, and Montpensier moved on to Lusignan, which surrendered on terms only on January 26, 1575, after a four-month siege. At Lusignan most of the problems posed by siege operations before well-defended places now reoccurred. With the help of the townspeople a relatively small garrison was able to endure heavy bombardment and throw back assaults at the breach. When the town was not quickly taken, the royal troops, unpaid and increasingly discouraged by their use as shock troops, deserted in droves, causing widespread disorders in the surrounding countryside, which had been stripped of provisions, draft animals, and laborers. In the end only a reduced force remained to accept the surrender of the city. Montpensier then dismissed many of the survivors and sent the remainder to garrisons elsewhere in the west, where their disorderly behavior soon evinced loud complaints and their presence did little to stop another Protestant insurrection from beginning the next summer.

In the meantime, political events were occurring which were to make the fifth civil war among the most complicated and confused of all the civil wars. In April, 1574, there was the critical defection of the experienced and powerful governor of Languedoc, Marshal Damville, who entered into a military alliance with the Huguenots of the Midi. Then in May the young prince of Condé, who had escaped from the court, arrived in Germany and immediately began trying to raise an army of mercenaries to bring to the aid of his coreligionists. Also in May, two of the marshals of France, Cossé and Montmorency (Damville's elder brother), were arrested and thrown in prison under suspicion of conspiring with the alienated duke of Alençon against the crown. Finally, on May 30, after a long illness, Charles IX died, leaving the queen mother in uncontested command of the government until Anjou could return to France from Poland. Eager for her favorite son to return to a military triumph, Catherine in August hurried to Lyon, where Henry was expected to arrive after crossing the Alps, and redoubled her efforts to assemble a large army for the operations along the Rhône.

Such was the situation when Henry III arrived in Lyon on September 6, 1574. Attempts at negotiations with Damville and the Huguenots had failed, and the court had no choice but to capitulate or continue the war. The royal army Catherine had assembled for operations along the Rhône, now under the command of the newly appointed marshal of France, Bellegarde, numbered about 17,000 men, including French, Swiss and Savoyard infantry, French and German cavalry, and a siege train of more than twenty guns. Bellegarde devoted the first two weeks of October to a siege of Pouzin, at the cost of many casualties. The siege of Livron, from December 17 to January 24, 1575, was an even bigger disaster. There were problems providing munitions for the breaching batteries and several assaults were bloodily repulsed. Despite a visit to the army by the new king to raise morale, the unpaid and mutinous troops began to desert in droves. In less than five weeks the vices and afflictions of a tough siege had again reduced the army to a shadow of itself. Bellegarde, who was widely criticized for the failure of the siege, had no choice but to retire, preventing the loss of the artillery train in his retreat only with the greatest difficulty. Henry III, eager to go to his coronation and a prospective wedding, abandoned the army, reaching Paris in March. The remaining royal forces on the Rhône were then split up to be used in a series of sporadic smaller-scale operations in Languedoc, Dauphiny, and Provence.

By the spring of 1575 the military situation was therefore bleak. The sieges of Lusignan and Livron, one ending in a victory, the other in defeat, had ground up the armies that had undertaken them. The coalition of Huguenots and Catholics led by Damville in Languedoc had formally erected a "state within a state" in January, and rumors were circulating that Condé was preparing to enter the kingdom with a large force of Germans. In fact, Condé's forces would not arrive in France until the winter of 1575–76. But to prepare for the eventuality of an invasion, Henry had to send out orders to raise more Swiss and German troops and in September he sent the duke of Guise and Biron towards the frontier with some 8,000 troops to establish a camp at Langres.

But the already muddled events of the war were further complicated at this point by the king's younger brother, Alençon, who on September 15 escaped the court and fled to Dreux, raising his banner of revolt and issuing a proclamation of personal grievances cloaked in a concern for the public good. To have a member of the royal family, especially the prince who stood next in line to the throne, in open revolt against the king, and perhaps even seeking an alliance with the Huguenots, was a potential political and military disaster of the first magnitude. Forces under Nevers were diverted to keep watch on him, the queen mother soon arrived for a series of interviews, and after much negotiation a formal truce was signed on November 22. As it turned out, Alençon had not attracted much of an armed following. He had little money to pay his men and few rewards to promise them, but to placate him the king now made arrangements to provide his tiny army with food and forage.

In order to deal with Alençon and to help with the looming invasion by Condé, the king had recalled forces from other parts of the kingdom, some of which he sent to reinforce Guise. With these forces Guise in October soundly defeated a small enemy advance force near Dormans, in Champagne. Badly wounded on the face during the battle, Guise had to relinquish his command, and his unpaid troops were dispersed into garrisons. But in December Condé and Casimir, the German mercenary chief, with an army of more than 25,000 men, began to move towards France. The defenses of Paris were strengthened and part of the available royal forces assembled at Gien under Henry's command, while the rest, under the command of Guise's brother, the duke of Mayenne, recently appointed lieutenant general by the king, camped at Vitry-le-François. Although the combined forces of the royal army numbered more than 22,000 men, they were in poor shape. The 10,000 men under Mayenne's direct command, unpaid and unfed, living off the countryside, their clothing in rags, suffering the extremes of the season, were in no shape to do anything other than shadow Casimir's army as it moved into France, reaching Dijon on January 31, 1576, and Moulins on March 4, 1576, where it was greeted by Alençon.

Now began one of the most confusing periods in the wars. Fighting continued in the west, where Montpensier's departure to bring reinforcements to the king had sparked a new Huguenot revolt, and in the south, where Damville remained unsubdued. To further complicate matters the king of Navarre also escaped from his captivity at the court and headed to his territories in the southwest where he began to rally forces of his own. But in the regions around Paris, despite the combined presence of as many as 50,000 troops, there was almost no fighting, just a series of truces and extended negotiations. The royal army, protecting Paris, was alternately dispersed and reassembled, competing with Casimir's force in its mistreatment of the civilian population. Finally, in April, impatient with the slowness of negotiations and suspecting that they were being drawn out simply in the hope that their army would disintegrate, Condé and Casimir threatened to move towards Paris. The royal army was hardly in shape to defend the capital and even less capable of fighting a battle, and the king was forced to sign peace terms on May 2, published as the Peace of Beaulieu on May 14, 1576.

The so-called Peace of Monsieur included the most liberal terms the Protestants were ever to receive during the civil wars. They were granted a large degree of religious freedom, given *chambres mi-partis*, or tribunals with equal numbers of Catholics and Protestants, in all the *parlements*, decreed full pardon and rehabilitation for all past transgressions and rebellious acts, and granted eight *places de sûreté*, two each in Languedoc, Guyenne, Dauphiny, and Provence.

The fifth civil war had been the longest of the wars begun during Charles IX's reign. The royal army had done most of its fighting in debilitating sieges of secondary provincial towns far from the most important centers of French Protestantism. From the beginning there had been chronic difficulties in paying and supplying the troops and as the campaign went on troop disorders increased. Moreover, by the time the initial round of sieges had come to an end there remained few large-scale military operations which the royal army was in any shape to undertake. The field army assembled with great difficulty by Henry and the Guises in late

1575 and early 1576 was too large to support financially and too weak to challenge the enemy, leaving the realm virtually defenseless. After fourteen years and five civil wars the royal army appeared no closer to a military defeat of the Huguenots than it had been at the beginning of the struggle.[22] The fact that the religious partition of France could not be significantly shifted by formal military operations after 1576, however, was to prove of little relevance to the greater nobility, Catholic and Protestant alike, whose own selfish interests were better served by perpetuation of the aimless and increasingly more destructive wars for which the fifth civil war provided a model.

[22] For a discussion of the long-term deterioration of royal forces see, besides chapter 6 on the artillery, the treatments of the infantry and cavalry forces in chapters 4 and 5, and chapter 11 on the cumulative financial costs to the crown of the first five wars.

The camp and army of the king

THE MILITARY LEGACY

The royal army was not created *de novo* for the purpose of fighting the civil wars. On the contrary, there were important aspects of the army as it existed at mid-century that could not and would not be modified as the wars unfolded. Some of these inherited aspects would make the royal army a formidable fighting force and contribute in large measure to its successes. But, as we shall see, some of these same continuities as well as other inherited features represented weaknesses and rigidities that, exacerbated by civil war, would significantly limit the army's effectiveness and contribute to its failures.

Weakness and limitations were probably not, however, on the mind of King Henry II of France as he and his retinue arrived at the village of Pierrepont, in Picardy, to review the royal army, on August 8, 1558 – near the midpoint of the last of the Hapsburg–Valois wars that had disturbed Europe's international affairs for more than half a century. According to François de Rabutin, the future historian of those wars, and one of the men-at-arms present at the review,

The king came to Pierrepont to see his army arrayed and ordered in battle formation, the place being, as I have said, convenient for the assembly of one of the finest and most complete armies ever put in the field by a king of France. Never in memory had so many Germans been seen, especially the cavalry, amounting to nearly 8,000 horses. So, the 8th of August, at one o'clock, after the duke of Guise had dined the King and all the princes who had accompanied his Majesty to Pierrepont, the King went to a knoll to review the army in formation in a lovely open countryside, below. Of this army thus ordered, I would like to provide here an ample account, having myself diligently and carefully witnessed such an event and considered it rare and worthy of being noted down and remembered. It might then serve as an example to those who follow the profession of arms.[1]

The army had marched out of its quarters early in the morning and been arranged unit by unit in the surrounding fields to form an open-ended rectangle, or half-moon formation more than two miles long, advance and rear guards forming the two wings and the main body of the army, the battle, the center.

Once this fine and fierce army had been arrayed, the King appeared, accompanied by several great princes of his kingdom, and wanted to inspect it from one end to another. Doubtless,

---

[1] Quoted in Lot, *Recherches*, 177.

his Majesty took great pleasure and gratification in seeing so many princes, great lords, captains, gentlemen, so many men in all, assembled there, presenting themselves to sacrifice their lives for his service and to support his cause.[2]

As he rode along the formed ranks of the army on his afternoon inspection – a journey which took about three hours to complete – Henry encountered the light cavalry of the advance guard, then units of reiters, the German pistol cavalry, and heavily armored French gendarmes of the battle, interspaced with massive blocks of pikemen and arquebusiers – German, Swiss, and French infantry – companies of pioneers, and fifty-three cannons with their crews, followed by more gendarmes and German cavalry in the rear guard.[3] To the 29,000 *gens de pied* and 11,000 cavalry taking part in this visual demonstration of the monarchy's armed might was added abundant aural proof of the army's technical and destructive powers.

What was even more impressive was that one could recognize the strange and awful powers and contrivances of the raging and bloodthirsty god Mars, by the thunder and roar of the artillery and by the discharges of the arquebuses and the pistol volleys of the reiters. One might rightly have said that the heavens and the earth burst into infinite thunderclaps, or that the Almighty wished by this blow to strike down the entire globe.[4]

At the end of the review, Rabutin added a less lyrical reminder of the impact of the more prosaic elements on the ordinary soldiers involved in the event:

After this general review, the King having retired that same evening to Marchets, each company returned to its quarters, each soldier finding himself, in my opinion, exhausted, completely spent, for having stood at arms from six or seven in the morning until four or five in the evening, barely fed, and moreover suffering from thirst due to the great heat of the day and the dust that was constantly stirred up, for all the usual drills that poor soldiers are used to having to endure.[5]

This tantalizing glimpse of force on display in the heat and dust of a summer afternoon can be used to suggest some of the strengths and vulnerabilities of the royal army, seven months before the signing of the treaty of Cateau-Cambrésis which was to end the Hapsburg–Valois wars and only a bit more than three years before the outbreak of the first war of religion. On the positive side, some of the forces assembled at Pierrepont represented the culmination of a century of effort by French monarchs to have at their disposal elements of a reliable and permanent army. Since the mid-fifteenth century the *gens d'ordonnance*, or gendarmerie, the mostly noble heavy cavalry, had formed the permanent core of the army, paid in peace as well as in war and functioning during the former as rotating garrisons in

---

[2] *Ibid.*, 179.
[3] For a detailed analysis of the royal army at Pierrepont, based on Rabutin's description but controlled by other documents of the times, see Lot, 176–86.
[4] *Ibid.*, 179.
[5] *Ibid.*

the provinces.[6] The fury of their armored charges with the lance had made them famous and they were still arguably the best heavy cavalry force in Europe. In addition, the cannons which had produced such thunder at Pierrepont were also, along with their technical personnel, part of the permanent native military establishment. They were the linear descendants of the mobile artillery train which had accompanied Charles VIII on his invasion of Italy in 1493, astounding the peninsula by their ability to overcome strong fortifications with rapid and continuous battery fire.[7] Absent from Rabutin's account but present at Pierrepont were the elements of the support services of the army whose job was to draw on the logistical riches of the kingdom: the teamsters whose horses pulled the guns and whose wagons carried ammunition and equipment (including a portable pontoon bridge), and 1,500 mules who carried the camp's daily bread rations.[8]

Though not part of any permanently maintained native force, the masses of foreign infantry anchoring the line of battle, particularly the Swiss, who were under contract to serve the king of France exclusively, were some of the finest combat troops in Europe.[9] The thousands of pistol-armed reiters were a relatively novel and successful attempt to marry the firearm technology of the century to the mobility and shock power of heavy columns of cavalry. Each of these major components of the army, in other words, represented the state of the art in military affairs at the mid-sixteenth century, whether indigenous forces developed over the preceding century and supported on a permanent basis or skilled mercenaries contractually obligated to serve the monarchy. What the king could not provide from the resources of his own kingdom, the review seemed to demonstrate, could be purchased with the enormous revenues he was entitled to collect from his loyal subjects.

Within several weeks of the review, as the campaign proceeded and the army's strength was increased by the arrival of additional French gendarmes and infantry as well as more Swiss, the "camp et armée du roy" came to dispose of close to 50,000 combatants, near to the maximum possible size the physical and technical limitations of the age imposed on a field army.[10] Such numbers represented final and conclusive proof of the military power of the kings of France. With the excep-

---

[6] For the formation of these permanent forces, especially for the gendarmerie, Contamine, *Guerre, état et société*, 277–551. For military forces in the first half of the sixteenth century see Lot, *passim*, and chapters 10 and 11 in *HM*, vol. 1. Chapter 13 of *HM*, which treats the wars of religion, also contains a great deal of information on the army midway through the century.

[7] Philippe Contamine, "L'Artillerie royale française à la veille des guerres d'Italie," *Annales de Bretagne*, 76, no. 2 (June, 1964), 221–61.

[8] Lot, 182.

[9] The best source on the Swiss component of the royal army during the civil wars is A. Ph.v. Segesser, *Ludwig Pfyffer und seine Zeit* (Bern, 1880–81), but Jean-René Bory, *La Suisse à la rencontre de l'Europe. L'épopée du service étranger* (Lausanne, 1978), provides a general overview of Swiss forces. See also Marcel Burin des Roziers, *Les capitulations militaires entre la Suisse et la France* (Paris, 1902). Chapter 4, below, contains a discussion of the battle worthiness of different types and nationalities of infantry.

[10] Lot, 186.

tion of the Hapsburgs, no other monarch in Europe had the resources to assemble such numbers in the field for months at a time and year after year.[11]

The review at Pierrepont also suggests to the historian blessed with hindsight some of the potential weaknesses and real inadequacies of the royal army. One of these limitations stemmed directly from the ostensible strength projected by the army's impressive size and formidable composition: it was hardly a French army at all. Slightly more than 70 percent of the troops on display were foreign mercenaries (8,000 German cavalry and more than 20,000 Swiss and German infantry).[12] This absolute preponderance of foreign mercenaries, especially among the cavalry, was a temporary product of a disastrous defeat at the battle of Saint-Quentin in the preceding year, and, as previously mentioned, more French troops (but also more Swiss) were to be added to the army within weeks of the review.[13] But the presence of such a large number of foreigners also reflected the failure of the crown, despite a number of initially promising initiatives over the previous century, to develop a permanent French infantry to match the quality of its native gendarmes and artillery. As we will see, a modest number of French infantry companies were kept in being at reduced strength as garrisons on the frontier between wars, but even at full strength they could not be counted on to firmly anchor a line of battle.[14] Dependence on foreign troops, then, was a function of a deficit in reliable native troops as much as any exaggerated faith in the fighting prowess of mercenaries, whose liabilities were well known: foreigners were more expensive than native troops (because their contracts called for higher wages and tremendous bonuses for their organizers and commanders); they would refuse to march or to fight if they were not regularly paid; their loyalty was sometimes suspect; and it was an extremely time-consuming process to collect them together from their various assembly points outside the kingdom. Yet without foreigners it would have been impossible for the crown to assemble on a consistent basis an army the size of that reviewed at Pierrepont.

The polyglot nature of the royal army also underlined another problem: at full strength the field army was in most respects an *ad hoc* and temporary conglomeration of units. The French and foreign contingents and even their leaders were often

---

[11] According to Parker, only in four out of thirty-nine years between 1567 and 1665, for which he has information, did the Army of Flanders number more than 80,000 men: *Flanders*, 28. According to Hale, *War*, 46–74, but especially 63–64, only twice between 1450 and 1620 did any European power (the Empire both times) raise armies larger than the Army of Flanders at its peak strength.

[12] Calculated from Lot, 176–86.

[13] Lot, 186, and for the immediately preceding campaign, 157–71.

[14] For the history of the French infantry and attempts to create a national militia see, besides Contamine, *Guerre* and *HM* and Lot; A. Communay, "Les Gascons dans les armées françaises," *Revue de l'Agenais*, 21 (1894), 379–91, 492–510, and 22 (1895), 165–76, 229–39, 392–406; and Louis Susane, *Histoire de l'infanterie française* (Paris, 1876), vol. 1, especially 120–25. Lot, 187–92 and 253–61, deals with royal forces on the eve of the civil wars, but depends on a purported 1562 "Abregé de l'éstat militaire de la france" published by Communay, "Gascons," 384–91, which to my knowledge does not exist in the archives.

unknown to one another, never seriously drilled or trained together, were not kept together long, and left each other's presence as soon as the few months of most campaigns ended. Though soldiers in individual companies may have served together for some time and individual companies and national contingents some-times drilled and practiced their own battle formations, there was no systematic and coordinated training. The embattling of units at Pierrepont, for example, as elabo-rate as it may have appeared, required from the troops little more than physical endurance, strong lungs, and the ability to shoot their firearms in the air. Given the time it took to mobilize all its units, it was a rare event for all of the army's elements to be assembled in one place and at one time. In some essential ways the royal army was always an army of strangers. Perhaps Rabutin's description of the Pierrepont review as a "rare" event, "worthy of being noted down and remembered," and serving as "an example to those who follow the profession of arms" suggests that the real novelty of the occasion had to do with the rare sight of the physically unified royal army at full strength forming a coherent battle line.[15]

In the heterogeneity of its army, however, France was not that much different than the other powers of the time: the armies of the Empire earlier in the century and those Spain was to use in the Low Countries demonstrated roughly the same amount of internal variety.[16] Lack of permanent formations aside, the *ad hoc* and temporary nature of the royal army also stemmed from the fact that it was almost impossible for the crown to keep such a sizeable force together and operational over long periods of time even if it had wished to. Large armies were delicate, if destruc-tive, creatures, susceptible to steady attrition from detachments, desertions, diseases, and casualties. If not continually replaced, such losses could reduce an army to some fraction of its original strength by the end of a campaign.[17] The assembly of the royal army, then, also marked the inevitable beginning of its steady dissolution, a process that was often speeded up by another important function of its formidable size: its cost. As we shall see, the royal army was ruinously expensive, both in the short run, when enormous sums of cash were needed to provide for its pay and sustenance and keep it in the field, and in the long run, to pay the enormous debts it was necessary to accumulate in order to have met such expenses in past wars.[18] It was this last weakness, state bankruptcy, as well as a desire to turn to the task of destroying the heretics who seemed to be multiplying in the realm, that led Henry II to conclude the treaty of Cateau-Cambrésis with Philip II of Spain in 1559, ending the long series of wars begun between their royal houses in 1493.

The territorial concessions required of France by the treaty of Cateau-Cambrésis were widely denounced at the time. With the exception of the acquisition of the bishoprics of Metz, Verdun, and Toul, and a small corner of Piedmont, the borders

---

[15] Lot, 177.
[16] Parker, *Flanders*, 25–49, especially Figure 4 on 28.
[17] *Ibid.*, 207–21, and *Military Revolution*, 52–58, for attrition rates.
[18] See chapter 11.

of France had been hardly changed at all by the almost constant fighting of the preceding sixty-five years. Especially disturbing was the relinquishing of possessions won in Italy, especially in Savoy, whose duke, wrote Brantôme, "peace made between our kings, in one hour and with one pen stroke, recovered all the possessions and lands which he had lost in thirty years of war."[19] But the historian may be allowed a different view of the significance of the type of "pen stroke" wielded by the kings of France.

On June 30, 1559, a few weeks after the signing of the treaty, Henry II was accidentally wounded in the head while jousting during the celebration of the marriage of his eldest daughter Elizabeth to Philip II of Spain, a dynastic union intended to seal the reconciliation of the two most powerful Catholic monarchs in Europe. By July 4 Henry had recovered enough to transact business with the constable, who got the king's signature on an order to pay the gendarme companies for their service during the second quarter of 1559 at musters to be held later in the month, after which they were to be assigned to garrison duties.[20] Six days later, on July 10, Henry II was dead, and one of the first acts of his successor, the 16-year-old François II, was to countersign his father's July 4 order and to sign an additional order assigning funds for the gendarmes' payment during the next two quarters of 1559, but drastically reducing their numbers. With a stroke of the pen the young king slashed the authorized strength of the gendarmerie by almost a third: from 8,800 to 6,275 men, a dismissal of 2,525 men which relieved the royal budget of a charge of some 700,000 *livres* per year. To achieve this reduction almost every one of the sixty-four existing companies, captained by the most prominent and powerful noblemen in the kingdom, had to be significantly reduced in strength.[21]

This exercise in the reduction of the gendarmerie, part of the larger process of demobilization following the peace treaty, suggests a final and most fundamental point about the royal army before the civil wars. Since the end of the Hundred Years War the French monarchy had continually and successfully sought to reserve to itself the right to organize and use armed forces. As the royal ordinances put it:

The King expressly forbids all his subjects of whatever quality or condition, or whatever dignity, title, office or charge they have in the kingdom, to undertake or have undertaken any levying or assembling of soldiers...under any pretext without explicit royal command, in the form of a royal letter patent, signed by the King's hand and countersigned by one of his secretaries of state and sealed with the great seal, under pain of being punished as rebels and guilty of high treason.[22]

Seen in this light, the creation of the permanent gendarmerie, with its large component of nobles, and an enormous artillery park can be interpreted as much as an attempt to establish control at home over these essential military resources as to

---

[19] Brantôme, *Oeuvres*, vol. 2, 145. See also Monluc, *Commentaires*, vol. 2, 376–79.
[20] BN Mss. Fr. 3,150, fols. 39–50.
[21] BN Mss. Fr. 21,543, fols. 28–47.
[22] Quoted in *HM*, p. 313, without other reference.

develop the wherewithal for foreign adventures. Only the king could maintain troops in peacetime, raise troops in wartime, dismiss the forces at his disposal at any time, and, given the military evolution of the preceding century, particularly the rise in the size and technical apparatus of armies, only the king could afford to pay the cost of the army in peace or war. French society in the mid-sixteenth century was not a stranger to violence, weapons, and martial displays, but for decades there had been no significant private armies and no great subjects with enough revenue to raise an army on a scale that could challenge the royal army. The only French army, for better or worse, in peace and war, was the royal army. During the civil wars these facts and assumptions were to be severely challenged.

THE ARMY IN PEACETIME

If François II's pen stroke can remind us of the monarchy's long established and largely successful claim to a monopoly on organized military force in France, it must also be recalled that financial exhaustion was the unseen hand which guided the king's signature, and that the reduction of the gendarmerie was only part of a larger demobilization of royal forces which followed the signing of the treaty of Cateau-Cambrésis. The artillery train, for example, was promptly disbanded at the end of the war, and the numerous foreign mercenaries paid off and marched to the frontier as quickly as possible. The French infantry companies, of which there may have been ninety in existence near the end of the war, were drastically cut by disbanding some, reducing the remainder to much smaller peacetime strengths as in the case of the gendarmerie, and sending them to garrison duty on the frontier. The process was complicated in 1559 by the return of almost all of French Piedmont to the duke of Savoy, which involved the evacuation of most of the French garrison there as well as an enormous artillery park.[23] Soon so many unemployed and impecunious captains crowded the court that the duke of Guise had to threaten all those who would not leave with capital punishment.[24] The widespread dismissals impressed contemporaries, some of whom blamed the coming of the wars of religion on the presence of large numbers of demobilized and discontented soldiers. After the Italian wars, wrote Brantôme: "France made peace and that was the cause of the civil wars, for a Frenchman never existed who did not want to fight; if not against foreigners, then against his countrymen."[25]

But, in fact, the army had always been disbanded between wars and deep reductions made in the strength of its remaining units. Neither the idea nor the reality of a large standing army existed in sixteenth-century France, and even the knowledge that continued warfare in the future was a near certainty could not offset the tremendous expense of maintaining larger forces in peacetime. The peacetime army

[23] See the inventory of artillery removed from relinquished places: BN Mss. Fr. 3,240, fols. 17–22.
[24] Brantôme, *Oeuvres*, vol. 4, 233.
[25] *Ibid.*, 120.

Table 2.1. *Gendarme companies in peacetime, 1559–74*

Year	Companies	Lances	Authorized strength
1559	64	2,510	6,275
1564	91	3,160	7,900
1566	91	3,060	7,650
1571	69	2,840	7,100
1574	68	2,530	6,325

was small, widely dispersed, and tied, where it existed in any strength at all, to the frontier provinces or the north of the kingdom – a strategic disposition intended primarily to defend France from foreign invasion at its most vulnerable points. The civil wars, as we will see, would do little to change this state of affairs, and as a result the royal army would confront the beginning of each civil war at a disadvantage, its forces inconveniently placed and numerically inadequate.

What forces could the crown count on having available in peacetime? The gendarmes or heavy cavalry companies which represented the most powerful offensive weapon of the army were the most important part of the peacetime forces. Because the gendarmerie was a permanent force, many of the documents which relate to its management have survived. This makes it possible to trace the number of gendarme companies maintained between the wars as well as estimate their total strength. Table 2.1 presents this information for five interwar years: in 1559, after the treaty of Cateau-Cambrésis but before the first war of religion; in 1564, immediately after the first war; in 1566, before the beginning of the second war; in 1571, between the third and fourth wars; and in 1574, before the beginning of the fifth war.[26]

In general, the crown maintained from 64 to 69 companies of heavy cavalry in peacetime, or about 2,500 to 2,800 lances (an archaic term which indicates the number of fully armored personnel) representing an authorized strength of between 6,275 and 7,100 men. These numbers were surpassed in the mid-1560s, in the aftermath of the first war, when for a short time a larger number of peacetime companies than usual (91) were maintained in an attempt to accommodate both loyal and Huguenot noble commanders while the search for a peaceful religious settlement continued. But the crown had decreed in late 1563 that no new companies could be created until enough had been disbanded by the death or resignation of their captains to reduce the number of gendarmes to a maximum allowable peace-

---

[26] For 1559 see BN Mss. Fr. 3,150. fols. 39–50; for 1564, Le General Susane, *Histoire de la cavalerie française* (Paris, 1874), vol. 1, 62–66; for 1566, BN Mss. Fr. 3,194, fols. 99–101; 1571, *OM* no. 153; 1574, *OM* no. 178, and for a little earlier in 1574, BN Mss. Fr. 3,193, fols. 184–93, which identifies companies that were to be reduced to partial pay.

Table 2.2. *Peacetime dispersal of gendarme companies, 1559–74*

	1559	1564	1566	1571	1574
Picardy	6	13	12	8	3
Champagne	13	15	15	11	9
Burgundy	4	5	6	6	4
Lyonnais	2	2	3	1	0
Dauphiny	1	3	3	4	3
Provence	1	1	1	1	2
Piedmont	6	0	2	1	1
Normandy	8	6	6	5	5
Ile de France	3	8	10	6	9
Orléannais	2	3	3	2	0
Brittany	1	4	3	2	2
Maine	1	2	3	3	1
Anjou-Touraine	1	2	2	2	1
Berry	2	2	0	1	1
Nivernais	0	1	0	0	1
Bourbonnais	2	3	2	0	0
Marche-Limousin	1	1	1	1	2
Auvergne	0	1	2	2	1
Poitou-Saintonge	6	8	7	5	6
Guyenne-Gascony	4	3	4	5	7
Languedoc	0	8	6	3	10
Total companies	64	91	91	69	68

time strength of 3,000 lances, or 7,500 men.[27] This goal had almost been reached by 1566 and we can safely take this total to represent an absolute maximum strength for the periods between the civil wars.

After every war the cavalry companies were widely dispersed throughout the kingdom, and it was a rare province that contained none at all. One of the most striking characteristics of peacetime distribution, however, as Table 2.2 indicates, is how small the numbers assigned to most provinces were.[28] Throughout the period ten of the twenty-one major provinces of the kingdom always had three or less companies assigned to them in peacetime. Even in regions with more companies, such as Ile-de-France or Champagne, they were not concentrated in a single body; instead, each individual company was assigned to a single locality. Since the typical company averaged 75–100 men, and usually only one-third of the companies were on garrison duty at any one time – the rest were furloughed to their homes – the net result was that large areas of the country were virtually empty of royal cavalry or,

[27] *OM* no. 51.
[28] Calculated from the stations identified in the documents cited in note 26.

Table 2.3. *Regional distributions of gendarme strength, 1559–74*

Year	In or north of Loire provinces		South of Loire provinces		Frontier	
	No.	%	No.	%	No.	%
1559	4,000	64	2,275	36	2,250	52
1564	5,100	65	2,800	35	3,475	44
1566	5,325	70	2,325	30	3,425	45
1571	4,850	68	2,250	22	3,375	48
1574	3,525	56	2,800	44	2,225	35

where the density of companies was higher, they were scattered in penny-packets all over the countryside. And if we calculate the proportion of all gendarmes assigned to some larger military regions, as in Table 2.3, the uneven nature of their presence is even more striking. Until 1574 about two-thirds of all the cavalry was stationed in or north of the Loire provinces and close to half on the northern and eastern frontiers. The net result of this concentration, an inheritance of the Hapsburg–Valois wars, was a relative denuding of the west and south of the country of cavalry. It was precisely in some parts of those regions that the Huguenots were to become most entrenched, but until 1574 the percentage of all horsemen assigned to the south steadily declined. Only then, during the uneasy truce between the fourth and fifth civil wars, was a more substantial portion of the gendarmerie than usual (44 percent) stationed south of the Loire provinces. But this late proportional increase, which took place primarily at the expense of the frontier garrisons in Picardy, Champagne, and Burgundy, involved very small absolute increases in the number of men assigned to the south.

After the gendarmerie, the infantry was the second major component of the peacetime army. At the beginning of every budgetary year infantry *états* were drawn up, one for the north and one for the south of the country, authorizing payment of the "gens de guerre à pied tenans garnison pour le service de sa Ma^te es villes chasteaux et places" of the kingdom. Only three of these annual infantry documents have survived, the 1566 *état* for the north and the 1572 *états* for both north and south.[29] But since the southern forces in 1566 can be pieced together from other sources, it is possible to reconstruct the crown's peacetime infantry establishment at both dates, the first about halfway between the first and second civil war, and the second just months before the Saint-Bartholomew's Day massacre.[30]

---

[29] For 1566, BN Mss. Fr. 3,243, fols. 103–13; for 1572, BN Mss. Fr. 3,193, fols. 203–10 (for the south, title quotation from 203r), 211–25 (for the north).

[30] For 1566, the presence of a 10-company regiment of French foot is attested by documents in Claude

The *états* show that the king planned to maintain, in 1566 and 1572, for the entire country, a total of 5,804 and 6,229 infantry, respectively, as well as, at both dates, close to 300 command and staff personnel (provincial lieutenants, captains and governors of towns and châteaux, regimental officers, engineers, gatekeepers, and scribes) and an unspecified number of pensioned supernumerary captains. It is clear from section A of Table 2.4, which provides a proportional breakdown of the infantry by province at both dates, how closely infantry garrisons continued throughout the civil wars to be wedded to a strategic placement inherited from the quarrels with France's neighbors in the first half of the century, rather than being disposed for quick mobilization against an internal enemy. In 1566, and again in 1572 – ten years after the outbreak of the civil wars – Picardy, the Pays Messin, and what remained of French possessions in Italy (Piedmont at both times, and in 1572 Mirandola as well) contained 62 percent of all the crown's infantry forces. In contrast, many internal provinces contained no soldiers at all or only a few garrisons.

Despite the putative concentration of infantry on the periphery of the kingdom, however, few of the places that had garrisons contained large numbers of soldiers. Of the more than 50 garrisons specified in the *états* at both times, only 21 in 1566 and 20 in 1572 (Table 2.4, section B) contained fifty or more troops, and at both dates more than half of the total royal infantry was accounted for by the three citadels of Calais, Metz, and Lyon, and the remaining French strongholds in Italy. So where sizeable concentrations were supported, they were wedded to the defense of places that (with the partial exception of Lyon, where a citadel had been constructed after the first war) looked outward past the frontiers rather than inward, where the civil wars were fought. Where the crown's garrisons were located away from the frontier, they were almost always very small. The largest concentration away from the frontiers at both dates was the 500 to 600-man French infantry regiment assigned to the peripatetic court.[31] The total number of companies of infantry which could be mobilized from the peacetime force was also quite small: it is possible to identify in 1566 only 43, and in 1572 only 45 reduced strength companies (50, 60, or 100 men) which could be mobilized to form the skeleton of a field army. From other sources we know that similar numbers of companies were all that

---

Devic and J. Vaissete, *Histoire générale de Languedoc* (Toulouse, 1889), vol. 12, 149, 794, 801–16. There are references to the forces at Lyon in Maurice Pallasse, *La sénéchaussée et siège présidial de Lyon* (Lyon, 1943), 293, note 3, and 423–25. Forces in Piedmont as well as the Bordeaux chateaux and Aigues-Mortes garrisons in 1566 can be identified by bracketing earlier and later payment *états* for Piedmont: the general assignation for Piedmont for 1565 is BN Mss. Fr. 4,553, fols. 1–6 and the *état* for the first quarter of 1565, BN Mss. Fr. 4,553, fols. 7–13; for first quarter of 1567, *ibid.*, fols. 21–25, and an April, 1567 *état*, BN Mss. Fr. 3,220, fols. 1–4.

[31] Two additional *états* specifying the royal bodyguard, or Strossi's regiment, in 1566 and 1572 are *OM* nos. 84 and 159. Of the 6,229 soldiers enumerated in 1572 some 75 were cavalrymen. Some of the command and staff personnel at both dates drew pay as rankers as well as pay for their higher position. The number of supernumerary captains was probably less than 100 (a handful appointed by the colonel general of infantry, 20 or so on the king's pension list, and a couple of score Italian captains appointed by the commander of French Piedmont)—it is impossible to be more exact.

Table 2.4. *The infantry establishment in 1566 and 1572*

A. *Locations of troops in garrisons*

Place or province	1566		1572	
	Number	%	Number	%
Picardy	1,069	18.4	1,284	20.6
Champagne	230	4.0	102	1.6
Pays Messin	1,457	25.1	1,307	21.0
Burgundy	56	1.0	102	1.6
Normandy	471	8.1	233	3.7
Anjou/Touraine	0	0	26	0.4
Brittany	27	0.5	70	1.2
Paris (Bastille)	14	0.2	20	0.3
Suite of king	550	9.5	600	9.6
Guyenne/Poitou	(21)	0.4	25	0.4
Languedoc	(560)	9.6	360	5.8
Lyonnais	270	4.7	456	7.3
Dauphiny	0	0	372	5.8
Piedmont	1,079	18.6	1,272	20.4
Total	5,804	100.1	6,229	100.0

B. *Size of garrisons*

1566		1572	
Troops	Places	Troops	Places
1,160	Metz	965	Metz
523	Savillon	600	Calais
500	Calais	456	Lyon
287	Pignerol	300	Mirandola
270	Lyon	212	Verdun
265	Carmaignolles	150	Monstreuil
206	Rocroi	130	Abbeville
162	Le Havre	100	Le Havre, Pignerol,
132	Verdun		Carmaignolles
112	Monstreuil	50–99	Belle-Isle,
100	Caen, Marsal		Aigues-Mortes,
50–99	Ardres, Rue, Doullens		Rouen, Chalon-sur-Sâone
	Corbie, La Capelle		Toul, Marsal,
	Rouen, Dieppe,		Rocroi, Doullens,
	Granville, Aigues-Mortes		Rue, Ardres

Table 2.5. Mortepaye *garrisons in 1571*

A. Location of *mortepayes* in garrison

Province	No. places	No. *mortepayes*
Champagne	8	92
Burgundy	10	232
Normandy	9	215
Brittany	4	246
Dauphiny	4	39
Provence	7	147
Languedoc	4	132
Guyenne	3	190
Total	49	1,293

B. Size of garrisons

Troops	Places
125	Auxonne
100	Bayonne
80	Nantes, Brest
70	Saint-Malo
67	Marseilles
50	Le Havre, Narbonne, Leucate, Acqs

remained in existence at other times after demobilization: 49 in 1564; 50 in 1573; and 49 in 1576.[32]

One other source of garrison troops supported by the crown in peacetime should be mentioned: the *mortepayes*. These were companies of sedentary soldiers, often older or hampered by wounds, not intended for field service, who were used primarily as château guards and were paid less than regular infantry. Information from the only surviving *état* for these soldiers shows (Table 2.5) that in 1571 some 1,293 *mortepayes* were to be supported, divided among 49 different places.[33] But only ten places had 50 or more *mortepayes* assigned to them and of those, only two had as many as 100 men. These troops were for the most part intended to supplement the frontier garrisons in the north and east and to provide a cheaper source of garrisons for certain strongpoints in the west and south which would otherwise

[32] For 1564 see BN Mss. Fr. 3,191, fol. 7 and Susane, *Infanterie*, vol. 1, 134–39; for 1573, *Henri III*, vol. 1, 279–81 and Nevers' daybook, BN Mss. Fr. 4,765, fol. 53r; for 1576, BN Mss. Fr. 3,256, fols. 23–24. The companies in existence after the sixth civil war are listed in the *ordonnance* of December, 1577, *OM* no. 248.

[33] BN Mss. Fr. 17,870, fols. 284–85.

The army in peacetime

Table 2.6. *The artillery in 1566*

A. Numbers and assignments of personnel

Category	At Paris	Outside Paris	Total
Grand master and his higher officers	30	22	52
Cannoneers	191	20	211
Technical staff and craftsmen	75	2	77
Total	296	44	340

B. Location of personnel outside Paris

13	Piedmont
9	Calais
7	Metz
4	Lyon
3	Marseilles
2	Amiens, Chalons-sur-Sâone, Tours
1	Monstreuil

have contained no royal troops at all. Though these very low-grade troops have to be considered in any accounting of royal forces, it is unclear just how many of them were actually serving, since as the troops with the lowest priority they were rarely paid on time: in 1573, for example, the company of fifty *mortepayes* at Narbonne had not received any pay for over 3½ years.[34]

The artillery, which in various guises had been in existence since the Hundred Years War, is the final component of the permanent peacetime establishment that remains to be considered. The grand master and his officials and technical staff were responsible for organizing and operating the field and siege artillery trains in wartime with their associated draft animals, laborers, materials, and ammunition. In peacetime, duties included founding and repairing guns, overseeing the collection of saltpeter and the confection of gunpowder, and inspecting the condition of weapons and munitions stored in the royal arsenals and depots. The survival of two almost identical annual artillery budget *états*, from 1564 and 1566, which list the individuals to be paid and where they were assigned, enables us to identify with some certainty this service's peacetime strength.[35] According to the 1566 *état* (Table 2.6, section A) the entire artillery personnel only numbered 340 men, the largest category of which were cannoneers, and 87 percent of that service total were assigned to Paris, primarily at the Arsenal. Table 2.6, section B, shows the locations outside of Paris to which artillery personnel, overwhelmingly administrative

[34] C. Douais, "Les guerres de religion en Languedoc," *Annales du Midi*, 4 (1892), 337.
[35] For 1564, BN Mss. Fr. 4,552, fols. 89–92; for 1566, *ibid.*, fols. 93–101.

Table 2.7. *The royal army in 1566 and 1572*

	Maximum strength	
Component	1566	1572
Maison du roy	700	700
Gendarmerie	7,650	7,100
Infantry	6,100	6,500
Mortepayes	(1,300)	1,300
Artillery	340	(340)
Total	16,090	15,940

commissioners of one type or another, were assigned, primarily to collect and oversee the munitions stored in the royal depots and arsenals near the frontiers.

All of the foregoing information puts us in a position to make a fairly accurate general assessment of the total strength of the royal army between wars. If we assume (as in Table 2.7) that the numbers of *mortepayes* and artillery personnel remained about the same in both 1566 and 1572, and if we also include the 700 soldiers of the *maison du roy*, the king's personal bodyguard,[36] then we can estimate a total strength for the royal forces of almost exactly 16,000 men in both 1566 and 1572. This was a large permanent establishment by sixteenth-century standards, but by those same standards France was also a very large country physically, and much of the king's permanent forces were locked into sedentary garrisons. The exact physical locations of those garrisons in 1572 are indicated on the map of military France presented in Figure 7.[37] At that time only 153 places contained garrisons consisting of at least three soldiers or more, whether *mortepayes*, gendarmes, or infantrymen. The *mortepayes* and probably half of the infantry never left their series of fortified towns and citadels, and once the rest of the infantry joined them in peacetime there was little movement of units. Only the gendarmerie, en route to their provincial musters and postings, were periodically on the move in any numbers, but, as we have seen, vast expanses of the countryside contained only small numbers of them. It would not have been that unusual for many of the inhabitants of the country, especially away from the garrison towns and off the main roads, to go for long periods of time without ever spotting any soldiers or, if they did spy some, only small numbers of them. France was, after all, the most populous country in Europe, with about 20 million inhabitants, which implies that only one out of every 1,250 of the king's subjects could claim to be an active professional soldier in peacetime, and that in a kingdom containing some 40,000 parishes,

[36] For the court units, see *HM*, vol. 1, 311. The 1572 gendarmes come from two 1572 general muster ordonnances: *OM*, nos. 161 and 165.
[37] Derived from assignments identified in the documents cited in notes 29, 33, 35, and 36 above.

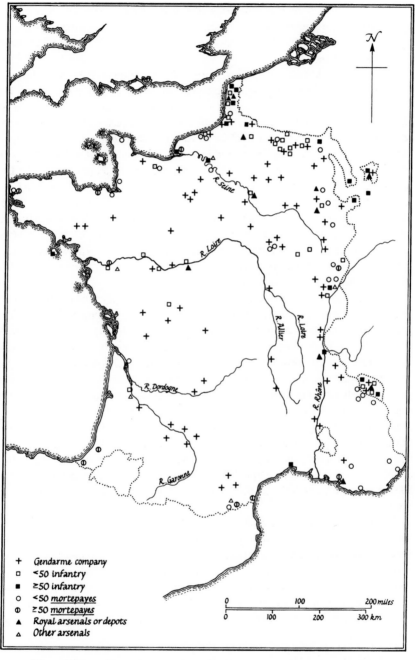

Fig. 7. Military France between the civil wars. Garrisons and arsenals, 1572

ringers of church bells may have been several times more common than soldiers. Compare this to contemporary France, with $2\frac{1}{2}$ times the population of the sixteenth century, armed forces 33 times as large, and one of every 107 inhabitants a soldier in peacetime.[38]

Though the burden of paying these 16,000 soldiers may have been an omnipresent weight on taxpayers, there were not, in other words, enough of them to create a dominant physical presence in most of the country apart from a few frontier citadels. Neither did they count for much in terms of realistic wartime requirements. If every soldier in France had been concentrated at a single place in 1566 or 1572, the resulting force would have been only about one-third the size of the royal army reviewed by Henry II in 1558, and entire components of the later force would have been missing. Foreign troops, for example, both infantry and cavalry, were an important part of the army in wartime, but with the exception of a few Swiss bodyguards, an occasional company of Italians in Piedmont or a handful of Corsicans in the south, no foreign troops were supported in peacetime. Missing also were the thousands of pioneers and hundreds of teamsters who were needed to repair roads and bridges, dig approach trenches and battery positions, pull cannons, and carry the army's food and munitions.

Even the way that existing forces were dispersed throughout the country did not lend itself very well to the operational requirements of fighting a civil war. The manner in which the heavy cavalry companies were spread out, for example, made it virtually impossible for the crown to achieve easily or quickly any kind of strategic concentration of this most important combat arm. With units scattered all over the map and understrength, with men often actually at their homes rather than in garrison, only rather obvious and lengthy pre-mobilization could concentrate large numbers of gendarmes. Such concentration was impossible to hide from the Huguenots and even if successful could not have produced the minimum number of companies thought necessary for a properly outfitted main field army.[39] As we will see, the main field army by itself in late 1567, during the second war, contained 87 full strength gendarme companies, and in the fall of 1568, during the third war, 88 companies, or practically all the gendarmes which existed in the entire kingdom in peacetime.[40]

When we turn to the infantry, an equally revealing picture of inadequate numbers and inconvenient troop placements emerges. Since the crown refused to denude citadels like Calais and Metz of troops even in a domestic emergency, a large portion of the small peacetime infantry force was unavailable even when civil war came. When war did break out, the number of companies of infantry had to be increased four or five-fold simply to supply the main field army (or armies).[41] Furthermore, mobilizing the old and new companies and moving them to the point

---

[38] *HM*, vol. 1, 304–6.
[39] Orders for recall were often published and publicly proclaimed in towns and cities.
[40] See pp. 131–33; Table 2.9 below, and Figure 10.
[41] See Table 2.9 below and Figure 10.

of assembly of the field army was a process not only made more difficult by peace-time dispositions but was one impossible to hide from the crown's internal enemies. Yet to depart from tradition was to risk war with the Huguenots. The outbreak of the second and third wars, in fact, can be directly traced to the two times that the crown tried to break this cycle – by the importation in 1567 of 6,000 Swiss and an increase in the numbers of French infantry, ostensibly to shield the eastern border from the duke of Alva's march to the Low Countries, and by the refusal of the crown in 1568 to disband most of the infantry and cavalry kept under arms after the Peace of Longjumeau under the pretext of escorting the German mercenaries of both sides out of the kingdom. It is to the efforts the crown made to bring the royal army to wartime strengths that we turn in the next section.

MOBILIZING FOR WAR, 1562–76

We are leaving Paris in order to prove that we are not prisoners, wrote the queen mother, Catherine de Medici, about herself and the young Charles IX in a May 18, 1562 letter to the French ambassador in Spain. Though there is hope for a peaceful accommodation, she continued, we are not losing any time in amassing forces from all sides, "So that if things cannot be resolved amicably, one can resort to the extreme remedy of arms to enforce obedience to my son the King."[42]

Little could the principals involved in the resort to arms on both sides of the religious issue have realized that their pursuit of "the extreme remedy" would throw the kingdom into more than three decades of turmoil, bloodshed, and despair. But if the waters of civil war that the crown was preparing to enter were in a general sense uncharted, the processes for the "amassing of forces from all sides" were, of course, well known to the experienced leaders of the royal army. We are fortunate to have, from this period, a basic strategic planning document which outlines their ideas and expectations at the very beginning of the first civil war, and of the types of structural factors and problems which accompanied the gathering of military forces and the outfitting of armies for the field.

The document, entitled "Les remèdes nécessaires qui semblent au roi de Navarre et aux seigneurs qui sont avec luy soubz le bon plaisir de la Royne," was submitted to the queen by the lieutenant general of the realm, Antoine de Bourbon, in early July, 1562, about a month into the army's advance against Orléans from Paris.[43] To liberate the kingdom from the Protestants the army chiefs proposed organizing four columns: one under Montpensier to march to Guyenne; another under Saint-André to retake Lyon; a third under Aumale to recapture Rouen; and a fourth, the royal army properly speaking, to proceed to the task of confronting

---

[42] *CDM*, vol. 1, 318–19.
[43] BN Mss. Fr. 15,877, fols. 84–85. Also printed in Alphonse de Ruble, *Antoine de Bourbon et Jeanne d'Albret* (Paris, 1881-6), vol. 4, 422–25, where it is misdated June, 1562 – internal evidence indicates it was written in early July.

Table 2.8. *Navarre's proposed "remedy" for 1562*

Type of force	No. companies	Estimated strength	% total force
Infantry			
French	85	17,000	37
Swiss	16	4,000	9
German	40	10,000	22
Italian	12	3,000	6
Spanish	12	3,000	6
Infantry subtotal	165	37,000	80
Cavalry			
Gendarmes	54	4,100	9
French light horse	7	650	1
Flemish gendarmes	20	2,000	4
German reiters	9	2,400	5
Savoyard horse	2	200	–
Cavalry subtotal	92	9,350	19
French subtotal	146	21,750	47
Foreign subtotal	111	24,600	53
Total	257	46,350	100

and defeating the main Huguenot force at Orléans. The forces designated for each of these tasks are also indicated and appear to have ranged from 6,500 men with Aumale to around 21,550 with Navarre. The three smaller columns were to procure their artillery, if any was needed, in the provinces they were to operate in, but for the main force Navarre specified requirements of 40 cannons, 10,000 balls, and 200,000 *livres* of powder drawn from the Picard depots close to Paris. The queen mother was also reminded of the army's need for money and of the necessity of diplomatic initiatives to prevent the Protestants from raising forces abroad.

From the information provided by the memo it is possible to calculate the total number and determine the provenance of the infantry and cavalry forces that Navarre and his lieutenants considered necessary for their operations. These rough estimates are given in Table 2.8.[44] It is evident from this information that the army's leaders intended to wage civil war with forces which in number and composition were practically the same as the typical major military efforts mounted by the crown during the preceding Hapsburg–Valois wars. Navarre hoped to command around

[44] When the number of companies or total strengths are given they are used; otherwise companies or strengths are converted from one to the other using the standard strengths of units as given in the many *états* and *capitulations* of the period. There are discussions of the standard unit sizes for infantry, cavalry, and artillery in chapters 4–6.

46,000 men overall, not including the artillery or garrisons outside the principal operational zones. Not quite half of these forces were to be French, which would require three times the number of peacetime infantry and practically the whole of the gendarmerie. A majority of the force, then, was to depend on foreign contingents: the traditional Swiss levy plus additional German, Flemish, Italian, and Spanish contingents. These were ambitious numbers, especially considering the fact that at the moment the plan was being submitted to the queen mother, some three months after the outbreak of hostilities, not a single one of the hoped-for foreign contingents had yet entered the kingdom.

As with most formal proposals submitted for royal approval during that epoch, the recipient, in this case the queen mother, responded with written notations to each individual section of the original document. Catherine approved the strategic division of forces and praised the choice of leaders for the various columns. But she also explicitly cautioned Navarre about the uncertainties surrounding the procurement of foreign troops. The king of Spain had promised aid in the form of 10,000 foot (the Spanish, Italians, and part of the German infantry) and 3,000 horse (the Flemish and part of the German reiters), but there was no word about the German infantry and the arrival of the cavalry was not a sure thing. Nor was there news yet of the German infantry raised on the crown's own account. The grand master of artillery could only provide twenty-two cannon from the resources of Amiens and the Arsenal and less than the desired number of balls and amount of powder from the storehouses in Champagne. Furthermore, so many areas were occupied by the enemy that it was impossible to raise the requisite number of draft animals and laborers for even this smaller train. As for funding, the queen noted, the most important foreign and domestic sources had already been approached or were being readied, and diplomatic initiatives to disrupt Protestant musters in Switzerland and Germany were also underway.[45]

Navarre's proposal and Catherine's response identify at the highest strategic level many of the chief concerns which would consistently influence the crown's decision-making and shape its military efforts during the reign of Charles IX: identification of appropriate strategic targets and goals; assessment of the overall number of troops required and the appropriate balance to maintain between native and foreign and between infantry and cavalry forces; the necessity to greatly expand French forces and to hire large numbers of foreign troops; obtaining enough material for an adequate artillery train (and the abandonment of secondary theaters to their own resources in this area); concerns about the Protestants' own efforts to recruit foreign mercenaries; the supply of funding; and, finally, consideration of the problems of time and distance to be overcome in gathering these forces and in organizing them into effective operational armies.

---

[45] The queen mother's annotations are interspaced with Navarre's points in the memo cited in note 43 above.

The enormous military efforts of the Valois in the first half of the century had gone far toward routinizing the waging of war by the French army at or across the frontiers. During its foreign wars the crown rarely had to fight on more than two fronts simultaneously. And whether the fighting was in Lorraine, Picardy, or Piedmont, well-established lines of advance and supply had been developed to control and support the movement of forces toward whichever front the fighting was on. The key to the efficient disposition of forces, of course, was that the interior of the country was free of fighting. Encouraging or coercing its subjects to co-operate in supplying and lodging troops was not an easy task, but at least the crown did not have to wage a chronic internal war on them.

The wars of religion were to change much of that. The Huguenots managed to seize towns and cities in many parts of the country as well as raise a large and dangerous field army. They had the advantage over previous rebellions, like the anti-*gabelle* revolts of the 1540s, of controlling the resources and skills of a number of urban centers, the adherence of large numbers of nobility, and the bankrolls of foreign governments. As a result, the field armies produced by the Huguenots were, in leadership, quality of troops (cavalry and foreign mercenaries), morale, and sometimes even numbers, not hopelessly mismatched against the royal army. Before there was ever a "state within the state" problem during the wars there was a "royal-like army against royal army" problem.[46]

All of these factors combined to confront the royal government during the early wars with perplexing military choices. On the one hand, the crown was institutionally and morally bound to protect its territory and loyal citizenry from attack and occupation by the Huguenots. On the other hand, the crown had to put together a powerful enough army not only to defend the territory it held and reconquer what it had lost, but also to defeat the Protestant army in the field. There was always the temptation and sometimes the duty to pursue multiple objectives. Towns had to be garrisoned and provincial lieutenants allowed to raise substantial forces of their own. The strategic situation sometimes mandated the raising of more than one main army. The consequences of defeat in battle, moreover, were quite sobering. The means to defend the kingdom could be irredeemably lost in a single afternoon of fighting. This meant very large numbers of troops were needed to meet both local and central contingencies.

But, as we have seen, the crown started each civil war at a disadvantage because of the small size and strategic dispersal of its standing forces. On the outbreak of war the crown had first to mobilize its domestic forces, which meant that to amass the numbers of native troops it needed it had to tap the resources of the entire kingdom. New infantry and light cavalry formations had to be raised in the

---

[46] There is no adequate study of the Huguenot military forces. Their ability to assemble dangerous field armies was based primarily on the adhesion to their cause of a significant portion of the nobility who made up their cavalry, and the ability to recruit large bodies of German mercenaries who differed little or not at all from many of the foreigners serving in the royal army.

provinces and sent to the main army and gendarme companies recalled from all parts of the country. To get these large numbers of troops to the main army took time, especially when the columns marching from the periphery (the west, south, and southeast) had to fight their way to the main army. The crown also, of course, immediately sent abroad for troops. And though the numbers procured varied, in all the civil wars foreigners constituted an important part of the royal army.[47] But providing these reinforcements often involved protracted negotiations (even with the Swiss, whose governing oligarchy was itself rent by religious divisions), long approach marches through difficult country, and, as a result, unpredictable delays in arrival.

The expense, difficulty, and uncertainty associated with foreign troops, of course, raises the question of why the crown so doggedly pursued their procurement. The answer is that the crown's dependence on reinforcements from outside the country was made unavoidable by the dearth of experienced formations at home. A proper field army capable of holding its own in battle with the Protestants required experienced troops. When mobilization began, the experienced pool of French infantry was quickly exhausted (or signed up by the Protestants), and most of the newly raised companies of foot were initially only capable of being trusted with secondary duties like garrisoning towns. For decades the crown had depended on the Swiss cantons for infantry to anchor, and on German mercenary troops to extend, its line of battle, and the civil wars would do little to change this. There was also a limit to the number of heavy cavalry that could be raised on short notice. So when the Protestants, as they did in five of the first six wars, hired large numbers of German cavalry, the crown was likewise forced to do so. While the recruitment of new companies of horse and foot in the provinces provided additional numbers, it was only from outside the kingdom, in other words, that large additional numbers of seasoned or specialized troops could be obtained, despite the delays this inevitably entailed.

The strategic problems the crown faced during the civil wars in coordinating the arrival of its forces and organizing them into effective operational unities were further complicated by the unyielding obstacles of time and distance. France was by sixteenth-century standards a vast country and the rudimentary state of communications presented many problems for armies. The terrain was often difficult or mountainous, cut up by numerous rivers with few crossings suitable for the movement of large numbers of soldiers and animals. The problems of moving and supplying troops were exacerbated by the fact that water communications across the interior of the country were not easy to use or were nonexistent. The borders of the country ran for hundreds of miles and either were relatively open or stretched over terrain that made it easy for a fast-moving force to elude pursuit. The military struggle, moreover, was spread out over the whole country rather than convenient-

---

[47] See Table 2.9 below, Figure 10 and Table 3.1.

ly concentrated in a single accessible region. At one point or another every part of the country, and usually several regions simultaneously, were in revolt. The geographic focus of campaigns was thus constantly shifting in an unpredictable manner from one part of the country to another, a factor that greatly complicated campaigning.

Some of the realities that the crown's military commanders had to overcome when marshalling their forces can be grasped by looking at standard marching times, as illustrated in Figure 8, which uses sixteenth-century itineraries of routes between cities and information on the *étapes* followed by marching troops in the early seventeenth century to identify zones representing one week of marching from the epicenter of Paris.[48] Standard daily march distances for troops changed little over the course of the sixteenth and seventeenth centuries, but since troops would have been rested on the march for one or two days out of every week, these weekly zones radiating out from the capital somewhat underestimate actual marching times. Of course in an emergency troops could be force marched at faster rates, but only at the cost of quickly wearing them out. What this map indicates is that to march troops without rest and without opposition and in perfect weather from Calais to Provence took at least six to seven weeks. To gather forces from northern France to Paris under the very best of circumstances took two weeks, and at least twice that when time is allowed for sending messages and assembling forces. Forces arriving at the eastern frontier were still more than two weeks' routine march away from the capital, and provincial contingents sent from the southwest had more than a month of constant marching before them, and this only if the most direct routes were not blocked by the enemy.

All of these factors made it difficult to get a campaign under way and the length of the period between the outbreak of hostilities to the first venturing out into the field of the royal army was always substantial. In all the wars it took at least two months and usually longer to assemble the initial core of the field army. This ponderousness had a price, for in none of the early wars did the crown assemble its forces quickly enough to seize the military initiative or prevent the Huguenots from mobilizing their own forces. In the first civil war, for example, the slowness of mobilization allowed the Protestants to seize scores of major towns and cities and to gather a powerful army at Orléans. In the second war, it took the army commanders six weeks before they could amass enough force to lift the blockade of Paris, and an additional month of preparation before they were ready to pursue the enemy. In the

---

[48] The map is derived from Charles Estienne, *La guide des chemins de France de 1553*, ed. Jean Bonnerot (Geneva, 1978) and the 1636 "Etat des estappes qui se peuvent dresser dans la Royaume de France pour y loger et faire vivre les gens de guerre," BN Mss. Fr. 18,587, fols. 1–22. See also Jean Bonnerot, "Esquisse de la vie des routes au XVIe siècle," *Revue des questions historiques*, 65 (July, 1931), 5–88 and George Livet, "La route royale et la civilization française de la fin du XVe au milieu du XVIIIe siècle," in Guy Michaud, ed., *Les Routes de France depuis les origines jusqu'à nos jours* (Paris, 1961), 57–100. See also chapters 1–3 of Parker, *Flanders*, 25–105, which deal in depth with questions of distance, military corridors, and the Spanish Road.

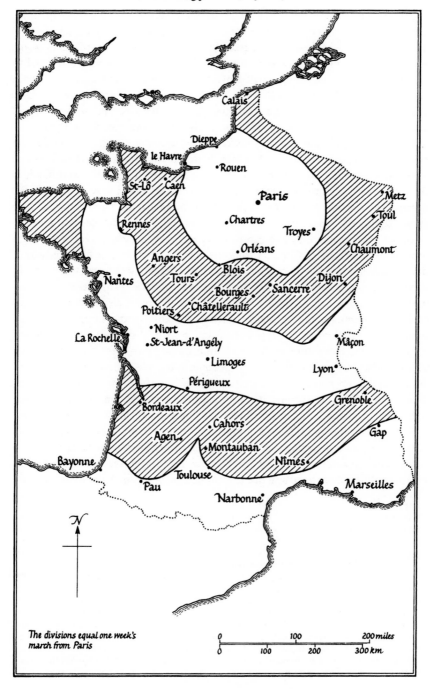

The divisions equal one week's
march from Paris

Fig. 8. Weekly march intervals from Paris

third war, serious operations had to be delayed almost three months until Anjou could arrive in Poitou from the main army's assembly point at Orléans, allowing the Huguenots plenty of time to begin assembling the most powerful army they would ever possess during the civil wars. Finally, during the fourth war, precipitated by the Paris massacre which eliminated much of the general staff and many of the cadres of the Huguenot army, the crown lost half a year before it was able to complete the investment of La Rochelle, allowing that city time to fortify itself sufficiently to withstand the terrible siege of the spring and summer of 1573.

Despite these delays and the uncertainties caused by staggered arrivals of reinforcements and foreign contingents, however, the crown was always able to assemble substantial forces in each of the first five civil wars. But it is difficult to determine with any precision exactly how many troops were raised and supported because the wartime fiscal control records of the monarchy for this period have almost completely disappeared, and this prevents the kind of detailed and accurate reconstruction of numbers and composition such as Geoffroy Parker was able to provide for the Army of Flanders from the marvelously complete fiscal records of the Spanish monarchy.[49] Though no centralized accounting of forces has survived, however, summary *états* and lists of the forces in the main areas of operation or with the main army itself do exist for almost every war. There are also useful references to major formations and strengths at various points in the campaigns in the command and diplomatic correspondence and in some of the contemporary histories, though the latter must be treated with caution. From these sources, original and secondary, direct and indirect, it is possible to provide some approximations of the size of the crown's military effort during each of the first five civil wars by identifying major troop formations, determining the number of companies of various types they contained, and estimating their approximate total strengths. These approximations appear in Table 2.9, but for an enumeration of the sources which were utilized in constructing the table, the reader is referred to the notes.[50]

No claims to absolute precision can be made for these figures, though a higher level of confidence can be placed in the identification of the total number of compa-

---

[49] *Ibid., passim.*

[50] Citations of the principal and most important archival sources on which not only the estimates in Table 2.9 are based, but also almost all the other major displays of army, branch, and contingent compositions and strength levels such as in Figure 10 on the makeup of field armies, Figure 16 on the gendarmerie, or Figure 27 on fluctuations in army size during the 1568–69 campaigns, can be found in the Appendix, Part C. I have tried in identifying the composition and estimating the strength of the royal army to apply a consistent methodology in order to facilitate comparisons across the wars. The initial problem was to identify the area of operations for the main army or armies in each war as well as locate ancillary forces which cooperated or were coordinated with the main force itself in the same general area. Once these major areas and groups were defined the next task was to identify the major branches or subdivisions into which the armies or forces in each area were organized, such as garrisons, the battle, the advance guard, etc., and then the main types of troops, i.e., infantry, cavalry, and artillery, that composed the subdivisions. The critical next step was to get an accurate count of company size units. That count could then be used in conjunction with muster figures, the round number totals often found in documents, and my own knowledge of average or typical company orga-

nies on hand at a specified time than the estimates of total strength for these formations, because in the absence of aggregate muster records nominal and imputed
strengths have had to be employed. But if these approximations are approached
with a large margin of error in mind, they can serve as a useful guide to the general
magnitude of military effort in each war and to the continuities and discontinuities
in the crown's military commitments across the period as a whole. The totals, it
should be noted, do not include every military unit which existed in France at the
indicated times – infantry garrisons on the frontiers or in places away from the main
areas of operations have not been included (though this might add anywhere from
3,000 to 6,000 additional troops to the totals). The table attempts, instead, to answer
the question: approximately what was the maximum number of troops the crown
had on hand for its main operations in each civil war and of what types of troops
were its forces composed?

Perhaps the first thing to note is the accuracy of the king of Navarre's projections
for the level of forces to be used in the first civil war. Recall that Navarre anticipated raising or hiring formations containing more than 250 companies and 46,000
men.[51] Though some of the strategic elements of his plan were overtaken by later
events, and 7,000 of the troops promised by Spain never actually arrived, enough
substitutes were found, including additional Swiss, Breton and Gascon contingents, and newly created gendarme companies, so that in the late fall and early
winter of 1562, near the time of the battle of Dreux, the crown's operational forces
reached their maximum total of about 288 companies of all types totaling (including the artillery train) approximately 48,000 troops. Some 62 percent of the royal
army at that date consisted of Frenchmen and 38 percent of foreign troops, a somewhat lower proportion than Navarre had anticipated, but nevertheless a substantial
number.

The forces assembled in late 1562 can serve as a useful point of comparison with
previous efforts and as a baseline against which later efforts can be judged. In its
numbers and composition, the 1562 army differed little from forces used earlier in
the Hapsburg–Valois wars. It included about double the number of peacetime
French infantry companies, an expanded native cavalry force, and a full artillery
train, but was anchored as always by substantial foreign forces. It did not, however,
represent the greatest efforts the crown made during the civil wars. In the second
war a maximum of 72,000 and in the third war a ceiling of 68,000 troops was

nizations and strengths to compute estimates of actual strength, that is, the number of effectives. This
information was then reaggregated to arrive at the higher level totals. I am absolutely confident that
no major formations or units were missed and that the numbers of companies identified are reasonably accurate. There is more room for error in the estimates of numbers of effectives and to be on the
safe side those figures should probably be treated as maximum strengths. Such estimates are probably
as near as we will ever get to a knowledge of real strengths. For the types of points and conclusions
these figures are designed to support no greater precision is necessary, and, in any case, would be difficult or impossible to produce from the documentary record that has survived.

[51] Pages 55–57 above.

Table 2.9. Estimated operational forces 1562–75

Troop type	1st war Nov/Dec 1562			2nd war Dec/Jan 1567–68			3rd war Dec/Jan 1568–69			4th war Apr/May 1573			5th war Dec 1574			5th war Dec 1575		
	Co.	No.	%	Co.	No.	%	Co.	No.	%	Co.	No.	%	Co.	No.	%	Co.	No.	%
French foot	97	18,150	38	154	31,450	44	221	33,150	49	157	30,900	64	107	21,400	47	103	15,450	53
Swiss	22	6,000	12	33	10,000	14	33	10,000	15	20	6,000	12	22	6,000	13	4	1,200	4
Landsknechts	21	5,250	11	–	–	–	–	–	–	–	–	–	–	–	–	–	–	–
Other foreign foot	24	5,500	11	21	1,885	2	–	–	–	–	–	–	23	4,500	10	–	–	–
Inf. subtotal	162	34,900	70	208	43,355	60	254	43,150	64	177	36,900	76	152	31,900	69	107	16,650	57
Gendarmes	80	7,200	15	143	10,725	15	180	13,500	20	87	6,525	14	68	6,120	13	102	7,650	26
French lt. cav.	41	2,650	5	48	3,940	5	7	600	1	4	200	–	6	350	1	6	550	2
German reiters	5	1,500	3	28	8,500	12	27	8,000	12	–	–	–	12	3,600	8	8	2,400	8
Other foreign horse	–	–	–	24	3,000	4	–	–	–	–	–	–	–	–	–	–	–	–
Cav. subtotal	126	11,350	23	243	26,165	36	214	22,100	33	91	6,725	14	86	10,070	22	116	10,600	36
Artillery train	–	2,150	4	–	2,710	4	–	2,460	4	–	4,650	10	–	4,000	9	–	2,000	7
French total	218	30,150	62	345	46,115	64	408	49,710	73	248	42,275	88	181	31,870	69	211	25,650	88
Foreign total	70	18,250	38	106	26,095	36	60	18,000	26	20	6,000	12	57	14,100	31	12	3,600	12
Grand total	288	48,400	99	451	72,210	100	468	67,710	101	268	48,275	100	238	45,970	100	223	29,250	100

reached. Later in the third war large contingents of Wallon and Italian troops which are not reflected in the table joined the army, but they merely served to offset losses partially, and this ceiling was never again reached in the third war. These supreme efforts, which depended on raising substantially larger numbers of native infantry than in the first war and doubling the size of the gendarmerie as well as hiring the largest numbers of foreign cavalry utilized during the reign, could not be sustained. In the fourth war only a maximum of 48,000 troops was reached, two-thirds of them French infantry dedicated for the most part to the single siege of La Rochelle. And though some 46,000 troops were again assembled in late 1574, during the fifth war, the number of native infantry raised dropped precipitously and it was only with the recruitment of some 4,000 notably unreliable Savoyard militia, who soon deserted, that the overall force level was even temporarily brought near that of the first war. The fifth war, of course, was the longest of the early wars, and was militarily divided into two chronologically separated periods of action. When, in late 1575, Henry III again attempted to reconstitute the royal army, but this time in the northeast near to Paris, the maximum attainable results had slipped to a total of only 29,000 troops (negotiations were also under way at that time for large numbers of Swiss infantry and German reiters who did not, however, appear until the spring of 1576).

Were we to draw a curve, then, of the military effort mounted by the crown across the whole period, it would reveal an initial mobilization of forces on the same scale as those encountered in the traditional wars at mid-century, followed by an intensification of effort including the maximum expansion of the number of native infantry and cavalry troops as well as the maximum usages of foreign troops. This supreme effort, however, was followed in the last two wars by a slowly deteriorating effort much more dependent on a shrinking supply of native troops and achieving strength levels much below the efforts put together in the late 1560s.

Obviously, some of the variation in the composition of the army was due to the strategy followed in each war. The much higher numbers of cavalry mobilized during the second and third wars, for example, were a direct result of an attempt to put together powerful field armies capable of pursuing and fighting battles with the main Huguenot army. But from 1572 onwards, the changing nature of the wars – predominantly siege warfare rather than open battles – is also reflected in the higher proportions of the army provided by infantry and in increases in the proportion of the forces represented by the artillery. Never again, after 1569, were such cavalry-heavy forces assembled, and, in general, the number of foreign troops used also declined because the crown simply could no longer continue to support such large numbers of them financially (the Savoyard militia available in late 1574 were supposed to be paid by the duke himself). Overall, the figures suggest a progressive exhaustion of resources, for the pool of available French troops was also in decline after the tremendous recruitments and losses of the late 1560s and the disaster at La Rochelle in 1573. It should be added that not only did the size of the maximum effort peak sharply and then decline, but also that the crown became increasingly incapable of sustaining even the lesser efforts of the fourth and fifth wars for very long compared to the more successful efforts to sustain larger forces for longer periods of time in the second and third wars.

Despite these significant variations, what should not be lost sight of is that, until the very end of the period, the crown was consistently able to gather at least 40,000 and at times more than 70,000 troops at a time for operations. This represented an enormous military effort by the standards of the day – certainly comparable in many respects to the much better known and studied operations of the Army of Flanders in the Low Countries during the same period.[52] The military aspects of the wars of religion are sometimes presented as small-scale warfare fought with tiny and unprofessional armies.[53] While this may have become more the norm as the military situation rapidly continued to deteriorate after 1576, the magnitude of this traditional military effort mounted by the monarchy against the Huguenots during Charles IX's reign has remained largely unappreciated. The financial implications of an effort on this scale will be explored in some detail later in the book, but suffice it to say at this point that any explanation of the failure of the crown to suppress its religious opponents must grapple with the fact that it failed despite what was by sixteenth-century terms an enormous marshaling and expenditure of military resources.

[52] Compare to Figure 4 in Parker, *Flanders*, 28.
[53] *HM*, vol. 1, 321–30, Lynn, "Tactical Evolution," and Parker, *Military Revolution*, 41–42.

3

The army in the field

"QUITE A FINE AND GREAT ARMY"

Monsieur du Lude, by my last letter, you will have heard of the victory God gave me over those who took up arms against me, and that if night had not separated us, I would have had my way with them completely. Since then, what remains of them fled from Saint Denis in great panic, for fear that I would make them a return visit; as they were leaving, I was forced to send after them my brother, the duke of Anjou, whom I have made my lieutenant general, with all the forces I have with me here, which makes quite a fine and great army.[1]

Thus with a mixture of pride and belligerency, Charles IX announced to the governor of Poitou in a letter of November 26, 1567, that his army had begun the pursuit of the Huguenots who had been forced to lift their blockade of Paris two weeks earlier by the battle of Saint-Denis. In the last chapter, we identified some of the difficulties involved in raising forces of the magnitude used by the crown during the civil wars. Though large forces were raised in each war, in no case did all the troops arrive at the same time, nor were they ever all assembled together at one place. As a result, the armies which fought the major battles and sieges were never to be as large as the overall force levels might suggest. What then, were the field armies like which fought the major campaigns of the civil wars? And what exactly did Charles mean when he referred to the army led by Anjou as "quite a fine and great army"?

We are fortunate to possess a document which describes, in some detail, the field army which Anjou was to lead eastward through Champagne in December of 1567. His army, it will be recalled, had moved out of Paris at the end of November to its camp at Nemours, where it gathered strength before beginning its march against the Huguenot army. On December 6, after his afternoon meal, the army's logbook notes that Anjou discussed until evening with his commanders "the order he desired his army to adopt on the march and the rank and place each should occupy." When the advance began, they decided, Montpensier would lead the advance guard while Anjou himself would command the *bataille*, or main body of the army. The rest of the details of the desired order of march were ordered to be transcribed into the logbook under the heading "The order according to which the army should march." With this order of march and other documents which have survived which

[1] M. Belisaire Ledain, ed., *Lettres adressées à Jean et Guy de Daillon, Comtes du Lude*, vol. 12, *Archives historiques du Poitou* (1882), 181–82. Henceforth cited as Lude.

describe this particular force as fully as any field army during the wars, we can construct a graphic and detailed picture of how the king's army would have appeared on its intended march, rendered schematically in Figure 9.[2]

Both of the two contingents into which the army was divided, the advance guard and the battle, or main body, were to march in large, roughly rectangular columns several hundred yards wide and up to a mile or two deep. Since the two bodies were themselves to be separated by a gap of a mile or two, it would have taken a good part of the day, given its numbers, for the whole army to have filed past. By this time in the campaign much of the colorful identifying materials worn by the troops in the absence of uniforms – scarfs, badges and vests of livery – would have been reduced to faded and stained rags by the wears and tears of camping in the open and marching over fallow fields and primitive roads in inclement weather. But as it marched, the army's internal articulation would have been clear enough to any observer from the distinct groupings of various types of soldiers and auxiliary personnel.

Leading the way for the advance guard was a mass of *chevaux-légers*, light cavalrymen armed with pistols and swords and protected by open-faced helmets and breastplates. Next, marching in parallel columns, were several tactical regiments of gendarmes, more fully armored, mounted on powerful horses, armed with great wooden lances, not differing much in appearance (except for the occasional pistol tucked into a saddle holster) from medieval knights. The presence of some of the greatest noblemen of the realm would be signaled by the quality of their clothing, armor, weapons, and mounts. Following the gendarmerie was a great mass of veteran French infantry, almost 9,000 strong. At the center of this infantry column, grouped with the company standards, would be the pikemen, protected by helmets, cuirasses, and bits and pieces of leg armor, long pikes sloped backward over their shoulders, flanked on both sides by the shot, arquebus armed infantrymen, unarmored except for their morions.

Scurrying after the rear of the infantry would come a company of several hundred pioneers, or conscripted peasant laborers, dressed in distinctive smocks, whose job it was to smooth the path and lend the strength of their shoulders to a baggage train of substantial dimensions: two-wheeled carts, four-wheeled freight wagons, strings of pack mules and horses, and spare mounts. Accompanying the

---

[2] BN Mss. Fr. 15,543, fols. 61–62. I have also used the slightly later "Lordre pour les logis de l'armée et se mettre en ordonnance par Regiment tant a marcher que pour le combat," PRO/SP 70/96, fol. 31, which specifies the number of gendarme companies in each tactical regiment. The marching orders are not unambiguous documents and the relative position of the different contingents could vary slightly according to interpretation; but the overall gestalt seems certain. The march order could, of course, also be influenced by factors such as navigating a defile, or passing a river, when the column would have been strung out in a much longer and more single file formation.

In calculating the relative strengths of the contingents I have used the documents specified in the Appendix, Part C. In representing the relative space requirements of the contingents I found Gigon, *passim*, very attentive to the physical requirements of the armies of the period on the march—he even provides some specific guidelines for making such calculations in notes B, F, G, and K, pages 362, 368–69, and 376–77.

"Quite a fine and great army"

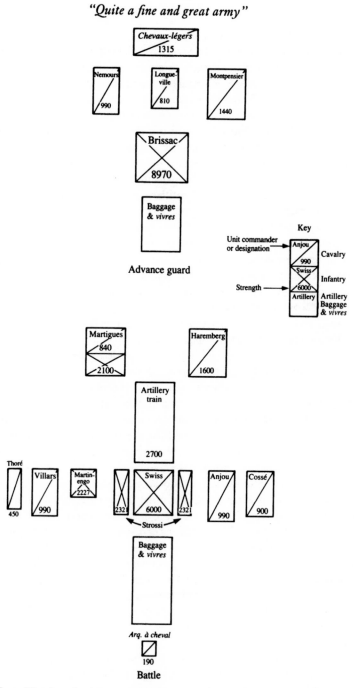

Fig. 9. "Lordre selon lequel larmee debvoyt marcher," December 6, 1567

cursing teamsters of the train, with its cargoes of personal belongings, tenting, spare lances and munitions, and several days' victuals, would be the inevitable camp followers, including pages, servants, camp women and children, provisioners, and miscellaneous unattached troublemakers. A pair of artillery pieces used to signal the main body when it followed at a distance brought up the rear.

After the advance guard came the main body of the army, composed mainly of the same types of troops, but with twice the numbers. Preceded on either forward shoulder by more regiments of gendarmes, the main body was to be led by an artillery train of ornate guns of various calibers, accompanied by several hundred ammunition and munitions wagons, many more pioneers, and the several hundred specialists of the grand master of artillery: gun loaders and layers, blacksmiths, powderers, carpenters, wheel-wrights, rope-makers – as well as a priest with a portable altar for the Mass. Immediately following the train, and serving in their traditional place of honor as its guard, was the hard core of all royal armies, a great block of Swiss infantry, some 6,000 strong, almost entirely pikemen. Flanking the Swiss on either side were more French infantry and then more columns of gendarmes, including Anjou's regiment, the most ornate of all. Behind the Swiss was to come a second great baggage train with its camp followers and then a convoy of foodstuffs and commissary personnel. Ordered to bring up the rear and to hurry stragglers along was a single company of gendarmes and some of the lightest of the cavalry, the *arquebusiers à cheval,* who also provided wide-ranging scouts for the army. Not assigned a definite place were the marshals of camp and their gendarme companies, on the march the most important officers in the army, responsible for keeping the column moving and deciding on the next day's campsite.

At this point in December the army contained close to 38,000 effectives, about two-thirds infantry and slightly more than one-quarter cavalry, the rest laborers and the crews of the artillery. With the camp followers of various stripes that it always attracted, the army would have contained close to 50,000 souls and, with mounts, transport animals, and livestock, close to 25,000 animals. In all the kingdom only at Paris and a handful of other major cities could a similar mass of humanity be found assembled in one place in such numbers. And of course to the visual spectacle of the army's subdivisions of cavalry, infantry, artillery, and baggage trains as it began its march would be added the sounds of thudding hoofbeats and tramping feet, rolling wheels, bumping and jarring vehicles, the jingling of spurs and harness, the clash of weapons against armor, the crack of whips, shouts of teamsters, the sounds of drums, fifes, and trumpets, and a babble of speech and song, including snatches of most western European languages – English, German, Italian, Flemish, and Spanish – and many varieties of French, as well as Breton, Gascon, and Provençal.

Such a multivariegated and numerous host was indeed entitled to be characterized, as Charles IX so aptly put it, "quite a fine and great army." But as an operational organism it was also by far the largest royal army ever put into the field

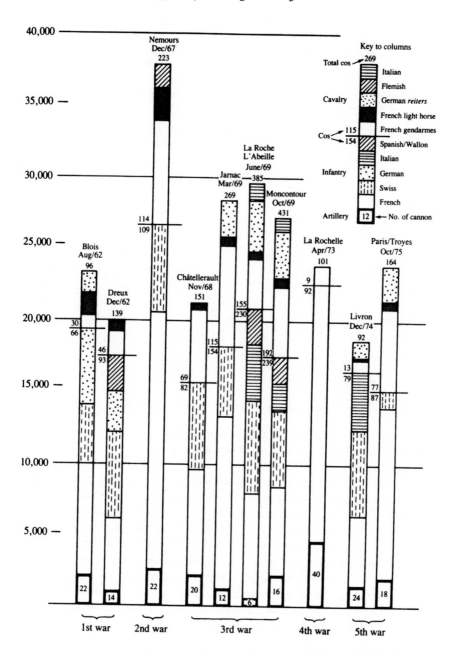

Fig. 10. Field army size and composition at key "moments" during the wars

Table 3.1. *Calculations of proportions of types of troops in the major field armies,*
1562–75

Army at	Estimated strength	Percentage			
		Foot	Horse	Artillery	French/foreign
1562					
Blois	23,350	75	17	9	40/60
Dreux	20,000	83	13	5	44/56
1567					
Nemours	37,725	63	29	7	80/20
1568					
Châtellerault	21,352	63	27	10	72/28
1569					
Jarnac	28,300	60	36	4	74/26
La Roche L'Abeille	29,550	69	29	2	40/60
Moncontour	27,100	60	36	4	51/49
1573					
La Rochelle	28,350	75	5	20	100/0
1574					
Livron	18,600	81	11	8	40/60
1575					
Paris/Troyes	23,850	55	36	8	85/15

during the civil wars and, in that sense, unique. Figure 10 uses the available primary evidence, as well as some useful secondary studies produced by an older school of military historians, to estimate and compare the size and composition of the main operational armies at ten important moments during the civil wars. These include, besides the force we have just described: those which were assembled at Blois in August, 1562, for the siege of Bourges and led out of Paris to the battle of Dreux in December, 1562; the combined force under Anjou and Montpensier which conducted the fall campaign of 1568 and the royal armies which fought the actions of Jarnac and La Roche L'Abeille and the battle of Moncontour, in 1569; the besieging army at La Rochelle in April of 1573; and, for the fifth war, the armies led by Marshal Bellegarde against Livron in December, 1574 and the combined forces assembled by Henry III and the Guises in late 1575. Table 3.1 provides further calculations of the percentage of various types of troops at those moments.[3]

[3] For sources see Appendix, Part C. It must also be noted that, apart from the primary documents, contemporary memoirs and histories often provide rich and reasonably accurate information on the armies of the period at certain climactic moments, such as the time of battles, which were objects of

All of these armies represent, as it were, important and sometimes famous moments in the military campaigns of the times. With the exception of Anjou's army in 1567, and Bellegarde's in 1574, all of these armies contained between 20,000 and 30,000 effectives. At times during the wars, especially as the campaigns wore on, or between successive waves of reinforcements, the royal army would have contained fewer numbers, but 20,000 fighting men seems to have been the threshold at which viable major actions could be undertaken.

If the army Anjou led out of Paris in 1567 was the largest of the era, it was also on the low side in terms of the proportion of foreign troops utilized (though more Swiss and Italians under Nevers would eventually rendezvous with Anjou at Vitry-le-François in January, 1568). As Table 3.1 recapitulates, during the first war a sizeable majority of the army was entrusted to foreigners, perhaps because so many of its regular formations were suspect, but this was also the case during the summer and fall of 1569, and at the siege of Livron in 1574. What is most striking, however, is how many different configurations and faces the armies put into the field by the monarchy had, with cavalry constituting anywhere from 5 (1573) to 36 percent (1569), infantry from 55 (1575) to 83 percent (1562), and foreigners from zero (1573) to 60 percent (1562, 1569, 1574). To a contemporary observer, the purpose of these multivariegated and numerous hosts would have been clear: to attack and defeat the enemy with the rudest of violence. Our understanding of the purpose of war and armies retains much of this meaning. But how could such, to modern eyes, shifting and instable combinations of men be led and commanded? How could they be organized for effective action? It is to an exploration of these problems that we turn in the rest of this chapter.

THE CHAIN OF COMMAND

During the first four civil wars the royal army was usually led in the field by the lieutenant general of the kingdom. The most recent appointment to this post before the treaty of Cateau-Cambrésis had been the duke of Guise, who was given overall command of royal forces when the constable had been made prisoner at the disastrous battle of Saint-Quentin, but the post had lapsed with the coming of the peace in 1559 and the release of Montmorency.[4] It was revived in 1561, primarily for political reasons, when the queen mother named the king of Navarre lieutenant general in order to counterbalance the influence of both the constable and Guise.[5] Navarre served as the nominal commander of the royal army in the first civil war

intense and detailed interest. Although there are differences between authors, those who were closest to the scene and in a position to know, such as Guise, Pfyffer, Tavannes, and Castelnau, generally differ only in details on composition and strengths. Sieges, perhaps because there was less glory to be won, are less well served, though there are often lively accounts of the storming of breaches.

[4] François de Lorraine, *Mémoires de François de Lorraine, duc d'Aumale et de Guise*, ed. J.-F. Michaud and J.-J.-F. Poujoulat (Paris, 1839), 387–90.

[5] Ruble, *Antoine et Jeanne*, vol. 3, 344–50.

until his death from wounds after the siege of Rouen, after which overall direction of the royal forces was exercised again briefly by the constable. After the battle of Dreux, where the constable was again made a prisoner, the army's leaders proclaimed Guise lieutenant general by acclamation. The queen mother was forced to confirm this praetorian promotion with formal investiture of the office and Guise functioned as an all-powerful generalissimo until his death at the siege of Orléans in 1563. After the end of the first civil war the position was left unfilled and military affairs were directed by the aging constable, under whose leadership the army was organized at Paris when war again broke out in October of 1567.[6] When Montmorency was killed at the battle of Saint-Denis in November, the queen mother successfully resisted pressure to choose one of a number of contending noble claimants (including Marshal Montmorency and the duke of Aumale) as the new constable, and instead persuaded the king to give overall direction of the military effort to his younger brother Anjou, for whom the post of lieutenant general of the realm was revived.[7] From late 1567 until his departure for Poland in late 1573, the army was always led in wartime by Anjou, who directed the great campaigns of the second and third wars and the siege of La Rochelle in the fourth.

To the extent then that a royal policy towards the highest military offices of state can be discerned during this period, it seems, after the experience of the first war, to have been to avoid appointing independent great subjects as constable or lieutenant general. After Montmorency's death, in fact, the office of constable was to remain unfilled until 1597. The army was instead controlled through the king's brother, elevated to the lieutenant generalcy. Among the sometimes dizzying political complications – intrigues, defections, betrayals, jealousies, and rivalries – which affected the army's top personnel during this period the lieutenant general generally provided whatever continuity in leadership the army received. When more than one major field army was necessary the commanders were always chosen from among the most loyal of the Catholic peers, like the dukes of Montpensier or Nevers, or the marshals of France, like Cossé or Bellegarde. But the marshalate also became a casualty of the political intrigue, and by 1574, at the time of the fifth civil war, marshals Cossé and Montmorency were prisoners in the Bastille on suspicion of disloyalty, and Damville was allied with the Huguenots of the Midi and leading an army against the crown. A fourth marshal, Bellegarde, was just beginning a career that would end within a few unfortunate years with his betrayal of French territory to the duke of Savoy.

Chaos at the very top of the army's command structure was offset by the considerable powers the lieutenant general was able to wield in pursuit of his duties in wartime. The letters of provision for the office, for example, gave him authority over:

---

[6] The best discussion I have found on the nature of military offices, commands, and commissions and the delegation of royal authority to soldiers is Helène Michaud, "Les institutions militaires."

[7] *OM* no. 106, dated November 12, 1567.

all the princes, constables, marshals and admirals of France, governors and lieutenants general of the provinces, master and captain general of our artillery, and all other lords, gentlemen and captains, of whatever condition and quality they be, to communicate to them any affairs he might wish to propose, and to order those present or absent to understand and to undertake any action appropriate to our service. Further, he may summon any captains and leaders of men-of-war that we maintain in our service, whether horse or foot: everyone under our authority, including our gendarme companies, light horse, pistoleers, or others, whatever be their rank, language or nation: captains of our places, fortresses and châteaux, together with our galleys and vessels, to command and to order all which seems expedient by virtue of their duties.[8]

He was also authorized to regulate the commanders and garrisons of fortresses, to recruit new units, to order the assembly and movement of troops throughout the kingdom, and to insure that the soldiers of the army conducted themselves according to the royal ordinances. He could issue orders directly to civil authorities on matters related to the defense of the kingdom, including demands for rations, munitions, and skilled and unskilled labor.[9]

In financial matters he was granted the power to issue mandates ordering payment of the army's expenses "as if they had been made and sent by ourselves," "representing our own person" as if the king "were himself present."[10] It was also expected that:

He will lead our troops and armies, joined and united as they will be, in all places and situations, for the execution of the enterprises he sees fit to carry out within our kingdom or outside of it. And with these forces he will besiege and attack towns and châteaux which he will assault and take, however he is able, by force or by concession. Further, he will engage in battles, combats, skirmishes and other acts and exploits of war.[11]

Such powers of administration and command carried a crushing burden of responsibility, and from the headquarters of the lieutenant general poured a continual torrent of letters and memos to the royal council, provincial governors, detached commands, foreign and mercenary leaders, local and civil authorities, and military officers of all kinds. Most of this correspondence is dominated by questions of money, supply, and personnel.[12] On day-to-day decisions in running the army and on questions of strategy the lieutenant general was assisted by a council of advisors made up primarily of the leaders of the major formations of the army, a relatively small group of great noblemen, all prominent military men in their own right. On critical occasions in a campaign, or when the crown wished to solicit advice on such questions as whether or not a battle should be risked, the advisors

---

[8] Ruble, *Antoine et Jeanne*, vol. 3, 346.
[9] See the letters cited in notes 4, 7, and 8, *passim*.
[10] *OM* no. 106, articles 10–11.
[11] *Ibid.*, articles 5–6.
[12] See, for example, the abstracted entries in the duke of Anjou's logbook for November 1567 through March 1568, which are interspersed with correspondence throughout BN Mss. Fr. 15,543 and

were asked to submit written opinions to be forwarded to the king.[13] The army's military council did not always operate peacefully or effectively. Personal ambitions and rivalries and the desire to avoid responsibility for setbacks often made it a cautious body, especially during the second civil war, when, under Cossé's leadership, it had failed to bring the Huguenots to battle, and it also appears, not surprisingly, to have worked less effectively when its numbers grew unmanageable, as at the siege of La Rochelle in 1573. It was most effective when its work was directed by a single, but capable, dominant personality like Tavannes, who was primarily responsible for the victories of Jarnac and Moncontour during the third civil war.

Apart from the lieutenant general himself, the number of higher-level commanders and support staff assigned to the field army was relatively small. An "Etats et appointments de officiers estans à la suicte du camp et armée du Roy", the authorization for such positions in Anjou's army, in December, 1567, has survived, and from it we can flesh out the composition and structure of the army's command and support staff below the level of the lieutenant general and his military council.[14]

It should be recalled that in late 1567 the crown actually had three forces operating in the northeast of the kingdom: the main army under Anjou, a small army under Nevers marching north from Burgundy, and an even smaller force under Aumale on the frontier. These columns were briefly united near Vitry-le-François in January of 1568, and at that time there were more than 50,000 royal troops concentrated in the northeast theater. To lead this force a total of 304 salaried appointments was authorized, 204 of which were assigned to Anjou and the army he was leading. It is the latter group of appointments, excluding smaller consignments to Nevers and Aumale, which are detailed in Table 3.2.[15]

With the exception of the bureaucrats from the world of the royal council, who collectively organized and ran the lieutenant general's secretariat – the secretary of state, an intendant of finances, and a royal secretary – the bulk of the staff appointments represented fairly humble positions: a couple of score messengers, translators, heralds, and trumpeters who provided the communications and signal staff for army headquarters and a small provision of physicians, surgeons, and pharmacists (only seventeen for an army of almost 40,000 men). More than half were

---

[13] See, for example, the formal written responses elicited at the end of May 1569 on the question of whether to give battle to the enemy (during the preliminaries of what would be the battle of La Roche L'Abeille): "Si pour la conservation du Royaulme et le mectre en Repos, Il est necessaire de donne la bataille, Laquelle resolution il fault prendre soubdayment, pour les Raisons que les Seigneurs y cappitaynes scavent, y soyens les opinions rapportees a Monsieur demain au matin, affin de les envoyer en diligence au Roy," BN Mss. Fr. 18,587, fols. 488–508.
For an example from November 1567, *CDM*, vol. 3, 80–81, note 2.

[14] BN Mss. Fr. 4,553, fols. 94–114. All the armies of the time were authorized such appointments. For 1562 see BN Vc de Colbert, vol. 84, fols. 235, 277–78; for 1569 see BN Mss. Fr. 4,554, fols. 19–20; and for 1577 during the sixth war BN Mss. Fr. 4,555, fols. 27–29. Even subsidiary operations were organized at the staff and command level like the main armies, though on a smaller scale: see the appointments to Nevers' column in 1567/68, BN Mss. Fr. 3,240, fols. 70–71.

[15] BN Mss. Fr. 4,553, fols. 94–114, minus the appointments to the smaller columns of Nevers and Aumale.

Table 3.2. *Authorized higher level officers and staff for Anjou's army, December, 1567*

Types of appointments	No.	% in category	Average monthly salary (*livres*)
Command		13	
Lieutenant general	I		2,000
Marshals of camp	3		300
Infantry colonel generals	2		300
Light cavalry colonel general	I		300
Colonels of infantry	3		300
Infantry regiment commanders (masters-of-camp)	8		200
Infantry regiment sergeant majors	8		100
Army headquarters		18	
Secretary of state	I		300
Intendant of finance	I		300
Royal secretary	I		100
Couriers and post	15		30–75
Heralds and trumpeters	16		30–40
Translators	2		50–100
Medical services		8	
Physicians	7		70–100
Surgeons	7		30–50
Apothecaries	3		50
Police		38	
Provosts	9		40
Clerks and archers	68		12
Lodging and transport		21	
Marshals of lodging	12		60–100
Fouriers	9		40
Baggage captains	2		40–60
Baggage archers	15		12.5
Tent handlers	5		8.5
Miscellaneous	5	2	
Total	204	100	

reserved for the military police and for the quartermaster types in charge of coordination of lodging and the direction of the baggage trains. Almost all of the latter positions were concerned with the daily functioning of the army: keeping order on the march, arranging suitable campsites and lodging, and enforcing basic discipline in the camp. In actuality, of course, more clerks and medical personnel than authorized traveled with the army, but they traveled as the private servants of their affluent masters, not as employees of the crown. *Aide-de-camp* functions were also performed by under-officers from the personal companies of the commanders (Anjou and all the major formation leaders were also captains of individual cavalry or infantry companies), and there were always a certain number of unattached gentlemen or captains without companies who were eager for employment and could be utilized to carry messages or undertake confidential missions.

The leadership's chain of command for the major formations of the army, as diagramed in Figure 11, was quite simple. The lieutenant general was assisted by his two marshals-of-camp (a third was assigned to the light cavalry) but the bulk of the command positions authorized by the *état* were those of the leaders of the major infantry groups and the regiments that made them up. Missing from the appointments *état* but included in the chain of command diagram were the colonel and small staff of the Swiss regiment and the grand master of artillery and his principal lieutenants.[16] Also included in Figure 11 are the prominent noble captains who led the temporary tactical regiments of cavalry companies, who are missing from the appointments sheet because they received no salary for their role nor any support staff.[17] The addition of these officers adds about a dozen more appointments to the command total of higher-grade commanders.

If these higher-level command appointments, as a group, constituted the brain of the army, then, like the central nervous system of a prehistoric monster, the size of the organ was quite small compared to the bulk of the beast itself, and most of its energy had to be dedicated primarily to the practical task of keeping the simple motor functioning of the animal going. No more than about forty individuals, out of a host of nearly 40,000, had command responsibilities beyond the level of an infantry or cavalry company. The organization of the chain of command was quite shallow, and there were few organizational steps between the commander-in-chief of the army itself and a captain of cavalry or infantry: from Anjou to a captain of gendarmes in the battle was only two steps, and to an infantry captain three steps. The organization was also quite undifferentiated horizontally. With the exception of the provision of a commander for the separate advance guard there was no intermediary commander between the lieutenant general himself and the handful of major formations which made up each division of the army.

---

[16] The staff appointments to the Swiss contingent are detailed by the *capitulation* of July 20, 1567, *OM* no. 96; for the staff of the grand master of artillery and the train in November and December 1567 see BN Mss. Fr. 4,554, fols. 10–14, and 4,553, fols. 95–100; for February 1568, see 4,554, fols. 1–3.

[17] The regiments in 1567 and early 1568 are identified in the sources cited in note 2 above.

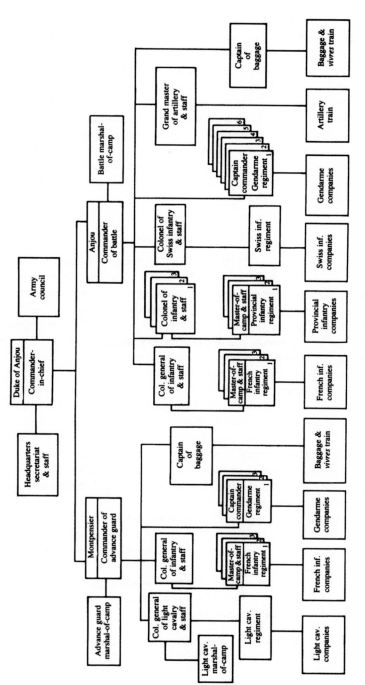

Fig. 11. Anjou's chain of command, December–January, 1567–68

The fact that less than one out of a thousand of the individuals in the army had command responsibilities above the company level, of course, meant that within the few larger groupings of troops it was at the company level itself that the principal functions of command and administration were provided. In Anjou's army company officers made up about 2 percent of the infantry and 5 percent of the cavalry.[18] This meant that around 95 percent of the slightly more than one thousand officers in his army in 1567 functioned purely at the company level. Their horizons and experience, and those of the ordinary horsemen and foot soldiers who made up at least 98 percent of the entire army, were provided by the several hundred homogeneous companies of infantry and cavalry and the artillery train. We will examine more closely the individuals and groups who made up the three principal combat arms of the army in chapters 4–6.

OPERATIONAL DIVISIONS

Between the company-level building blocks of military formations and the commander-in-chief of the army were the major divisions of the army and the higher-level troop formations designed for marching and fighting, which remained consistently the same for all royal armies throughout the period and which were clearly identified in the December, 1567, order of march illustrated in Figure 9.[19] At the highest level the army was divided into two major divisions, the advance guard and the battle, each containing a sizeable infantry and cavalry component as well as its own baggage and supply train. Apart from the concentration of the light cavalry in the advance guard, and the presence of the artillery with the battle, there was little besides numbers to distinguish between them. This relatively simple and clear division allowed some tactical flexibility by enabling one part of the army to defend or pursue while the other maneuvered to reinforce the action or escape the enemy. It also enabled the army to utilize the primitive road network more efficiently by marching in separate columns and to ease the logistical and lodging burdens on the communities and countryside the army passed through by staggering the arrival of the different divisions.

Within both the advance guard and the battle, soldiers and equipment were organized into a relatively small number of tactical groups strictly segregated by troop type, nationality, and specialized function. Anjou's advance guard of about 15,000 men, for example, consisted of only one infantry and four cavalry groups plus a baggage train while the 22,000 soldiers of the battle were organized into four infantry and six cavalry groups, the artillery, and a baggage train. The simple intermediary formations of large blocks of infantry and cavalry (in 1567 from 2,000 to

---

[18] There were generally three officers and two sergeants in the typical 200-man infantry company and five officers in the typical 75-horse gendarme company. For more on the structure of such companies see chapters 4 and 5.
[19] See page 69 above.

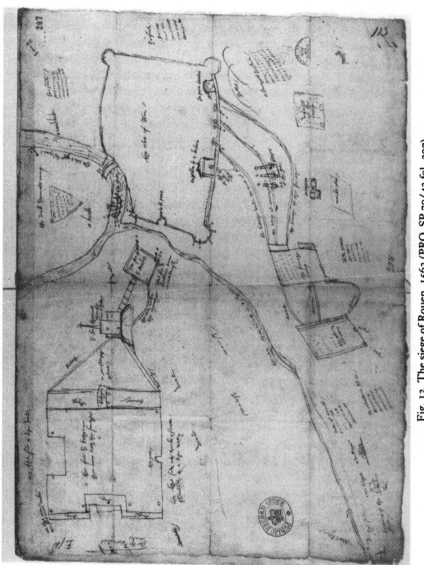

Fig. 12. The siege of Rouen, 1562 (PRO, SP 70/42 fol. 207)

9,000 infantry, and from 400 to 1,600 horse) and a unified artillery train, are absolutely characteristic of all royal armies during the civil wars. The essential organizational form is shown again, for example, in a plan drawn of the royal camp at the siege of Rouen, in 1562, which is reproduced in Figure 12.[20] This illustration captures a moment near the end of the siege when the army, which was about half the size of Anjou's in 1567, had captured the fortifications on Saint-Catherine's hill, which dominated the city, and were using them to provide artillery positions for flanking fire on the ramparts of the side of the city where the main attacks were to be made. Another large battery of twenty-two guns concentrated its fire on the wall and gates which were the targets of the approach trenches and where assaults by the royal troops were finally to penetrate the defenses and cause the fall of the city.

The camp of the besiegers was clearly organized in the same general manner as it would be in 1567. There were three separate infantry (French, German, and Swiss) and five cavalry groups, including one of German reiters, camped so as to close off every side of the city except on the opposite bank of the Seine, where the duke of Aumale, camped with an unspecified force, completed the investment of the city. A separate camp for the pioneers was located near the heads of the approach trenches and the main artillery battery and further off there was a market place and a supply depot for foodstuffs.

The same limited and simple formations that defined the internal organization of the army on the march, in other words, were equally characteristic of the organization of the army in camp and at sieges, and the rudimentary nature of the higher-level organization is quite striking: in 1567, for example, Anjou's army of almost 40,000 combatants was subdivided into less than a score of distinctive and homogeneous formations. The separation of soldiers into a small number of clearly distinct groups based on arms, nationality, and language simplified, of course, in an age before uniforms were adopted, the identification of personnel, was useful in enforcing order and discipline on the march, in camp, or in battle, and simplified security. The simple internal articulation also reflects the merger of tactical and administrative functions, and the organizational constraints that an absence of quick and accurate ways of communicating orders imposed. Unlike in modern armies, the higher level formations served simultaneously as the chief administrative, operational, and tactical units – in the field the army marched, camped, and fought in exactly the same formations. The 1567 order of march, for example, also served as an order of battle. A 90° turn to the right or left, or a filing into line on one of the flanks of the advance guard by the battle produced a continuous line of tactical blocks of troops like that illustrated in Figure 13.

This eyewitness sketch of the battle of Saint-Denis shows the deployment in November of 1567 of many of the same formations that would be included in

[20] PRO/SP 70/42, fol. 207.

82

Fig. 13. The battle of Saint-Denis, 1567 (PRO, MPF 313, Nov. 10, 1567)

Anjou's December order of march.[21] The army had marched out of Paris in its traditional divisions and deployed for battle against the Huguenots. This naive sketch, which tries to combine both a formal presentation of the army's main units with the blurring rapidity of what was primarily a cavalry action, shows the conventional fighting formation used by all armies of the time, with most of the cavalry on the wings and the infantry and artillery concentrated in the center. Though no labels are provided, the dense infantry formations commanded by colonel generals Brissac and Strossi, the Swiss infantry, the field artillery battery, and various regiments of cavalry, are clearly shown.

Simple forms then, flowed from the singular functions of the upper levels of the army's organization and command. Having a limited number of tactical formations, each with a strictly defined combat or support function, considerably simplified the problems of command and communication of orders. When the enemy was encountered little time needed to be wasted reorganizing and redeploying the army's subdivisions, since they were already in battle formation. Their basic combat missions did not need to be specified either, since what the homogeneous combat groups were tactically capable of was almost entirely preordained by their troop type or equipment. In other words, the need for complicated orders and time-consuming communication of commands was avoided because they were already directly built into the actual functioning of the major formations of the army. The price of the efficiency achieved by rigidly building function into the organization of formations rather than providing it with a more lavish provision of upper-level commanders or a larger number of smaller formations was a lack of flexibility, interchangeability, and redundancy, all qualities which modern higher command and formation organization seeks to embody.

Just visible in the left foreground of Figure 13 is a depiction of the mortal wounding of the elderly constable in a cavalry melee at the battle of Saint-Denis. The contrast of the handful of solid blocks of troops with the entanglement of the nominal commander of the royal army in a cavalry charge helps to illustrate these points even further. Once the action was joined orders were fairly useless, and the battle was won or lost according to the skill of deployment, the inherent fighting qualities of the few large formations, and chance. It is thus no accident that the commanders of both the advance guard and main body of Anjou's army served as the tactical combat commanders of two of the powerful cavalry groups. At the moment of action their roles would quickly be reduced to the tactical leadership of their respective cavalry regiments. In that respect the practice of leadership in the army was still closer to that of ancient and medieval rather than modern times, as reaction to the conduct of the duke of Guise at the battle of Dreux, in 1562, proves. Guise had refused to prematurely commit himself and the relatively small number

---

[21] PRO, MPF 313, *CSPF/E* dated November 10, 1567, and probably sketched by the son of Sir Henry Norris, the English ambassador to France, who had witnessed the battle from the heights of Montmarte.

of troops under his direct command until they could be used to carry the day at the very end of the battle. His exercise of what in retrospect looks like "modern" generalship was interpreted by some at the time as cowardice or even a calculated act intended to allow his rivals to be eliminated. That he even had an opportunity to act in the way he did, however, depended on the fact that the other top leaders of the army had long before in the action abandoned any attempt to exercise overall command in order to lead the charges of their individual cavalry contingents, which was, of course exactly what they were intended to do.[22]

[22] For Guise's role in the battle of Dreux, see chapter 7.

4

"The footmen of the king"

THE "OLD CREW"

In September, 1567, about two weeks before the Huguenot attack on the royal court at Meaux precipitated the second civil war, Melchion Gatico, *commissaire extraordinaire des guerres*, and Jehan Girard, *commis par le roy au conteroolle de ses guerres*, conducted musters of two companies of veteran French infantry stationed at the piedmontese fortress city of Pignerol. One of the units was a regular infantry company commanded by the young Count Brissac, colonel general of all French infantry stationed beyond the mountains and son of the recently deceased Marshal Brissac. The other was the garrison company of the citadel of Pignerol, commanded by its governor, Jehan de Monluc, son of the famous Blaise de Monluc, the future marshal of France.

Commissioners Gatico and Girard pursued two different purposes at the muster. The first was simply to pay the men of both companies for their service during the previous months of July and August. The second was to compile a *roolle signale* of each company, that is, a roster containing a detailed individual description of each soldier.[1] An order to compile such rosters had been sent earlier in 1567 to the duke of Nevers, the military governor of French Piedmont, and reissued to the commissioners a week before the muster. The information that the king wished the commissioners to collect was quite extensive.

They must take the name and surname, the age and place of birth of the soldier, and the house where he is lodged. They should note his height and general description and learn from him if he has ever had some wound by which he might be identified; they should inspect it if it is in a place suitable to be shown, and describe it on the roster. Furthermore, they must learn each man's rate and pay and have each paid personally in the presence of the commissioners. And if their captains lent them money, the men shall then repay it. Then, they should make two registers, one to keep to themselves, and the other to dispatch to me, which shall be signed by the captain or lieutenant and the said commissioner and controller.[2]

---

[1] BN Mss. Fr. 4,553, fols. 42–49 for the Monluc muster on September 18, and fols. 50–62 for the Brissac muster on September 13, 1567.

[2] BN Mss. Fr. 3,240, fol. 51, dated September 5, 1567.

Intended primarily to prevent fraudulent substitutions at future reviews, the *roolles* produced by the musters of Brissac's and Montluc's men contain precious and suggestive information about the ordinary veteran soldiers of the royal army. Their information gives us a rare opportunity to examine the social origins and individual physical characteristics of these men, to compare a regular company intended for combat with that of a sedentary garrison company, and to contrast the social profiles of both companies to the larger civilian society.

Brissac's company, with an authorized strength of 180 men, was a veteran combat company, one of the forty or fifty such veteran companies always preserved, though often at reduced strength, even in peacetime. In time of war it would be concentrated with other such companies to form the major infantry groups of the field army identified in the previous chapter. As part of the garrison of French Piedmont it was maintained at a higher level of strength than most peacetime companies, and at the time of the muster 170 of its men were present. Its captain, Brissac, was one of the most important general officers in the royal army, dividing command of the French infantry at that time with the other colonel general of infantry, Andelot. As a great nobleman in his own right, the son of one marshal of France and nephew of another, Brissac would not have devoted much attention to his company, so it is not surprising that he and the company's lieutenant, Honoux, were absent on leave, the company being led at the muster by its ensign. When war came Brissac would be found at Paris early in October organizing the infantry of the advance guard of the army, not personally leading his company, and his lieutenant, Honoux, would command one of the regiments under him.

Monluc's company, by contrast, was not intended to play a combat role during wartime. A pure garrison company with an authorized strength of 100 men, 98 of whom were present at the muster, its mission was simply to guard the citadel of Pignerol in both peace and war. Similar permanent companies provided the garrisons of the fortified towns of Picardy and Champagne, as well as citadels like Metz, mentioned in chapter 2. Unlike Brissac, Monluc himself was present at his company's muster, but he would not be at Pignerol for long. As the ambitious son of another prominent military leader, Jehan de Monluc's horizons extended far beyond the captaincy of a simple 100-man garrison company. A complaint he filed about this time over conflicting military jurisdictions within Pignerol suggests that he was dissatisfied with his position, and at the outbreak of civil war he was granted a leave of absence from his post by Nevers in order to rejoin his father in Guyenne.[3] Once there he was appointed colonel of one of the two regiments of Gascon infantry the senior Monluc was organizing to send as reinforcements to the royal army at Paris, where the younger Monluc would, among other things, become embroiled in a command dispute with Brissac.

---

[3] See Nevers' granting of leave, BN Mss. Fr. 3,220, fol. 7.

Table 4.1. *Brissac and Monluc company tables of organization*

Rank or specialty	Brissac		Monluc	
	No. men	Monthly pay range (*livres*)	No. men	Monthly pay range (*livres*)
Cadre				
Captain	1	106	1	106
Lieutenant	1	56	1	56
Ensign	1	36	–	–
Sergeant	2	20	1	20
Corporal	4	20	3	12
Fourier	1	12	1	12
Musician	2	12	1	12
Cadre summary	12	12–106	8	12–106
Polearms				
Lanspessade pike	16	12–16	9	9
Corseleted pike	37	8–9	10	8
Corseleted halberd	9	8	–	–
Pike	17	7	38	7–8
Pike seiches	–	–	6	6
Polearms summary	89	7–16	63	6–9
Arquebusiers				
Lanspessades	4	13	–	–
Arquebusiers morinées	55	8–9	10	9
Arquebusiers	20	7	19	7
Arquebusier summary	79	7–13	29	7–9
Totals summary	180	7–106	100	6–106

Table 4.1 presents the tables of organization for both companies, which were typical for their type and size.[4] The quite variegated nature of their internal structure of ranks, specialties, and pay grades is striking. Brissac's larger and more elaborate combat company, for example, included three grades of officers, two types of noncommissioned officers, a quartermaster, musicians, three types of pikemen,

---

[4] Documents detailing the standard tables of organization for companies of all kinds are one of the most ubiquitous types of document encountered in the archives, being kept on file both by the central government and armies in the field for the use of paymasters in their preparations for musters. See also note 28 below.

halberdiers, and three types of arquebusiers, fourteen distinct grades of troops in all. To accommodate this variety of troops, there were eleven different pay rates, from 7 *livres* a month for an arquebusier without helmet to 106 *livres* per month for the captain, which, when applied to the fourteen grades of troops, produced twenty-one different combinations of specialty and wages. Monluc's smaller garrison company had a slightly simpler structure with twelve grades of troops and eight pay steps, making fourteen different distinct combinations of specialty with pay.

Apart from the officers, noncoms, musicians, and quartermaster, the common soldiers were categorized and paid according to their weapon and their armor, with the corselets, or more heavily armored men among the pikemen and halberdiers, and the men equipped with morions, or helmets, among the arquebusiers, receiving higher pay. Within this group the highest pay went to the *lanspessades*, or bonus men. These positions were originally created to enable captains to recruit gentlemen volunteers – the *lanspessades* of Monluc's company, for example, were all young gentlemen from Guyenne and Gascony – but essentially it permitted captains to reward their best or most loyal men with some extra pay, a custom which was common to infantry companies all over Europe.[5] The range of variation in the rates of pay meant that the noncommissioned officers (at 20 *livres* per month) were paid somewhat more than twice as much per month as the average ranker and anywhere from a quarter to two-thirds more than the *lanspessades*.

The multiplicity of grades and salaries within the two companies left room for those minor but significant combinations of promotions, incentives, and favoritism which have always been the daily bread of military societies. It also suggests a complicated little social world which mirrored the fondness for gradations of rank and distinction so characteristic of all levels of early modern French society. But basic differences between types of troops were also based on the tactical requirements of the day and the relative danger of the place a soldier's equipment prepared him for. When the army was organized, many companies similar to Brissac's would be combined to produce the large tactical blocks of infantry so evident from the orders of march and battlefield formations of the era. The pikemen were intended for the center of the infantry formations and the shot for the wings, and the more heavily protected a soldier was, the closer he was stationed to the front ranks of the deep formations. The combining of pike and shot, of course, was the principal tactical innovation of the century – the pike protected the shot and, indeed, the whole formation from being overrun by heavy cavalry while the shot was used for offensive fire and to protect the otherwise defenseless pikes from the enemy's firearm troops. The one anachronism in Brissac's table of organization was the provision of halberdiers, who were unable to fulfill either of these two functions on the battlefield. The second civil war would change this, however, for in February, 1568, the

---

[5] In the contracts signed with German and Swiss mercenary contingents this usually took the form of a set number of extra pays to be assigned by the colonel to their "plus apparente."

Table 4.2 *Birthplaces of Brissac and Monluc company men*

A. *Provincial origins*

Province	Brissac No.	Brissac %	Monluc No.	Monluc %
Picardy, Champagne	6	4	2	2
Normandy, Ile-de-France	16	10	2	2
Nevernais, Berry, Orléannais	6	4	–	–
Anjou, Maine	5	3	1	1
Poitou, Aunis-Saintonge	7	4	1	1
Auvergne, Marche-Limousin	1	1	2	2
Lyonnais, Burgundy	2	1	5	5
Subtotal:	43	27	13	14
Languedoc	20	12	12	13
Guyenne, Gascony, Béarn	39	24	38	41
Provence, Dauphiny, papal enclave	41	25	19	21
Foreign (Piedmont, Italy)	19	12	10	11
Subtotal	119	73	79	86
Total	162	100	92	100

B. *Localities*

Number of men	Places
6	Turin
5	Embrun
4	Pignerol, Grenoble
3	Agen, Grenade, Stafort-pres-Agen, Apt, Avignon, Montpellier, Dieppe, Lyon
2	Marmande–en-Agenois, Luc-en-Agenois, Montauban, Cahors, Condom, Biar, Cisteron, Romans, Gap, Bussière, L'Ile Vénaissin, Toulouse, L'Ile Jourdain, Sommières, Pézenas, Rouen, Paris, Maçon
1	175 different places

king ordered the halberds discarded and replaced by arquebuses, thereby reducing the weapon types to just two.[6]

Both Monluc's and Brissac's companies had been involved in the Italian theater for many years and the historical pattern of their recruitment and deployment was well reflected in the provincial origins of their men, presented in Table 4.2A.[7] Sixty

[6] BN Mss. Fr. 15,544, fol. 257: "Sera commande aux conte de brissac y sr Strossi, de oster toutes les halebardes qui sont en leurs compagnies et de navoir que harquebusiers y picques comme lon a acoustemmes."

[7] The displays and analysis presented in this section are all derived from the Brissac/Monluc musters cited in note 1 above.

-two percent of Brissac's and 75 percent of Monluc's men were originally from the south and southeastern part of the kingdom and foreigners, almost all Italians, made up another 11–12 percent of each company. This kind of regional flavoring is not surprising. The regular companies who had been stationed in Picardy or Champagne for some time would no doubt, and for similar reasons, have shown a very high proportion of men from the north of the kingdom. What is more impressive than the overall southern cast of the men is the significant multi-provincial origins of the companies' personnel. Seventeen major provinces are represented in Brissac's company, and twelve in Monluc's, plus representatives from Béarn, the papal enclave, and Italy in both companies. Brissac's company had a significant portion of men, more than a quarter, who hailed from the center and north of France, reflecting the fact that it had served in France at the time of the first civil war and at the siege of Le Havre, before retracing its steps to its peacetime station in the Piedmont.

That soldiers came from the same provinces, of course, does not necessarily mean that they were related, or that they were acquaintances at the time they enlisted. When the actual localities men came from are examined, in fact, it becomes clear that the companies cast a very wide net indeed for their membership. The 162 men in Brissac's company for whom some indication of place of origin is given came from 144 different localities, and only 30 men shared the same place of origin with even one other man. The 92 men in Monluc's company came from 71 different locales with 34 men sharing a common place of origin with at least one other man. When we compare the origins of the men of each company to one another as well, eight additional dyadic pairs of common places of origin turn up. The combined 254 men of both companies came from a total of 205 different places, and only 17 percent of the men shared a common place of origin with at least two other soldiers.

But do the relatively modest numbers of common places of origin point towards some prior relationship? A closer look at the common places of origin presented in Table 4.2B reveals that almost without exception they were towns and cities rather than obscure country parishes, which would seem to lessen even further the possibility of any prior links between men. Indeed, the very strong urban nature of the men's origins is striking. At least 46 percent of Brissac's and 59 percent of Monluc's company (and a majority overall, 51 percent) come from towns and cities that are instantly identifiable on a modern road map of France, and even more if we count even smaller towns, market villages, bourgades, and the immediate hinterlands of larger places that may also have had an urban flavor.

It is, of course, possible that men from the same places, or even different places, were related by blood or through marriage. But a comparison of surnames suggests an overwhelming lack of interrelatedness. Both within and between companies, 231 of 263 men, or 88 percent, had unique surnames which they shared with no other soldier. Only twelve dyadic pairs and two quartets of men shared common last names, and of those only one pair also shared a common place of origin (two men

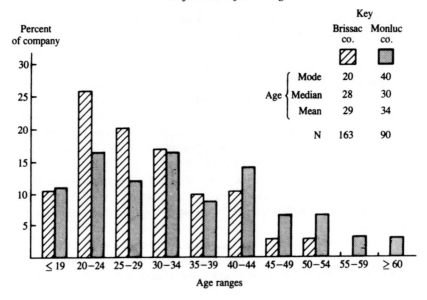

Fig. 14. Ages of Brissac and Monluc company men

named de Fosse, from Dieppe, in Normandy, near where the army had operated in 1562–63). This does not mean that there were no family relationships within the companies – at least one member of Brissac's company was the natural son of Lieutenant Honoux and we cannot completely rule out the possibility of matrilineal ties. But the evidence seems overwhelming that prior ties of family and place appear not to have played a very important role in the recruitment and composition of these companies of regular soldiers.

When we turn to an examination of the other personal characteristics noted by the muster masters, several more illuminating facts emerge. They recorded, for example, the ages of 253 men, 163 in Brissac's, and 90 in Monluc's company. If we look closely at this information, presented in Figure 14, we find that there are notable differences in the age structures of the two companies. Simply put, the men of Monluc's garrison company were significantly older, on average, than those of Brissac's combat company. The modal age of Brissac men was 20, that of Monluc, 40, and the respective means were 29 and 34. Over a third of Monluc's company were 40 years of age or over, twice the proportion in Brissac's company. Significantly, when the latter were 40 or over they tended to be younger than the men in that same category in Monluc's company, which included six men over 54 years old including a 60-year-old sergeant and an 80-year-old veteran. Overall, 56 percent of Brissac's men were less than 30 years old versus 40 percent in Monluc's company and here also Brissac avoided the extremes, enrolling no one younger than 17 whereas Monluc had enrolled four boys aged 13 to 16.

These differences in age structure reflected the different roles the two companies were expected to perform and they remind us that even in the sixteenth century active soldiering favored the relatively young. Older, even elderly men, the proverbial greybeards, could continue to serve usefully in a garrison company even after they passed into their late forties or fifties, ages at which some of the physical qualities required of a member of a unit like Brissac's, especially the endurance to make long marches and to withstand extreme conditions, had begun to diminish. Nevertheless, the wide range of ages represented in both companies is striking. Very much unlike modern armies, only about a tenth of their strength was composed of teenagers. And a very sizeable portion of both companies were fully mature men between the ages of 30 and 49 (41 percent in Brissac, 47 percent in Monluc). The vocation of soldier, then, provided a place not just for younger men starting out in the world, but one with plenty of room for experienced adult men as well, testified to by the presence of so many mature veterans.[8]

The most significant of other characteristics recorded by the commissioners, like hair and skin color, hirsuteness, facial expressions, and identifying scars from wounds, were the height and body type of soldiers. The commissioners recorded the height of 147 of Brissac's and 80 of Monluc's men, and the body type of 167 and 96 men, respectively. This physical information is presented in Table 4.3, A and B.

In a military world without significant mechanical aids, and in an occupation where differences in physical strength and dexterity could be important in the handling of weapons, an examination of the physical endowments of these soldiers indicates that, as a group, but especially in Brissac's combat company, they exhibited some physical singularities. Though the physical descriptions are not recorded with great exactitude, what we find in Table 4.3A is that 45 percent of the men were reported to be tall, very tall, or of good height, 35 percent of medium height, and 20 percent were described as short. A third of the men in Table 4.3B were described as big, powerful, strong, stocky, or well-knit, 29 percent as thin, slender, or gaunt, and we can presume 40 percent had an average body frame. When we correlate height with body type, as in Table 4.3C, 58 percent of the 227 for whom descriptions on both dimensions are given were either tall or full bodied, powerful men, or a combination of both. Another 37 percent were neither big nor tall but were instead either of medium height or build, or a combination of the two. Only 13 of the 227 men, or 6 percent, were both thin and short. The types of ordinal categories used by the muster masters were, of course, imprecise and relative (what if they themselves were very short men!), but it is difficult to believe that a random group of adult men drawn from areas so heavily tilted to southern France would have contained so many big, powerful, and tall men and so few short and thin men.

The possibility that veteran soldiers may have been on the average taller and more powerful than the adult men of the general population seems to be increased

---

[8] The same preponderance of men in their twenties and thirties but with not insignificant numbers of older men seems also to have been the norm in the Army of Flanders: Parker, *Flanders*, 36–37.

Table 4.3. *Physical characteristics of Brissac and Monluc company men*

	Brissac		Monluc		Combined
	No.	%	No.	%	%
A. *Height*					
Very tall	19	13	5	6	11
Tall	43	29	20	25	28
Good height	10	7	6	8	7
Subtotal	72	49	31	39	45
Medium	47	32	32	40	35
Short	28	19	17	21	20
Total	147	100	80	100	100
B. *Build*					
Powerful	12	7	3	3	6
Big, strong	32	19	14	15	17
Stocky, well-knit	13	8	9	9	8
Subtotal	57	34	26	27	32
Medium (assumed)	74	44	30	31	40
Thin, slender, gaunt	36	22	40	42	29
Total	167	100	96	100	100

C. *Height and build* (number of men)

	Height			
Build	Tall	Medium	Short	Total
Powerful, big, strong, stocky, well-knit	39	18	10	67
Medium (assumed)	29	42	22	93
Thin, slender, gaunt	35	19	13	67
Total	103	79	45	227

by the significant differences in height and body type between the two companies. Brissac's company, intended for combat, contained a higher proportion of the taller, larger, and more powerful men than Monluc's garrison company. Almost half of Brissac's men (49 percent) were described as tall compared to 34 percent of the garrison company, and only half as many, proportionately (22 to 42 percent), were described as thin. Moreover, in Brissac's company height and build were significant predictors of troop type, bonuses, and leadership functions. Seventy-five percent of the biggest, heaviest, strongest, and most well-knit or stocky men were either noncoms, *lanspessades*, or the most heavily armored pikemen and halberdiers, whereas 76 percent of the arquebusiers were men of slender or medium frame. Only 3 percent of noncoms and *lanspessades* were short men, and 60 percent were tall men.

Brissac's men, intended for a fighting role, were therefore in addition to being younger, more physically imposing than the men in Monluc's sedentary garrison company. But the desires of officers and sergeants for imposing recruits aside, what incentives might account for the tendency of younger and bigger men to enroll in Brissac's company rather than Monluc's? A comment by the duke of Estampes during the first civil war suggests that pay was the prime consideration of soldiers. Ordered by the queen mother in July 1562, for economy reasons, to let go some of the soldiers he had assembled in Brittany, he remonstrated that "If the said duke of Estampes dismisses his men, there is a great danger that he will weaken himself and reinforce his enemies, *for such men follow the éscu.*"[9] Pay played a crucial part in the lives of ordinary soldiers, since without it they had no means to feed, clothe, house, or entertain themselves. And it is clear from their varied origins that they were thoroughly uprooted from the kinds of community and family ties that might have provided assistance under other circumstances.[10]

If we discount the possibility of significant individual differences in temperament, thirst for action, and constitutional belligerency, it seems possible that an important role in determining at least some of the distinctions between the personnel of field and garrison units may have been played by differences in pay incentives. When, as in Figure 15, we calculate the average wage of the soldiers in each age group in both companies we find that Brissac's men, especially those old enough to be considered experienced veterans, were paid on average a higher wage than men in the same age groups in Monluc's company. A major part of this imbalance is explained by the existence of more of the higher pay steps in Brissac's company, but the steps are also distributed in a pattern clearly based on seniority. When they joined Brissac's company very young soldiers were not paid much differently than the youngest soldiers in Monluc's company. But once an apprenticeship had been served, they could anticipate, if they survived, a fairly steady rise in their wages between ages 25 and 49, exactly the kind of premium for experience and veteran status that any long-term soldier would want. The precipitous drop in average wage for soldiers 50 or over in Brissac's company on the other hand represents a clear

---

[9] A. Lublinskaya, *Documents pour servir à l'histoire des guerres civiles en France (1561–65)* (Moscow, 1962), 97.

[10] The Monluc/Brissac musters also contain information on where in Pignerol each soldier was lodged. With the exception of several small clusters who cohabited with various officers (or at the home of a deceased officer), it is difficult to discern any pattern of boarding together based on surname or place of origin. The overwhelming majority of Monluc's men lived at the château itself. Brissac's men were spread out all over the town, almost entirely as single boarders in homes and businesses. For many of Brissac's men the lack of connection to the townspeople they were boarded on is revealed by the frequent notation "ne scait le nom hoste."

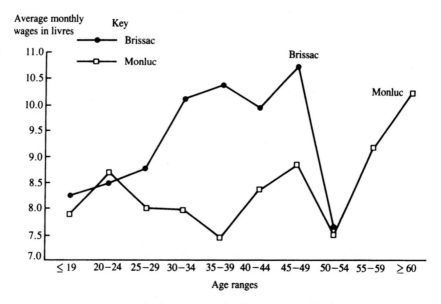

Fig. 15. Average wage by age category in Brissac and Monluc companies

disincentive paid to elderly men in a combat company. In Monluc's company, by contrast, length of service did not receive much of a premium until after age 45 and young soldiers, unless they ended up as noncoms, could not expect to make much more as their career went along than they had received at the time they enlisted. In a sedentary company, however, there was little need to pay elderly men less if they had achieved noncom status. Brissac's combat company, therefore, provided premiums which attracted younger and more physically imposing men, and guaranteed the most experienced of them, between the ages of 30 and 49, up to 2 *livres* more per month in pay on average than men of comparable age and experience in a simple garrison company.

Besides underlining some of the distinctions between the personnel of field and garrison units, and between the physical attributes of soldiers and civilians, all of this information clearly leads towards an even more interesting conclusion. Everything we know about the social organization of groups and communities in sixteenth-century France shows that they were chiefly defined by ties of class, family, intermarriage, locality, and occupation. But in its permanent veteran companies of French infantry, both garrison and field, the crown had created a quite singular type of social organization of self-selected, unrelated, and nationally recruited men of all ages whose major commonalities, besides more imposing physiques and a tendency towards urban origins, were only their shared membership in the company and its activities.

Brantôme, in a famous passage about the ordinary soldiers of the veteran French infantry companies, one of which he himself had commanded, noted:

And what I most admire in these infantrymen is that you see young men come from the villages, the plow, the shops, the schools, the palaces, the posts, the forges, the stables, and lackeydom, and from similar low and mean places, and no sooner do they dwell among this infantry for even the shortest time, than you see them promptly become hardened and fashioned into warriors, and that from the nothing they were, they come to be captains and the equals of gentlemen, having their honor to recommend them as much as the most noble, and performing deeds as virtuous and noble as the greatest gentlemen.[11]

Two things are interesting about this statement. The first, of course, is the implied widespread, though humble, social origins of the young men who entered the army, and, in fact, only a very small proportion of the men of these units were gentlemen (six in each company). Even if we take into account the officers, who were all nobles, far more than 90 percent of the men in these companies were from relatively humble origins. But, even if their origins were humble compared, as we shall see, to the gendarmerie, their urban origins strongly suggest that the veteran French infantry was by no means an army only of peasant boys, and that here Brantôme may have spoken more accurately than he is usually given credit for, because when we examine a little more closely the places from which the men with common origins came, we find them almost without exception to have been centers of many of the types of occupations – artisans, domestics, students, and paralegals – named by Brantôme as the prime sources of soldiers.

An explanation for the second part of Brantôme's description, with its reference to the ability of young soldiers of humble origins to act as bravely and honorably as their social betters, might best be sought in the shared values of the fighting men of what was to some extent an artificially and rationally constructed military community. Geoffrey Parker has written about the way in which veteran status distinguished the useful from worthless unit in armies throughout early modern Europe.[12] The men of Brissac's and similar companies, the soldiers of the *vielles bandes*, the men who so impressed the Parisian bourgeoisie when they marched in from Calais, or Metz, or Piedmont, were exactly the kinds of veterans the crown needed to wage war successfully. The problem with the "old crew," as the English Ambassador Norris so aptly named them, was not, as we will see, to be found in their fighting quality, but in the fact that there were never enough of them.[13]

---

[11] Brantôme, *Oeuvres*, vol. 5, 367–68.
[12] Parker, *Military Revolution*, 50–52.
[13] Norris' reference was to the veteran French infantry companies Strossi brought with him to Paris from the Picard frontier in October 1567; see *CSPF/E*, vol. 8, no. 1,756.

COMPANY STRENGTHS AND ARMAMENTS

Only a short interval separated the musters of Brissac's and Monluc's companies from the arrival at Pignerol of news of the Huguenot attempt on the king at Meaux, and of the outbreak of renewed hostilities. The duke of Nevers, urged on by the queen mother, promptly threw himself into an effort to organize a sizeable column to bring to France from the Piedmont. On both larger and smaller scales, royal commanders all over the kingdom were engaged in exactly the same type of activity which, where the infantry forces were concerned, involved bringing the regular companies up to full strength, raising new companies of native or foreign troops, and arranging for the replacement of companies removed from garrison duties. The key to a successful mobilization lay with the activities of the company captains, the military entrepreneurs who could recruit men, integrating them into existing, or organizing them into new, formations. The fortunate survival of some key documents from Nevers' command in 1567 allows us to reconstruct how this process worked and the type of infantry companies the process produced.

Soon after the arrival of the dispatch alerting him to the renewal of civil war, Nevers wrote to the duke of Albequerque, the Spanish military governor of Milan, to obtain permission to raise troops in Italy. He explained that he had been

> commanded to raise Italian infantry and cavalry for service in France...For this reason, Monseigneur the duke of Nevers asks Monseigneur the duke of Albequerque that he be so kind as to grant permission to all soldiers of good will, whether horsemen or footmen, who are subjects of his Catholic Majesty, to enroll and be in the pay of the very-Christian king, under captains that Monseigneur the duke of Nevers will deputize to carry out the recruitment and to lead them to the service of His Majesty. He will also please permit the said Seigneur duke to have his captains sound the drum in Milanese territory and to procure such arms as are necessary to equip their company. To that same end, let those who wish to go on horseback arm themselves, mount their horses, and leave the territory with their horses and arms, in order in like manner to come to the service of His Majesty.[14]

As military governor of Piedmont, which had been for so long during the Hapsburg–Valois wars the center of French military involvement in Italy, Nevers was authorized a number of small pensions in his annual budget which were used to keep dozens of unemployed captains, mostly Italian, on retainer. Both of the colonel generals of infantry also had budgetary allotments for this purpose, as, of course, did the king himself.[15] In Pignerol lists of available captains were soon produced,

---

[14] BN Mss. Fr. 3,220, fol. 81.

[15] An example of the royal list is BN Mss. Fr. 3,312, fols. 44–45; *OM* nos. 84 and 159 indicate the standard appointments of captains allowed Andelot in 1566 and Strossi in 1572. Two examples of captains kept on retainer by the governor of Piedmont are: for 1559, BN Mss. Fr. 4,552, fols. 1–6 and for 1567, BN Mss. Fr. 3,220, fols. 1–4. For dramatic evidence that such appointments were not simply nominal see the very interesting document, BN Mss. Fr. 4,552, fols. 87–88, dated August 14, 1563, which lists Italian captains on the Piedmont rolls who had crossed the Alps to serve during the first civil war but were stranded by hard circumstances – nonpayment of pensions, evaporation of promised places, or wounds.

the names of those to be chosen to raise companies ticked off, and notations made of the amount of recruiting money advanced to them so that they could begin to collect their men.[16] Captains would give money to under-officers, or to civilian contacts, often old soldiers, to help with the recruiting, or to the recruits themselves for their room and board money as they made their way in small groups to camp.[17] Not all captains were equally adept at raising men, so there were always variations in the sizes of companies, and the promise of a company sometimes had to be rescinded, though usually with some recompense, when a captain was unable to raise the minimum number of men required or when his company had to be broken up to help fill up other understrength companies.[18] But a lack of captains or of recruits does not seem to have been a serious problem at the immediate beginning of each war – on the contrary, the problem was to choose from among a superfluity of unemployed captains eager to be allowed to organize companies.

The force that Nevers assembled for the march down into France included the five veteran French infantry companies stationed in the Piedmont, one of them Brissac's, and twenty-one companies of newly raised Italian troops. An additional eight Italian companies were later to be raised to join the remaining citadel companies, like Monluc's, in the Piedmont garrison. A summary of the payment made by the newly appointed muster masters at the assembly point at Carmaignolles, if it can be trusted, indicates that by mid-October, 1567, the five French companies had been brought up to their full complement of 180 men each while the twenty-one Italian companies had an average strength of 90 men each.[19] By mid-November, this force had arrived at Belleville, in the Rhône valley north of Lyon, where it was joined by an additional force of 4,000 newly raised Swiss infantry. Fully organized, Nevers' little army of about 8,000 men, including cavalry, with its headquarters, staff, and tactical organization, was a smaller mirror image of Anjou's army at Paris.[20] But the infantry companies which had marched from Piedmont in October had already begun to slim down, as the records of a muster of the French and Italian troops held at Belleville on November 18 clearly show. The elaborate niceties of the *roolle signale* were abandoned, an early victim of the realities of war, and the muster masters were instructed simply to count the number of soldiers in each company with an eye out for obvious *passe-volants* and to note how each soldier was armed. The five French companies averaged 139 men each, varying in size from 110 to 155

---

[16] BN Mss. Fr. 4,553, fol. 84, and 3,240, fols. 60–61.

[17] For a good example of the finances of recruiting and the manner in which recruits dribbled in to the assembly point, see the document presented in Douais, vol. 5, 89–92.

[18] BN Mss. Fr. 3,240, fols. 70v–70r for Nevers' November 1567 *état* approving recompense to two Italian captains who had been promised companies.

[19] BN Mss. Fr. 4,553, fols. 89–90. For Nevers' appointment of commissioners and muster masters, see BN Mss. Fr. 3,220, fol. 89. The replacement of the extra Italian companies raised to garrison Piedmont during the second war is noted in the March, 1568, *état*, ibid., fol. 85.

[20] His force can be reconstructed in some detail using BN Mss. Fr. 4,553, fols. 88–93, 103 (October and December *états*, including the Swiss); 3,212, fols. 151–52 (November *état*); and 3,240, fols. 70–71 (November staff and command appointments).

Table 4.4. *Organization and equipment of five French and eighteen Italian companies mustered at Belleville, November, 1567*

Rank and/or armament	French		Italian	
	No.	%	No.	%
Cadre				
Officers and sergeants	25	4	72	5
Musicians	–	–	18	18
Subtotal	25	4	90	7
Polearms				
Halberds	–	–	46	4
Corseleted pike	190	27	67	5
Pikes seiches	11	2	–	–
Subtotal	201	29	113	10
Arquebuses				
Morion	441	63	993	74
No morion	–	–	110	8
Subtotal	441	63	1,103	83
Other				
No weapon or sword only	29	4	12	1
Total	696	100	1,336	100
Average company size:	139 men		74 men	

men, with Brissac's company, the *colonelle* of the regiment, mustering 146 men. The eighteen Italian companies enumerated had a much lower average strength – 74 men each (72 if the strengths of two unenumerated companies are counted) – and an even wider variation in sizes, from a low of 57 to a high of 130 men.[21]

The details of the information contained in the surviving muster sheet, presented in Table 4.4, also indicate differences in the way the French and Italian troops were armed. In the French companies firearms outnumbered pikes by a ratio of about 2:1 and all the men who carried weapons had at least a morion for protection though, interestingly, some 29 of 696 men had no offensive arms at all or only a sword, though a few of them had brought nags with them. The polearm contingent in the eighteen enumerated Italian companies was much smaller – only 10 percent of the total 1,336 men whose weapons were indicated, 83 percent of whom carried

---

[21] BN Mss. Fr. 3,212, fols. 151–52.

arquebuses. When we consider that almost half of the Italian corselets were armed with obsolete halberds (no French soldiers were) and that more than 100 of the arquebusiers did not even have the minimal protection of a helmet, it seems clear that the Italians were both more lightly equipped and less ready for action in the field than the French troops. This fact may have contributed to a sharp defeat inflicted on them later in the campaign by Huguenot cavalry and must certainly have played a role in Nevers' decision right after the muster to use his French infantry, rather than the Italian bands, to storm the city of Mâcon, captured earlier in the war by the Protestants, at the beginning of his march north to Champagne.

After the troops were enumerated, the muster masters administered the oath. The five *vielles bandes* of the French regiment pledged "We swear and promise God to well and capably serve the King with our all and against all, without exception or reservation as it will be commanded and ordered by Monseigneur the duke of Nevers, our general, or by Monseigneur the count of Brissac, our colonel."[22] The eight Italian companies assigned with the French regiment to the advance guard of the army and the twelve assigned with the Swiss to the battle swore the same simple oath, but in Italian, substituting the names of their own colonels.[23] Shortly after the musters Nevers began his advance, taking Mâcon on December 4 and linking up in January, 1568, as we have seen, with Anjou's and Aumale's forces near Vitry-le-François, where the senior company of the French regiment was briefly reunited with its captain, Colonel General Brissac, commander of the regiments of French infantry in the vanguard of Anjou's army. Anjou, curious to see the French units from Piedmont, asked to review them. To honor him they fired a salvo and took part in a mock skirmish, but tired from their long march and their rough handling at the storming of Mâcon, their performance was so desultory it embarrassed their colonel.[24]

How typical of the French and foreign infantry which served the king were the strength and armament of the companies mustered at Belleville? About the same time that Nevers was gathering his companies of French and Italian troops at Carmaignolles, Brissac himself, as one of the colonel generals of infantry, was holding a muster at Paris of twenty companies of French infantry which were to form the initial core of the major infantry formation of the advance guard of the royal army under the constable at the battle of Saint-Denis and later in the year under Anjou. As at Belleville, the muster commissioners recorded the number of men in each company and how they were equipped, information which is presented in Table 4.5.[25] The twenty companies enumerated (including one which had 150

[22] *Ibid.*, 152.
[23] *Ibid.*
[24] See Nevers' provisional letter granting to his principal commanders spoils from the taking of Mâcon, BN Mss. Fr. 3,240, fol. 69. Brantôme gives an account of the tepid mock skirmish, *Oeuvres*, vol. 6, 153–55.
[25] BN Mss. Fr. 3,197, fols. 59–60, dated 12 October, 1567, two weeks after Meaux.

Table 4.5. *Organization and equipment of twenty French infantry companies at Paris, October,* 1567

Armament	No. of men	%
Polearms		
Corselet	437	18
Pike seiche	706	28
Halberds	20	1
Subtotal	1,163	47
Arquebuses		
With morions	1,118	45
Without morions	177	7
Subtotal	1,295	52
Other		
No armor or weapons besides swords	30	1
Total	2,488	100
Average company strength	132 men	

of its men on detached duty) had already reached an average strength of 132 men per company (135 if officers are counted) less than two weeks after the beginning of hostilities. The smallest company contained 89 and the largest 277 men. Some of these companies, in other words, were already at or were well on their way to becoming full strength units, and, if an overall summary of the army's numbers is to be believed, had reached an average strength of 204 men per company by the time the army had reached its camp at Nemours in early December.[26] Like Nevers' French infantry there were more firearms than polearms within the units, though the overall ratio (52 to 47 percent) of the weapons was more even. Substantial numbers of men, more than a third, were completely unarmored pikemen and arquebusiers (28 and 7 percent respectively), and 30 out of the 2,488 men enumerated had no arms at all except swords. One of the main purposes of such an initial review, of course, was to determine the equipment needs of the units, and any defaults could be made good from the resources of the Arsenal at Paris, from which wagonloads of weapons and armor could be dispatched to units in the field.[27] But this basic mixture of weapons and armor (minus the halberds, soon converted to arquebuses) was to be the standard for regular French infantry companies serving with the royal army throughout the rest of the early wars.

[26] BN Mss. Fr. 4,553, fol. 101.
[27] See the reference to the expense of sending arms and armor from the Arsenal to the army by wagon in the December 1567 artillery *état*, BN Mss. Fr. 4,553, fol. 99r.

The planning documents of the time show that, on paper at least, the crown supported an enormous variety of company organizations for its native troops. A list from the early 1560s, for example, summarizes the number and type of soldiers, their wages, and total monthly unit costs, of twenty-nine different types of French infantry companies, ranging in size from 50 to 400 men.[28] But the type of unit containing 180–200 men, organized like Brissac's company, seems to have become the norm for full-strength French infantry companies with the field army from early in the wars of religion. Such standard infantry companies probably achieved strengths very near to their official authorized levels at the beginning of a campaign. The returns for nineteen active companies of French infantry stationed in Picardy at the beginning of the fourth civil war, for example, the core of two of the infantry regiments which were to fight at the siege of La Rochelle, mustered an average of 171 men in late August, 1572, and by October, 190 men each, or 95 percent of full strength.[29] Sometimes, in fact, companies began the campaign with even larger numbers. At the beginning of the siege of La Rochelle Biron had to deal with an enormous and ill-disciplined company brought into camp by a Captain Saint-Martin. He wrote to the king of

the company of Saint-Martin, which has entered this camp with 500 men, and we do not know how to support them. It is a huge, unruly company. Nevertheless, it is a mine of men, and the said Saint-Martin promises to perform miracles...[but] you could say, Sire, that having sent me to besiege La Rochelle, I find myself instead besieged by the said Saint-Martin and by his men...and I assure you, Sire, that I am more afraid of him than of those of La Rochelle, which is why I have lodged them apart from myself and my men.[30]

Summary army returns for the two Gascon regiments which joined Anjou's army in late 1567 (one of them led by Jehan de Monluc) reported average company strengths of 268 and 228 men, and we can determine that as late as March, 1568, according to the bread ration records of the siege of Chartres, some of these companies still mustered close to 200 men.[31]

As for foreign troops, the capitulations of the time show that Swiss and German infantry were hired in large regiments of at least ten and more usually twenty companies of 250 to 300 men each in which the stipulated ratio of polearm to firearm weapons was approximately 9:1 and 7:3 respectively.[32] Such Landsknecht and Swiss companies tended to be very close to full strength, if not actually over

[28] "Etat par le menu de la forme du payment des compagnies de gens de guerre a pied qui sont au service dur Roy. Tant Francois, Suisses que Lansquenetz": BN Mss. Fr. 3,150, fols. 87–105.

[29] BN Mss. Fr. 29,508, fols. 221–23 and 224–34.

[30] Biron, *AHG*, 62–63, 67; letters of January 10, 1573.

[31] BN Mss. Fr. 4,553, fol. 101; Merlet, "Etat des dépenses faites par la ville de Chartres", *Bulletin historique et philologique* (1840), *passim*, esp. 404–6; for strengths for the original garrison companies and Martinengo's column, *ibid.*, 396–97 and 400–1.

[32] Capitulations for the Swiss in 1567, 1568, and 1570 in *OM* nos. 96, 125, and 139; Landsknechts in 1562 in BN Mss. Fr. 4,552, fols. 83–85 and 4,553, fols. 35–36; reiters in 1568, *OM* no. 128 and BN Mss. Fr. 15,608, fols. 30–33, and in 1577, *OM* no. 237. See also Table 4.7 below.

strength, at the start of a campaign, and their company sized units were consistently larger than the average French unit. Nevers' Italian regiment, then, with much smaller and more lightly equipped companies, represented a weaker and lower grade type of foreign contingent than the Swiss and German infantry hired during the wars of religion.

But if the veteran French companies and the Swiss and German units started the campaign near full strength or achieved it within a few weeks, the trajectory of infantry strengths after several months of service, or even sooner, as the Belleville muster reminds us, was steadily downward. All of the contemporary accounts and recollections show that hard marching and hard fighting, not to mention illness, reduced company strengths rapidly. Tavannes, for example, claimed that at the end of the fall, 1568 campaign, the thirty-odd infantry companies of the regiments under the command of Brissac could only muster some 300 men.[33] And in June, 1569, at the nadir of the royal army's fortunes in the sterile country around Limoges during the following campaign, the bread ration lists show an average strength of only 81 men for 137 companies of French infantry.[34] Sieges in particular seem to have quickly resulted in greatly reduced strengths. In a January 10, 1573, letter to the king about the inadequacy of the infantry force assigned to the siege of La Rochelle, Biron warned:

Having learned that the corps of Swiss will not be brought and that the table of strength contains only 57 French companies, I want to well alert you, Monseigneur, that you should not expect more than 100 men per company; for at the muster because of *passe-volants*, illness and absentees, there are companies which hardly amount to more than that. And when they stand guard, some will be sick, and others will absent themselves to go pillaging. Therefore, you should expect no more than 100 men per company.[35]

Biron's prediction that companies counted as full strength could in actuality only provide 100 serviceable men at the siege may actually have been an overestimate once combat casualties are also taken into account. Anjou was to recall in his official report on the siege of La Rochelle that as battle casualties and sickness mounted companies were reduced to such small size that when a regiment entered the trenches all that could be seen was a cluster of company flags.[36] Biron was willing to tolerate an oversized if disorderly company at the beginning of the siege exactly because it could indeed be a mine of replacements for other companies.

When companies were reduced beyond a certain point, generally less than 30–40 men, their utility was markedly reduced. They could not be used for the many company sized tasks: guard of a sector of the camp or the trenches, for example. As original and reinforcing companies became greatly reduced in manpower, they also

---

[33] Gaspard de Saulx, *Mémoires de Gaspard de Saulx, Seigneur de Tavannes*, ed. M. Petitot (Paris, 1822), vol. 25, 56.
[34] BN Mss. Fr. 4,554, fol. 14.
[35] Biron, *AHG*, 69, letter of January 10, 1573.
[36] BN Mss. Fr. 4,765, fol. 72r.

became relatively more expensive to maintain, since their officers and cadre continued to be paid at a high rate even as they were leading fewer and fewer men. The expense of providing food was also affected as companies continued to demand bread rations at their old strengths – a claim that was hard to refute because since pay was usually in arrears there was often no current muster sheet which could be used to certify their actual numbers.

One solution to the problem of diminishing numbers was to allow territorially raised contingents to leave the army temporarily in order to recruit themselves back up to strength at their home. But for the veteran French infantry companies, often hundreds of miles from their peacetime stations, this was not usually possible. Some local recruiting in the area of operations always took place (as the presence of a dozen or so Normans in Brissac's company reminds us) and this method of raising troops was thought preferable by Biron, among others, who argued that by enlisting men in the area of operation you denied them to Huguenot captains.[37]

In the end, however, the most effective solution to the problem of understrength companies was to consolidate their personnel into a smaller number of fuller companies. Such "reductions" involved the disbanding of some units and the transfer of their remaining soldiers to other companies. Though always bitterly resented by the captains who lost their companies, the process made both financial and military sense, and reduction of companies was used in the royal army in every campaign to keep the French infantry companies up to a serviceable strength. After the battle of Dreux, for example, Guise reduced the worn-out French infantry with the army from 45 to 30 companies, and at the siege of Saint-Jean-d'Angély in 1569 more than 100 companies were consolidated into six regiments of 10 companies each. Anjou also directed a drastic reduction after a succession of failed assaults at the siege of La Rochelle had reduced many of the French infantry companies there to 25–30 men.[38]

Reductions were sometimes an opportunity to get rid of undisciplined or mutinous units. During the fifth civil war a conspiracy by many of the officers and men of Bussy D'Amboise's regiment in Perigord to murder and rob a unit of German reiters was discovered. In the reduction that followed the ringleaders and their followers were dismissed, the companies reorganized, and the regiment given a new commander.[39] Reductions also played an important role at the end of campaigns, when large numbers of companies were disbanded. At that time almost all new companies would be dismissed and the number of veteran companies reduced to the numbers needed for peacetime duty.[40] Such consolidations must have proved helpful to the veteran captains whose companies survived because they allowed them to

---

[37] Biron, *LD*, vol. 1, 62–63.
[38] Guise, *Mémoires*, 501–3; *Henri III*, vol. 1, 136; BN Mss. Fr. 4,756, fol. 72r.
[39] Brantôme, *Oeuvres*, vol. 4, 34–35.
[40] See the royal order for early 1564, BN Mss. 3,191, fol. 10, and the reductions and *départements* of 1576 and 1577, BN Mss. Fr. 3,256, fols. 23–24, and *OM* no. 248, respectively.

discard sick, wounded, or worn out men and pick and choose among the best of the released troops to fill up their ranks. The solid nucleus of vigorous and hardened veterans that we found in an "old crew" company like that of Count Brissac is in part attributable to this system of triage. But the role the reduction system played cannot be properly appreciated without reference to the framework in which it operated, the single true organizational innovation introduced into the army during the wars of religion, a change that in some respects marks the beginning of the modern French army, the organization of permanent infantry regiments.

THE BIRTH OF INFANTRY REGIMENTS

The organization of permanent infantry regiments was not a single or a straightforward process, nor was the idea itself original to France. The famous Spanish *tercios* of the first half of the century and the German and Swiss troops who were routinely being organized into regiments long before the time of the wars of religion appear to have furnished the models. The essential need that regimental organization met was the creation of an organization above the company level but below the level of the massive blocks of troops into which infantry were concentrated for tactical purposes on the march and the battlefield, thereby providing an intermediary operational unit strong enough to undertake independent assignments yet small enough to ease logistical and deployment problems. The creation of regimental level officers was also intended to enhance discipline and reduce disorders by providing closer surveillance of the captains of individual companies and, although this was not at first the case in France, to regularize recruiting practices by assigning each regiment to garrison duties in a single set area during peacetime.[41]

Before the civil wars the French infantry had been organized into a pair of large loose commands under the two colonel generals of infantry. One, stationed at Calais, was responsible for administration of all French infantry in metropolitan France, and included the right to appoint their company captains. The other, a holdover of the Italian wars, was headquartered at Pignerol, and had similar authority over the French infantry stationed in Piedmont. Both were assisted by small staffs and provided with funds to keep a limited number of captains without commands on retainer. When war came they functioned as the chief commanding officers of the main bodies of French troops in the armies. But when the infantry was split up among a number of different assignments the lack of a flexible intermediary form of organization above the company level made the exercise of command a cumbersome process and when troops were detached from the immediate surveillance of a colonel general it created confusing lines of authority.

---

[41] By far the best of older treatments of this subject is Susane, *Infanterie*, especially his chapter on the origin of the regimental system, vol. 1, 126–79. *Ibid.*, vol. 2 contains histories of individual regiments which are also sometimes useful. Susane must, however, be used with care, especially for the earlier periods – he over-relies on Brantôme sometimes, and is inaccurate in some of his dating.

The birth of infantry regiments

Credit is usually given to the duke of Guise, whose affection for and attention to the infantry was well known, for attempting to solve these problems by organizing the first French infantry regiments, though there is some confusion as to whether this innovation took place during the short reign of François II while Guise was involved in the drastic reductions in forces following the end of the Hapsburg–Valois wars, or at the very beginning of the first civil war. But in either case the initial organization of the first three regiments – each containing twelve companies of 200 men each, commanded by a master-of-camp, his sergeant major and camp marshal, and a small provostial and medical staff – was also motivated by a pressing political problem. Andelot, Admiral Coligny's brother, and a confirmed Protestant, held the post of colonel general in metropolitan France, and from this position was able to favor captains loyal to himself. By organizing the first regiments Guise was therefore also attempting to erect a competing level of experienced commanders with authority over a number of veteran companies who were loyal to the crown yet not of high enough rank to overtly challenge Andelot's authority.[42] Such a precaution was well taken, for at the beginning of the first civil war, when Andelot deserted to help his brother and Condé led the Huguenot army, the captains and men of Andelot's *colonelles*, the senior companies of the "old crew," promptly deserted and threw themselves into Rouen where they served valiantly as the backbone of the Huguenot garrison that defended the city against the royal army in the fall of 1562.[43] The original three regiments organized by Guise formed the initial core of the French infantry in the royal army which marched from Paris against Orléans, and during that campaign of 1562 an additional five similar regiments were organized in the provinces, including a regiment of the French companies commanded by Brissac, the other colonel general, in Piedmont. All of these regiments made their way at various times to the main army during the first war or to the siege of Le Havre immediately afterwards and played an important role in the major actions of the army under the direction of a new colonel general, Randan, and after his death at Rouen, the count of Martigues. But the coming of peace posed two problems for the new regimental commands. The first was that the crown had promised to disband its regiments after the recapture of Le Havre. The second was that Andelot had been restored to his office and was determined to resist the existence of competing levels of command between himself and the company captains over which he was supposed to have authority. As a result, and also as an economy measure, all of the regiments which had fought in the first civil war had been disbanded by the time of the renewal of war in 1567. The sole remaining regiment was that of the king's guard, eleven companies strong, organized on the initiative of the queen mother from the best companies of the disbanded regiments after the siege of Le

---

[42] I find Susane's explanation, vol. 1, 130, convincing.
[43] Brantôme, *Discours*, 120–21.

Havre in order to provide a sizeable and loyal bodyguard of veteran troops for the young king entirely removed from Andelot's jurisdiction.[44]

At the beginning of the second civil war Andelot again defected and the king named the commander of the royal guard, Strossi, son of the deceased marshal, one of the many naturalized Italian soldiers in the crown's employ, to the metropolitan post of colonel general of infantry. A number of infantry regiments were then created from both old and new companies and command of them divided between Strossi and Brissac, the other colonel general, who each then commanded one of the large French infantry formations assigned to the battle and the advance guard of the army. From 1567 on the main challenge to the system came not from the Protestants but from soldiers like Jehan de Monluc, who claimed the right to be entitled to the rank of colonel of the territorially raised regiment he brought to the army and to escape the authority of either colonel general.[45] But this struggle was finally won by Strossi and Brissac and their dual command over the organized regiments of French infantry continued during the brief interwar period and into the third civil war until Brissac's death at the siege of Aubterre in May, 1569, whereupon the crown took advantage of the contemporaneous death of Andelot to consolidate the two colonel general positions into a single unified infantry command under Strossi, who would wield overall authority over all French infantry regiments during the rest of the third war, at the siege of La Rochelle in 1573, and during the fifth civil war.[46]

By the early seventeenth century the supposed founding date of regiments had become important in arguments over seniority and claims of precedence, and during the rest of the old regime and even after the Revolution, military archivists and historians of the French infantry made attempts to sort out the exact sequence of creation and survival of what had become at a later date the permanent territorially named regiments.[47] Until well past the end date for this study, however, it is difficult to trace an incontrovertibly continuous life for even a single French regiment, since their integral infantry companies were often shifted around and sometimes disbanded during reductions and the regiments themselves often did not return to exactly the same peacetime stations. The only one of the regiments to survive from before the second civil war, the king's guard, was itself disbanded at the instance of the Huguenots after the siege of La Rochelle because it had been an active participant in the earlier massacre in Paris, though its companies were hurriedly reassembled in 1574 for service in the fifth civil war.[48] Nevertheless, from the time of the

---

[44] Susane, *Infanterie*, vol. 1, 134–39, and *OM* no. 84, an infantry *état* for 1566 authorizing payment of Strossi's regiment independently of Andelot's command.

[45] The *CDM* and Anjou's logbook are replete with references to this quarrel and also to others, for example between Meru and Martigues, during the second war. Brantôme, *Oeuvres*, vol. 6, 135, also notes this quarrel over the authority of the colonel generals over other infantry colonels.

[46] Susane, *Infanterie*, vol. 1, 146–49.

[47] Establishing precedence, of course, was one of Susane's main purposes, see *ibid.*, vol. 2.

[48] *Ibid.*, 19–20.

Table 4.6. *Regiments of French infantry, 1562–1577*

Period	Regiments	Approximate no. companies
Prewar	3	36
1st war, 1562–63	8	86
Postwar, 1564	3	30
Postwar, 1567	1	11
2nd war, 1567–68	11	118
Postwar, 1568	9	83
3rd war, 1568	14	190
3rd war, June, 1569	12	172
3rd war, October, 1569	9	189
Postwar, 1572	8	42
4th war, 1572–73	11	127
Postwar, 1573	6	50
5th war, 1574–76	11	114
Postwar, 1576	8	49
Postwar, 1577	5	62

second civil war on regiments were always preserved in peacetime, most, though not always the same ones, stationed as garrisons on the frontier. By the end of the sixth civil war, in 1577, the postwar stationing of French infantry regiments was being printed up and distributed publicly as part of the peace agreement and by 1580, when the king assigned definite fixed geographical recruiting regions to individual regiments, the continual existence of such famous formations as the Picardy, Champagne, Piedmont, and King's Guard regiment were well established.[49]

During the first five civil wars, however, regiments were referred to primarily by the name of their master-of-camp, or regimental commander, rather than their provincial stations. As Table 4.6 shows, during wartime anywhere from 8 to 14 such regiments, with 11 being the usual number, were supported, and during peacetime anywhere from 5 to 8 such commands were maintained, their companies usually reduced to fifty men each.[50] Though a portion of the native infantry companies

[49] *OM* no. 248; and the recruiting areas stipulated in the "Reglement que le Roy veult estre observe par les cappnes des Regimens de gens de pied francois en faisant les creues de leurs compaignyes," BN Mss. Fr. 21,541, fol. 4.
[50] Identifications of regiments are culled from a number of the sources, too many to be cited, but especially those in the Appendix, Part C, and this chapter. Often companies from the same regiment could be scattered across several provinces, but their existence is revealed by the presence of their specialized command staffs, the masters-of-camp and sergeant majors. Despite a great deal of effort used to track the regiments across time, many obscurities remain, but I am confident that Table 4.6 is reasonably accurate.

raised in each war escaped such organization, especially those raised purely for garrison duty and local operations, from the first war on a steadily higher proportion of the French infantry which served with the main field armies were organized into regiments, and the number of companies included in the regimental organizations provides a good guide to the intensity of the crown's military effort in the different wars. It was to the regimental masters-of-camp of these regiments, as well as the general officers of the French infantry, of course, that Brantôme dedicated his *Discours sur les colonels de l'infanterie de France*, from which an excellent idea of the personal qualities and relationships of these leaders and their milieu of camp and army can be gleaned.[51] Though infantry commanders – regimental commanders and for that matter company officers – were almost always nobles, with the exception of the colonel generals they seem to have come from relatively modest noble families. Their chance for further advancement was small and few of them were ever awarded with higher commands or even the command of a gendarme company, which were reserved for the most part for the greater nobility. The most conspicuous quality they shared was an exemplary personal courage which is reflected in the high proportion of them who were wounded or killed in action. As we shall see, it was on the officers and men of the regiments and companies of veteran French infantry that the brunt of the army's fighting fell.

"HOMMES D'ASSAULT"

As Geoffrey Parker has so well elucidated for the Army of Flanders, early modern military observers considered different nationalities of troops to possess different and distinct characters, fighting qualities, and skills.[52] Some observers of the wars of religion considered French troops to have severe liabilities. La Noue, for example, accused his countrymen of "the natural impatience of the French nation, which upon failing to perceive promptly enough the effects of her plans, becomes disgusted and then complains about it."[53] And during the preliminary preparations for the siege of La Rochelle the English ambassador wrote that "Soldiers of judge-

---

[51] Brantôme is a gold mine of information on the milieu of the regiments, especially his *Discours sur les colonels de l'infanterie de France*, in its most modern edition by Etienne Vaucheret. The biggest drawback to using Brantôme is not a lack of accuracy, which can usually be controlled for and was in any case seldom intentional, but in his work's sprawling and disorganized construction. But as he himself points out, "Or je pense bien que plusieurs personnes qui me liront diront bien que je suis un grand extravaguant en mes discours & que je suis fort confus; mais qu'on prenne le cas que j'en faictz comme les cuysiniers, qui font un pot-pourry de plusieurs viandes qui ne laissent pourtant a estre tres-bonnes & bien friandes: de mesmes en sera la confusion de mes propos &, si elle ne plaist aux uns, possible plaira elle aux autres, en tel ordre qu'ilz puissent estre," *ibid.*, 84–85. Those with the patience to read carefully the *Grands capitaines* and *Discours* will be well rewarded, for they are as rich a sixteenth-century stew as can be imagined, and only this author's exercise of extreme discipline prevented an entertaining, illuminating, and appropriate Brantôme quote from appearing on nearly every page of this work.

[52] Parker, *Flanders*, 13–16, 27–35.

[53] François de la Noue, *Discours politiques et militaires*, ed. F.E. Sutcliffe (Geneva, 1967), 643–44.

Table 4.7. *Weapon and armor proportions in French and and foreign infantry formations*

Formation (no. companies)	% formation		
	Pike	(Corselets)	Shot
Pfyffer's Swiss, 1567 (20)	87	(10)	13
Rhingrave's Landsknechts, 1562 (21)	68	(40)	32
Brissac's company organization, 1567 (1)	53	(43)	47
Brissac's regiment, Paris, 1568 (20)	47	(19)	53
Nevers' French, Belleville, 1567 (5)	31	(29)	69
Nevers' Italian, Belleville, 1567 (18)	10	(10)	90

ment here conclude that without either the Swiss or Almains the king cannot besiege Rochelle, for the Frenchmen are not fit for the keeping of artillery or to make the body of the battle of footmen."[54] But in the first part of this opinion Ambassador Wilson was certainly mistaken, for if the foreign infantry engaged by the crown were considered necessary to anchor the army's battleline in open combat, they were much less useful than the French infantry in most other duties. A review of the relative proportions of polearm to firearm weapons found within the infantry formations of the various nationalities, as in Table 4.7, will be both helpful and suggestive in this regard and remind us that even though foreign infantry, the Landsknechts, Italians, and especially the Swiss made up at times a large portion of the royal army's infantry, they were intended to be utilized in a somewhat different manner than the French infantry.[55] The Swiss, for example, were especially highly valued for their discipline and bravery. Their performance at the battle of Dreux, where their formation withstood repeated attacks and suffered heavy casualties, probably saved the royal army from a crushing defeat. But their customary post as guards for the artillery train had little to do with any exceptional skills or aptitude. The fact was that their organization and weaponry severely restricted their usefulness off the battlefield. Almost nine out of ten of them were armed with pikes. Only a very small proportion were protected by corselets, or full armor, and at sieges that and their almost complete lack of firearms limited their role to the guarding of the artillery park and trenches. Perhaps conscious of their limitations, they refused as a matter of course to take part in the storming of breaches though, curiously, individual Swiss soldiers were always willing to volunteer to earn extra pay by doing the manual labor associated with the lowly pioneers.[56]

[54] *CSPF/E*, vol. 10, no. 673.
[55] In descending order: *OM* no. 96; BN Mss. Fr. 4,552, fols. 83–85 and 4,553, fols. 35–36; ibid., fols. 50–62; BN Mss. Fr. 3,197, fols. 59–60; and BN Mss. Fr. 3,212, fols. 51–52 for the last two examples.
[56] BN Mss. Fr. 4,765, fol. 71.

The German troops who served in the first civil war also contained a very high proportion of polearms, but enough firearms and armor protection to be more actively involved in siegework and one of the approach trenches at the siege of Rouen in 1562 was entrusted to them. In Biron's opinion the German Landsknechts were much to be preferred because they could be utilized in many different roles.

> I will venture to say that the French infantry have given up carrying pikes. Therefore, there must be joined to them a nation which does carry pikes, for expeditions in great as well as small force, according as the occasion offers itself, and especially for assaults. It would therefore be very good to have one or two good *Landsknecht* regiments, all the while claiming that the Swiss would be even better. The truth is that I rate the Swiss more highly for a day of combat in open country in large formation. But they are indeed not easy to lead, refusing to go on expeditions, or escorts, even in no matter how small a detachment, to support your arquebusiers with their corselets in a skirmish or at an assault. But if well-selected *Landsknechts* go in large numbers, as is their custom, with the French arquebusiers, there is neither town nor commune which can hold against them. They are also well suited to support the artillery and to assist its conduct in escorts, in the trenches, even to be put to work sapping, mining or toiling in ditches; for in a ditch where they set themselves to toil, they will do more work than 500 pioneers could do in one night.[57]

But Brantôme recalled that "I have heard great captains say that such manner of *Landsknechts* are worthless in a besieged place, because they have a strong tendency to mutiny if they do not have everything they need. They are spendthrift, ungovernable, destructive and dissipated."[58] And in any case, after the first civil war German infantry did not play a large role in the royal army, though they remained quite important to the Huguenots.

Italian infantry was much more important in the early wars, but they were often relatively low-grade troops, poorly protected and armed, like the bands raised by Nevers in 1567. They had too few polearms to stand in battleline and too little armor to be of much use in storming a breach. Though considered brave enough, they proved particularly rapacious in their treatment of civilians and were denounced as sodomites by Protestant historians. They were generally relegated to garrison duties and on those few occasions when they did take part in heavy combat, such as attempting to stand against Huguenot cavalry in early 1568, as already mentioned, or to storm a breach as at Châtellerault in 1569, they suffered bloody repulses.

Those formations in Table 4.7 with the highest proportions of polearms and therefore the best chance to defeat cavalry on the field of battle, the Swiss and Landsknechts, can be seen to rank at the top of a crude hierarchy representing infantry battle worthiness, and the Italians at the bottom. As can be seen, the regular French infantry's table of organization called for slightly more pikes than

---

[57] Biron, *LD*, vol. 1, 63.
[58] Brantôme, *Oeuvres*, vol. 6, 224.

firearms and a large proportion of the pikes were supposed to be corseleted. If the fall of 1568 is any guide, it may have been hard to attain these exact proportions in practice because there was a great lack of standardization among companies. But the French infantry were certainly better and more heavily armed than the Italians and than most purely provincial formations of infantry, including the Huguenot French infantry, which suffered throughout the wars from a shortage of trained pikemen. They were less well equipped for the phalanx-type role envisaged for the Swiss and the Landsknechts though veteran units could serve adequately enough in battleline, if need be, as at Dreux.[59] But the French infantry was actually better equipped for many of the most important tasks called for by the civil wars, for they had a high enough portion of firearms and armor to man the trenches, fight the sorties, and provide the shock troops capable of storming or defending the breaches in city fortifications. As a result, the crown came to rely almost exclusively on the French infantry regiments for the bulk of the most dangerous and dirty fighting of the civil wars. Catherine de Medici, for example, during the siege of Rouen, after several assaults had failed to gain entry into the city, wrote to Monluc in Guyenne to hurry a regiment of Gascons to her because the army had suffered many casualties and needed his "hommes d'assault."[60] As war followed war and the already rare ranged battle practically disappeared, it was the French infantry rather than the foreign infantry who always functioned as the army's "hommes d'assault" at the numerous sieges of the time.

Yet as Brantôme reminds us, experienced soldiers who had fought in both battles and sieges reported that "In a single hour of a siege, you are in greater danger than in an entire day of battle."[61] Not only was the kind of hand-to-hand combat which occurred at the breach deadly, but the adaptation of the still relatively recently developed gunpowder small-arms weapons to the defense of places made the approach to the walls and trench duty much more potentially lethal than in medieval times.[62] The unsuitability of the hired foreign infantry for siegework meant that it was largely on the regiments of French infantry that the burden of such fighting fell, a fact that is well attested by the high casualty rates suffered by these formations during the wars. Three of the four Catholic colonel generals during this period met a violent end at sieges, and eleven of the fourteen regimental commanders who lost their lives during the first six civil wars were killed in action at sieges, almost all shot by firearm weapons.[63] Indeed higher officers who

---

[59] See Chapter 7 for the saga of the Swiss at Dreux.

[60] *CDM*, vol. 1, 421.

[61] Brantôme, *Oeuvres*, vol. 6, 20.

[62] The clearest treatment of this issue is Pepper and Adams, *Firearms and Fortifications*, 3–31.

[63] Randan (Rouen, 1562), Brissac (Mussidan, 1569), Martigues (Saint-Jean-d'Angely, 1569), Richelieu (Le Havre, 1563), Ardelay (Chartres, 1568), Honoux (Poitiers, 1569), Foissy (Vezélay, 1569), Gouas, Cosseins, Poilliac, and Foillou (La Rochelle, 1573), Sainte-Colombe (St. Lô, 1574), Lucé (Lusignan, 1574), Martinengo (La Charité, 1577). Many others were grievously wounded at sieges. The number of such officers who survived to old age was quite small, since they tended to continue to serve as long as they survived the dangers of war and their sometimes lethal personal quarrels.

had not sustained several serious wounds were considered somewhat of a curiosity.[64] But company officers also sustained high levels of casualties, as an example from the siege of Rouen in 1562 will demonstrate.

After the recapture of Rouen the duke of Guise ordered a list made of the officers and sergeants of French companies at the siege who had suffered wounds. The information contained in this list, intended to be used as a guide to distribution of combat bonuses, suggests a strikingly high casualty rate for officers and sergeants.[65] As Table 4.8A indicates, out of seventeen companies' total maximum paper strength of 85 cadre, 38 had been wounded, or at least 45 percent of all officers and sergeants. Keeping in mind the fact that Guise's list did not identify those officers and sergeants who had been killed (we know some were but not the exact number) and that the seventeen companies were almost certainly not at full strength (since the campaign was already entering its eighth month), this 45 percent wounded rate can only be considered a minimum total casualty rate, and the total casualty rate must certainly have amounted to more than half of the company leaders of those units.

Guise's list also identified where on their bodies the 38 officers and sergeants were wounded and what kind of weapon inflicted the wound. This information, summarized in Table 4.8B and C, dramatically underlines exactly the deadly consequences the particular sixteenth-century combination of gunpowder and fortifications had for the king's native regiments. The 38 surviving officer and noncom casualties shared forty-nine total wounds only three of which were by hand-to-hand weapons, confirming a combat environment full of lethal missiles capable of inflicting multiple wounds. But when the sources of wounds are more closely examined it is clear that about one-third of the missile wounds came not from the century's equivalent of high technology weapons, that is firearms, mostly arquebuses, but from thrown rocks. We can deduce they were thrown, or dropped on the attackers because of where they impacted – all sixteen such wounds were inflicted on the soldiers' hands, arms, and heads, obviously dropped from above as they attempted to storm the breaches. The impact points of bullets, on the other hand, were far more evenly distributed over the whole body, indicating the ability of firearms to inflict wounds at a distance on the head and upper body of officers oper-

---

[64] See, for an illuminating discussion of the relation of wounds, chance, valor, and reputation, Brantôme, *Discours*, 79–85. *Ibid.*, 81–82, quotes the young duke of Guise, who, like himself, had not yet acquired a wound at La Rochelle, as complaining, "Si faut il que nous nous facions un peu blesser, au moins quoy qui soit, pour nous faire estimer comme les autres & parler de nous. Ce n'est point nostre faute, ny de Monsieur d'Estrozze, ny de moy, ny de vous; car il n'y a hasard que nous ne recherchions, il n'y a factions que nous ne recuillons autant ou plus qu'il y en ayt ici, & pourtant le malheur est tel pour nous que nous ne pouvons recevoir aucun petit coup heureux que nous remarque & signale. Il faut bien dire que l'honneur nous fuit; & quand a moy, je fairay dire une Messe demain, qui est le jour de l'assaut, afin que je prie Dieu qu'il m'envoye quelque petite heureuse harquebusade, & qu'en retourne plus glorieux au moins, puisque la gloire de nostre Court & des Dames consiste aux coups receuz & non aux coups donnez."

[65] BN Mss. Fr. 15,877, fols. 347–49 for this and what follows.

Table 4.8. *Wounds and casualty rates suffered by officers and sergeants of seventeen French infantry companies at the siege of Rouen, 1562*

A. *Casualty Rates*

Paper strength and rank	Actual no. wounded	Minimum % casualty rate
17 Captains	8	47
17 Lieutenants	3	18
17 Ensigns	9	53
34 Sergeants	18	53
Total 85 Cadre	38	45

B. *Cause of Wounds*

Weapon type	No. wounds	% wounds
Pikes	3	6
Rocks and boulders	16	33
Arquebuses	28	57
Musket	1	2
Light artillery	1	2
Total	49	100

C. *Cause of wound and place wounded*

Place wounded	Cause of wound			Total	(%)
	Pike	Rocks	Firearms		
Head, face, and neck	1	8	4	13	(27)
Upper limbs, arms, hand	1	8	10	19	(39)
Trunk of body	–	–	5	5	(10)
Lower limbs	1	–	11	12	(24)
Total	3	16	30	49	(100)
(Percentage)	(6)	(33)	(61)	(100)	

ating in the approach trenches and on the whole body, including the lower limbs, once the attackers exposed themselves as they left their trenches to cross the moat and scale the breach. What is missing from these dismal snapshots of the type of carnage sieges could inflict on the attacker (and the defender) is also significant. There were very few trunk (including abdomen) wounds – possibly because of armor protection but equally as likely because almost any projectile wound that penetrated the body cavities was fatal, and Guise's list does not include those who had been killed or died from their wounds. There were also no wounds listed from incendiary devices probably again because any kind of direct hit by such a weapon was invariably fatal. Randan, the officer who replaced Andelot as colonel general of

Table 4.9. *Source and place of wound scars on Brissac and Monluc company men*

A. *Identified sources of wound scars*

Source of wound	No. wounds	% wounds
Missiles		
Arrow	2	2
Stone	13	10
Arquebus	39	31
Subtotal	54	43
Hand-to-Hand		
Sword	68	54
Pike and Other	5	4
Subtotal	73	57
Total	127	100

B. *Place of wound scars*

Place of Scar	No. scars	% scars
Head, face, neck	96	43
Upper limbs, arm, hand	83	37
Trunk of body	14	6
Lower limbs	31	14
Total	224	100

infantry at the beginning of the first civil war, had in fact suffered fatal burns from such a device earlier in the siege in an assault on the defenses on Saint-Catherine's hill.[66]

Though we have no comparable after action report on the casualties and wounds among the ordinary French soldiers at Rouen, it is possible to glean some physical evidence of the types of fighting the veteran French infantry were used for from the scars from wounds recorded by commissioners Gatico and Girard during their muster of the soldiers of Brissac's and Monluc's companies in September, 1567, presented in Table 4.9A and B. Only 36 (22 percent) of 167 men in Brissac's company and 36 (38 percent) out of 95 in Monluc's company had no scar or wound to show the commissioners (though some had natural marks like moles). In Brissac's company, 131 men shared 157 scars and in 92 cases the weapon which caused the mark was specified. The 59 marked men of Monluc's company shared 65 scars, the source of 35 of which was identified. Many of the unidentified sources of wounds were of the concussive type, but 43 percent of the identified wounds were inflicted by projectiles, mostly arquebuses but some from rocks and stones. Fifty-

[66] Brantôme, *Discours*, 143.

seven percent of the total came from hand-to-hand weapons, mostly sword and pike thrusts and sword slashes. When we look at the places men had been wounded we find generally similar proportions to those of the wounded officers and sergeants at Rouen, with more than four-fifths of the wounds to the head and upper limbs, and very few survived wounds to the body. Among ordinary soldiers wounds to the legs were also relatively rare and the reason is not far to seek, for a truly lame man could not serve as an infantryman (only one of 262 soldiers was described as gimpy).

A recital of the circumstances under which these wounds had been received reveals, in brief, a history of the royal army itself. Pierre Bergiers, 60-year-old sergeant of Monluc's company, had taken an arquebus ball in the side at the battle of Cerisolles. Claude La Sale, a 40-year-old corporal, had been shot in the left arm at the escalade of Cayrase. The greybeard Antoine Sechet, the oldest of all the soldiers at 80 years, "having borne arms in the service of the King for 42 years in this company" and still spry enough to wear a corselet, had half his left hand burned and maimed. Bernard Torniel, a 50-year-old Béarnese, had taken a blow through his nose and the left side of his face at the siege of Thionville, while Arnauld de Soulmon, a Gascon, had a pike wound in his right thigh, "received during the recent troubles at Lectore while at the side of Monsieur Monluc."[67]

The list could be extended, a litany of distant and recent combats, confirming on the bodies of ordinary soldiers as it had on those of their officers and sergeants at Rouen the effects of a combination of the oldest and most primitive of weapons, like rocks and swords, with the latest in military technology, gunpowder weapons, that dominated the combat environment of sieges in which the crown depended for success on its regiments of French infantry. This survey of Brissac's and Monluc's men also returns us to the opening scene of the first section of this chapter and to its conclusion about the type of social organization the veteran companies of French infantry represented. It was suggested there that the most important commonality binding these groups together was their shared membership in the company's activities. The information on scars and wounds presented in this section suggests that for both officers and men the principal element lending itself to the cohesion of such groups, and distinguishing them clearly and starkly from most of the rest of society, was a community of shared dangers signified by the marks left by the violence of mid-sixteenth-century warfare on the bodies of the men who survived it.[68]

---

[67] BN Mss. Fr. 4,553, fols. 42r, 42v, 43v, 44r, 45v.

[68] Brantôme, *Discours*, 84, reveals both stoicism about the dangers involved in war and resentment about the differential rewards risk-taking earned for the *grands* compared to humbler folk: "car enfin quand nous allons a la guerre, nous y allons comme a un marche (ainsi que disoit un bon Capitaine que j'ay cognu) la ou nous contentons d'avoir & achepter ce que nous trouvons; de mesmes a la guerre, nous y amassons ce que l'on donne & seme &, si nous n'y allons, jamais nous n'aurons rien. La Fortune est bonne en cela pour ceux qui sont grandz & de grand qualite: la moindre blessure ou rafflade qu'ilz recoivent, les voila haut eslevez en gloire pour jamais; nous autres, petitz compaignons, nous nous en contentons de peu & tout ce que nous faisons ce ne sont que petitz eschantillons au pris de grandes pieces des Grandz, qui scavent mieux faire sonner la trompette de leur renommee que nous, qui ne pouvons passer par tout comm'eux a publier nos playes & valeurs."

The scarred bodies of the veterans of the native infantry regiments also remind us that such soldiers were expendable, unlike the nobility in the gendarme companies who, as we will see in the next section, largely for reasons of class, the crown and the army's leaders were always loath to risk on the battlefield or at the breach. At their maximum strength, the royal infantry regiments deployed in action seldom exceeded a total of 25,000 men for the entire kingdom, and in the main field army alone, rarely more than 15,000 men. This was not a large manpower reserve and due to the circumstances of the warfare of the times the attrition and exhaustion of these units was eventually to severely limit the ability of the royal army to fight extended campaigns.

5

The gendarmes

The day after the battle of Dreux, Admiral Coligny, leader of the Huguenot army, wrote a dispatch describing the battle and its outcome to Queen Elizabeth of England. In the dispatch, which was soon to be published widely abroad, Coligny listed a number of great Catholic noblemen whom he believed to have been killed or seriously wounded in the battle. In addition, some others,

chevaliers of the order, along with several leaders, lieutenants and men-at-arms, prisoners, up to a hundred or more, who have not yet been identified; such that in truth, if they had suffered any higher losses, their army would have been entirely ruined. On our side, the capture of the Prince of Condé is a great misfortune...Besides that, we have lost some infantry captains and some gentlemen and soldiers, but in very small numbers. We thank God that our losses do not even compare to those suffered by our enemies. Not a single one of our principal leaders was wounded...They have but one sole point of advantage: because of the night and lack of horses, we left them four field pieces. But we consider that more than compensated for by the loss they sustained of so many great lords and captains.[1]

Two days later in yet another dispatch to Elizabeth he again regretted that the battle had led to the capture of the prince of Condé but emphasized,

but this was at the cost of such a great loss, indeed the ruin of their cavalry, the greater part of their leaders and principal captains having been taken, wounded, or killed. But our cavalry, which stayed intact and which did its execution without having lost more than eighty or a hundred horse, is resolved to continue the present enterprise with all its power and all its might.[2]

Another pair of letters to the queen soon after the battle, but from her ambassador to France, Throckmorton, who had been present with the Huguenot army and was made a prisoner, reemphasized these points. According to Throckmorton's first letter, since Guise had lost 300 gentlemen killed and another 120 or so taken prisoner and the admiral had lost only 140 horsemen, "the victory may be called doubtful and not advantageous to the Prince's adversaries..." Though all the conventional signs of victory belonged to the duke, "who behaved himself like a great

---

[1] PRO/SP 70/47, fols. 18–21, quote from fols. 19v-20.
[2] *Ibid.*, fol. 101.

and valiant captain," because of the number of leaders and gentlemen lost, "being victors their damage is greater than those who are defeated."[3] Writing again to report on the fate of some of the wounded notables, he increased the number of cavalrymen conceded to have been lost by the royal army to eight hundred gentlemen.[4]

Now, both Coligny and Throckmorton were engaged, obviously, in a sixteenth-century effort at diplomatic damage control. In point of fact, the battle of Dreux had been in most respects a disaster for the Protestants. Their Landsknecht infantry regiment had been entirely slaughtered or captured, those of their French infantry who had escaped being slain were routed and dispersed, and most of their small artillery train was lost in the retreat from the field. Strategically the way was now open for the royal army to advance to capture Orléans, which had served from the beginning of the war as headquarters for the Huguenot cause and was now the only remaining major Protestant stronghold north of the Loire river. As selective and self-serving as Coligny's and Throckmorton's views were, however, their analysis of the significance of the battle's outcome was also shrewd and close to the truth, and their claims suggest a number of insights into the role and importance for the royal army of its cavalry and their leaders.

At the forefront was the simple quantitative calculation that they had killed, disabled, or captured more gentlemen of the king's heavy cavalry than they themselves had lost, and that among the royal army's casualties were a number of prominent noble captains and officers while the Huguenots had lost few men of note. The crown's victory "may be called doubtful and not advantageous" because they had inflicted enough losses on the king's cavalry to seriously compromise its effectiveness as a battlefield force while the Huguenot cavalry, including their German mercenary reiters, remained intact. Behind this claim was the unspoken knowledge that strong cavalry forces were an essential part of any army which intended to take the field, because their mobility and offensive shock power made them perfectly capable of playing a dominant and decisive role on the battlefield. To have this arm seriously crippled or destroyed in battle was a military disaster against which the six or seven thousand bodies of dead foot soldiers which littered the battlefield near Dreux ultimately counted for very little.[5]

Furthermore, unlike the infantry, the cavalry, especially the gendarmerie, was composed of gentlemen and noblemen of note, including the greatest lords of the land, who in addition to providing models of courage and leadership based on class-conscious notions of honor, furnished all of the higher leadership of the army and represented, collectively, the dominant political and social group in the kingdom.

---

[3] PRO/SP 70/48, fols. 25–30, especially 25–26.
[4] *Ibid.*, fols. 192–93.
[5] Much of my argument in this chapter points to the conclusion that at mid-sixteenth century heavy cavalry was still, despite the development of infantry forces and firearms, a powerful and sometimes decisive battlefield force. The eclipse of cavalry, if it occurred at all during the wars of religion, may have been a result of a decline in the number of formal, open-field battles, rather than some diminution of gendarmerie effectiveness on the battlefield.

High losses among this group would not only potentially cripple the heart and core of the army's noble leadership but would have an important effect beyond the purely military in any overall calculus of the political affairs of the kingdom. With this basic assessment of the central military and political importance of heavy cavalry and of the nobility who dominated both its ranks and the army's leadership, the Catholic generals would have been in broad agreement, as their actions in relation to the specific impact of the battle of Dreux on the gendarmerie at the time and their treatment of the royal cavalry as a whole over the entire course of the early civil wars show.

The royal army's cavalry, in fact, had been badly handled at the battle of Dreux by the Huguenots and their German allies. All but one of the seven tactical regiments into which the gendarmerie and light cavalry had been divided at the beginning of the battle had been mauled or routed from the field – some riders in their panic not stopping until they reached Paris the next morning, where they erroneously reported a terrible defeat for the royal army. The exact total of casualties is not known, but of the thirty-six companies of gendarmes which took part in the battle, at least seven had their captains killed or mortally wounded, and four or five had captains who were seriously wounded or captured.[6] If we can surmise from this a casualty rate including prisoners of close to one-third of the gendarme effectives then Throckmorton's claim of 800 gentlemen lost may have been quite accurate. The casualty rate among the leaders of the tactical regiments, who were the most prominent noble leaders in the army, was particularly high, with four of the eight killed or seriously wounded and one, the constable, commander of the army, captured. At his busy headquarters after the battle, then, Guise faced a formidable problem, for the ranks of his heavy cavalry were in fact considerably reduced and therefore in the field the still intact Protestant cavalry retained its superiority.

Although the tactical results of Dreux exacerbated the situation, however, weakness in the cavalry arm had haunted the royal army since the beginning of the civil war. Some sixty-five gendarme companies had been in existence at the start of the war, but four of these had gone over entirely to the Huguenots, leaving only sixty-one units, and the leaders of several of those were also considered suspect.[7] Moreover, besides the obvious and dramatic defections, like Condé or Coligny, the gendarmerie in general was the hardest hit of all the arms by the civil war. Many ordinary gentlemen and even some officers deserted their companies and

---

[6] No single list of the gendarme companies at the battle exists, but from the various sources cited in the Appendix, Part C, the presence and identity of 36 companies can be deduced. La Brosse, Givry, Annebault, Montbrun, Ossun, Saint-André, and Nevers, according to different sources, were killed or died of wounds. Aumale, the constable, Beauvais, Piennes, and Saint-Heran were grievously wounded or captured. For casualty lists and replacements see PRO/SP 70/48, fols. 184–87 and Henri de la Popelinière, *L'histoire de France enrichie de plus notable occurrences*... (La Rochelle, 1581), vol. 1, fol. 349r. See chapter 7 for a fuller discussion of casualties at Dreux.

[7] Condé, Coligny, La Rochefoucauld, and Genlis were the most prominent captains of gendarme companies to defect to the Huguenot side.

Protestant recruiting strength among the rural nobility as a whole meant that the Huguenot heavy cavalry from the beginning of the war was a match for the cavalry with the royal army because so many gendarme units were pinned down in the struggles in the provinces. When the royal army marched from Paris against Orléans in June of 1562, for example, it contained only twenty-two companies of gendarmes.[8] To bolster this arm and to replace early casualties and defections, the crown and the army leadership authorized during the late summer the creation of about twenty-two new companies and *creues* (increases in strength) for many exist-ing companies. About three-quarters of the new companies were intended to bolster the cavalry strength of the main army and, in fact, at Dreux the army's heavy cavalry had increased to thirty-six companies of gendarmes. But the campaigning had drastically reduced the strength of many companies and in his after action report Guise himself had estimated the army's total cavalry strength at Dreux at only 2,000 horse, or much less than the Protestant strength in cavalry, about half of whom were the mercenary German pistol cavalry, the reiters.[9]

The weight of numbers then, as much perhaps as fighting prowess, had con-tributed to the rout of much of the army's cavalry at Dreux, and in the aftermath of the battle the crown had only about seventy-two companies of gendarmes available for operations in the kingdom as a whole, not many more units than it had begun the war with. Faced with this dilemma, Guise initiated an unprecedented further expansion of the gendarmerie, naming new captains to the vacancies, authorizing the creation of eighteen additional brand new companies, as well as allowing further increases in the strengths of many existing companies. By the time of the siege of Orléans in February, 1563, almost a hundred units of gendarmes were in existence with an authorized total strength of approximately 10,000 men. When, after the peace, the handful of previously existing companies belonging to the major Protestant leaders were reintegrated into the gendarmerie, the total number of units reached 103, an unprecedented number that, as we will see in the next section, soon was to be dwarfed by the continuing creation of ever more new units, the method the crown would choose to increase the strength of the gendarmerie, with mixed results, throughout the early wars.[10]

But heavy cavalry companies were not, as we have mentioned, simply military units. They were a public manifestation of royal favor and trust, the mark, bar none, of high status and often political power as well, forming the core of the retinues of

---

[8] See Sainte-Croix's report in Jean Aymon, *Actes ecclésiastiques* (La Haye, 1710), vol. 1, 168. The royal cavalry at this time can be contrasted to the cavalry resources claimed by the Huguenot party, which, according to an "Estat de parties," PRO/SP 70/41, fols. 46–52, amounted to some 4,439 horse, including six former gendarme company captains. Some uncertainable but significant number of nobles and even some captains who had initially adhered to the Protestant cause, probably because of clientage ties, rallied to the royal cause over the course of the first war.

[9] Guise, *Mémoires*, 497.

[10] Calculated using sources in the Appendix, Part C, especially the end of the war *département*, *OM* no. 48. The post-Dreux documents cited in note 6 above and the partial *département* of February, 1563, also help to establish new creations. On numbers in general see ahead, p. 128.

all provincial governors and most lieutenant governors.[11] They were, in other words, the most glittering awards of the complicated system of patronage and clientage among the upper nobility, and Guise's choices of the men to fill the vacant captaincies, to receive increases in the strengths of their existing companies, or to command new companies show careful calculation and a fine sense of balancing factional groups. Rather than simply reward his family and followers, though he did that too, Guise also rewarded members of the rival Montmorency and Bourbon clans, provincial leaders who had distinguished themselves fighting the Protestants (like Joyeuse and Maugiron), soldiers who had distinguished themselves through their service with the main army (Biron and Martigues), a few Italian mercenary captains, and marshals of France and their relatives (young Brissac and Gonnor, later Marshal Cossé).[12] It was from this expanded group of gendarme company captains that almost all the major leaders of the royal army would come until the very end of Charles IX's reign, and nearly half of them owed their promotion directly or indirectly to the events of the first civil war and especially the heavy casualties suffered at Dreux, the single major ranged battle fought by the royal army during the first civil war.

The battle of Dreux, then, had a number of consequences for the royal army and its heavy cavalry forces. The large number of gendarme and leader casualties at Dreux, which were in part a result of numerical weakness, seems to have galvanized the crown and its military leaders to the determination never again to operate at a disadvantage in heavy cavalry. Besides choosing the creation of new units as its primary response to the problem of numbers, the crown also had to face up to the challenge posed by the German mercenaries hired by the Protestants. The regiments of these heavy cavalrymen, operating in deep formations and utilizing maneuvers designed to maximize the impact of the firepower generated by the several wheel-lock pistols with which each rider was equipped, had played an important role in the overthrow of the gendarmerie at Dreux, greatly impressing a generation of French military leaders and observers. The immediate conclusion drawn by the crown seemed to be the necessity of matching the Protestant reiters by hiring mercenaries of its own. In all of the rest of the wars until 1576, with the exception of the fourth war, which was dominated by the siege of La Rochelle, the crown attempted to hire substantial numbers of such mercenaries and they came to play an important role in the army's cavalry arm. But besides being prohibitively expensive, such troops required an inordinate amount of special handling and delicate diplomacy. They frequently refused to fight (as in June, 1569, before the battle of La Roche L'Abeille) and were of all the foreign troops involved in the civil wars absolutely the most hated and feared for their destructiveness, cupidity, and cruelty. Their introduction in large numbers into France was one of the fundamental resentments held against the Protestant leadership.

[11] Harding, *Provincial Governors*, 21–22.
[12] For the creations immediately after Dreux see note 6 above.

Reiter forces were felt to be a necessary addition to the royal army not just because of their supposed fighting prowess, however, but also in order to shield the gendarmerie from the heavy casualties it was assumed they would incur from fighting the deep columns of the Protestant mercenaries. For the shock from the casualties to the heavy cavalry at Dreux continued to reverberate long after the battle itself was only a distant memory. One of the main strategic concerns of the crown and the army's leadership became the need to protect the nobility, that is, the gendarmerie, from destruction. One reason for this was the realization, at least during the early wars, that heavy casualties among the French nobility, whether Catholic or Protestant, worked only to the advantage of France's traditional enemies abroad: Spain, England, and the Empire. This nascent type of patriotic concern, obviously, did little to prevent widespread internecine bloodshed during the wars. But it interacted in an influential manner with the natural conservatism of the monarchy and the army's leadership to produce at various times a reluctance to risk the kingdom's army and especially its nobility because their destruction would leave the country defenseless against outsiders.

Such concerns played an important part in the second civil war. The gendarmerie had again made a poor showing against the Huguenot cavalry at the battle of Saint-Denis and then as far as the court was concerned demonstrated considerable reluctance to come to grips with the small Huguenot army it was pursuing across Champagne. After the Huguenots had finally escaped and were on their way to unite with their German allies, King Charles revoked his earlier order to bring them to battle, explaining that "At present, he did not wish to risk his kingdom or his nobles, who are not so strong that in risking a single battle enough of them would remain to him to fight a second in order to conserve his estate."[13] Instead he suggested sending part of the army eastward to the duke of Aumale to combat the enemy, but the latter, perhaps with memories of Dreux or Saint-Denis in mind, responded: "And as for my advice on whether the whole army should march together to combat what is approaching, Monseigneur knows how perilous it is to fight ten thousand concentrated cavalry. He also knows the King's command not to risk his estate against men who have hardly anything to lose."[14]

Anjou himself, however, still wished to push on and defeat the now formidable enemy but the reason he advanced was curiously a concern that when the German cavalry being raised for the crown arrived they might combine with the reiters in Condé's pay against the interests of France.[15] In the end it was the duke of Nevers' advice which was followed,

not to fight, and in the meantime, not to endanger that which we hold securely...Once the King's reiters come, to go right at them and easily defeat them, in the meantime not

---

[13] BN Mss. Fr. 15,443, fol. 113r.
[14] *Ibid.*, fol. 115v.
[15] BN Mss. Fr. 15,544, fol. 1.

concerning ourselves with the devastation they would inflict at their whim upon the towns of France. A country kept is worth more than a country lost, as it would be, if we lost a single battle now.[16]

But, in the event, the reiters that the king and the army's leaders hoped to hire to checkmate the Protestants' German cavalry and to protect the gendarmerie from having to risk exorbitant losses by fighting them alone did not arrive in time to see action, and the army shamefully avoided a major battle until the coming of the peace in March, 1568.

A similar situation occurred in late May of 1569, not long after the victory at the battle of Jarnac, when the army council had to consider whether to risk a battle with the duke of Zweibrücken's army of German mercenaries which was approaching Limousin in an attempt to rendezvous with Coligny and his French Huguenot army. Even though at this point in the campaign the army, particularly the gendarmerie, was in poor shape, most of the council spoke in favor of battle in the written opinions they submitted to Anjou.[17] But Tavannes, who dominated the council, reminded Anjou of the decision taken in the previous war,

that for lack of a second army with the King at Paris, it was resolved not to hazard everything at one time...As for giving battle in order to preserve the kingdom, that could not be done without risk even if the forces were near in strength to one another by one or two thousand cavalrymen. I would always prefer to be 8,000 horsemen trying to conquer than 10,000 horsemen who have something to lose, and it would not matter a bit if the attacker had a third less infantry as long as the principal part of his army consisted of cavalry. And to engage in battle with these people and risk all is not to combat your true enemies, who, once defeated, will call on the princes of the German league aroused by their loss to have a new army in France tomorrow, while a great part of your principal captains will have been killed, perhaps even the commanding general himself, God forbid, such that even with such a victory, there would remain the princes of Navarre and Condé and the Admiral with their party and their forces...That is to say, I will never be of a mind to gamble all of the Kingdom on the fortune of a single battle. And if my servant counseled me to gamble my lands against a trickster who possessed nothing, I would think that he wanted to trick me, and the first thing I would do would be nothing other than to give him the boot.[18]

The desire to preserve the nobility also played an important role in Anjou's conduct of the siege of La Rochelle in 1573. Though only a handful of gendarme companies were needed at any one time at the siege, close to half of all the companies in the kingdom rotated through service there, and their officers and gentlemen, along with the greatest nobles in the kingdom, are prominent in the casualty lists. As the siege wore on, in fact, and the ordinary infantry was reduced to a shadow of its original strength by sickness and casualties, Anjou was forced to rely more and more on these noble volunteers for even the most mundane tasks, like

---

[16] *CDM*, vol. 3, 107–8, note 1.
[17] BN Mss. Fr. 18,587, fols. 488–508.
[18] *Ibid.*, fol. 500.

providing guards for the trenches. At the last major attack, on May 26, Anjou held back the nobility from the assault when the breach appeared to be dangerously unassailable, "which made me hold back fearing that in taking the city, I would cause you to lose the nobility, and as much as I was strongly determined to take it, I did not want to hazard that outcome."[19] Near the very end of the siege Anjou defended to the king his agreement to an eight-day truce with the defenders on the grounds

that I had no hopes of taking the city by force, nor the means to undertake another assault, which I did not wish to risk, since the princes and the nobility would have been entirely responsible for such an effort, which could lead to a greater loss for you than not to take the town. Seeing thus that it was your will to make peace, I did not wish to risk anything.[20]

In the political and strategic calculus of the crown and its military leaders, then, the preservation of the gendarmerie and the nobility had a high value. Whether it was a decision not to hazard the destruction of the gendarmerie and its leaders and risk the safety of the kingdom on the outcome of a single battle against the Huguenots and their German cavalry, men who had little to lose, or the conviction that if it entailed the sacrifice of the nobility it might be preferable not to take a city like La Rochelle, there was a clear reluctance to risk them. It was no accident that from the second civil war onward there would never again be as large a battle loss inflicted on the gendarmerie as at Dreux. They were wholeheartedly committed to battle several more times, but only when the leadership thought they had an advantage in numbers or situation such as at Moncontour. Unlike the infantry, they were not considered expendable. The combination of the care with which they were committed on a large scale to combat with the decline in the number of battles and increase in the number of sieges fought by the army resulted in very low levels of battle casualties for them during the rest of the early wars. This development was, of course, exactly the opposite from that of the French infantry, whose heavy usage increased in proportion to the number of sieges fought, and for whom no such similar considerations of social value needed to be entertained.

"OUR GENDARMERIE BE THE PRINCIPAL FORCE"

On March 8, 1574, a few days after the Huguenot Mardi Gras insurrection precipitated the fifth civil war, Charles IX issued an *ordonnance* mobilizing his gendarme companies for war. In the declaration the king noted how he had worked to keep the kingdom in repose since the pacification of the preceding July had brought the siege of La Rochelle, and the fourth civil war, to a close. But his enemies had hatched secret plans culminating in February in an uprising and attempts to take many of the cities of the kingdom by surprise. He was therefore compelled to assemble his

---

[19] BN Mss. Fr. 4,765, fol. 71r.
[20] *Ibid.*, fol. 74r.

own forces and because "our gendarmerie be the principal force which might help and serve us on such occasions," its companies were ordered to travel in sufficient numbers to prevent being surprised, and in good order, to assembly points throughout the kingdom where, fully equipped and ready to serve, they were to receive their pay at musters scheduled for April 20.[21] More than a score of such declarations, issued at the beginning of and sometimes at various points within a campaign and listing the assignments of all the gendarme companies, have survived from the first six civil wars. When compared to peacetime enumerations they enable us to track with considerable precision both the mobilization and demobilization of companies and the assignments they were given from 1562 through 1578.

Recent scholarship has tended to dwell on the supposed decline and disappearance of the gendarmerie during the civil wars.[22] But no account of this decline has utilized in any systematic way the wealth of documents at the national level that enable a detailed and balanced analysis of the fate of the monarchy's "principal force" during the earlier period. It is true that as France wended its painful way through the 1580s and early 1590s almost all government and military institutions ceased to operate very well under the twin stressors of splintered loyalties and financial impoverishment. But when a national focus is adopted and the primacy of the needs of the royal army itself are properly appreciated, the history of the heavy cavalry forces of the crown turns out to be somewhat at odds with current assumptions about the fate of the gendarme system, which turn out to have greatly exaggerated its decline.

Figure 16 tracks changes in the number of gendarme companies in existence from the peace of Cateau-Cambrésis in 1559 to the period immediately following the end of the sixth civil war, the first war fought completely within Henry III's reign, in 1578.[23] The curve traced by the expansion and contraction of the gendarmerie directly reflects in a most revealing manner the changing intensity of the crown's war efforts over the period and the place that the gendarmerie had in them.

[21] For the March 8, 1574, declaration see the preamble to *OM* no. 178.

[22] Harding, *Provincial Governors*, especially 71–80.

[23] Though some of the *départements*, *états*, and *mandats* on which Figure 16 is based have previously been cited, references to its major sources are consolidated here in order not only to provide a unified list for it, but also for most of the other displays that follow in this chapter. For 1559, BN Mss. Fr. 3,150, fols. 39–50 (July); 1560, BN Mss. Fr. 21,543, fols. 28–47 (January) and *OM* no. 29 (October); 1561, BN Mss. Fr. 3,243, fols. 45–46 (February); 1562, Communay, "Gascons," 384–86 (early 1562); 1563, *OM* no. 48 (May); 1564, Susane, *Cavalerie*, vol. 1, 62–66 (April); 1565, BN Mss. Fr. 3,243, fols. 57–58 (January); 1566, BN Mss. Fr. 3,194, fols. 102–4 (March) and *ibid.*, fols. 94–101 (September); 1567, BN Mss. Fr. 4,552, fols. 18–26 (February) and 3,187, fols. 38–39 (March); 1568, BN Mss. Fr. 4,553, fols. 108–10 (February), *OM* nos. 120 and 122 (September), and BN Mss. Fr. 3,193, fols. 195–201 (October); 1569, *OM* no. 129 (February) and PRO/SP 70/107, fols. 310–11 (July); 1570, BN Mss. Fr. 21,543, fols. 69–75 (an October *état* of officials including company paymasters); 1571, *OM* no. 153 (June); 1572, *OM* nos. 161 (March) and 165 (August); 1573, BN Mss. Fr. 21,543, fols. 77–93 (January) and *OM* no. 173 (September); 1574, BN Mss. Fr. 3,193, fols. 184–93 (January) and *OM* no. 173 (March); 1575, *OM* nos. 199 (August) and 208 (December); 1576, *OM* no. 212 (February) and BN Mss. Fr. 3,256, fols. 21–22 (June); 1577, *OM* nos. 226 (February) and 235 (July); 1578, BN Mss. Fr. 21,543, fols. 95–106 (January).

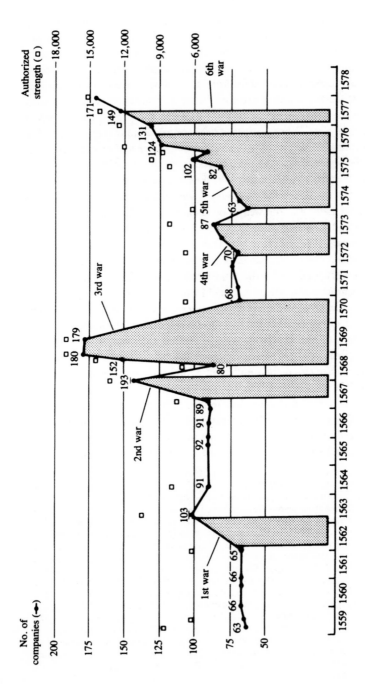

Fig. 16. Number of gendarme companies, 1559–78

The first great increase, as we noted in the previous section, entailed an unprecedented two-thirds expansion in the number of companies during the first civil war. This expansion was only partially rolled back during the first interwar period, when the number of companies (including those of a few prominent Protestant leaders) remained some 50 percent higher than in the prewar period. From this expanded base a second and much more massive increase occurred during the second and third civil wars when, at its peak strength in 1569, there were three times as many gendarme companies in existence as at the beginning of the era of religious troubles. This enormous expansion, it should be remembered, coincided with the crown's effort to bring every possible resource it could to bear on the goal of destroying the main Huguenot army in the field. The result by 1570 was physical and financial exhaustion, demobilization, and then major retrenchments in the second major interwar period which reduced the number of gendarme companies back almost to the level of the original prewar period itself. During the fourth and at the beginning of the fifth civil war modest expansions occurred which never reached the level of even the first civil war. However, as the fifth war continued and the crown attempted to assemble a cavalry-heavy field army near Paris in order to block Condé and Casimir's invading German mercenaries, more and more companies were created, beginning a third great expansion that, continuing through the sixth war and afterwards, equalled the great efforts of the second and third war period and led at least nominally to the highest levels of postwar numbers in the whole period.

There are two great ironies imbedded in the tremendous but episodic mobilizations of heavy cavalry by the crown. The first, of course, is in the contrast of the despair felt by many nobles immediately following the treaty of Cateau-Cambrésis when it seemed that the kingdom was entering a period of longterm military inactivity and retrenchment, with the actually quite extensive opportunities for promotion to captain which the civil wars were to provide. The second is that the expansion of the gendarmerie during the civil wars was sustained only at the cost of the absorption of most of the light cavalry of the army. Rather than decline, the period actually witnessed the triumph of the gendarmerie through the convergence of different types of battle cavalry into a single overwhelmingly favored type of heavy cavalry.

We can calculate that from the beginning of the first war in 1562 (when about 60 loyal companies remained) to the end of the fifth civil war, a cumulative total of at least 309 new companies of gendarmes were raised at one time or another, and a total of at least 383 by the beginning of 1578. Only about 9 percent of these companies were raised in the two interwar periods and almost two-thirds (62 percent) of all the new companies raised during the first five civil wars had been created by the end of the third civil war. Almost all the companies raised to the end of the third war were genuinely new, that is they had never previously served as part of the gendarmerie nor had their commanders ever been captains of gendarmes before. This represents, then, a genuine wave of first-time promotions, though, as we will see below, this expansion may have exhausted the cavalry resources of the kingdom for some time. By contrast, 60 percent of the newly raised companies during the fourth and fifth wars were organized by captains who had served sometime in the past as gendarme captains, but had lost their previous command in the reductions following the end of the third and fourth wars. For many of those captains cashiered or demobilized after the great campaigns of 1569, in other words, as well as those remobilized after some significant lapse of time towards the end of the period, one of the original major meanings of gendarme status, permanent support in both war *and* peace, had been lost, though they and their men continued to serve the same military function and have the same equipment as those companies of heavy battle-field cavalry which were not disbanded between wars.

The gendarmes, of course, were not the only type of cavalry which existed in France. During the first and at the beginning of the second war substantial numbers of *chevaux-légers* and *arquebusiers à cheval* were also utilized. The latter type, in fact, was well on its way to becoming the most ubiquitous form of light cavalry during the wars, serving primarily in units of fifty men as scouts, escorts, mounted infantry, and mobile garrison troops. Much cheaper than other types of cavalry, these mounted infantrymen were particularly useful in the small-scale wars in the provinces and though some always served with the main armies their numbers in that role do not appear to have increased much if at all over the course of the early wars. The *chevaux-légers*, on the other hand, became the primary source for the major expansions of the gendarmerie. These units, whose history is obscure and which are sometimes confused with the less heavily armored archers of the gen-darme companies, were in fact a distinct branch of cavalry, usually composed of noble volunteers organized in 100-man companies, more lightly armored than the gendarmerie, but still expected to play a role as battle cavalry organized in a single tactical regiment under the command of their own colonel general. In the pre-civil war period, perhaps because the numbers of gendarme companies remained rela-tively small, these companies seem to have been able to recruit good quality human material, men eager to serve or seek their fortune in the cavalry but unable to obtain a place in a regular gendarme company. From various sources it seems that such units were usually organized from the gentlemen volunteers who flocked to the side of local commanders at the beginning of each war or of nobles who chose service rather than a financial contribution to fulfill their obligation when the *ban* and *arrière-ban* was called out.[24] From the first war onward, however, it was decided that in fighting the Huguenot gendarmes or their pistol-armed German allies, it was heavier rather than lighter cavalry that was required. As a result, the *chevaux-légers* companies with the army, their equipment partially upgraded, were converted *en*

---

[24] See, for example, the July 1562 muster of more than 200 gentlemen who accompanied Maugiron, the lieutenant general of Dauphiny, and the count of Clermont during their service with Tavannes' army against Lyon during the first civil war, a subset of whom were later ordered to be organized as Maugiron's newly created gendarme company, Lot, 258–61, and *CDM*, vol. 1, 466.

masse during the second war into gendarme companies and served that way from late in the second war and throughout the third war, indistinguishable from the existing gendarme companies or those which had been created from scratch. From the end of the second civil war onward, the *chevaux-légers* as a type of distinct light cavalry practically disappear from the rolls of the main field armies.[25] The great expansion of the gendarmerie in the second and third wars, then, owed most of its magnitude to the conversion and absorption of these lighter units, though this may have been, as we will discuss below, a flawed experiment.

From the second to the end of the fifth civil war, then, the overwhelming majority of the French cavalry attached to the main field army were gendarmes, from approximately 77 percent in late 1568 (compared to about 61 percent at Dreux) to over 90 percent during the fall of 1568, in 1569 at Jarnac and Moncontour, and near Paris in late 1575.[26] The lack of light cavalry carried on the army's rolls seems not to have been considered a problem, for when foreign cavalry were sought or bought to bolster the army's strength, they were almost always either more gendarme types, such as Flemish horse sent by the duke of Alva in 1567 or the Italian cavalry sent by the pope in 1569, or German reiter types hired by the crown for the king's service – both types of heavy cavalry intended for a battlefield role. As far as the crown and the army leadership were concerned, apparently, there could never be too much heavy cavalry.

An analysis of the assignments of gendarme companies during the wars helps to make clearer this emphasis on heavy cavalry and its maximum possible expansion. Figure 17 calculates the proportion of all gendarme companies serving with the main field army at various times during the first five civil wars as well as the proportion serving in important secondary concentrations (those containing at least 10 percent of all gendarme companies and those assigned elsewhere than the royal army or its secondary concentrations which were almost without exception dispersed in small groups under the command of the governors and lieutenant governors who were fighting the local wars outside the main areas of operations.[27] So what this display indicates, first of all, is the extent to which the gendarmerie was utilized as a concentrated force of battle-capable cavalry by the crown. From right before the battle of Dreux in the first war to the end of the period, at least 40 percent and more often closer to 60 percent of all the gendarme companies in the kingdom were concentrated with the main royal army whose purpose was to defeat

---

[25] This process can be closely followed by tracking the troops brought from Brittany to the main army by Martigues at the beginning of the second war, listed in BN Mss. Fr. 3,898, fols. 228–35. The six *chevaux-léger* companies on the roster in November 1567 are in December listed as "compagnies hommes d'armes nouvellement fait dont y en a aulcuns compagnies de chevaux legiers," and in January 1568 disappear from the Breton contingent's roster, only to reappear on the general gendarme *état* in February, 1568, BN Mss. Fr. 4,553, fols. 108–10.

[26] Calculated by comparing the sources for Figure 16, which usually provide information on the areas of the country and the armies to which companies were assigned, to the information on main armies on which Figure 10 is based, and the overall operational forces detailed in Table 2.9

[27] *Ibid.*

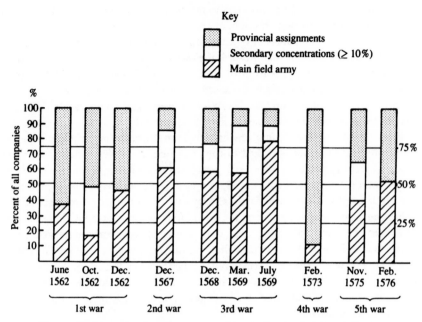

Fig. 17. Assignments of gendarme companies during the first five civil wars

the Huguenot army on the battlefield. To the extent that sizeable secondary concentrations of companies were organized, they were intended to intercept on the periphery of the kingdom the German mercenary cavalry hired by the Protestants during all but the fourth civil war. During the crucial second and third wars, in fact, at least 75 and usually more than 80 percent of the total gendarmerie was devoted to both these purposes and during the fifth war two-thirds were devoted to one or the other. The gendarmerie's near exclusive devotion to these tasks highlights the reasons for the crown's concern with expanding its heavy cavalry forces, for light cavalry was of little use against what was identified as the most dangerous component of the enemy forces. Ironically, all of the attempts to intercept the Huguenots' German allies failed, perhaps because the forces delegated for this purpose were always too weak. The depth of the concern, however, which dated from the experiences of the first civil war, is also reflected in the crown's constant attempts to hire German mercenaries of its own.

The great exception to this development, of course, is the fourth war, dominated by the siege of La Rochelle, which required little cavalry and was the only war in which there was no need to organize one of the substantial secondary concentrations of heavy cavalry to intercept the enemy's reiters. By the fifth war the proportion of the gendarmes devoted to battlefield functions, while still high, had diminished somewhat, reflecting the concentration on sieges and the splintered nature of the early campaigns of that war. But by then as we shall see, the changing nature of campaigns, financial exhaustion, and the shifting mental horizons of captains were combining to leave the royal cavalry, converted by then to a slightly less heavy gendarme type, in a state of advancing disarray that the disintegration of Catholic unity in the 1580s only deepened.

In terms of the wider military struggle during the early wars of religion the other most notable conclusion to be drawn from Figure 17 is the way in which the main and secondary royal armies drew to themselves such a high proportion of the kingdom's military resources in cavalry for use in the conventional military campaigns against Huguenot armies. To the extent that the struggle was being decided on the local level, this meant that the representatives of royal power in the provinces were deprived of the kind of resources they needed to wage more effective campaigns or to prevent the reoccurrence of Protestant rebellions that usually flared up again as soon as the main army moved on. From the point of view of local governors, forced to operate without much of the best cavalry in the country, it may have seemed that the institution of heavy cavalry itself had declined, at least as they remembered its provincial importance during the prewar period.[28] This also highlights the absolutely crucial role played by the Huguenot noble cavalry and their German mercenaries in the long-term survival of local Protestant communities. By maintaining or purchasing conventional cavalry-heavy field armies, the Huguenots forced the crown to invest a disproportionate amount of military resources in its own very expensive heavy cavalry long after the great mobile campaigns of the second and third wars had come to an end, at a time when expansion or at least more stable support of the assault infantry needed for the reconquest of towns and territories in the west and south of the kingdom might perhaps have been a more productive investment of military resources. What was at work in the decline of light cavalry and its conversion to gendarme types as well as the overall expansion of the gendarmerie itself, then, was not simply the class prejudices of the noble leaders of the army and the royal council, but a kind of sixteenth-century heavy cavalry brinksmanship grounded in assumptions and experience of the still formidable military effectiveness, on the battlefield, of heavily armored cavalry.

THE ORGANIZATION AND IDENTITY OF THE GENDARMERIE

The basic organization for cavalry, like infantry, was the company. Light cavalry was generally organized in standard sized units of 50 or 100 men, but gendarme companies continued until the end of the period to compute their strength in "lances," a term that in the middle ages referred to the retinue a knight was obligated to bring with himself on service and which continued to be used as a unit of account when the permanent gendarmerie was founded in the mid-fifteenth century. At the

---

[28] Harding, 75–77.

outbreak of the wars of religion a lance represented an abstract unit of two and one half horsemen, one of which was a more heavily armored *homme d'armes*. But as other than an accounting term which also conveyed immediately the number of *hommes d'armes* in a gendarme company the lance had no real-life military equivalent.

By this usage, then, a company of 30 lances would have a total strength of 75 men – 30 *hommes d'armes* and 45 of the more lightly armored archers, and companies of 20, 30, 40, 50, 60, 80, 100, and 120 lances are encountered in the documents of the time corresponding to authorized strengths varying from 50 to 320 men.[29] The largest companies, however, were quite rare and by quite early in the period the vast majority of companies, in a ratio of about 4:1, were composed of 30 and 60 lances respectively, though the situation was complicated by reductions in strengths after wars and *creues* during wars, as well as the fact that letters of commission for captains refer only to companies of 50 and 100 lances. Such 50 and 100 lance commissions, however, were only *en titre*, and as a practical matter referred to companies with actual strengths of 30 and 60 lances, or 75 and 150 men. As the queen mother wrote to the lieutenant governor of Dauphiny, Maugiron, one of the captains given a company after the battle of Dreux,

so that you will know that I have not forgotten you, as I never would those whom I know to have a sincere and strict affection for the service of the King, my son, I have had him grant you the captaincy of a company of fifty men-at-arms, which I request you fill with the best and most valiant men, and as soon as you are able, to aid him on such occasions as present themselves, while waiting for the letters of provision that I have dispatched to you. *It is for thirty lances, to which all of the companies of this quality have been reduced.*[30]

Contemporaries who grasped these distinctions more clearly often simply referred to the larger companies as "double" companies, and in representing real strengths the ratio per lance of one and one half times as many archers as *hommes d'armes* remained stable throughout the period. Some variation in authorized strengths of individual companies can of course always be found, and in the 1570s there was a trend towards larger numbers of 20 lance, or 50 man, companies. But the typical size of companies serving through most of the period was of 30 or 60 lances, and the manner in which such standard companies were organized and paid is presented in Table 5.1.[31]

With only seven specialties or ranks and six separate pay steps, the internal organization of such companies was somewhat simpler than that of a standard infantry company. There were really only two troop types, the *homme d'armes* and the archer, and the officers also served as *hommes d'armes* for which they received pay in addition to their officer salaries (the two have been combined in the table).

---

[29] Many examples could be given, but see, for 1559, BN Mss. Fr. 3,150, fols. 39–50, for 1567 BN Mss. Fr. 4,552, fols. 18–26, and for 1574 BN Mss. Fr. 3,193, fols. 184–93.

[30] *CDM*, vol. 1, 466. My italics.

[31] From the sources in note 29 above.

Table 5.1. *Gendarme company organization*

Rank or specialty	Double company of 60 lances		Company of 30 lances	
	No.	Pay (*livres* per month)	No.	Pay (*livres* per month)
Captain	1	267	1	183
Lieutenant	1	108	1	88
Ensign	1	83	1	67
Guidon	1	83	1	67
Marshal de logis	1	50	1	46
Cadre subtotal	5		5	
Hommes d'armes	55	33	25	33
Archers	90	17	45	17
Trooper subtotal	145		70	
Total strength	150		75	

The main distinction between these two standard companies besides size was the fact that the officers of the larger company received substantially higher pay, a prime reason for constant scheming by the captains of smaller companies to get their status elevated from *en titre de cinquante* to *en titre de cent hommes d'armes*, but the larger companies were usually reserved for the grandees. The base pay for *hommes d'armes* and archers remained the same despite company sizes.

In general, gendarme officers were paid somewhat more than twice as much as officers of analogous rank in infantry companies and even a simple *homme d'armes*, at 33 *livres* per month, was paid more than all but an infantry ensign, lieutenant, or captain, while the lowest paid rank of archer could expect at 17 *livres* per month a slightly higher salary than even the highest paid infantry *lanspessade*. These salaries, incidentally, which remained stable from the second through the sixth war, are slightly lower (by 3 and 1 *livres* per month, respectively, for *hommes d'armes* and archers) than the rate paid during the first civil war and reflect the retrenchment attempted after 1563.

Compared to the infantry, gendarme salaries may appear lavish, and certainly in the aggregate such rates meant that heavy cavalry units were quite expensive, but in actuality not all of the salary was free and clear of daily expenses like feeding for man and beast nor, of course, did wages cover the initial investment for equipment and horses which the regulations of the time required of gendarmes. The general regulations of 1574 for the gendarmerie, for example, required of an *homme d'armes* a closed helm (lighter morions were expressly excluded), a good cuirass, upper arm and forearm armor, thigh, haunch, and knee pieces, and a fully armored saddle in addition to a pistol and a "bonne et fort" lance. Their horses were also required, theoretically at least, to be barded, that is, to have head and chest armor as well as flank protection. Archers were also required to possess a good closed helmet, cuirass, arm protection, thigh and haunch armor, and a pistol and a lance, but they were excused from wearing knee pieces and there was no barding requirement for their horses. *Hommes d'armes* were required to have on campaign two great warhorses and one nag for riding and baggage, archers a single warhorse and one nag.[32]

At the beginning of the wars of religion the lance armed *hommes d'armes* on their barded horses must have looked very much like medieval knights. But by 1574 the regulations, though still requiring barding, also excused those *hommes d'armes* who did not have it on their warhorses as long as they promised to provide it as soon as they could afford to, a tacit admission that it was no longer widely used.[33] So over the course of the early wars movement towards a merger of the *hommes d'armes* and archer types was occurring, primarily through the lightening of horse protection, as the two types were armed practically the same, with pistol and lance. This also made it possible to transform pistol armed *chevaux-légers* with a slight upgrading of mount and armor into an *homme d'armes* or archer type. The premium in wages that continued to be paid to *hommes d'armes*, then, rested primarily on the fact that they had to support two warhorses, carried a little more armor protection, and had the most dangerous tactical assignment of fighting in the first rank of the *ligne en haye* formation favored by the royal gendarmes throughout the period.

The equipment and horses that gendarmes were required to have quite clearly marked them off from infantrymen as men of at least some modest means. A conservative estimate of the cost to properly outfit an archer and his two horses comes to about 400 *livres*, and for an *hommes d'armes* with three horses a minimum of 600–700 *livres*, ten to fifteen times the cost of equipping even the most heavily armored pikeman.[34] A cavalryman of course also had to pay for the feed his mounts consumed, and an estimate of the time calculates this expense, at normal prices, at

---

[32] The February 1, 1574, printed "Ordonnance du Roy sur le reiglement de sa gendarmerie, forme de vivre & payement d'icelle," *OM* no. 177, contains 63 very full clauses; the ones in question are clauses 15–17.

[33] *Ibid.*, clause 15.

[34] Calculating 200 *livres* for a warhorse and 60 for a nag. The 1574 "Ordonnance," clause 17, prices a lance, pistol, and saddle for a total of 27 *livres*. Perhaps 100 *livres* for the rest of the defensive armor and a sword. This very rough estimate may be an underestimate and would not in any case apply to the quality of equipment carried by *les grands*. Clause 6 of the "Ordonnance" tries to limit the price captains could pay for the distinctive livery of their men. Good quality horses were extremely expensive. A technical discussion of the artillery of the day assigns a cost of 120 *écus* for a good quality draft horse, BN Mss. 3,193, fol. 233r. The queen mother was outraged when Condé reneged on his personal promise to her to spare the royal stud farm which had fallen into his possession during the first civil war and instead distributed twenty-two stallions to his captains: Alphonse de Ruble, "Documents inédits sur la guerre civile de 1562 en Berry," *Société des Antiquaires du Centre Bourges*, 15 (1887–88), 142–43.

8.33 and 12.75 *livres* per month, respectively, for an archer and an *homme d'armes*.[35] Disregarding other expenses, this left an archer 8.67 *livres* to support himself on each month, or only about the pay of the average infantryman. The *homme d'armes* was in better shape with 20.25 *livres* clear each month, or about the equivalent of an infantry sergeant's pay. But after deducting other expenses and including the cost of providing food for the ubiquitous pages and servants which always traveled with the company, it is hard to imagine that any gendarme could get rich off his pay, especially if, as often happened, the campaign took place in time of scarcity and elevated food prices.

The gendarmes, however, were a much less expensive proposition than the other most common type of cavalry to be found in the royal armies of the times: the German mercenary reiters. Reiters were hired in regiments of two to four companies of 300 men each, a size which dwarfed even the largest double company of gendarmes. Reiter companies had a less varied internal organization than gendarme companies since all men without exception were supposed to be "good and valiant cavalrymen, men of war and service, true Germans, well mounted and armed with corselet, mail gloves, gauntlets, morion, and equipped with two pistols each, a cutlass and a mace."[36] Troopers were paid 21 *livres* per month, somewhat more than an archer but less than an *homme d'armes*, about the same as the average wage in a gendarme company when the cost of both types of troopers are combined. But a reiter company also carried on its payroll a number of specialists not found, or at least not supported by the crown, in gendarme companies, such as a pistol worker, a fourier, a surgeon, and four *rottmeister*, or troop commanders. Each company was also paid 6 *livres* per month for each of the 100 draft horses it was allowed to have to draw 25 large or 50 small baggage wagons. The top officers, moreover, were paid at a significantly higher rate than the equivalent gendarme officers. Finally, the fact that the reiters were hired by the regiment added another whole layer of expenses, for the colonel of a four company regiment received 1,800 *livres* per month salary and his lieutenant 471 *livres* (the same as a reiter company captain) and the regimental staff itself contained another thirty-seven paid places including, among others, two trumpeters, a translator, a chaplain, seventeen military police, an executioner, officers of the watch, a master of baggage, a quartermaster, and a remount officer.[37] Gendarme companies operating in the provinces, by contrast, were never

---

[35] For the estimate of feeding costs, see BN 3,085, fol. 78. See also *OM* no. 177, clause 19, for the extra mounts and baggage horses allowed, which added to the expense, especially for officers. A 30-lance company in the field, mustering 75 men, at full regulation strength required 192 horses. In garrison the same 75-man company was allowed by regulation 279 horses. BN 4,555, fol. 40, a 1577 royal order commanding the furnishing of *vivres* to Nevers' gendarme company as it went into garrison at Douzy and Poully, stipulates the number of horses to be supplied and the amounts of feed and forage the inhabitants were to provide each day for every horse.

[36] BN Mss. Fr. 15,608, fol. 32r, a *capitulation* with a Colonel Lunebourg.

[37] *Capitulations* with reiter colonels are: *OM* no. 128 (1568); BN Mss. Fr. 15,608, fols. 30–33 (1568); and *OM* no. 237 (1577).

organized in regiments, and even the heavy cavalry regiments with the main army, which grouped together from five to a dozen companies of gendarmes, contained no organized paid staff or regimental commanders, leadership being simply exercised by the most senior or prestigious company captain.

But besides pay and the initial cost of their equipment and mounts, the most important differences between the gendarmerie and the army's infantry were the class and social status of leaders and men and a higher prevalence of common geographical origins and kinship and clientele ties. The gendarmes were regarded by all contemporaries as the most aristocratic of the army's military formations – considered in fact coterminous with the nobility by the king and army leaders, as we saw in the first section of this chapter – and all the available historical evidence overwhelmingly supports this conclusion. Even a casual examination of the many *départements* and mobilization documents of the era quickly reveals that the most elevated and powerful noblemen in the kingdom dominated the ranks of gendarme captains. The postwar 1563 *département*, for example, contains a rabelaisian profusion of titles: seven princes, fourteen dukes, twelve marquises and counts, four marshals of France, the admiral, and the constable, and even the names of those captains whose titles were not recorded on the list, such as Tavannes, Biron, Cossé, Damville, Martigues, Monluc, Matignon, and Joyeuse, are as immediately recognizable by any serious student of the era as they would have been thoroughly familiar to any well-informed contemporary.[38] Forming a basic core of captains were the governors and lieutenant governors of provinces and important places, royal princes, holders of major military posts, relatives of the grands, a few foreign rulers, and more rarely a foreign, usually Italian, mercenary soldier. As the gendarmerie expanded it drew its new captains from less grand but nonetheless locally prominent men who were often serving as officers in existing companies, the lieutenants and clientele of provincial potentates, and, as mentioned above, captains of *chevaux-légers* companies. What all the captains had in common was their noble status, a condition seemingly shared without exception by the officers of their companies, as any analysis of the thousands of names of company officers present at musters published in Vindry's *Dictionnaire de l'état-major français au XVIe siècle*, will confirm.[39]

But most *hommes d'armes* seem also to have been nobles and many, perhaps most, of the archers as well. So besides the expense of mounts and equipment, the shared aristocratic origins of members of the gendarmerie dramatically set them apart

---

[38] *OM* no. 48.

[39] Fleury Vindry, *Dictionnaire de l'état-major français au XVIe siècle* (Paris, 1901), 1 vol. plus *Atlas*. A large number of gendarme muster documents survive in the *Bibliothèque nationale*. For the period covered by this work, Vindry's *Atlas* cites more than 1,700 monstres in the *Manuscrits français*, *Nouvelles acquisitions français*, and Clairambault series and lists the officers identified in the muster documents. The relatively large numbers of such documents that survive from this period compared to infantry musters is due to the fact that they were essential pieces of genealogical evidence for families trying to prove their quarterings long after the wars of religion were over.

from the infantry as a group and contributed to a very different internal social organization of their companies. Unlike the widely recruited and unrelated soldiers of the regular infantry companies, gendarme companies were virtually family and clientele related operations. An in-depth study of more than one thousand members of ten different gendarme companies between 1568 and 1574 by Robert Harding found, first, that an average of 75 percent of the gendarmes in these companies came from the same governorship, that is province, as their commander, and in some cases more than 90 percent. An analysis of surnames and kinship related terms shows that the companies included numerous relatives both of the captain and other members of the company, including fathers and sons, and brothers, and related *hommes d'armes* and archers. In Blaise de Monluc's company, for example, 40 percent of the men shared a surname with another member of the company.[40] Compare this to Brissac's and Jehan Monluc's infantry companies where, out of 263 men, we were able to find only one pair of men with matched surnames from the same locality. Although Harding did not do a close analysis of troopers' ages, his general impression, which is validated by Vindry, is that captains were generally battle-hardened veterans of a mature age and that the companies, as the name matches might suggest, were multigenerational associations of mature men aged from 17 to 59 years old.[41] The number of upper age range men may have been slightly more truncated than among the infantry, however, for there was no equivalent to the purely sedentary infantry company and the prime requirement of an ability to withstand the rigors of sitting a saddle for long periods of time must have worked against the inclusion of most older men, the example of Constable Montmorency, still leading charges in his seventies, notwithstanding.

It was Harding's impression that the gendarmerie may have actually become more aristocratic during the period of the wars of religion.[42] By law, at least, this should have been the case, for the 1574 general ordinance regulating the gendarmerie states a requirement that enlistees be exclusively gentlemen.[43] That the *hommes d'armes* were overwhelmingly noble seems clear, but it is equally evident that though non-nobles served as archers, many archers were noblemen and during wartime significant numbers of promotions from archer to *homme d'armes* always took place. Given that recruitment of gendarmes was generally from a much smaller portion of the population than infantry and concentrated primarily within more limited geographical areas, the more close-knit nature of the heavy cavalry companies seems clear – even if not related, men may have been more apt to have known each other or a previous or serving member of the company before enlisting. This mixture of family and clientele recruitment made the companies much more the personal instrument of their captains than infantry companies and as such

---

[40] Harding, *Provincial Governors*, 23–24.
[41] Ibid., 24–25.
[42] Ibid., 23.
[43] *OM* no. 177, clause 17.

contributed to a certain independence from higher authority that became increasingly hard for the crown to control as warlordism increased in the provinces in the last decade of civil war. It also made it difficult to reduce companies and remix their personnel in the same impersonal manner adopted for the infantry. If a company was not continued by a new commission granted to the son or client of a retiring or deceased captain it was generally completely disbanded, though released troopers would surely have tried to sign on with other companies. Captains, unlike in the infantry, were not treated as interchangeable, which says something about their more elevated personal status and meant that the heavy cavalry still carried a certain feudal character that was missing from the royal infantry and its newly organized regiments.

But the primacy of interrelatedness and association for gendarme company personnel can be overestimated. Not only, as we shall see in the next section, was the existence of many companies precarious and short-lived, but many gendarmes themselves were involved in strategies of self-advancement which led them to switch from company to company, a practice consistently and loudly condemned by the various ordinances of the times.[44] As Monluc explained, "when soldiers know of a captain who has achieved some glory early in his career, all brave men seek to join him, hoping that since he had such a glorious beginning, his career will continue in like manner, and thus they will continue to be employed."[45]

We can, then, distinguish at least three or four levels of social mobility at work in the gendarme companies. At the lowest level was the occasional *roturier* volunteer whose service certainly tended to associate himself with the gentlemen and perhaps, over time, led to the achievement of noble status. Second, archers could aspire to be elevated to *hommes d'armes* with a chance beyond that, perhaps, one of the lower officer positions like *guidon* or *marshal de logis*. Third, officers from lieutenant down might hope to elevate themselves if they followed Monluc's advice to "make yourself worthy of the praise and esteem of the grandees, and in this way, through their support you will be known to the King, from whom we must all hope for compensation for our services and labors."[46] Such notice might even lead to the command of their own company of heavy cavalry. And captains, of course, might aspire to lieutenantships and governorships of places or provinces, higher level army posts such as marshal-of-camp, or at least to be rewarded for their services by a gift or grant. And though, as the ladder of opportunity was climbed, the number of men elevated from archer to *homme d'armes*, to company officer and then to company captain, and on to higher responsibility shrank rapidly – there were only about a hundred such higher positions in the entire kingdom, most reserved for grandees – at the lower levels constant turnover meant that there was often plenty of room for advancement.

[44] For example, *CSPF/E*, vol. 8, no. 1942, January 14, 1568.
[45] Monluc, *Commentaires*, vol. 1, 59.
[46] *Ibid.*

As with the infantry, over the course of a campaign attrition took its toll. Reiter companies always were hired at full strength and even after several months campaigning seem to have maintained their initial strengths fairly well, perhaps because even though regulations prohibited it they could find replacements among their pages and draft horses. Five reiter companies serving in the regiment of the marquis of Baden, who mustered out in May of 1568, for example, were still at 91 percent (1,640 out of 1,800 present) strength after four months of service though without combat.[47] A study of gendarme company strengths during the third war by Gigon based on a sample of 27 company musters showed an average strength of 82, 65, and 49 men, or 85, 72, and 65 percent of authorized strength after three, nine, and fourteen months of service, respectively.[48] Individual companies, of course, could sink to much lower levels (Gigon records an individual low of 33 men), but as a general guide this and other information seems to indicate that the gendarmerie as a whole entered campaigns very near to an average authorized strength of about 90 men per company which was reduced by about one-third after six months of service and to half by service of more than a year (or a steady attrition rate of 3–4 percent per month). Obviously, over the course of a campaign there was a great need for replacements and many opportunities for promotion within companies. When very reduced strengths were reached companies were furloughed, if possible, to bring themselves back up to strength, but new companies were also raised, and most common of all, more of the existing companies outside the main area of operations were ordered to join the field army. Over the course of a campaign, as we have noted, a very high proportion of all companies in the kingdom were often drawn to the royal army by such means.

Despite significantly more stable ties between personnel within gendarme companies compared to the infantry, the fact is that turnover within even the most secure of companies could be quite high. An analysis of changes in the personnel of Blaise de Monluc's company of gendarmes from the end of the second war in March, 1568, to around the time of Moncontour, in September, 1569, during the third war, will make this clear. Monluc, of course, was a famous captain and provincial governor who devoted much of his time to promoting his relatives and lieutenants as well as his personal interests. His company had been actively involved in local campaigning in the south and west during the second war. In the third war it was again actively involved in local operations but also took part in important secondary operations in conjunction with the main army, and at one point briefly joined it in the spring of 1569. In March and October of 1568 the company was rated as 40 lances, but later in the fall of 1568 it was granted a *creue* which was supposed to transform it into a 60-lance company, the same status it had about a year later in September, 1569. Two surviving musters from the beginning and the end of this 18-month period make it possible to work out the changes in personnel

---

[47] BN Mss. Fr. 15,608, fols. 100–1.
[48] Gigon, 356–62.

which had taken place by three intermediate dates, between the second and third war, in October, and in December of 1568. The results of this reconstruction are presented in Figure 18.[49]

The first point to be drawn from this data is the impressive turnover in the company from March, 1568, to September, 1569. As can be seen, after nineteen months the great majority of the company's personnel had changed. Only fourteen of the original 40 *hommes d'armes* and 10 of the original 60 archers remained. Seven more of the original archers who had been promoted to *hommes d'armes* during the period can also be counted as holdovers, bringing the total of survivors to 31 out of the original strength of 100 men. This computes to a gross attrition rate of 69 percent over the whole period of nineteen months, or 3.6 percent per month.

A closer examination of the turnover figures, however, also highlights another important point, that the turnover rate within the company was actually less during the third war than over the period between wars from March to October, 1568. Seventy-eight of the ninety-five men present in October, 1568, were still there in September, 1569, a gross attrition rate of 17.9 percent in twelve months, or 1.5 percent per month. And of the total of 136 men who we know served in the company over the course of the third war, only 26 failed to show up again in September, 1569, a gross attrition of 19 percent, or 1.6 percent per month.

Though the company stood at full strength in March, 1568, and at 95 percent of its authorized strength at the beginning of the third war, the nominal increase in size of 50 men, or 50 percent, from the *creue* to 60 lances, had resulted in a real increase of only 14 men in December, 1568, and 10 men in September, 1569, or an average of 12 percent, leaving the 60-lance company at about 75 percent of authorized strength through most of the war. This suggests that given the competition for troopers in the greatly expanded gendarme forces during the third war, even the most famous commander was hard pressed to increase the size of his company over its strength at the beginning of the war, whether or not he was granted extra lances. It also suggests that to maintain its average strength of around one hundred men roughly double that many men had to cycle through the company every two or so years.

What does such a replacement ratio imply when compared to the total number of nobles available for service with the royal army? Most estimates of the total number of nobles in sixteenth-century France fluctuate between 1.5 and 2 percent of a total population of roughly 20 million people. For the purposes of this model, we will assume the higher figure is correct and that the total number of nobles was about 400,000 in the 1560s. Once allowance is made for children, women, the very elderly, and those nobles holding non-military occupations or office, we are left with a military age adult male noble population of perhaps 80,000. We know that some

---

[49] The originals, according to Vindry, are BN Mss. Fr. 21,528, no. 1890 (March 18, 1568) and 21,530, no. 1978 (September 20, 1569).

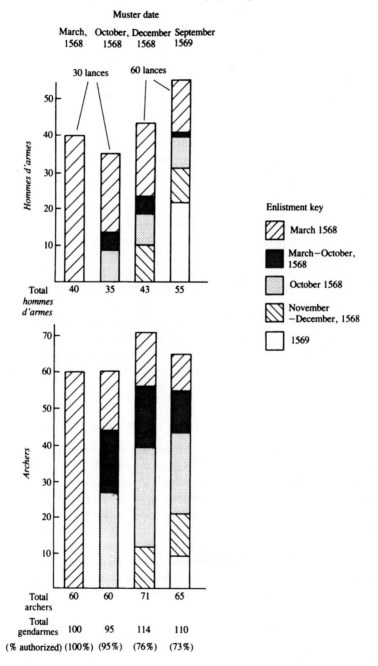

Fig. 18. Personnel changes in Blaise de Monluc's gendarme company, 1568–69

143

sizeable portion of these men tried to avoid military service (the Sire de Gouberville comes to mind) or commuted it to monetary payment or had too few resources to afford the cost of a gendarme's equipment. If we also take into account the Huguenots and estimate that around half of the rural nobility converted to Protestantism, we are then left with an admittedly very rough total of perhaps 25,000–30,000 catholic adult male nobles available, able, and willing to serve.[50] During wartime the infantry would have offered places to perhaps 2,000 men as officers and gentlemen volunteers. At the height of the expansion of the heavy cavalry, in early 1569, the authorized strength of the gendarmerie was slightly over 16,000 men. Even if all the gendarme companies in France had mustered in at only three-quarters strength and quickly dropped to half-strength, to have maintained even 8,000 gendarmes over a four-year period, if Monluc's 2:1 replacement rate every two years held true for all companies (and his company was obviously much less worn down than many) would have sucked up almost every eligible and willing nobleman in the kingdom. The king and army leaders, therefore, may have been more right than they imagined in their intuition that the nobility was not numerous enough to form a second royal army if the first was lost. The critical factor here was the high defection rate among the rural gentry to Protestantism, which impacted in a singular fashion on the gendarmerie. The great expansion of 1567–69, then, scraped very close to the bottom of the barrel of manpower reserves as far as the nobility was concerned. This put an enormous strain on the viability of companies which when combined with the financial strains affecting the pay of the gendarmes and their captains led to increasing signs of instability and exhaustion by the end of the period.

TRANSFORMATION OR DEMISE OF THE GENDARMERIE?

In his study of royal governors in Renaissance France Robert Harding dates the "Demise of the gendarmerie" (one of his chapter subheadings) rather precisely to 1579, at which time, he argues, it had ceased to provide nobles with permanent careers. Harding also adduces the disappearance of open-field battles, the relative cheapness of "mercenary" cavalry substitutes, and the growing indiscipline of the gendarmerie as important factors in its decline.[51] But can we really speak of a "demise" of the gendarmerie? Harding's perspective was that of the impact of growing disorder on the regime of provincial governors who were usually distant from the major operations of the royal army (which he characterizes incorrectly as being "comprised mainly" of foreign mercenaries).[52] As we have tried to show in

---

[50] This may be an overestimate of noble numbers. For a different calculation of the number of nobles in service, see J.Russell Major, *From Renaissance Monarchy to Absolute Monarchy: French Kings, Nobles, and States* (Baltimore, 1994), 54–55.

[51] Harding, 74.

[52] *Ibid.*, 77.

the preceding section, however, the period to 1578 witnessed not the demise of the gendarmerie but its near total triumph over lighter types which it absorbed as it became the singular type of cavalry which predominated in the royal armies. Rather than a demise of the gendarmerie, in most of the civil wars the crown constantly sought to greatly expand the number of units of such horsemen, and during the sixth civil war and after, in 1578, just about the time Harding designates as the end of the gendarmerie, there were more units in existence than at any point in the civil wars except 1569.

Yet Harding is certainly correct in that much of the evidence he brings to bear on the case of the gendarmerie in the context of the clientage systems of local governors undeniably shows increasingly bad discipline and disorder. He is particularly astute in sensing that an important aspect of the coming crisis of the 1580s was the disintegration at the level of individual companies of expectations of assured support from the crown.[53] But such disintegration of older certainties and expectations spared few traditional institutions and affected all levels of French society in the last decade of civil war. Over the course of the first five wars, as we will see, the composition and conditions of service of the gendarmerie did significantly change, but the disarray which can be detected at the end of this period had more to do with growing exhaustion, financial problems, and the changed mental horizons of a new generation of captains than with the military obsolescence of the institution of heavy battle cavalry.

We can illustrate the process that was at work by examining changes in the composition of the gendarmerie over time based on the origins and longevity of individual companies. Figure 19 traces the cycles of creation and survival of the hundreds of gendarme companies which took part in the wars. The figure allows us to identify the age and longevity of companies and therefore the continuing importance of particular cohorts of companies created at different moments in the wars. The bars in the graph represent the gendarme companies (except for the occasional Protestant companies, which have been ignored) in existence at sixteen different dates from the beginning of the first civil war in 1562 to after the sixth war, in 1578. The subdivisions within each bar indicate the percentage of companies at that date that could trace their origins to one of ten specific periods of creation: the period just before the first civil war, the first civil war, the first interwar period, the second and third wars, the second interwar period, the fourth, fifth, and sixth wars, and the immediate post-sixth war period.[54]

There were, as we know, three great expansions of the number of gendarme companies: during the first war, the second and third wars, and the fifth and sixth wars. If we take as the original cohort of companies those companies existing at the beginning of or created during the first civil war we see that though overshadowed by the newest companies in the second and third wars, they continued to provide

---

[53] *Ibid.*, 71–75.
[54] Derived from the sources in note 23 above and Vindry.

By percentage, 1562–1578

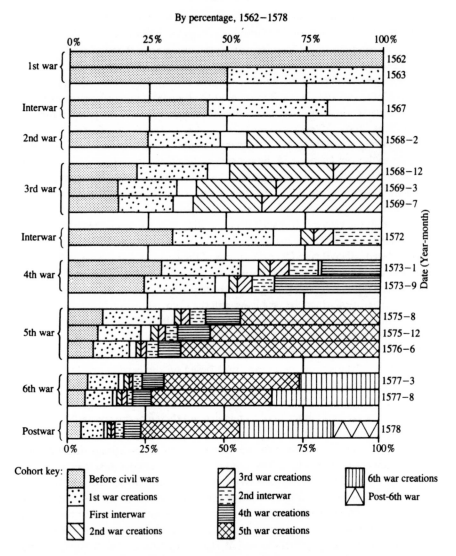

Fig. 19. Origins of gendarme companies. By percentage, 1562–78

half or almost half of the reduced size gendarmerie during the fourth war and as much as a quarter of all companies even at the beginning of the fifth war. They are then swamped by the creations of the fifth and sixth war until by 1578 they only constitute about 10 percent of the expanded peacetime gendarmerie. When the lapse of time between the beginning of the era of the civil wars and the disappearance of these companies is considered, however, it is not the decline of the original companies but their relative staying power which appears impressive. Half of them had been in existence since before the civil wars and most of those from before the time of the treaty of Cateau-Cambrésis in 1559. By 1578, in other words, the surviving companies had been in service for more than sixteen years and in many cases more than two decades. The twin natural processes of advancing age and cumulative casualties over a period of two decades combine to explain the diminution of this oldest cohort of captains and companies. Although it is impossible to discover the fate of all these original captains, a comparison of the captains of this cohort with the biographical information of Vindry's *Dictionnaire* shows that at least 21.4 percent of the 112 men who held captaincies during the 1562–63 period were killed in action or assassinated during the course of the wars. Many others suffered crippling wounds or died of accidents or illnesses contracted in camp.[55] By 1578 most of the great nobles who had formed the core of the original cohort of gendarme captains and who had provided the top leadership for the royal army both before and at the beginning of the civil war period were dead or retired. Antoine de Bourbon, Constable Montmorency, Guise, Aumale, Monluc, Tavannes, the Brissacs, Martigues – the list could easily be lengthened – and many more of slightly lesser rank, had departed from the scene, or were approaching old age if they had managed to survive.

By contrast, the large cohort of new captains and their companies created during the second and third wars, while they contributed a majority of all companies at those times, leave hardly a trace after 1569. Some of the captains of these companies were later called on again to raise new companies, but only after a significant number of years had passed, and most simply disappear from the ranks of the gendarmerie, even though we know that actual battle casualties among the gendarmes during those campaigns were quite low. Even the relatively few companies raised during the debacle of the fourth civil war seem to have lasted longer than the cohort formed from the second great expansion and though it has not been possible to trace the companies of the third wave of creations, during the fifth and sixth civil wars, beyond early 1578, to the extent that we are able to trace them over the short run they seem to have lasted longer than those of the second wave. These new companies created during the fifth and sixth wars (albeit often raised by men who had previously commanded companies) so dominate the gendarmerie by 1577–78 that it is clear that a decisive generational change had occurred, producing a differently constituted gendarmerie than that which began the civil wars. What proportion of the inflated number of companies in 1576 or 1578 were actually receiving adequate support from the crown at any one point in time is debatable, but in terms of the overall complexion of the heavy cavalry, the vast majority of companies were certainly new and relatively inexperienced.

---

[55] The basic source for the survival of captains is Vindry, but the captains of the 1562–63 cohort were prominent enough men that their death by military action during the civil wars is usually mentioned in the contemporary memoirs and histories.

Table 5.2 *Length of service of gendarme companies, 1559–1578*

| | | Still in existence after: | | | | | | | |
| | | 2 years | | 5 years | | 10 years | | 15 years | |
Cohort	Companies at start	No.	%	No.	%	No.	%	No.	%
1559	64	53	83	37	58	22	34	12	19
Prewar	10	9	90	9	90	6	60	12	20
Ist war	49	36	73	33	67	23	47	13	27
Interwar	15	14	93	6	40	3	20	–	–
2nd war	62	47	76	3	5	2	3	–	–
3rd war	61	6	10	4	7	2	3	–	–
4th war	29	18	62	9	31	–	–	–	–
5th war	54	39	72	–	–	–	–	–	–
Total	344	222		101		58		37	
Percentage	100	65		35		22		22	

The key questions that need to be answered, then, are what explains the disappearance of the second great cohort of creations and the longevity of the first, and what were the historical implications for the royal army on the eve of the 1580s, of the reconstitution of the gendarmerie amid growing governmental paralysis? Let us begin by attempting to actually measure and compare the staying power in years of different cohorts of companies, as is done in Table 5.2. We are able to trace all of the cohorts raised before the fourth war over at least a decade and before the fifth war over at least five years. But because the documentary trail practically disappears in the chaos of the last decade of civil war, we are not able to trace the cohorts raised near the end of the period over as long a time span as the earlier cohorts. Nevertheless, what we find is that over the whole period 65 percent of 344 companies we can trace were still in existence at least two years after they were raised, 35 percent after five years, and 22 percent after ten and fifteen years. But when we compare the experience of individual cohorts to these averages, the staying power of the companies already in existence in 1559 or created before the first war far exceeds that of later creations, though the cohort raised during the first civil war itself was not far behind. Even the first interwar cohort had a longer life span, on average, than later cohorts. And to the extent that we can measure it, the fourth war cohort was significantly longer lived over a five-year period than the companies of the second and third war cohort, out of which only 7 of 123 companies survived five years. These data suggest two points. The first is to recognize the traumatic truncation of the gendarmerie after 1569, lasting until 1575. We see here one of the costs engendered by the Jarnac–Mocontour campaign – that even though the Huguenot field army had been largely destroyed the effort it took and its aftermath nearly in turn destroyed the royal army. But the tiny number of these second cohort companies which survived the reductions is not, I think, explained totally by postwar economy measures. When the third large wave of creations began from 1575 onward many, perhaps a majority, of the captains dismissed after 1569 were never again asked to raise another gendarme company. This suggests that many of the new companies of the second and third wars, whether raised from scratch or converted from *chevaux-légers*, had not performed well or had encountered so many difficulties in recruiting or maintaining themselves on campaign that they and their captains were no longer considered to be viable as gendarmes.

This brings us to a second and related conclusion: that the original cohort of companies was more viable because their captains were of higher station and wealthier than the captains of later companies. What is clear is that the men awarded companies during the first war and its immediate aftermath were all men of considerable status and means, comparable in all respects to the commanders of the gendarmerie at the time of the treaty of Cateau-Cambrésis. The initial expansion of companies, then, probably involved tapping a surplus of qualified noblemen who had not received companies primarily because of the crown's attempted parsimony after 1559, the type of nobles for whom a captaincy was simply part of a larger complex of appointments and rewards and who were not overly dependent on their captain's pay to survive or succeed – the type, in other words, who could raise a gendarme company and still weather out the financial problems of the period. But later waves of creation must have quickly exhausted the number of suitable candidates as the number of nobles who had been tapped to raise companies increased rapidly from around 100 at the end of the first war to more than 200 by the end of the third war and then well over 300 by the end of the fifth war (with comparable expansions of lieutenancies). Given the defection of so many Protestant nobles the pool of well qualified gentlemen must have quickly been drained and the crown forced to make its selections increasingly further below the level of the great nobility. The new men being tapped to raise companies, it should be noted, were usually distinguished enough – they were not simple *hobereaux* and certainly not commoners – but their status and resources simply did not, nor could not, given the stratification of wealth among the nobility, compare to the greatest nobles in the land who dominated the gendarmerie in 1562.

If the crown had been able to fully support its gendarme companies this partial decline in the status and quality of captains may not have mattered. But the new captains were entering service at a time when companies were often dismissed after increasingly short service and even on campaign could count less and less on being regularly paid, which was critical to their men even if individual captains could weather such conditions. And though it anticipates somewhat subjects to be discussed further below, when we assemble all the information that has survived about how often the gendarmerie actually received its pay as the period of the civil wars unfolded, the results are important and suggestive. Table 5.3 simply indicates the number of quarters in each year between 1554 and 1576 in which it is certain that

Table 5.3. *Quarters of service paid to the gendarmerie by year, 1554–1576*

Year	Quarters paid	Year	Quarters paid
1554	4	1566	2
1555	4	1567	3
1556	4	1568	2
1557	4	1569	1
1558	3	1570	0
1559	3	1571	2
1560	4	1572	2
1561	3	1573	2
1562	3	1574	1
1563	2	1575	3
1564	3	1576	1
1565	2		

Total quarters paid: 46 of 92, or 50 percent

all the gendarme companies received a general pay, even though it should be remembered that pay for a particular quarter was often received months or even years after service was performed.[56] Individual companies may have mustered and received pay at other times and it is possible that because of the fragmentation of the documentation some general pays have been missed, but the overall picture is quite clear. In the aftermath of Cateau-Cambrésis and from 1560 on, as the era of the wars proceeded, gendarmes never received four quarters of pay and in some years no pay at all or a single pay. From 1562 to 1576 general pays were managed for only 29 of 60 quarters and from 1569 on for only 12 of 32 quarters. Obviously, in any year where an archer received even only half his due his entire income could be consumed by his horses alone, and an *homme d'armes* would find himself reduced to the level of an infantryman's salary. The burden of providing interim financing for their men, of course, fell on the captains, but as we have argued, probably increasingly fewer of these men had the wealth to continually support their companies from their means alone or the status that would allow them to demand preferential individual treatment.

---

[56] *OM* no. 82, "Extraict de lestat des montres, et des quartiers, pour lesquels a este faict payement aux compaignies de gendarmerie depuis l'annee 1554 jusques a l'annee 1565" summarizes the pattern of payment through 1565. For the period from 1566 onward, a survey of all the documents that could be found concerning the gendarmerie, *états*, *départements*, etc., provides evidence that a quarter's pay was announced on at least twenty-five other occasions. The uneven survival of records and the fact that single companies sometimes received partial pay in individual *montres* arranged with local funding, make it impossible to verify, by comparing them to the musters listed by Vindry, whether the announcements were accompanied by actual payment. The information on quarters paid from 1566 onward, therefore, must be considered a maximum figure, and many companies may not have received even this portion of the money due them.

Transformation or demise of the gendarmerie?

Money problems were of course the constant obsession and despair of the crown as well, and as conditions of support continued to deteriorate all kinds of measures were taken to try to preserve the heavy cavalry on which, after all, most leaders were convinced the ultimate safety of the kingdom rested. Many captains were retained on half pay rather than simply dismissed, more companies were reduced to 20 lances, and units were mobilized for service for only one quarter of the year. This enabled the crown to carry higher numbers of companies on the books in the inter-war periods, like 1576 and 1578, when up to double the usual number of peacetime companies were preserved. But even if the preservation of a larger number of companies at reduced wages meant that the gendarmerie was at least nominally larger from 1576 onward, the fact is that most of those companies were on permanent reserve status and unpaid, which meant companies had to fend for themselves or lose their men. And when companies were created or mobilized to fight, as in the fifth and sixth wars, lack of pay or the hope for any better support led to widespread disobedience and dereliction of duty. The horizons of the few survivors of the second wave of expansion and the many new and remobilized captains of the third expansion were very different from that of the cohort of gendarme captains who began the civil wars. Not only could they not look forward to any reasonably stable existence or fairly reliable pay, their own financial means were not great enough to constantly substitute for royal support. Such conditions undercut their ability to recruit and maintain men of quality – the pool of potential troopers which was itself limited and becoming significantly more exhausted as time wore on. By the time of the fifth war the situation was becoming critical and there are clear and widespread signs of exhaustion among cavalry captains who often simply failed as never before to show up at assembly points with their units. Henry III, for example, issued orders in August of 1575 to assemble all gendarme companies, promising that they would be paid for the first quarter of that year. The promise that arrears would be made up apparently did not convince all captains to bring their companies to the assembly points. The earlier order had to be repeated in October, and again in December, accompanied by complaints that many companies ordered to report had still not arrived. A further order issued in February, 1576, repeated the same complaint.[57] The crown's ill-conceived solution to this problem – exacerbated perhaps by Henry III's distrust of many of the captains created by his brother and his wish to hurriedly create his own coterie of favorites (the appointments of Bellegarde and Retz as marshals come to mind) – was to multiply the number of new companies but never to call a very significant portion of them together for a very extended period of time.

As the older generation of leaders and companies passed on, they were replaced by a new generation of officers whose practical experiences and intellectual formation was quite different. Table 5.4, for example, shows the origins of captains' first

[57] *OM* nos. 199, 205, 206, 208, 212.

Table 5.4. *Origins of initial appointments as gendarme captains, 1564-1578*

	No. captains in:				
Made captain in:	1564	1571	1574	1576	1578
1559 or before	40	23	13	16	12
1560-64	51	34	29	31	29
1565-71		11	15	31	43
1572-74			11	15	16
1575-76				31	28
1577-78					43
Total:	91	68	68	124	171

commissions at various points of demobilization from 1564 to 1578. As early as 1564, only 40 of 91 captains of gendarme companies (or 44 percent) had commanded companies in or before 1559. By 1574, in the aftermath of the Saint-Bartholomew's Day massacre and the fourth war, the figure was only 13 of 68 captains (19 percent) and in 1578 it was only 12 of 171 (7 percent). By 1578 a majority of gendarme captains had first become captains *after* the massacre. At that time 93 percent of heavy cavalry captains had never led their gendarme companies against a foreign foe – their military horizons had come to consist exclusively of the experience of fighting fellow Frenchmen. Were it possible to trace the careers of infantry officers a similar picture would surely emerge.

By the late 1570s, then, a whole generation of officers had been initiated into command positions who knew little except an environment of an increasingly unsuccessful series of civil wars. The first and third wars, at least, had included some great victories. But the fourth war ended with the frustrated siege of La Rochelle and the fifth war with a combined Huguenot and German mercenary army encamped in the center of France dictating peace terms. Habits of ill-discipline, disobedience, depredations, and venality – the warlordism that was to plague national and local politics until the end of the civil wars – were already well under way, and in the increasing chaos contemporaries specifically singled out the gendarmerie for its atrocious behavior.[58] This should come as no surprise, given the conditions they were operating under, and the fact that the officer corps as a whole for all practical purposes had been purged of elements who could remember a unified country and wars against foreign foes. In the late 1570s the gendarmerie and its leaders, experienced for the most part only in increasingly aimless civil war, stood ready to contribute in even greater measure to the agonies France was to suffer during the 1580s and 1590s.

[58] Harding, 75–76.

6

The artillery train

"FOR WANT OF A NAIL ..."

"My good man, I am beside myself that if only I had had six cannons and enough ammunition to fire two thousand rounds, this town was ours," wrote the duke of Guise to Gonnor, later Marshal Cossé, from Orléans on February 7, 1563.[1] After pausing for rest and reorganization after the battle of Dreux, the royal army under his leadership had marched against Orléans and in a swift attack seized the faubourg of Le Portereau, and the Tournelles, the twin towers guarding the bridge which passed over the Loire to the heavily defended island of Les Mottes and thence into the city itself. But despite this initial success the attack was stillborn, for the army's heavy artillery train was missing, mired in a primitive road network made impassable by heavy winter rains. Guise's army would have to wait several weeks before receiving enough of the thirty-odd heavy guns and munitions it would eventually deploy in its preparations for a final assault on the city.[2] But in the meantime the duke himself, mortally wounded by an assassin, would be removed from the scene, leaving the queen mother in a position to negotiate an end to the war and the peaceful surrender of Orléans.

Similar frustration was voiced by the duke of Anjou, in March, 1569, just days after his victory at Jarnac, which caused Condé's death and the dispersal of the Huguenot army in the west, when he urged his royal brother to hurry the dispatch of a siege train from Paris.

The enemy having withdrawn into fortified places, it is nearly impossible...for us to advance our affairs without the artillery and equipment necessary to attack them. I humbly beg you

---

[1] Guise, *Mémoires*, 505.

[2] On the departure of the train from Paris and the hampering weather: Paschal, *1562*, 120; *CSPF/E*, vol. 6, no. 9; and A.H. Layard, "Dispatches of Michele Suriano and of Marc' Antonio Barbara," *Publications of the Huguenot Society of London*, 6 (Lymington, 1891), 73; Guise, *Mémoires*, 503; and *CDM*, vol. 1, 479–80. There were efforts in mid-February to reinforce the train with more heavy guns from Paris shipped by water to Montargis, where they were to be met by doubled teams of draft horses from the camp; see letters of February 11 and 12, 1563, in *CDM*, vol. 1, 502, and February 12 in Guise, *Mémoires*, 505. Efforts to assemble a large train for the siege of Orléans may have been affected by a somewhat premature order by the queen mother to Gonnor (later Marshal Cossé) in mid-January 1563 to begin preparations for another enormous train intended for the siege of Le Havre, *CDM*, vol. 1, 473, and certainly by the explosion of the Arsenal's powder reserves on January 28, 1563, which caused great destruction.

to command that the twenty cannons and their equipages you have ordered for this army be sent to us with all possible speed, for otherwise, this army will be useless and will serve only as an expense.[3]

In fact, at the time Anjou wrote the king the siege guns had not even left Paris and would not arrive at Châtellerault by water until mid-April, long after the opportunity to fully exploit Jarnac had passed.

But it was not just the actual presence of heavy guns, their crews, and equipment that was important. For both practical and psychological reasons, the skill and rapidity with which they were deployed was equally critical. In an advice written for Anjou at the beginning of the siege of La Rochelle Blaise de Monluc urged the subordination of all other issues to the needs of establishing the artillery batteries and advancing them as close to the walls as possible, stressing that not an hour was to be wasted.

First of all, when a man is besieged, if he is astute, he observes how the enemy disposes itself to assail him, quickly determining from which side they begin their trenches, and, having recognized this, he will immediately understand where they wish to attack and will toil with great diligence, night and day, to oppose and remedy all the harm the attacker could inflict. And if the besieger proceeds slowly in his preparations for a prompt and diligent attack, having failed to execute the necessary groundwork, the besieged gains the time to make himself twice as strong as he was beforehand in the part attacked. And if the new works are added to the strength of the old defenses in the time given to him, the place will be very difficult to capture. And, on the contrary, when he sees his enemy advancing rapidly night and day, he will cower, and unless he is very alert and experienced he will be lost and will not know how to command against the great works he will see approaching.[4]

But, in fact, failure to implement Monluc's advice would play a significant role in the defeat of the royal army at La Rochelle, and problems with the artillery were certainly on Anjou's mind when in July of 1573 he dictated his final report on the failed siege to the king.

It will please you to know that the three things that are most important and necessary in the siege of a city are a good and grand artillery train, a good number of soldiers, and quantities of food supplies. Because if I have cannon without soldiers, that does not serve me at all; and if soldiers are without cannon, they will be able to do nothing; and if all of that is there, but the food supplies fail, I have to lift the siege.

I had an unprecedented lack of all three of those things, as you may have heard, for the artillery equipment limped in piece by piece and at a snail's pace, and I lacked good soldiers, so that I could not totally invest the city or have the means to prepare three batteries and three breaches...As for powder, I was never able to learn for certain how much there really was. Besides, it came only in such small amounts that at times I ran out completely; and, when I had powder, I lacked cannon balls. All this did I endure.[5]

[3] Letter of March 18, 1569, quoted in Gigon, 221.
[4] Philippe Tamisay de Larroque, "Quelques pages inédites de Blaise de Monluc," *Receuil des travaux de la société d'agriculture, sciences et arts d'Agen* (1863), 322–31; quote on 323–34.
[5] BN Mss. Fr. 4,765, fols. 75v, 76v-77r.

The critical importance and unique problems of the artillery were again brought home to Anjou, now Henry III, in a January, 1577, *mémoire* by the grand master Biron. The king had asked his principal advisors to submit their views on peace and war as he contemplated renewing the military struggle – what would in fact later become the sixth civil war. Biron, after making the conventional observation that without proper finances nothing could be done, went on to say:

The next most important consideration is that the artillery be a great, cumbersome, and heavy contrivance, and if anything is lacking, the whole thing is useless. Indeed, any service and utility one claims to derive from an army resides in its artillery, without which all its expense and force are useless.

That is why it is necessary to promptly see to its needs...for as far as artillery is concerned, beyond the expense which is normally estimated to be one third of that of the army, it requires time to assemble the equipment and everything involved in it.[6]

The import of all these views and statements is quite clear. The royal army ran the risk of being a very expensive and useless tool without an adequate provision of artillery. In a war in which cities constituted the main prizes even great victories on the battlefield would prove empty if there was no means to silence defending artillery and to batter the breaches that enabled the infantry to mount their assaults. And in this execution adequate and well-coordinated stocks of material were essential. Without powder, guns could not fire and without cannon balls, powder was useless. Without adequate horsepower, artillery could not be moved. Without pioneers and cannoneers, guns could not be deployed or operated. Absence of only a single element of the many needed to operate the artillery could cause delay and in the context of a siege any delay allowed the defender time to initiate effective countermeasures. Yet, as Biron warned, because of its cumbersome nature and because so many of its essential elements required time to prepare, assemble, and move, foresight and long-term planning were needed if, indeed, the crown was to field an adequate artillery train in time of war.

The French monarchy had historically in fact been a pioneer in the deployment and use of the mobile artillery trains which had played such decisive roles in the campaigns of the later Hundred Years War and the invasions of Italy from 1494. By the mid-sixteenth century there was a well-developed system, centered on the Arsenal in Paris, for procuring essential minerals like saltpeter, manufacturing and storing the three principal grades of gunpowder, and casting and mounting new, lighter, and more efficient bronze cannons of several different standardized calibers.[7] The complicated task of planning, coordinating, and conducting the

---

[6] Biron, *LD*, vol. 1, 61.

[7] Susane, *Artillerie*, 97–130, especially 100–1, for the earlier calibers, and a very informative manuscript artillery manual from the reign of Francis I, BN Mss. Fr. 2,068, fols. 1–65. See also Contamine, *passim*: "Les industries de guerre," and *Guerre, état et société*, and *HM*, vol. 1, for earlier developments. Gigon provides a very useful chart of the technical dimensions of the reformed six calibers of France at the time of the civil wars, 18–19. See also Paul Lecestre, "Notice sur l'arsenal royal de Paris

affairs of the artillery was given to the "maistre et cappitaine general de notred. artillerie" who was given wide authority over

> all officers, commissioners, gunners, foundrymen, carpenters, wheelwrights, blacksmiths, dischargers, captains, conductors of the train, and other men, both ordinary and extraordinary, of our said artillery, including the sappers, masons, carpenters, teamsters and horses which are and will be able to be called up for the conduct, exploitation and service of our said artillery...[and] all and each of the artillery pieces, the large ones as well as the small ones, cannon balls, powder, saltpeter, sulfur, copper, tin, lead, iron, wood for remounts and all other kinds of materials and munitions, weapons and equipment, pioneer tools, craftsmen and laborers, in our arsenals, cities, châteaux and fortresses of our kingdom and regions under our obedience, as well as our ships, galleys and other vessels of war...and the authority to augment, change and restock these munitions according to the needs of our service. Moreover, he will be responsible for the casting of guns, mounts, remounting, and their equipment, manufacturing powder, large and small grain, and fine, also our saltpeter and sulfur, and to conduct, lead and operate, in armies, enterprises and sieges, by land or by sea, for the security of our cities, forts and other locations as necessary, such number of pieces of our artillery, powder, cannons and other kinds of munitions as need dictates.[8]

The post of grand master, therefore, was critical in preparing the defenses of the kingdom during peacetime and in organizing and leading the powerful artillery trains that were an essential component of the royal army in war. Throughout the early civil wars the monarchy was blessed with outstandingly competent grand masters: Jean d'Estrées, though a Huguenot, in the first war, followed by his son-in-law, the Sieur De La Bourdaisière, in the second and third wars, and, after the latter's death in November 1569, during the early stages of the Saint-Jean-d'Angély campaign after Moncontour, Armand de Gontault, the Sieur de Biron. Though, as we shall see, there was no lack of difficulties to be overcome in the royal artillery service, especially as time went on, the resources of the Arsenal did give the royal army a tremendous initial military advantage, particularly when it came to attacking and taking well-defended cities. But even on those few occasions that field artillery was able to play a brief role in battles, as at Dreux, or before Moncontour, the royal artillery was handled with efficiency and the Huguenot artillery was not. The Huguenot armies of the times were never well supplied with artillery and the equipment of even the small trains they sometimes possessed was always substandard and in poor shape. In perhaps no other area was the disparity between the armies of the two sides so pronounced, and the Huguenot captain La Noue considered this a critical weakness, because it meant that the Huguenots had to attack cities like Chartres or Poitiers *à l'improviste*, hoping to compensate with

---

jusqu'à la mort de Henri IV," *Société de l'histoire de Paris et l'Ile-de-France*, vols. 42 (1915), 185–281, and 43 (1916), 1–82; Jean-Pierre Babelon, "Le palais de l'arsenal à Paris," *Bulletin Monumental*, 128 (1970), 267–310, and *Nouvelle histoire de Paris. Le XVIe siècle* (Paris, 1986), 239, the front and endpiece map of Paris, and illustrations of parts of the Arsenal on 281 and 377.

[8] Biron's commission of November 6, 1569 in Biron, *LD*, vol. 2, 534–41; quote, 536–37.

speed and surprise for the deliberate approaches and thorough artillery preparation denied to them by their lack of guns and resources.[9]

"A GREAT, CUMBERSOME, AND HEAVY CONTRIVANCE"

The key to effective deployment of artillery, as the citations in the previous section suggest, lay first of all in planning and coordination, which in turn depended on a thorough knowledge of the material, animal, and human resources needed to put a proper artillery train into the field. Though the assembly of an artillery train was an immensely complicated and time-consuming task, it was also a task whose dimensions could almost exactly be calibrated to the number and types of guns it was intended to put in the field. By the time of the civil wars the lack of standardization so characteristic of artillery inventories in the first century of effective gunpowder weapons had been considerably ameliorated, and the royal ordinances recognized only six types of guns of diminishing size and weight: the cannon, great culverin, bastarde, moyenne, faucon, and fauconneau.[10] Of these six recognized calibers of France only the first four were serviceable in the field and only the first two of any use in serious siege work. Though the faucon and fauconneau, along with a ubiquitous type of heavy mounted musket, the *arquebuse à croc*, continued to exist in large numbers, they were primarily useful as anti-personnel weapons in fixed fortifications, being too lightweight to make much impression on the defensive works of the era or the massive troop blocks on the battlefield. Even the two intermediate guns, the bastarde and especially the moyenne, both shorter and lighter types of culverins, though useful in the field, threw such a lightweight ball that they were also of little use in knocking down fortifications. This left the cannon and the great culverin, usually employed in a ratio of three cannon to one culverin, as the two great siege pieces of the day, particularly the cannon, which threw a ball twice the weight of that of the great culverin, whose most effective use was in counterbattery and suppressive fire rather than pounding a breach.

Table 6.1 gives a brief summary for the four heaviest guns of the technical parameters within which the grand master and his principal lieutenants had to operate as they made their plans to assemble the train.[11] Since the material, animal, and human resources needed to work a gun of any of these categories was fairly fixed, the exact requirements for a train were determined, as we have said, by the numbers of each type gun which were to compose it, and whether or not it was to function primarily as a field train accompanying the army on the march and available for battle action, if need be, or exclusively as a siege train. Obviously, the heavier the

---

[9] La Noue, *Discours*, 757.

[10] Gigon, 18–19.

[11] *Ibid.*, and planning documents from 1568, BN Mss. Fr. 17,870, fols. 298–99r, and 1577, BN Mss. Fr. 4,555, fols. 23–25, which provide information on cargo capacities, horse and munitions requirements, rates of fire, and powder consumption.

Table 6.1. Technical specifications and throw-weight efficiencies of the train's artillery pieces

A. *Technical specifications*

	Weight (*livres*)			Crew		
Gun	Gun mounted	Shot	Powder charge	Gun	Pioneers	Team horses
Cannon	8,000	32	20	5	30	23
G. culverine	6,500	15	16	4	24	17
Bastarde	4,400	7	12	3	12	13
Moyenne	2,200	2	5	3	6	9

B. *Throw-weight ratio per thousand rounds fired*

	Total requirements				Throw-weight in *livres* per		
Gun	Men	Horses	Powder	Shot (*livres*)	Man	Horse	*Livre* charge
Cannon	90	223	20,000	32,000	356	143	1.6
G. culverine	83	141	16,000	15,000	181	106	.9
Bastarde	38	93	7,000	12,000	184	75	.6
Moyenne	18	37	2,000	5,000	111	54	.4

gun, the more horses that were needed to haul it; the more crew and laborers that were needed to manhandle, load, and fire it; and the higher the poundage of shot and powder that was needed to be transported in order to fire a single round.

The increased number of men and horses and quantities of munitions required for the heavier guns, especially the cannon, however, were much offset by the increased efficiency in throw-weight that, up to a point, the larger and heavier guns enjoyed, a factor of considerable importance in any type of siege work. Table 6.1B estimates the logistics of firing one thousand rounds from a single gun of each of the four heaviest calibers, that is, it counts the number of crewmen and pioneers needed to operate the guns, the quantity of munitions needed to fire one thousand rounds, and the number of horses and teamsters needed to haul both the guns and the munitions (based on the standard two-wheel, four-horse cart, with one driver, which could carry one *millier*, or one thousand *livres* of cargo). These totals are then used to calculate throw-weight ratios, that is, the number of pounds of iron shot each type of gun could throw per thousand rounds for each man or horse in its equipage and for each pound of powder it expended.[12]

[12] *Ibid.* The throw-weight statistic is my contrivance rather than a contemporary sixteenth-century measure. A *millier*, or 1,000 *livres*, is about two-thirds of a modern US ton.

"A great, cumbersome, and heavy contrivance"

As can be seen, in terms of throw-weight ratios, the heaviest gun, the cannon, was more efficient in operation than the other three calibers by up to a factor of three or four in all the comparative categories, while the great culverin, except in the throw-weight per man category, was about one-quarter to one-third more efficient than the bastarde. The moyenne was hopelessly outclassed by the two heaviest guns – for slightly less than three times the number of horses required to support a thousand rounds of moyenne fire and only a little more than four times as many personnel, a cannon could throw more than six times as much iron, or more than three times as much throw-weight per man. Most of the increased efficiency came from the fact that the heavier the gun, the less powder it took to fire a pound of shot, an efficiency curve whose upper bounds were set more by the practical immobility of guns much heavier than the cannon rather than any technical limitations in gun design or metallurgy. But offsetting the gains in throw-weight efficiency of the larger guns, of course, was the fact that in absolute terms they were inordinately more greedy consumers of munitions. To fire one thousand cannon rounds took 32,000 *livres* of iron shot and 20 *milliers* of gunpowder, more than six times as much shot and ten times as much powder as a thousand rounds fired from a moyenne.

The tradeoffs between size, projectile weight, and munitions consumption (all of which were directly linked to the number of wagons, horses, teamsters, and crew needed to service a single gun) were of course well understood by the artillery personnel and recur often in the planning and technical documents of the time. A train of lighter guns was somewhat more maneuverable and less expensive to support in absolute terms than a train of heavy guns. But before any type of fortifications the bastarde and moyenne were practically useless. To demolish defenses throw-weight and speed of fire were the keys. The technique for demolishing fortifications depended on maintaining a practically uninterrupted fire against a portion of wall or bastion, scoring its facing over and over again by rapidly successive salvoes by a number of guns until it collapsed or a breach was opened.[13] In work of this type the field mobility of lighter guns was really of no use because the minimum mobility needed was simply the ability to get the gun drawn to the place being besieged – once there and in firing position mobility ceased to be a serious consideration. Much more important was the increased kinetic energy of the heavier cannonballs and the rate of fire, and the heavier guns, which could fire three to four rounds an hour (50 rounds per summer, and 30 rounds per winter day by contemporary reckonings) did not take significantly longer to fire than the smaller pieces.[14] A cannon, firing at only half the rate of a bastarde, for example, could still land more than twice the latter's weight in shot on target in an hour of operation.

Given all these considerations, and in the absence of numerous open-field battles which involved the ponderous guns, it is not surprising that when the royal army's

[13] Pepper and Adams, *Firearms and Fortifications*, 8–14.
[14] The rounds per day from which hourly rates can be computed are noted in BN Mss. Fr. 17,870, 299r.

artillery train was put together at the beginning of each campaign the predominant pieces were the heaviest and most efficient: cannons and great culverins with some bastardes thrown in to serve as maneuverable field pieces or signal guns. Moyennes, not to mention the even lighter pieces like faucons and fauconneaux, were almost never included. This had implications for the usefulness of the weapons and ammunition stockpiled in royal arsenals which will be explored below. But the tendency towards larger guns with their gargantuan appetites for munitions, more numerous personnel, and more extensive equipages gave a definitive shape to the artillery trains assembled by the crown to serve with the royal army throughout the period.

The material and human dimensions which had to be considered in putting together a typical artillery train are reflected quite well by a planning document from September, 1568, entitled "Estat du train et bande d'artillerie que le Roy a ordonné estre mis en campaigne pour servir au camp et armée que sa Majesté a faict dresser au mois de Septembre, mil Vc soixante y huict."[15] It will be recalled that in the fall of 1568 after the flight of Condé and Coligny to the west general mobilization orders were issued which specified Orléans as the assembly point for the army Anjou was to lead south to join Montpensier at Châtellerault in early November. The king was determined in this campaign to use the royal army to destroy the Protestant army in the west and reduce any cities there that continued to hold out for the Huguenots. To help accomplish those tasks Anjou's army was to be given a train of 20 guns: 8 cannons, 6 great culverins, and 6 bastardes, a mixture weighted towards siege work but with an ample number of the most mobile of the heavier pieces for battlefield work, 5,000 cannon balls in proportion, and 91 *milliers* of powder. To draw the guns, the document calculated, would require 348 draft horses and to carry the shot and powder 192 wagons drawn by 782 more horses. An additional 430 horses were needed to draw the 30 wagons of the pontoon bridge section, 20 wagons were to be assigned for the baggage of the grand master and his principal officers, and 41 wagons were to haul workmen's tools, spare parts, forges, extra wheels and limbers, ropes and pulleys, bar iron, lead, nails, pioneer implements, medical supplies, and tenting. In all, according to the document, a total of 283 wagons of all types and 1,550 draft horses would be required, four-fifths of the horses and all of the wagons assigned to the support tail, rather than the firing end, of the column. In addition to its animals and material the train would also require 2,620 personnel of all types to operate the train, an average of 131 men per gun.[16]

Such documents, with projections of the resources needed for an army's artillery train, did not long remain paper exercises. Contemporary accounts note the arrival with Anjou at Châtellerault in early November of 1568 of a well-equiped 20-gun artillery train and surviving financial documents authorize the payment for the preceding September of 2,371 personnel, including 316 teamsters, 241 Arsenal

---

[15] BN Mss. Fr. 17,870, fols. 298–99r, and for the accompanying *assignation* estimate, *ibid.*, fols. 299v–300.

personnel, 1,814 pioneers, and 1,653 horses, and for the preceding October of 2,056 personnel, including 300 teamsters, the same 241 artillery personnel, 1,515 pioneers, and 1,590 horses who had served with the train.[17] Field trains of this approximate size and number of guns also served in the other early wars. In the first civil war, the royal army left Paris in June of 1562 with 22 guns and again deployed 22 guns at the battle of Dreux in December.[18] During the second civil war payment was authorized for 2,612 personnel and 927 horses, and 2,590 personnel and 1,130 horses for service in December, 1567 and February, 1568, respectively.[19] An even larger number of guns served with the train during sieges. In August, 1562, the 20 guns at the siege of Bourges were supplemented by 10 additional heavy guns; there were some 45 pieces of artillery and 3,000 pioneers in action at Rouen in September and October; and, once the army's transport difficulties had been overcome and the train was reinforced by 10 more heavy guns from Paris, 32 guns in operation at Orléans in February of 1563. For the siege of La Rochelle in 1573 the crown made a supreme effort, perhaps the greatest of the entire civil war period, assembling some 42 cannons and great culverins, 354 Arsenal personnel, about 220 teamsters, and some 4,350 pioneers, close to 5,000 total personnel, or double the size of the field trains which marched with the army in the first three civil wars.[20]

To have moved the train intended for La Rochelle in single file by road would have required a column at least six miles in length. This was indeed a "great, cumbersome, and heavy contrivance" and from the beginning of the civil wars there would be difficulties in providing such artillery trains for the army. Some of these

---

[17] See the September and October 1568 *états*: BN Mss. Fr. 4,553, fols. 118–19, BN Mss. Fr. 4,554, fols. 5–7, and 4,553, fols. 122–24.

[18] No artillery *états* survive for the first civil war, but for the dimensions of the train, Paschal, *1562*, 41, 45, reports 25 guns leaving the Arsenal and then 22 leaving Paris in June, 1562; Middlemore reported 30 guns in Guise's camp in late June, *CPSF/E*, vol. 4, no. 238; and Raymond de Coynart, *L'Année 1562 et la bataille de Dreux* (Paris, 1894), 15, for the 22 guns at Dreux.

[19] For the November and December, 1567, and the February, 1568, artillery train see BN Mss. Fr. 4,554, fols. 9–14, 4,553, fols. 95–100, and 4,554, fols. 1–3.

[20] The Venetian ambassador, "Dispatches," Layard, 55, reported 42 cannon in action at Rouen in October 1562 and the sketch of the army's siege works described in chapter 3 indicates a camp for 3,000 pioneers. The dispatch of guns to the siege of Orléans in January and February, 1563, is noted in *CSPF/E*, vol. 6, no. 9 and the sources cited in note 2 above. According to the Venetian ambassador, *op. cit.*, 106, 40 guns were deployed against Le Havre in the summer of 1563, and Marshal Brissac's dispatch to the queen mother of June 14, *Documents*, Lublinskaya, 270–72, especially 272, mentions 3,200 pioneers levied, while a letter from the queen mother on June 21 claims that 40 cannon and 4,000 pioneers were ready for the siege, *CDM*, vol. 2, 62. For La Rochelle, Phillipe Cauriana, *Histoire du siege de la Rochelle en 1573* (La Rochelle, 1856), 19, reports 40 brass guns; Guillaume le Riche, *Journal de Guillaume et de Michel Le Riche* (Geneva, 1971), 117–35, counted over the period November 1572 – May 1573 23 cannon and 220 cartloads of munitions on their way to the siege, as well as pioneer contingents from various *élections* which by reference to the standard levy sizes identified by the sources cited in note 19 above would have come to about 3,500 men. We also know from Biron's letter of January 21, 1573 to Anjou, *AHG*, 78, that besides those reported by Le Riche, an additional 1,000 pioneers were levied in the Auvergne and La Marche–Limousin regions. Anjou's post-siege demobilization report to the king, *Henri III*, vol. 1, 281, mentions 34 cannon and 8 culverins to be returned to arsenals.

difficulties were predictable accompaniments to the normal frictions of war, but the civil wars themselves also created new difficulties which, as we will see, had begun to reach crisis proportions as early as the campaign of 1569, three years before the siege of La Rochelle, as operations shifted away from the artillery service's major sources of personnel and resources at the Arsenal in Paris and in northern France.

THE ENTERPRISE'S LABOR FORCE

At least as important as the large numbers of animals and massive quantities of material required by the artillery train was its very large human component. The 2,620 personnel the planning documents of 1568 projected as necessary for the operation of the train fell into three distinct groups: 233 men were to be drawn directly from the royal artillery establishment at Paris, and 367 teamsters were to be hired as independent contractors or levied, along with 2,000 pioneers, on surrounding tax districts. The numbers of different types of personnel within those broad categories and their monthly salary rates are summarized in Table 6.2.[21]

The men of the Arsenal have been briefly touched upon in chapter 2.[22] To provide the 233 men previsioned by the planners required almost the entire peacetime complement of artillery personnel. The Arsenal contingent can be divided into three main groups: executive officers and their assistants, skilled workers, and gunners. The officers, from the grand master himself to the provost's clerk, who constituted about a third of the Arsenal's contingent though only 3 percent of the train's total personnel, were dedicated to the executive functions of overall command and coordination of the gunners, craftsmen, pioneers, and teamsters as well as the logistics and deployment of the train. The skilled workers, some forty-six wheelwrights, foundrymen, blacksmiths, carpenters, barrel makers, powderers, boatmen, and tent masters, were responsible for repairing broken equipment and in general seeing to the smooth mechanical functioning of the train. The gunners, the men who actually loaded, laid, and fired the guns, constituted slightly more than half of the Arsenal personnel. If we add to them a few of the officers who would assume direct command of the batteries into which the park would be divided in action (at least two, and as many as four or five batteries, depending on the job to be done), we find that only about 5 percent of the total personnel of the train was directly involved in the end product of its vast labors: the laying of iron shot onto the target; though several hundred of the pioneers would also have been assigned to the batteries to provide the muscle power to draw the guns back up to their firing position after each discharge and to carry roundshot and powder to the gun positions.

---

[21] BN Mss. Fr. 17,870, fols. 298–300. There is detailed salary information in the artillery *états* and *assignations* identified in notes 17 and 19 above.

[22] Chapter 2, pp. 51–52.

Table 6.2. *Projected personnel and salaries for the artillery train, September, 1568*

Position	No.	Monthly pay in *livres*
Arsenal personnel		
Grand master	1	500
Controller general	1	100
Clerks of the C.G.	4	45
Regular commissioners	10	100
Extra commissioners	6	25
Garde general	1	60
Clerks of the G.G.	2	30
Deschargeurs	3	15
Gunners	120	10
Skilled craftsmen	30	15
Captain gen. of train	1	50
Captains of train	8	30
Conducteurs and guides	4	25
Colonel of pioneers	1	50
Captains of pioneers	5	20
Provost	1	50
Provost's clerk	1	25
Archers	4	15
Chaplain	1	30
Quartermaster	1	50
Fouriers	3	20
Master tenters	3	20
Tenter assistants	3	15
Physician	1	100
Surgeons	4	30
Apothecary	1	25
Apothecary's assistant	1	15
Captain of pontoons	1	50
Lieutenant of pontoons	1	25
Pontoon craftsmen and boatmen	10	15
Arsenal subtotal	233	
Teamsters	387	15
Pioneer captains	20	12
Pioneer carpenters	20	9
Pioneers	1,960	6
Total	2,620	

Despite social differences, it is clear that the group from the Arsenal must have had a fairly definite group identity, for its members worked together in peace and served together in war, had common geographical origins, and shared a common technical culture. Almost all the artillerymen were of urban, indeed almost exclusively Parisian, background, the world of guilds and handicrafts, mysteries and tools, masters and their assistants, the *atelier*, the *écurie*, and the minor levels of officialdom. Only the grand master and a few of his principal lieutenants were nobles, and the surviving general *états*, which show little turnover in personnel over periods of several years at a time, suggest stable lifetime vocations interrupted only by accidents, death, or old age, as requests for payment of the pensions due retired officers at the end of the annual budgets remind us.[23]

The second major source of the train's personnel in 1568 was to be the 387 teamsters who would serve as drivers of the draft horses which drew the train's guns and the wagons which carried its huge logistical apparatus. Constituting about 15 percent of the entire train's personnel, the teamsters outnumbered the artillerymen as a group, but unlike them were neither permanent members of the artillery nor were they drawn from a single locality. Some were entrepreneurs who had enough capital to provide their own horses and carts to the train at traditional monthly wage rates (their own salary plus a cash payment for each horse). But the vast majority of teamsters and horses were to be levied by the officials of the surrounding *élections* and sent in groups of up to twenty-five four-horse wagons, each driven by a single teamster, to the train's assembly point at Paris. Coordination of the horses and wagons of the train was provided by the Arsenal staff in the form of the captain general of train, his eight captains, and the four train conductors.[24]

Though the social profile of the teamsters provided for the army is fairly self-evident, they constituted only a temporary skilled labor force and, coming from widely scattered areas and localities, unlike the regular artillery personnel, they must have been largely unknown to one another. It is not clear if the animals and men requisitioned for the train had any previous experience of working together as teams, though those originating from a single locality may have. And though they have to be considered skilled workers, the teamsters and the draught resources raised by requisitioning may not have always been of the best quality. Levies of men, wagons, and horses were a heavy burden on the communities which had to supply them and there is evidence that at least some of the teams sent to the army were rejected as substandard and unable to serve.[25] A technical memorandum of the times suggests that part of the reluctance of districts to provide horses was based on the experience that when and if the horses were returned they were invariably in

---

[23] See entries for "commissaires & cannoniers vielz y impotens," in the 1564 and 1566 artillery *états*: BN Mss. Fr. 4,552, fols. 91v, and 99r. The November 1567 *assignation*, BN Mss. Fr. 4,554, fol. 13v, mentions back wages owed to a serving official while the December *assignation*, 4,553, fol. 99, includes back wages from as far back as 1559 owed to a deceased official!

[24] Cf. notes 17 and 19 above.

[25] See, for example, the December 1567 entry, BN Mss. Fr. 4,553, fol. 95v.

poor shape because the teamsters they were assigned to were abusive or negligent in the care of animals which were not their private property.[26]

The third major group of personnel, the pioneers, brought little to the army besides the strength of their arms and backs. Of all the elements in the army they were the lowest, humblest, and most poorly paid. Raised in the tax districts in companies of up to 200 men, including a captain and a small number of men with carpentry skills, they were assigned in work gangs, under the direction of the colonel and overseer captains provided from the Arsenal cadre, to the unenviable tasks of repairing roadways, lending their shoulders to the wagons and guns in bad going, loading, unloading, and carrying the munitions of the convoy, running loaded guns up to firing position, constructing camps and depots, digging battery positions and approach trenches under frequently severe fire at sieges, and taking part in highly dangerous mining and countermining operations. It is a mark of their status that the tasks to which they were regularly assigned were considered so lowly that not even infantry were expected to perform them. French soldiers were exempted from such manual labor and when, on occasion, Swiss soldiers were willing to hire themselves out individually as manual laborers, it was a matter of some note.[27]

A receipt for the delivery of a company of Norman pioneers to the siege of La Rochelle provides a clue to the nature of service as a pioneer.

Pierre Sixlivres, merchant of Bernay, presented us in this city of Niort the number and quantity of 50 pioneers and a captain, including three carpenters, a standard bearer, and a drummer, ordered raised by the king in the *élection* of Bernay...We found these pioneers, carpenters, and captain to be good men, healthy and equipped with the proper tools...fit to serve the king in the artillery train that his Majesty has assembled for the siege of La Rochelle. Each one was attired and arrayed in red caps, and cassocks and hose of green woolen cloth with two white crosses and the first and last letters of the name of their election sewn on the front and back of their garments. After they took and received the accustomed oath for such an occasion, we received them into the service of His Majesty.[28]

Aside from the fact that they took an oath to serve the king, which put them under military justice, this description of a group of obviously very humble men with ordinary tools, paid a daily wage, and led to camp by a merchant who was filling in for a local official who could not leave his post, seems, except for one detail, to describe a typical industrial or agricultural work gang more than a military formation. That detail, of course, is their distinctive dress. Of all the men and units

---

[26] BN Mss. Fr. 3,193, fol. 234r. See also the interesting minute of the king's council at Niort after the siege of Saint-Jean d'Angely, which discusses what to do with the artillery horses of the train, BN Mss. Fr. 21,544, fols. 61–62.

[27] Cf. notes 17 and 19 above. For the Swiss at La Rochelle, BN Mss. Fr. 4,765, fols. 71r, 72r. According to Anjou, *ibid.*, 75r: "Quant aux pionniers la faulte en a este si grande que telle fois il a fallu se servier des goujatz de bandes, telle fois des Suisses, authrefois des paisans volontaires, et bien souvant ne faire rien par faulte diceuls." Note that the possibility of using some of the more than 20,000 French infantry at the siege for labor is not mentioned.

[28] Biron, *LD*, vol. 2, 575–77.

in the army, it was only the pioneers who were issued uniforms, dramatically setting them off not only from the soldiers, who could be identified by their armor and weapons, but also from the servants and grooms who voluntarily made up the vast majority of the army's noncombatant camp followers. Clearly, the uniforms were not intended as a mark of distinction or honor, or even to enhance morale (though one can imagine that for the simplest of men this may indeed have been an initial reaction). On the contrary, the uniforms fulfill the clear penal function of marking the identity of prisoners or coerced men (galley slaves also wore uniforms) so they could not easily escape. The curious alphabetized marking of each man's uniform also contributes to a sense that they differed little from the other factors of production, also stamped with lading marks, which traveled in the field train's wagons. Given the disagreeable and often extremely dangerous tasks to which the pioneers were assigned and their low pay – a *teston*, a small silver coin, was to be considered a suitable enough bonus to induce them to risk their lives to recover spent cannon balls under direct enemy fire at the siege of La Rochelle – it is not surprising that they suffered very high rates of attrition, including the massive desertions that their convict uniforms were designed to prevent.[29]

When we examine the relation of the functions performed by the men of the artillery to their wages, the striking industrial enterprise nature of the organization of the train compared to the overwhelmingly social and/or military organization of the infantry and cavalry forces becomes clear. When, as in Table 6.3, we collapse the many kinds of officers and workers identified in Table 6.2 into a few major functional groups, calculate an average monthly wage for the members of each group, and provide some points of comparison to the wage levels of typical types of infantry and cavalrymen, the train's complicated internal division of labor seems to reflect in a rather straightforward manner both a clear hierarchy of labor and the effect of the market rationalization of labor wages.[30] The hierarchy that is defined by average wage level descends smoothly from executive administrators to managerial, to skilled, and finally unskilled workers. Less than 3 percent of the personnel performed executive administrative, managerial, or overseer functions (not counting the medical staff and chaplain), 22 percent performed skilled labor tasks, and three-quarters were unskilled workers. To carry the industrial analogy another step, some 90 percent of the train's labor force can be classified as temporary or seasonal workers. Within the labor hierarchy, interestingly enough, the gunners themselves occupied a position at the bottom of the ranks of skilled workers but above the unskilled pioneers. Premiums were to be paid, in other words, primarily to those who oversaw or actually organized and led the work gangs or directed the transport and supply of other factors of production to the batteries whose principal product was to deliver massive weights of iron shot onto the target.

---

[29] Both Nevers and Anjou, BN Mss. Fr. 4,765, 29v and 65v, note the rate of one *teston* per returned shot.
[30] BN Mss. Fr. 17,870, fols. 298–300 and sources in notes 17 and 19. For the comparative infantry rates, see page 88, and for the gendarmerie, page 135.

Table 6.3. *Functional groups and comparative wage levels in the artillery train, 1568*

Group	No.	%	Average monthly wage	Comparison group monthly wage (*livres*)
Officer-administrators	19	0.7	93.9	106 (Inf. captain)
Clerks and archers	6	0.2	40.0	
Medical and chaplain	8	0.3	36.3	33 (*Hommes d'armes*)
Provostial	6	0.2	22.5	
Managers/overseers	45	1.7	21.4	20 (Inf. sergeant)
Teamsters	387	14.8	15.0	17 (Gendarme archer)
Skilled workers	66	2.5	13.4	12-14 (*Lanspessade*)
Gunners	123	4.7	10.1	8-9 (Most infantry)
Unskilled workers	1,960	74.8	6.0	7 (Lowest paid infantryman)
Total	2,620	100.0		

Of the 2,620 personnel proposed for the train in 1568 only the grand master himself, at 500 *livres* per month, was to enjoy a salary that was higher than that of a simple captain of an infantry company. The salaries of his eleven principal lieutenants or commissioners, at 100 *livres* per month, came close to the pay of an infantry captain but besides them only the single physician in the train, also at 100 *livres* per month, was to receive comparable pay. The absence of higher salaries might seem surprising given the skills of many of its functionaries and the importance of the train to the military operations of the army as a whole. But when we compare average wage rates to the wages of other types of soldiers, we actually find a much higher proportion overall of more highly paid men in the artillery. Of all the personnel in the train only the pioneers were paid less than the lowest paid infantryman and all the rest of the personnel, starting with the gunners, at 10 *livres* per month, were paid a higher wage than the 8–9 *livres* per month received by the average pikeman or arquebusier. Skilled craftsmen and teamsters were paid about the same or even slightly more than infantry *lanspessades*, and the managerial and provostial categories about the same as an infantry sergeant. It is only in comparison with the *hommes d'armes* of the gendarmerie that the wages of artillerymen start to seem at a disadvantage. At 33 *livres* per month the *hommes d'armes* who constituted 40 percent of the heavy cavalry received better pay than almost 99 percent of the artillery personnel, and even if we deduct the upkeep of their mounts, each *homme d'armes* still received 20.3 *livres* per month, or more than 97 percent of the artillerymen. But the gendarmerie's archers, though nominally receiving 17 *livres* per month, which would have put them in the most highly paid 4 percent of the artillery, cleared only 8.7 *livres* after the upkeep of their mounts is deducted, about half of the monthly wage of conscripted teamsters, and less per month than all the artillery personnel except pioneers.[31]

In an army-wide labor hierarchy dominated at the top by noble military commanders and officers and at the bottom by the unskilled pioneers, the regular artillerymen and skilled workers who assisted them ranked below the noble *hommes d'armes* but above most infantrymen and all the archers of the gendarmerie. This intermediate position almost exactly paralleled the intermediate economic and social position to which their training, skills, and resources would have placed them in civilian society and is a reflection of the economic rationality, tempered by the premiums given to noble status, which underlay the royal army's hierarchy of labor and reward systems.

SUPPLYING THE TRAIN

France at the beginning of the wars of religion seemed to be rich in artillery resources. The Arsenal, where most of the foundry work for new guns was done and which also served as the crown's central depot for munitions, contained large stocks of gun barrels and hundreds of *milliers* of powder. Other arsenals across the kingdom, such as Nantes, Narbonne, Marseilles, Orléans, and Dijon also contained quantities of guns and munitions, some of it originating from the 1559 evacuation from French Piedmont of 487 guns (including 48 cannons and great culverins, 38 bastardes, and over 300 *arquebuses à croc*), 22,268 roundshot for the five heaviest types of guns, and 268 *milliers* of gunpowder.[32] Even on the eve of the civil war, however, Piedmont still remained one of the two principal areas of concentration of artillery resources outside Paris. In November, 1561, just four months before the outbreak of civil war, an inventory of artillery in Piedmont reveals 583 guns including 49 cannons and 23 grand culverins, 30,943 roundshot of the six calibers of France (including 12,700 for cannon) and 151 *milliers* of powder.[33] We do not possess a similar inventory for that date of the second principal concentration of artillery outside Paris, in the cities and fortified places of Picardy. But the result of

---

[31] *Ibid.*; on the calculation of net pay for the gendarmes and archers of the heavy cavalry see chapter 5, pp. 137–38.

[32] See the November 1559 inventory of guns and munitions evacuated from Piedmont, BN Mss. Fr. 3,240, fols. 17–22.

[33] BN Mss. Fr. 4,552, fol. 81.

Table 6.4. *Artillery in Picardy in 1577*

Location	Gun type						Total
	Can.	G.C.	Bas.	Moy.	Fau.	Faucn.	
Calais	10	9	2	15	17	4	57
Guise	4	3	6	9	4	16	42
Doullens	4	3	2	4	6	12	31
Ardres	4	–	3	11	3	9	30
Boulogne	2	7	6	8	1	6	30
Monstreuil	7	8	6	5	–	1	27
Peronne	4	5	–	8	1	4	22
Abbeville	3	2	2	2	5	7	21
La Cappelle	2	2	2	2	4	7	19
Rue	–	1	3	6	3	3	16
Amiens	4	2	6	2	1	–	15
St.-Quentin	–	–	2	–	5	5	12
Corbie	1	2	2	2	2	2	11
Mondidier	–	–	–	2	–	3	5
La Fère	–	–	2	1	1	2	6
Ham	–	–	1	1	–	–	2
Roye	–	–	–	–	–	5	5
Castellet	–	–	1	2	2	–	5
Monthulin	–	–	–	3	–	1	4
Total	45	44	46	83	55	87	360

an inventory of guns located in Picardy in the late 1570s or early 1580s, presented in Table 6.4, is worth examining in some detail, for it allows us to draw some general conclusions about the availability of different types of guns.[34]

The first point to be made is that though there were a large number of guns stationed on the northern frontier, they were very widely scattered; 360 guns of various calibers were divided among nineteen different places, their number and distribution determined by the defensive needs of specific locations. The number and proportion of guns that would be useful for offensive operations was relatively small. Only 45 of the 360 weapons, or 13 percent, were cannons, and another 44, or 12 percent, great culverins. Almost two-thirds (63 percent) of the guns were the lightweight moyennes, faucons, and fauconneaux. Only Calais and Monstreuil contained a combined total of as many as 10 cannons and great culverins. To strip large numbers of the heaviest weapons from these locations would have been extremely foolhardy, since in most cases their defensive works had been carefully designed with a certain minimum number of guns in mind to provide mutually supporting

[34] BN Mss. Fr. 4,555, fol. 50. Though included among documents from the sixth civil war in 1577 it is possible that this document originates from a slightly later date.

fire, and weakening even a single sector of defenses endangered the whole. We can be sure that similar constraints also applied to the artillery of Piedmont. Only 82 of the guns that were there in 1561, or 14 percent of the total, were cannons or great culverins, and later inventories indicate that slightly more than half of the serviceable heavy guns were required to provide the minimum number needed in the stationary defenses of the seven main fortresses left to the crown in Piedmont.[35] Furthermore, many of the guns in strongplaces were mounted on old or rotten limbers or not mounted on carriages at all and were therefore unavailable for action.[36] The existence of large numbers of guns alone, in other words, did not necessarily guarantee an equally large number of serviceable heavy guns for offensive action.

Such constraints made themselves felt from the beginning of the civil wars. It will be recalled, for example, that when early in the first war Navarre had demanded a field train of 40 guns, the queen mother had reported that the grand master could only initially supply 20 guns for the field. One reason for the delay in the supply of a larger number of serviceable guns was the fact that, according to the English ambassador, though the Arsenal contained many guns, most of them were not yet mounted; and some portion of those that had mounts had to be diverted downriver in June of 1562 for an abortive first siege of Rouen.[37] In order to put together the initial field train for the main royal army, somewhat more than a dozen serviceable guns were transferred from the northern frontier and places in Champagne, but that was about the extent of the aid that apparently could be provided with safety from those areas.[38] The initial shortfall of guns at Paris, however, was more a result of a lack of preparedness due to the unexpected outbreak of civil war rather than to a lack of resources per se. From the second civil war on enough serviceable heavy guns seem to have been kept on hand at Paris – at least 40 and perhaps as many as 60 at a time – to outfit the field train.

The absolutely central role that Paris played in the provision of serviceable heavy guns, however, while at first advantageous for the crown's military operations, over time became increasingly disadvantageous. The demands of the stationary defenses of the two other principal areas of concentrations of artillery resources – Picardy and Piedmont – denied those resources in the main to the series of wars fought in the interior of the country. Both Picardy and Piedmont, after all, had been the repository of vast resources because in addition to their defensive importance they

---

[35] Cf. note 33 above. For later inventories of the artillery in French Piedmont, see, for 1567, BN Mss. Fr. 3,220, fols. 13–25 and 56–59; and 4,554, fols. 112–17 for 1573. See also BN Mss. Fr. 3,164, fol. 33, and Biron, *LD*, vol. 2, 567–68.

[36] See BN Mss. Fr. 3,220, fols. 69–70 for conditions in 1567, and *ibid.*, fol. 63 for needs in 1569 or 1570, but especially the very detailed 1573 inventory, 4,554, fols. 112–17. There are 1568 and 1569 inventories of the Rouen arsenal in BN Mss. Fr. fols. 50–55, of Marscilles in 1571, 4,554, fols. 33–37, and of Narbonne, the principal arsenal in the south in 1572–73, in Douais, "Les guerres de religion," vol. 4, 65–67, and 331–42.

[37] Paschal, *1562*, 50, 51, and 59; *CSPF/E*, vol. 4, no. 1058.

[38] *Ibid.*; Paschal, *1562*, 28.

were also principal staging areas for offensive action outside the kingdom. Neither was particularly well placed to support offensive actions oriented to the interior of the country. Much of Picardy, while well within supporting distance of operations in upper Normandy or the Ile-de-France, was at a disadvantage as a staging area for operations that moved far to the south of Paris. Piedmont suffered from being cut off from the interior by the Alps, which made the moving of any sizeable amount of munitions to the Rhône very expensive, and, because of the presence of Huguenot bandits in Dauphiny, perilous as well. As a result the large stockpiles of guns, equipment, and munitions which remained behind in Piedmont after 1559 were essentially left to rot, and by the time of the final liquidation of the French garrison in Piedmont in 1575 the crown was borrowing heavy guns from the duke of Savoy to fill out the artillery train for the siege of Livron.[39]

Given the mostly peripheral importance of the frontier fortresses for the prosecution of interior wars, a very good case can be made that Paris would by default if for no other reason have served as the singular source of artillery resources for the royal army during the civil wars. The Arsenal and its personnel, after all, had functioned as the main depot of the kingdom and as the central headquarters of the grand master's command even before 1562. The major shift during the civil wars was that Parisian resources were to be marshalled almost exclusively for the offensive tasks assigned to the royal army rather than supplying the munitions and modernizing and upgrading the defensive capabilities of the artillery of the fortified places which guarded the kingdom from outside aggression. Also, the fact is that the main military campaigns of the first two civil wars largely unrolled in or near the capital, whose geographical centrality and political and economic importance made it the natural lynchpin of the crown's drive to defeat the Huguenot army and reconquer the cities of the north which had fallen to the Protestants.

During the first civil war in particular, the location of Paris at the heart of the riverine system of northern France worked to the royal army's advantage. It was a relatively short trip by boat or barge west from Paris to Rouen or Le Havre, south to the Montargis terminus, and east as far as Châlons-sur-Marne. In the first stages of the war, during its march around Orléans to Blois and then across the province of Berry to the siege of Bourges, the royal army was unable to take advantage of the interior lines provided by water transportation. But after the fall of Bourges the army frequently used the Montargis–Paris–Rouen route to shift guns and supplies back and forth through the capital, sending guns in this manner to the siege of Rouen, returning artillery to Paris before the battle of Dreux, dispatching additional heavy guns to the siege of Orléans, and transporting some forty guns back down the Seine to the siege of Le Havre after the peace.[40] In the second civil war the river

---

[39] June 1574 dispatches in *CDM*, vol. 5, 64 and 67 and October dispatches in *Henri III*, vol. 2, 39, 41, 51–53.

[40] See, for example, the queen mother's reference to transshipment to Montargis from Paris, *CDM*, vol. 1, 502, and Brissac's use of the Seine in preparations for the siege of Le Havre, Lublinskya, *Documents*, 270–72.

system also came in handy. Though the main train took the land route with the army to Châlons-sur-Marne, much of it returned by water to Paris later in the war, and at one point additional guns were sent up river from Paris to Melun to be used for a possible attack on Auxerre.[41]

Besides being relatively cheap and reasonably rapid, water transport had the advantage that it involved little wear and tear on the guns: a technical discussion of the time which urged water travel pointed out that travel by land was in fact more wearing on the big guns than their actual operation in battery during a siege.[42] Water travel was also reasonably secure. Recall that another of the grand master's reasons for not being able to provide more than a 20-gun train in the early summer of 1562 was the fact that it was impossible to gather enough horses and pioneers because the enemy controlled or threatened large stretches of territory in the north. Anxiety about the security of convoys of guns and munitions moving from Paris to the army runs like a litany through the command correspondence of the time, and, given their lack of artillery, the glittering prospect of capturing a substantial artillery convoy always hung before the eyes of Huguenot leaders. Here the city of Paris again played an important role by sending large detachments from its otherwise largely useless militia to provide convoy protection as the artillery moved to and from the capital. Much beyond Paris, however, the army itself had to provide not insubstantial forces to the guard of land-bound convoys, sometimes to no avail. One of the most spectacular military exploits of the entire civil war – one that so impressed contemporaries that it is mentioned in all the histories of the time – occurred in early September, 1562, when Coligny successfully managed to ambush a reinforcement of six heavy guns and a large amount of powder on the road from Chartres to Châteaudun. Only the escape of the convoy's draft horses prevented the Huguenots from taking the guns as prizes and they instead had to settle for blowing up the whole convoy with its own stock of gunpowder.[43] Such relatively minor coups, contemporaries understood, could potentially have major consequences: in this case the destroyed convoy was headed to Bourges where the expenditure of almost all of the army's powder in the initial bombardments of the siege had failed to make an assaultable breach. The loss of the convoy's powder would have compelled the royal army to lift the siege, which could very easily have given an entirely different complexion to the events of the campaign, but before word of Coligny's attack reached camp the city was unnecessarily and disgracefully surrendered by its Huguenot commander.

---

[41] The December 1567 artillery *assignation*, BN Mss. Fr. 4,553, fol. 99r, mentions river transport of six cannons; Anjou's dispatch of January 14, 1568, orders cannons moved by barge from Paris to Auxerre; and the February, 1568 *assignation*, BN Mss. Fr. 4,554, fol. 2r, mentions the return riverine trip of munitions to the Paris Arsenal from Châlons-sur-Marne.

[42] BN Mss. Fr. 3,193, fol. 234r.

[43] See, for an account, Theodore de Bèze, *Histoire ecclésiastique des églises reformées au royaume de France* (Nieuwkoop, 1974), vol. 2, 172–73.

From the beginning of the third war in the fall of 1568, however, the centering of the royal army's artillery service on Paris and the north of France seems to have begun to work against the monarchy. The shift of operations to the south and west in the third and fourth wars and to the Rhône valley as well in the fifth war reversed the favorable transportation calculus the crown had earlier been able to take advantage of. To move the train from Paris to Poitou or the Charente or to La Rochelle added weeks of travel. Since there was no direct internal water link to the southwest the train had to move by land to the Loire and then southwards to Châtellerault for transshipment, again by land, to other points. Use of the long alternative sea route, down the Seine from Paris, along the Norman coast, around Brittany, and then up the Loire, bypassed one of the major land obstacles, but was made quite dangerous by Huguenot inspired piracy and the risk of losing the precious guns and equipment to shipwreck. At the beginning of the fifth war, for example, after Matignon had followed his capture of Montgommery by using the train sent from Paris to reconquer places in Lower Normandy, the queen mother ordered him to send his artillery south to Montpensier for the sieges of Fontenay and Lusignan, suggesting that he use seaborne transportation if he thought it safe enough, but otherwise to send it, as in the event he did, by land escorted by much of his infantry and with doubled horse teams to speed up the long and wearing journey overland to Poitou.[44]

Water transport, however, continued to be important during demobilizations. After the siege of La Rochelle in 1573, for example, the train was divided into two groups, one of which was sent by sea to Nantes and then up the Loire and thence by land to Paris, the other by sea to Le Havre and up the Seine to the Arsenal.[45] But the return of the train to Paris after each war meant that the long trip to below the Loire had to be repeated each time war recommenced, and also made it more difficult to send follow-up support. During the fall campaign of 1568, for example, the 20-gun train used by Anjou had turned out to be too cumbersome for operations in the cut-up and wooded regions south and east of Poitiers and Châtellerault. Some of the heavier guns were returned to Paris in December when Anjou decided to improve the army's mobility during the next year's campaign with a somewhat smaller and lighter 12-gun train, but a separate siege train of twenty heavy guns was supposed to be held in readiness for transport from Paris. But in the event, as we know, the siege train was delayed in leaving Paris, probably for financial reasons, and arrived at Châtellerault too late after the battle of Jarnac to be of offensive use (though some of the guns proved useful in the defense of Poitiers) until the beginning of the siege of Saint-Jean-d'Angély in November of 1569, when it was again late in arriving due to poor weather and roads and a lack of draft horses.[46]

As the main areas of the army's operations moved steadily further to the south from the fall of 1568 onwards, tripling or quadrupling the distances involved for the

[44] Letter of July 1, 1574, *CDM*, vol. 5, 45–47.
[45] *Henri III*, vol. 1, 281.
[46] *Ibid.*, p. 128.

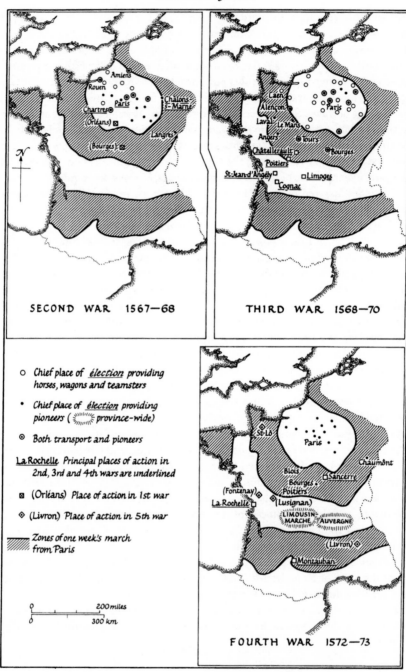

Fig. 20. Levies of horses, wagons, teamsters, and pioneers, 1567–73

movement and supply of the trains, the artillery's reliance on Paris was hardly modified at all. Figure 20, which indicates the *chef-lieux* of *élections* that were called on to furnish horses, wagons, teamsters, and pioneers during the second and third, and pioneers (all we have information on) during the fourth civil war illustrates the dimensions of this continued dependence.[47] The vast majority of horses and pioneers during these wars were always raised from *élections* within about one week's infantry march from the capital, and though we do not possess such detailed information for the first civil war we can be sure that the pioneers at the sieges of Rouen or Havre as well as the hundreds of horses that left Paris with the train in the summer of 1562 were drawn from exactly these same areas. But even during the movement of the train southward at the beginning of the third war very little of the total requisitions came from slightly beyond a week's march from Paris and during the siege of La Rochelle at least two-thirds of the pioneers of the train continued to be levied from the region around Paris.

This reliance on Paris and northern France for horses and labor was determined, of course, by a number of factors. The first was the fact that it was exactly in that region that the crown had never lost or had quickly reestablished its political authority during most of the early wars. There was a longstanding infrastructure of royal officials in the surrounding areas who from earlier times had ample experience in marshaling the required resources. The fact that the train continued to be assembled at Paris at the beginning of each war also set practical limits on the extent of territory from which it could draw transport and labor resources, especially draft horses and vehicles, since the length of time it would have taken to collect them from farther away would have led to unacceptable delays and they would have arrived in the area of operations already in a fairly worn-out state. But it was not just the certainty of Paris-oriented resources that have to be borne in mind. Equally important was the fact that the areas the army was traveling to and fighting in were usually highly contested and disrupted, and the chances of being able to raise comparable resources on the spot were quite slim and, when attempted, always fraught with difficulties. During the later stages of the siege of La Rochelle, for example, when the original pioneer detachments had been reduced by attrition to a few hundred men, Anjou was unsuccessful in raising additional labor in Saintonge and Poitou and even offers of high daily wages in the midst of one of the worst famines in memory did not suffice to draw men to the dangers of the siege.[48] It would therefore have been extremely foolhardy to arrive at the campaign area without a full complement of horses and laborers since, as Biron reminds us, if any one single element of the train was deficient the whole was rendered useless, and it was only in the north that such resources could be found in requisite quantities.

The same strictures applied to the provision of munitions, specifically powder and

---

[47] Derived from the sources cited in notes 17 and 19 above and Le Riche, *Journal*, 117–35. For a levy of pioneers in 1577 during the sixth civil war, BN Mss. Fr. 4,554, fol. 142.
[48] Le Riche, 137; BN Mss. Fr. 4,765, fol. 75v.

Table 6.5. *Powder reserves available for the siege of La Rochelle in 1572–73*

	Grain (*livres*)			
Location	Large	Medium	Total	%
Paris				
Arsenal	142,600	23,600	166,200	43.2
Hôtel-de-Ville	12,000	–	12,000	3.1
Picardy and Normandy				
Amiens	80,000	–	80,000	20.8
Abbeville	30,000	–	30,000	7.8
Peronne	12,000	–	12,000	3.1
Rouen	20,000	–	20,000	5.2
Loire river				
Tours	10,597	2,299	12,896	3.3
Chinon	2,400	100	2,500	.6
Angers	9,000	1,000	10,000	2.6
Poitou–Saintonge–Angoumois				
Niort	6,600	1,200	7,800	2.0
Saint-Jean-d'Angély	4,500	300	4,800	1.2
Poitiers	18,800	1,600	20,400	5.3
Angoulême	6,400	100	6,500	1.7
Total	354,897	30,199	385,096	99.9

roundshot, for the train's guns. An *état* of the location of powder reserves drawn up during the planning for the siege of La Rochelle illustrates the problem.[49] As Table 6.5 indicates, the reserves available for the siege consisted of 385,096 *livres* of large and medium grain powder located in twelve different cities. Paris, with the Arsenal and its Hôtel-de-Ville was by far the richest source for powder in the kingdom – 178,200 *livres*, or 46.3 percent of the total. Next in importance were several of the frontier places in Picardy and the Norman capital of Rouen, which together contained 36.9 percent of reserves. Towns along the Loire had only 6.5 percent of the total. The powder available in the Poitou–Saintonge–Angoumois region closest to La Rochelle (Poitiers, Niort, Saint-Jean-d'Angély, and Angoulême) amounted to only 39,500 *livres*, or 10.2 percent of reserves. Eighty-three percent, in other words, of all available powder reserves was located on or north of the Seine.

These were not, of course, all the powder reserves in the kingdom. Narbonne, the principal depot for Languedoc, had about 50 *milliers* of powder of all grades on hand in 1572 and there were about 126 *milliers* of powder still in existence in

---

[49] BN Mss. Fr. 3,240, fol. 54.

Table 6.6. *Origins of shot at La Rochelle, 1573*

Place	No. balls	%
Paris	7,500	28.0
Orléans	9,856	36.8
North subtotal	17,356	64.8
Poitiers	662	2.5
Niort	455	1.7
Melle	240	0.9
Saint-Jean-d'Angély	1,298	4.8
Angoulême	95	0.4
Western cities subtotal	2,750	10.3
Monberon forges	6,082	22.7
Galleys	600	2.2
Other sources subtotal	6,682	24.9
Total	26,788	100.0

Piedmont in 1573.[50] We also know that in 1574 30 *milliers* of powder were ordered from the depots of Champagne for the siege of Livron.[51] Total national reserves, then, probably amounted to roughly more than 600 *milliers* of powder. But half of the Narbonne reserves were to be used by Damville in operations in Languedoc during 1572–73, and as far as the siege of La Rochelle was concerned the Piedmont reserves may as well have been on the moon.[52] Biron was to claim that his batteries fired 25,000 rounds during the siege of La Rochelle, which would have required the consumption of about 500 *milliers* of powder, or almost all of the national reserves.[53] This may have been a slight exaggeration, but the magnitudes involved make it quite clear that prosecution of a major siege at a site hundreds of miles from Paris was still completely dependent on the gathering and transport of the hundreds of *milliers* of powder that could only be provided by the capital and the regions in the north of the kingdom. The provision of shot for the siege, as is indicated in Table 6.6, was just as complicated. We know from a second-hand report that the original convoy of munitions from the Arsenal in Paris unloaded about 7,500 roundshot at Châtellerault on its way to La Rochelle.[54] Almost all of those rounds were expended in the preparatory bombardments and the earliest assaults on the city in March

---

[50] For Narbonne, Douais, "Les guerres de religion," vol. 4, 332, and for Piedmont, BN Mss. Fr. 4,554, fols. 112–17.
[51] *CDM*, vol. 4, 64, 67.
[52] Comparison of Douais, vol. 4, 332 and 335.
[53] As reported to Anjou, BN Mss. Fr. 4,765, 75v.
[54] Le Riche, 119.

and April of 1573, leading to a critical shortage of shot, and a search for additional supplies from other sources.[55] Table 6.6 combines the information on the shot sent from Paris with information from an inventory of the points of origin of cannon-balls in depot at La Rochelle in mid-May, 1573, to show the origins of the round-shot available during the siege.[56] Almost two-thirds of the 26,788 balls had come from Paris and Orléans (64.8 percent). Another 23 percent of the shot had actually been manufactured by the conveniently located Monberon forges in nearby Angoumois. But the towns in the operational region managed to provide only about one-tenth of the total. Local resources, therefore, would have sufficed for only perhaps a third of the shot requirements for the siege, once again underlining the dependence on Paris and regions north of the Loire. As the presence of products of the Monberon forges suggest, however, it may have been easier to procure at least some quantities of ironshot locally than powder, which was more complicated to manufacture. But utilization of nearby manufacturers always entailed negotiations and up-front cash payments, and put the fortunes of the army partially into the hands of local merchants. This could lead to serious problems. In the fifth civil war, for example, Burgundian merchant forgemasters set such a high cartel price on production of shot for the batteries intended for the siege of Livron that the queen mother refused to pay it, and in the end, after much delay, only a threat by the newly arrived Henry III to revoke their privileges to manufacture bar iron compelled them to cooperate.[57] But the imbroglio led directly to miscoordination of the bombardment of Livron which, according to Bellegarde, was the main reason for the ignominious failure of that siege.[58]

THE DECLINE OF THE ARTILLERY

On April 22, 1562, just three weeks after the Huguenot seizure of Orléans precipitated the first civil war, the king, the queen mother, the king of Navarre, the constable, and the duke of Guise paid a highly visible visit to the Arsenal, where they dined, inspected the artillery, and fired some test rounds.[59] Such visits to the Arsenal were often repeated during the civil wars. Besides satisfying the curiosity that contemporaries seem to have had about the huge artillery guns which, with the exception of ships and buildings, were the largest and most beautiful technical artifacts of the era, the royal inspections were also designed to remind subjects of a type and quantity of military might that was available, because of its tremendous expense, only to great sovereigns. The possession of vast parks of artillery was a source of pride, and certainly one to be publicly flaunted, the great guns' booming

---

[55] See pp. 248–53.
[56] Inventory of May 1573, BN Mss. Fr. fols. 76–78.
[57] Letter to Tavannes of January 24, 1575, *Henri III*, vol. 2, 100–1.
[58] Eugéne Arnaud, *Histoire des Protestants du Dauphiné* (3 vols., Geneva, 1970), vol. 1, 319.
[59] Paschal, *1562*, 28. For a good study of Paris during the early wars see Diefendorf, *Beneath the Cross*.

salvos serving simultaneously to warn foes and comfort loyal subjects. The transfer of the great guns from the Arsenal through the streets of the capital to the outer fortifications where they assembled to form the army's train was also a well-attended public ritual which accompanied the beginning of each civil war.[60]

But in contrast to the era of the Hapsburg–Valois wars, civil war created new problems for the artillery which went quite beyond the normal difficulties of renovating deteriorating stockpiles of munitions and weapons, grappling with inadequate or uncertain government finances, and providing for the defense of a vast country's frontiers. In logistical terms alone the civil wars had from the beginning put a strain on the artillery resources of the kingdom. Over time the extensive campaigns completely disrupted the normal process of maintaining adequate stockpiles of weapons and munitions and led to abandonment of the task of modernizing and upgrading the crown's frontier defenses. Furthermore, over the course of its campaigning much of the artillery's equipment had been left scattered in various locations far from Paris while collapsing royal finances at the end of each war brought to an end such activities as the transfer of worn-out guns to the Arsenal for refounding. This disarray was becoming critical even before the siege of La Rochelle. As the grand master Biron wrote to King Charles in November of 1571:

Sire, I fear that I will not be in time for the approval of the budgets to object to the deficiencies in your Majesty's artillery, in all the provinces of your kingdom, deficiencies which are great and extreme because in the past wars, everyone disposed of everything without order and there was confusion and waste, such that all your provinces are lacking munitions and guns, excepting Picardie, which I have seen to the best I could. In all your towns, it is necessary to remount the cannons because the limbers are all rotted for the lack of care that has been taken in providing cover for them. Also, in several provinces, it is necessary to cast new guns, while in others it is easier to send in the pieces, to store the odd parts, and to take the broken and damaged ones to the Arsenal, for there is a shortage of copper. And to let Your Majesty know what was accomplished this year, not a pound of powder was made nor a hammer wielded to fashion equipment, except the few guns I was able to have cast on my own credit and the sixty *milliers* of powder and 1,500 shot I delivered to Picardy.

Your Majesty often receives complaints from the governors of the provinces and towns and their inhabitants of the shortages which exist. And remember, Sire, that the most honorable excuse of those who surrender a fortified place is the lack of powder. For a hundred years there has not been such a severe shortage nor has so little been made as in the last year. Sire, your service and the preservation of your state and crown are at stake: if the needs of the artillery are not carefully seen to regularly, all the treasure in the world is useless to produce them when they are needed. Your Majesty should not pay attention to what some have told you that it is necessary to economize in peacetime, and that, therefore, it is not necessary to spend on the artillery, as it pleased you to tell me at Blois. Certainly, economize in things that can be produced at will. Some may tell Your Majesty this is too great an expense, but the total cost of current operations, ordinary and extraordinary, only amounts to about the cost of two gendarme companies of one hundred men at arms each. For the production of powder, the

---

[60] See, for example, Paschal, *1562*, 41.

purchase of shot, and wood for remounts, the casting and remounting of certain pieces, and throughout the kingdom the repair of magazines, transport of broken pieces, remnants, and powder and shot to the Arsenal, and for something to be sent where there is need, for the extra pay of my provincial lieutenants, clerks and controllers and guards to conduct a general inventory, which has not been done in twenty-five years – so that you can know with certainty which pieces and munitions are in your towns...I could see to all the above if I took delivery of 70,000 *livres* for this year. This does not include the regular budget for personnel, saltpeter and construction at the Arsenal. Sire, besides the fact that it is a great and important service to you, and one of the cornerstones of the preservation of your state, it is because I am infinitely jealous of protecting my reputation that I write you such a long discourse. I therefore beg, importune and plead with you to consider this as much as its importance requires.[61]

Given the state of royal finances in 1571, it is doubtful that Biron got the financial allotment he was requesting, but in one respect at least his importuning was taken seriously, because within months he received a royal commission in which the king acknowledged that

Having been warned by you of the great disorder and confusion which have plagued the affairs of our artillery during these recent wars, due to necessary changes, movement, and transport of our guns, powder, shot, and other munitions in several different places of our Kingdom, we have been advised that in order to re-establish the regulations and order which must reign in our said artillery affairs, and in order to have a true accounting of the number of artillery pieces and munitions we possess and what is serviceable, it is very necessary to have a general inventory taken throughout the Kingdom of all the artillery pieces, weapons, powder, shot, sulfur, saltpeter, copper, tin, lead, iron, wood for remounts, fireworks and incendiaries, picks, shovels, hoes, ropes and other munitions and weapons...in our magazines, cities, châteaux and fortresses.[62]

The work of preparing a general inventory of artillery resources was actually begun in the spring of 1572, but it was cut short by the outbreak of the fourth civil war and the siege of La Rochelle, and in the turmoil of the fifth war largely abandoned. The few inventories of arsenals that survive from 1572–73 show that though the crown possessed hundreds of gun tubes in its various arsenals and fortresses, many of them were actually in no condition to serve. Barrels were burst, ventholes enlarged, carriages and wheels rotted, cables and harnesses old and worn out. Imploring letters from local commissioners catalog the mounting need for refurbishment, repair, and shelter of guns and supplies. The arsenal at Narbonne, for example, reported 93 guns of all types in storage, but only 51, including some large guns of irregular caliber, were considered serviceable, and many of these were dismounted.[63] An inventory of 1573 reports a total of 241 guns in the fortified places of Piedmont, but 43 percent of the 72 canons and grand culverines, and 60 percent of

---

[61] Biron's 1571 report to Charles IX, *AHG*, 49–51.
[62] Biron, *LD*, vol. 2, 571–72.
[63] Douais, vol. 4, 65–66, 331, 334; and other inventories and requests cited in notes 35 and 36 above.

the 67 bastardes and all but four of the 102 guns of the three smaller royal calibers were either completely dismounted or mounted on old and rotting carriages. Only 8.3 percent of all the guns in Piedmont in 1573 had recently constructed mounts.[64]

From the third war onward, then, there are increasing signs of exhaustion and disarray in the artillery service. And to the wear and tear of almost constant campaigning from 1567 through 1570 and the chronic neglect of the vital infrastructure and stockpiles of the artillery can be added, of course, the strain of the enormous effort put together for the siege of La Rochelle. As Anjou noted in his report, problems with the lack of materials and shortfalls of critical munitions at various moments during the siege had greatly hampered operations, for which he blamed Biron, remarking "It seems to me that if one is unable to ready the things necessary for a siege in three months' time on the spot, it will be nearly impossible to do so once the attack begins."[65] But Biron might have excused himself in his distinctive Gascon manner as he had in an earlier letter to the king when he pointed out: "The caretaker is not considered skilled when with much, he does much, but when with little, he does much."[66] And, in fact, years of campaigning and repeated demands for men and horses were leading to chronic shortages or met with delays due to the reluctance of increasingly uncooperative officials. Such difficulties, of course, often exasperated those military authorities who had an essentially rationalistic and goal-oriented cast of mind. Biron reported a typical example of non-cooperation to the king in January 1573, as he awaited Anjou's arrival at La Rochelle and as he attempted to complete the initial investment of the city.

And so that Your Majesty see how he is served: the forty thousand livres which it pleased you to order for the artillery for the month of December has been ready in Tours for twenty-five days now. Nonetheless, the treasury clerk, unable to transport it himself, came to this camp to fetch two carts for its transport. In so doing, he saved 40 livres, but for the month of December, no funds came. It was therefore necessary to live off loans until now, which is a very pernicious state of affairs for such an equipage of artillery when the money does not come on time.[67]

But while Biron's indignation is understandable, the reluctance of a more humble official to advance money he would probably never see again reminds us of the highly commercial realities of the operation of the artillery train. To Biron what was principally at stake was his reputation which he was "infinitely jealous of protecting."[68] But to most members of the artillery train it was money, rather than reputation, or honor, that guaranteed their involvement. As Biron himself wrote in 1577: "For as much as the conducting and handling of the train is done by hired

[64] BN Mss. Fr. 4,554, fols. 112–17.
[65] BN Mss. Fr. 4,765, fol. 75r.
[66] Biron, *AHG*, 82.
[67] *Ibid.*, 65.
[68] *Ibid.*, 51.

horses, gunners, craftsmen and poor workers who live from day to day, unable to leave the artillery train, it is important that pay not be lacking."[69]

The artillery train, perhaps more than any other segment of the army, resembled an industrial enterprise in its organization, and one can assume, the assumptions of its labor force. In previous wars the crown had been very careful to ensure the prompt payment of the professional artillery personnel. But from early 1569 on, when even the best will could not substitute for empty coffers, there is evidence of increasing dissatisfaction among the men drawn from the permanent staff of the Arsenal. In April of 1569 the artillerymen at Châtellerault refused to unload the siege guns sent by water from Paris because they had not been paid, and in the spring of 1574, Matignon's operations in Normandy were nearly brought to a halt by the threat of a strike by unpaid artillerymen, a threat averted only by Catherine de Medici's quick arrangement for local financing of the needed sums.[70]

There may also have been growing personnel problems due to casualties, though, unfortunately, we have no information on the cumulative losses among artillery personnel over the period. But it is hard to believe that in this area, as with the exhaustion of the kingdom's munitions, the siege of La Rochelle did not deliver a final critical blow to the artillery service. We know from a roll drawn up in February, 1573, that the Arsenal's contingent at the beginning of the siege numbered 354 personnel of all types.[71] But by May 18 the bread ration list for the artillery (excluding pioneers and teamsters) only contained 95 men in the batteries and depot, or 27 percent of the original contingent, a 73 percent loss in strength in three months of service, though what proportion of those losses was due to casualties, sickness, or desertion we have no way of determining.[72]

By the time of the fifth civil war financial difficulties, supply shortages, casualties, and the strain of continued operations far to the south of the only reliable and readily available artillery resources in the kingdom had finally, it seems, reduced the artillery service to a shadow of its former self. None of the siege operations in 1574–75 deployed more than about twenty heavy guns, that is, one-third to one-half fewer guns than the army had used at sieges during the first four civil wars. Furthermore, the trains that were assembled for the sieges of Fontenay and Lusignan by Montpensier and for Livron by Bellegarde depended heavily on widely scattered local resources, and Paris seems to have contributed only the ten heavy guns sent first to Normandy and then forwarded by Matignon to Poitou. In the Rhône valley campaign, as mentioned, Henry III was forced to borrow four guns from the duke of Savoy, and after liquidation of the last French strongholds in Piedmont in 1575, when the rest of the duke's lands were returned to him, the possibility of supply

[69] Biron, *LD*, vol. 1, 61.
[70] Anjou to the king, May 2, 1569, Gigon, 394–96, especially 396; Charles IX to Matignon, May 29, 1574, *CDM*, vol. 4, 308–9, note 1, and the queen mother to Matignon, June 19, *ibid.*, vol. 5, 28–29.
[71] BN Mss. Fr. 3,240, fols. 100–6.
[72] *Ibid.*, fols. 86–88.

from there no longer remained even a theoretical possibility. Even when the crown managed to put together a 14-piece train for the duke of Guise's army in Champagne in late 1575, there were not enough personnel or funds to sustain it and it spent the rest of the war rotting in scattered depots all over the northeastern part of the kingdom. As was the case with the cavalry and the infantry, the strains of war had finally caught up to the artillery, and when, at the beginning of the sixth civil war in 1577 the planners sat down again to calculate the size of the train which was intended for the siege of La Charité, successive drafts quickly reduced its dimensions from 20 guns, 429 wagons, and 2,156 horses to 10 guns, 104 wagons, and 670 horses.[73]

The substitution of smaller scale and increasingly localized artillery operations for the powerful and effective trains which accompanied the royal army from Paris in the first four civil wars did not, however, represent the nadir of the service's fortunes during the later civil wars. The final blow to the royal artillery service painstakingly built up by the monarchy since the fifteenth century was to come during the days of the Catholic League, when the citizens of Paris, who had contributed so much to the artillery service, seized and sacked the Arsenal itself, leaving it a damaged and empty shell and a fitting symbol of the complete disintegration of royal authority and power during the last years of civil war.

[73] BN Mss. Fr. 4,555, fols. 23–24, 25, 334; the reduction is noted on 23v.

7

In search of a battle: Dreux, 1562

Though they loom large in the contemporary accounts and early histories of the wars of religion, the number of major standup battles fought by the royal army was actually quite few. In the nine years from 1562 to 1570 the main army fought only seven major battles: Dreux, Saint-Denis, Jazeneuil, Jarnac, La Roche-L'Abeille, Moncontour, and Arnay-le-Duc. That there were few ranged battles, however, was not always for lack of trying – in the first three civil wars, especially, campaigns usually revolved around attempts by one or both sides to bring the other's army to battle. On perhaps a dozen other occasions before 1570 there were also near battles, that is, times when the opposing armies or major components of them were actually in sight of one another but one or both held back from battle, as at Talcy, or were unable to come to grips because of the weather, as at Loudon, or successfully sought to disengage, as at Notre-Dame-L'Epine. And on many other occasions the armies were close enough to one another for there to be skirmishes between cavalry outriders, but no battle or near battle developed. After 1570, however, battle almost completely disappeared from the major campaigns. The royal army fought no open field battles at all during the fourth war, and only one serious action, at Dormans, during the fifth war.

The disappearance of large-scale battles after 1570 was influenced by both the weakness of the Huguenots after the great massacre as well as the growing ascendancy of siege operations. But even before these developments battles had only very infrequently been fought. The fact was that a battle was an extremely difficult event to arrange unless both sides simultaneously sought one, a condition that, for a number of tactical and strategic reasons, was quite rare. Battles were also extremely risky and chaotic events whose outcome was impossible to predict or control. And though lengthy siege operations certainly caused more casualties overall during the early wars, battles could result in enormous casualties and even the near complete destruction of an army in a very short length of time. As destructive as they could be for the loser, battles also could prove equally destructive and disorganizing for the victor. Though the results of a major battle could literally change the complexion of a campaign overnight, it was almost always impossible to quickly follow up or exploit even a great victory. In contrast to the great inherent risks involved in giving battle, they tended, no matter how dramatic the outcome, to be curiously indecisive events. An analysis of the battle of Dreux, on December 19, 1562 – the first major battle fought by the royal army during the civil wars – can serve to illustrate all these attributes: difficulty of arrangement, high risk, unpredictable results, destructiveness, and indecisiveness, as well as the kind of long-lasting influence the lessons drawn from such singularly dramatic events could have on the organization and strategic direction of the royal army.

Like most battles of the epoch, Dreux almost did not happen, and the fact that it did take place was at least as much the result of accident as of consciously laid plans or an unequivocal desire to combat on either side.[1] It will be recalled that the Huguenot army, consisting of almost 13,000 combatants, more than half of them German mercenaries, had appeared before Paris in mid-November, 1562, where it delayed for several weeks, skirmishing with the royal garrison, mounting a series of probing attacks on the defenses of the faubourgs, and negotiating in vain for a favorable peace settlement. By the end of the first week in December it was clear to the Huguenot leaders that the royal army, which had been receiving reinforcements almost daily, was preparing to attack its camp with superior numbers. So, early on the morning of December 10 the Huguenots decamped, marching in a southwesterly direction towards Chartres (see Figure 21(a)). Their march was constantly slowed by breakdowns in their small artillery train which necessitated a two-day delay for repairs at Saint-Arnoult. Their unpaid and increasingly mutinous German mercenaries were also a concern as were increasing desertions by their French troops. But a larger problem was a lack of clear strategic direction for the army and disagreement between its two principal leaders, Condé and Coligny. Contemporary accounts suggest that their initial idea had been to mount an assault on Chartres, but this was stymied by news of the presence of a substantial royal garrison and the growing realization that the royal army had left Paris in pursuit of them. At a meeting of the army's council at the village of Ablis on December 16 Condé argued for an audacious retrograde movement on Paris, now denuded of most of its garrison. Coligny argued for a march to Normandy, where the funds sent by Queen Elizabeth of England to pay the army's German troops had arrived and where the numerically inferior Huguenots could strengthen themselves with men from the English expeditionary force occupying Le Havre. There was also a suggestion by local Protestants, though it turned out to be wrong, that they could arrange the betrayal of the city of Dreux situated on the road to Normandy.

In the end it was Coligny's plan that was adopted and the army turned to the northwest, crossing the Eure river at Maintenon on December 17. Here delay and disagreement again intervened. A mixup by the masters-of-camp had resulted in the battle, or main body of the army under Condé, passing and camping at Ormoy ahead of the advance guard under Coligny at Néron, and an extra day's delay was

---

[1] See Appendix, Part D.

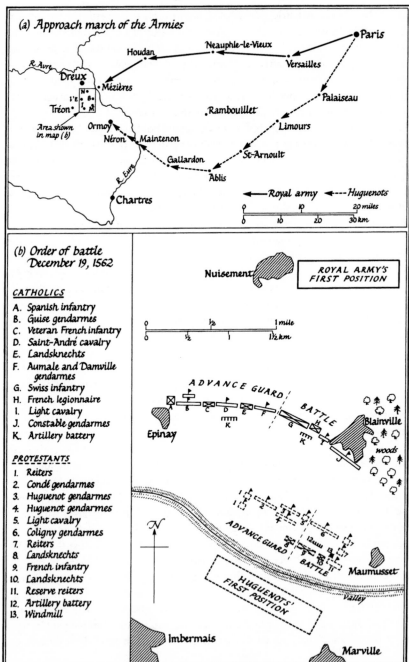

Fig. 21. The approach to the battle of Dreux

agreed upon in order to sort out the confusion. On the evening of the 18th, scouts reported the enemy had crossed the Eure and was appearing on the right flank of the route the army planned to pursue on the morrow. The army went on alert, but when the news proved to be unsubstantiated went back to its camps. The next morning Condé, who had been certain for several days that there would be a battle, waited impatiently for Coligny, who obstinately clung to his conviction that the royal army would not dare to risk a battle because it was inferior in cavalry, and was very late in getting the advance guard on the road so it could pass Condé and begin the day's march in its proper place. Finally, the Huguenots, drums beating, began their march towards Tréon, a village south of Dreux, but the basic carelessness which had characterized the army since Paris continued. No scouts had been left behind during the night to guard the river crossings where the previous evening's false alarms had originated, and when word finally came, about 10 a.m., that the royal army had been discovered drawn up for battle on the right flank of their intended route, no battle plan had been issued to subordinate formations and some of the cavalry were not even wearing their armor.

The unexpected arrival of the royal army on the open plains south of Dreux was itself the product of only a slightly less accidental and contingent string of events and decisions. In the glow of burning villages around Paris which signified the deliverance of the city and the departure of the Huguenots, the queen mother, according to Guise

with great regret, to see thus this war continue, nevertheless, not wanting to allow him [Condé] to carry out his enterprises, immediately dispatched Messieurs de Guise and the Constable and Marshall Saint-André to follow him with all the forces then assembled in Paris, having first warned these lords that for the conduct of these great and important affairs which would present themselves, she thought it impossible to make any better nor more certain choice than they, whom the late King Henry, her husband, had always trusted so much, and whom she knew to be prudent and greatly experienced, and moreover greatly devoted and loyal to the crown, as is their obligation. Drawing confidence from this, she had no difficulty whatsoever in freely committing to their hands all the forces of the King her son and all the power and means she had at her disposal to sustain his estate, in order to diligently pursue and terminate this war, as it was very necessary that it quickly be ended one way or another, being certain that the longer it went on the more new and very damaging problems would appear daily, to the total ruin of the kingdom. For her part, she would continue constantly to pursue a peaceful end, whilst they sought to end the war with arms, without letting pass an opportunity to fight and give battle when the time and the place required it, trusting that with their habitual prudence and virtue, they would take no unnecessary risks, and when the time came that they would report certain victory.[2]

The royal army that marched from Paris on December 11 numbered about 19,000 combatants, superior in overall strength to the Huguenots, but markedly inferior in cavalry (about 2,500 royal cavalry to 4,500 Huguenot horse). This caused

[2] Guise, *Mémoires*, 497.

the Triumvirate to lead the army on a more northerly path roughly parallel to the enemy along very bad roads in less open country where their superiority in infantry could guarantee them safe passage. For several days it was not known exactly what the eventual goal of the Huguenot march was to be, nor if, despite its headstart, the enemy army would move slowly enough to allow themselves to be overtaken. As it became clearer that there was a good chance that the Huguenots might choose to move to the west and north in an attempt to force a passage to Normandy, the leaders of the royal army, who knew they were in a position to intercept the enemy by moving rapidly to the west, reported to Paris that they thought a battle might be imminent within four or five days. According to Castelnau, who arrived in Paris with the dispatch, the Triumvirate, despite their lavish mandate for action, were hesitant to risk a battle against other Frenchmen without more explicit royal permission, a bit of news that the queen mother adroitly deflected by remarking "that she was stunned that the Constable, the duke of Guise, and Saint-André, being good, prudent, and experienced captains, should send for the advice of a woman and a child who were full of regret to see things in such an extreme state as to be reduced to the hazards of a civil battle."[3] And, summoning the king's Huguenot nurse, sarcastically asked: "The time has come that they ask the advice of women on whether or not they should give battle, what is your opinion?"[4] The nurse, it turned out, favored battle, but at a meeting of the royal council later that day it was resolved "that those in charge of the instrument of war should ask for neither advice nor orders from the Court...such that all decisions be left entirely to the wisdom of the leaders of the army, who will do whatever they deem necessary, given the forces under their command."[5]

Armed with this ambiguous support, the army continued its march, but was forced to halt at Mézières, on the east bank of the Eure, on the afternoon of the 18th because it was too late in the day to effect an immediate crossing and because the old constable was suffering from an illness. Only a few miles now separated the royal army from the Huguenot army, which had crossed the Eure, as we noted, at Maintenon on the 17th but had to spend the whole of the 18th in place while the mixup which had left the vanguard behind the battle was sorted out. It was some scouts from the royal army sent across the Eure who had excited the false alarm that temporarily put the Huguenots on alert in the early evening of the 18th.

After several hours' rest, the royal army began to cross the river in silence about midnight, and before dawn on the 19th all of its elements, including the artillery and the baggage trains, had successfully passed over the river without being observed and were planted in line of battle in a strong position to the south of the town of Dreux between the villages of Nuisement and Le Lucate. It was at this place, shortly after daybreak, that scouts reported to the Triumvirate hearing the

[3] Michel de Castelnau, *Les mémoires de Michel de Castelnau* (3 vols., Brussels, 1731), vol. 1, 122.
[4] *Ibid.*
[5] *Ibid.*, 123.

drums of the Protestant army as it approached the village of Imberdais, some two miles to the south (see Figure 21(b)). At a brief council of the army leadership it was resolved to attempt to intercept the enemy and to force it to give battle at a disadvantage by occupying a strong position threatening its line of march. To this end, after instructing the captains of the plan and their places, the army, leaving its baggage and camp at Nuisement, advanced about three-quarters of a mile further south to a position between the villages of Epinay and Blainville, forming a continuous line with the advance guard on the right and the main battle on the left.[6]

Yet even now, with only about a mile of mostly open plain separating them, it was still uncertain if either side would commit itself to battle. Finally alert to the threat that faced them, the Huguenot leaders hurriedly formed a line of battle in front of the village of Imberdais and immediately to the south of the little Maumusset valley, facing the royal army's new position. Andelot was sent ahead to reconnoiter the Catholic position, which he concluded was too strong to attack. So for about two hours the two armies remained standing in sight of one another, and La Noue was probably not far wrong in saying of many of the Frenchmen present:

Each one braced himself for battle, contemplating that the men he saw coming were neither Spanish, English, nor Italians, but French, indeed the bravest of them, among whom could be found his own comrades, relatives and friends, and that within the hour it would be necessary to start killing one another. This added some horror to the scene.[7]

Finally, about noon Coligny, who continued to maintain stubbornly that the Catholic leaders would not risk an advance across terrain that was perfectly suited for the Huguenots' superior cavalry, persuaded Condé to continue the march, and the advance guard began to disengage from the line and march west towards Tréon. But as the movement began some light cavalry and a regiment of reiters from the battle which had ridden forward on the left towards Epinay to screen the march suddenly were cannonaded by a 14-gun battery which had been placed in front of the Catholic vanguard's position and retreated in a panic to the shelter of the Maumusset valley. Condé, concluding that to continue the march was now too risky, recalled the elements of the advance guard that had begun to march off and amidst some confusion the Protestant army was again placed in line of battle, but this time north of the valley, the vanguard on the right and the battle on the left, just in time to begin an attack against the left of the royal army, whose cavalry had begun a precipitous advance on the right of the Protestant line. After nine days of maneuvering, strategic confusion, and last minute hesitations, battle was joined only because both armies finally found themselves in a position where withdrawal was neither unilaterally nor mutually feasible.

[6] De Coynart, vi-viii, plans 1–6, and pages 15–31, gives a good account of the march to the battle and a convincing topographical reconstruction of the battlefield and the initial positions of the armies. His locating of the various contingents generally conforms as well to the contemporary illustrations by Tortorel and Perrissin, see note 8 below.

[7] La Noue, 661.

THE COURSE OF THE BATTLE

But the hesitancy of both sides to actually come to grips with the enemy, which is literally what had to happen for there to be a battle, was the result not so much of caution as of close calculation. Wise military leadership involved taking into account the strategic situation, the composition of the opposing forces, the condition of the army, time and place, terrain, and weather. Such factors could be weighed and measured for relative advantage and disadvantage and even controlled to a certain extent by decisions of when and when not to engage. But the tolerance for risk in these areas had to be fairly low because the uncontrollable risks in battle were inevitably quite high.

As in most of the battles of the epoch the course of the fighting and to a great extent the shape of the outcome of the battle were heavily influenced by the initial tactical dispositions of units. For the battle of Dreux, the nature of these dispositions is known rather exactly, and they are presented diagramatically in Figure 21(b), along with a detailed order of battle, and portrayed in the first of the famous series of six engravings of the course of the battle published in 1570 by Tortorel and Perrissin, which are reproduced in Figure 23.[8] The royal army's battleline extended across a front of slightly more than a mile between the villages of Epinay and Blainville. On the right flank, anchored on Epinay, were the elements of the advance guard, commanded by Guise and Saint-André, first the Spanish infantry, then Guise with his gendarme regiment, followed by a block of veteran French infantry under Martigues, then Saint-André with more cavalry, the regiment of German Landsknecht infantry, and the gendarme regiments of Aumale and Damville. Next to the latter and beginning the battle, under the command of the constable, was the largest unit on the field, the block of Swiss pikemen, abutted by another block of French infantry – *légionnaire* troops from Picardy and Britanny – then a unit of *chevaux-légers* under Sansac, and finally the rest of the gendarmes under Montmorency himself. About the middle and in front of the line occupied by the advance guard was the battery of fourteen guns covered by some detached infantry skirmishers, the so-called *enfants perdues*, and immediately in front of the left flank of the Swiss another battery of eight guns and more skirmishers. The infantry of the battleline was organized in deep formations of ten ranks, but the cavalry seems to have been deployed *en haye*, or in a single rank.

The royal army's position was a strong one, with both flanks protected by villages, though because of the length of the line the constable's gendarmes had been deployed in front of Blainville when the army advanced from its first position near Nuisement earlier in the morning. The interspersing of horse and foot units was a

---

[8] Figures 21b and 22, on the phases of the battle, are derived from the many accounts of the time and from De Coynart's plans as well as the six engravings by J. Tortorel and J. Perrissin which appear in Figure 23: Alfred Franklin, *Les grandes scènes historiques du XVIe siècle. Reproduction en fac-similé du recueil de J. Tortorel et J. Perrissin publié sous la direction de M. Alfred Franklin* (Paris, 1886).

deliberate attempt to minimize the royal army's inferiority in cavalry and take advantage in an unflankable position of the defensive strengths of its numerically superior infantry. The hope, obviously, was to entice the Huguenots to attack a strong defensive position, but the key to holding the position depended on its line of mutually supporting units remaining intact, for besides the villages on either flank the entire battlefield was basically an open plain, sloping gently down to the Protestant position and ideal for cavalry deployment.[9]

The Huguenot army had formed its line about a half mile in front of the left half of the Catholic army, with the battle, under Condé, on the left and the advance guard, under Coligny, on the right. The army was organized in two lines, the most forward of which was made up entirely of cavalry, anchored on its left by two regiments of reiters in column, followed by Condé's gendarme regiment, then two more gendarme regiments, one behind the other, a unit of light cavalry, then a regiment of gendarmes under Coligny and, closing the right flank, two more regiments of reiters in column. The second line contained all the Protestant infantry – a large block of French foot flanked on either side by the two regiments of Landsknechts – and on the extreme right a reserve regiment of German reiters. The small Protestant field gun battery was deployed in front of the French infantry. Like the royal army, the Huguenot infantry regiments were organized in rectangular blocks about ten ranks deep, and the French cavalry in single rank formation; the German reiters, however, were organized in massive columns sixteen ranks deep. From these dispositions it is clear that the Protestants expected their first line of cavalry to bear the brunt of the fighting while the second line, containing infantry in which little confidence was placed, served as an anchor or rallying point for the first line.

It was from these initial positions on a field about a mile wide and half a mile deep, crowded with more than 30,000 men, that the battle began. Once begun, the action was wild, confused, and bloody, but as they later attempted to describe, understand, and explain the battle, participants, eyewitnesses, contemporary chroniclers, and even modern historians all divided the action into a varying number of distinct phases. Guise, for example, distinguished six distinct phases in his after-action report; Coligny's dispatch to Queen Elizabeth divided the battle into three major phases marked by charges; and Tortorel and Perrissin's series of engravings of the battle illustrated four charges and a retreat (Figure 23b–f).[10]

In order to give an overview of the course and outcome of the battle Figure 22 adopts a fourfold schema.[11] In the first phase, lasting about an hour, the Protestant first line threw itself at the left half of the royal army (Figures 22a and 23b). On

---

[9] De Coynart's plans also provide indications of the contour gradients.

[10] Guise, *Mémoires*, 498–500; for Coligny, M.L. Cimber and F. d'Anjou, *Archives curieuses de l'histoire de France* (30 vols., Paris, 1834–41), vol. 5, 76–79; and Tortorel and Perrissin, *op. cit.*

[11] The adoption of these four phases of action seemed to me on balance to best illustrate the overall sequencing of the battle as well as suggest the varied but connected experiences of the participants. But see John Keegan, *The Face of Battle*, 13–77, on the pitfalls of writing battle narrative.

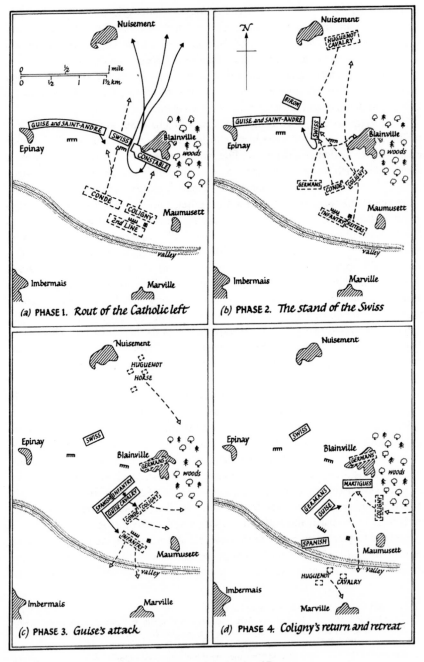

Fig. 22. Phases of the battle of Dreux

Condé's side the Huguenot cavalry launched a series of charges which penetrated through the Swiss phalanx, which was also attacked by Condé's German cavalry, which inflicted a number of casualties with their pistol fire. Coligny's cavalry attacked and routed the constable's cavalry, capturing Montmorency in the process, and bowled over the *légionnaire* formation, which disintegrated in panic. In a very short time the entire left wing of the royal army, with the exception of the Swiss, was fleeing to the rear, hotly pursued by much of the Huguenot cavalry all the way to the baggage train at Nuisement and to the Eure. During this period, with the exception of the cavalry under Aumale and Damville, who tried to stop the attack on the Swiss but were themselves routed by part of the reiters, the forces under Guise and Saint-André remained in place.

The inactivity of the right wing of the royal army, with the exception of a force of cavalry under Biron placed at the rear of the line, facing towards Nuisement, in order to protect those men and riders from the constable's side of the battlefield who had managed to rally to the advance guard and to protect the forces near Epinay from attacks by returning Huguenot horse, continued during the second phase of the battle, which also lasted about one hour (Figures 22b and 23c). Virtually the entire burden of the royal army's fighting during this period was borne by the Swiss, who were attacked again by the cavalry returning from Nuisement. Then the leftmost Landsknecht regiment of the Huguenot's second line opportunistically advanced against the Swiss, but were charged so ferociously by them that after little fighting the Germans panicked and retreated into the village of Blainville, where they barricaded themselves in a large courtyard. The Swiss then tried to recapture the artillery battery to their front, which precipitated another series of cavalry charges against them, including the last of the Huguenot's uncommitted gendarmerie. These final cavalry assaults broke the Swiss formation into small groups who retreated, still fighting and attempting to rally, towards the rest of the royal army at Epinay. Seeing the Swiss broken up, most of the German cavalry, including the reserve regiment in the Huguenot second line, shouted "Victory!" and streamed north across the plain to Nuisement to take part in the ongoing looting of the Catholic baggage train. Condé and Coligny, who knew that a major portion of the Catholic army remained untouched, desperately attempted to rally their cavalry, which was dispersed on blown horses all over the plain, south of Blainville. The remaining French and German infantry in their second line were now completely bereft of cavalry support.

At this critical moment, about two hours after the fighting had begun, Guise and Saint-André, who from their position at Epinay were able to see the entire battlefield and who had observed the movement of much of the enemy's cavalry to the looting at Nuisement, decided to advance (Figures 22c and 23d). On they came, with a front line composed of their cavalry and a second line of infantry, Germans in the center and Spanish and French on the right and left, respectively. This advance seemed at first to sweep the Huguenots from the field. A unit of gendarmes

(a)

(b)

Fig. 23. Engravings of the battle of Dreux by Torterel and Perrissin (1570), from Franklin, A. *Les grandes scènes historiques du XVIe siècle* (Paris, 1886)

(c)

(d)

(e)

(f)

supported by the Spanish attacked the shaky Huguenot French infantry, who were poorly armed and had few pikemen. As the Spanish discharged several volleys and lowered their pikes to charge, the rear ranks of the Huguenot formation broke and ran, leaving the front ranks to be slaughtered. The Huguenots' sole remaining Landsknecht regiment, having observed the Catholic advance, abandoned its position without striking a blow and retired as rapidly as it could across the little valley to its rear. After some hard fighting the tired and disorganized Huguenot cavalry retreated as best it could through the woods on the eastern side of the battlefield but in this withdrawal Condé was captured. Suddenly, with the Protestant infantry in flight to the south and the Huguenot cavalry withdrawn to the east, it seemed, as dusk was coming on, that the field belonged entirely to the royal army, and Guise now approached Blainville to negotiate the surrender of the Landsknecht regiment barricaded there.

But behind the woods and out of sight of the Catholics Coligny had managed to rally around a thousand French and German horsemen and hurriedly organizing them into a line re-emerged from the woods to begin the final phase of the battle, which was to last about half an hour (Figures 22d and 23e-f). The Catholics initially thought that this advance from the woods was of enemy troops who wished to surrender, and the few hundred remaining disorganized Catholic cavalry were now outnumbered by the returning Huguenot horse. The fortune of battle might have shifted again to the Huguenots had Guise not ordered up his sole remaining reliable reserve, the veteran French infantry under Martigues (the German foot regiment which had not yet fought was considered unreliable), who formed square directly to the south of Blainville and began to pour arquebus fire into the approaching enemy cavalry. The Huguenot cavalry, having used up their lances, could find no break in the formation through which to attack. At this point, some four hours after the beginning of the battle, with darkness making it increasingly impossible to distinguish friend from foe, Coligny ordered a retreat and the Huguenot cavalry withdrew to the south from the battlefield, followed for a few minutes, but not attacked, by royal troops, who then returned to the field.

THE COST OF BATTLE

For some time in the immediate aftermath of the battle there was a question of who the victor was. The reiter escort which had hustled the captured constable to Orléans proclaimed a great victory for the Huguenots while the Catholics who fled the field in the first hour of battle, some of whom reached Paris by the next day, spread news of a disastrous defeat for the royal army.[12] Over the next few days, as

---

[12] Bèze, vol. 2, 312–13; Vieilleville, *Mémoires*, Michaud and Poujoulat, vol. 9, 322, and 323–25, which embellishes Vieilleville's role but reports the bare facts correctly enough; *CDM*, vol. 1, 455 and note 1, 454, which quotes a misinformation letter by Francis Hotman; A.H. Layard, "Dispatches of Michele Suriano and of Marc' Antonio Barbaro," *Publications of the Huguenot Society of London*, 6 (Lymington, 1891), 69–70; and Paschal, *1562*, 117.

more accurate reports came in, it became clear that the royal army had won a great though costly victory. As we have seen, Coligny and the Huguenots promptly disputed Catholic claims of victory on the grounds that they had killed enough Catholic leaders and gentlemen cavalry to cripple the royal army. They also maintained that the Catholics could not claim to have driven them from the field because they retired in good order, claiming that they had reappeared the next day to renew the battle but that the Catholics had refused to re-engage.

In fact, by all the conventional measures of success the royal army was victorious: it had caused the enemy to retreat, had slept on the battlefield, captured the enemy's artillery, and many standards. As La Noue judiciously analyzed the situation:

Some were of the opinion that there was no defeat because the losers had not been routed. But they were fooling themselves, for he who wins the field of battle, captures the artillery and the standards of the infantry, has enough evidence of victory. Nevertheless, it can be said that the victory was not total, as when a rout has occurred.[13]

Formal claims to victory aside, the consequences of the battle in terms of the human costs of the fighting were appalling on both sides. All the immediate reports of the battle and the earliest historical treatments agreed that the battle was one of the longest, most obstinately contested, and bloody battles of the century. The fighting had not been continuous, for as La Noue recalled:

It nevertheless must not be imagined that the fighting went on continuously during this time, because there were several lulls in the battle; and then there were re-engagements by smaller charges and sometimes by larger charges, which carried off the best men and which continued into the dark of night. There was certainly tremendous animosity on both sides, of which the number of deaths provides adequate evidence...Most of the dead were killed fighting and not in flight.[14]

The battle had ended in the darkness of a night which, the Huguenot trooper Jean de Mergey recalled, "was the coldest I ever felt."[15] Small groups of men from both armies still wandered over the battlefield in the dark trying to regain their units and avoid capture. Dead and injured men, victims of arquebus or pistol ball, lance or pike blow, sword thrusts, or simply falls and spills, littered the ground. Most of the unwounded survivors sought shelter, as did Guise with his prisoner Condé, in the surrounding villages and hamlets or even in the town of Dreux itself. But others, including local civilians, camp followers, and probably many ordinary soldiers, were already hard at work stripping and looting the bodies which covered the field.[16]

---

[13] La Noue, 666.
[14] *Ibid.*, 664.
[15] Jean de Mergey, *Mémoires*; Michaud and Poujoulat, vol. 9, 570–71.
[16] The sixth and final engraving of the battle by Tortorel and Perrissin, entitled "La retraite de la bataille de Dreux," shows the beginning of the looting of the battlefield and of the dead by men, women, and children even before the end of the battle.

The following morning Guise ordered some of the cannons left on the field to be fired in order to recall his dispersed troops. The Swiss lieutenant, Hans Krieg, described the scene starkly in a letter to his father:

When the battle continued into the night, as you can well imagine, neither could find or recognize the other, for it was quite dark when we withdrew. In the morning, however, together with others from all areas we went out to search for our own. Thus we found on the battlefield our colonel Gebhard Tammann from Lucerne ... [and other officers] ... all completely naked and undressed. Then we loaded them up and transported them into the above-mentioned city [Dreux], and buried them in the cathedral there, as is befitting and due a knight. May God have mercy on their souls. Then, when we compared notes, we found that many and the majority of our officers had been lost and severely wounded ... The number of deceased is not yet clear, but is estimated at 4,000 on both sides.[17]

Guise ordered the naked bodies laid out for identification and the wounded who had survived the night were removed to shelter in in the town of Dreux while the civilian population was set to digging a mass grave in the hardened ground for the cadavers.[18] The famous surgeon Ambroise Paré, dispatched to the army by the king to care for a wounded grandee, described:

The day after I arrived, I wanted to go to the field where the battle had been fought to see the dead bodies. I observed for a good league all around the ground completely covered: the estimate was of twenty-five thousand dead or more, all dispatched in less than two hours ... While I was at Dreux, I visited and treated a great number of gentlemen and poor soldiers, and among others, many Swiss captains. I treated fourteen of them in a single room, all wounded by pistol shots and by other diabolical firearms, and not one of the fourteen died ... Surgeons came from Paris, who attended as best they could to the wounded ... and I returned to Paris, where I met up with many of the wounded gentlemen who had retired there after the battle to have their wounds dressed.[19]

While we do not know exactly how many dead and wounded there were, Paré's estimate was much too high and Lieutenant Krieg's probably too low. Castelnau claims to have heard a report to Guise that 8–9,000 dead lay on the field, but notes that others present estimated 6,000 bodies.[20] The account in the Protestant *Histoire ecclésiastique*, almost surely contributed by Theodore de Bèze himself, who was an eyewitness, claimed that apart from the wounded there were 5,000 dead bodies on the field.[21] Other estimates ranged from 5-6,000 to more than 10,000 combined dead for both armies.[22] When we discount some of the casualties as belonging to the

---

[17] Hans Krieg, letter in Segesser, vol. 1., 625–26, note 1.

[18] Bèze, vol. 2, 314; Castelnau, vol. 1, 129; Throckmorton's January 3, 1563, dispatch, PRO/SP 70/48, fol. 25v.

[19] Ambroise Paré, *Oeuvres complètes* (Reprint of 1840–41 edition, Geneva, 1970), vol. 3, 724.

[20] Castelnau, vol. 1, 128.

[21] Bèze, vol. 2, 305.

[22] *CDM*, vol. 1, 454, claimed 5–6,000 dead. A letter of Charles IX, *ibid.*, 453, note 1, boasts of 9–10,000 Protestant dead; Guise, *Mémoires*, 500, reported 8,000 Protestant casualties; a report in French intended for the English court, PRO/SP 70/47, fol. 31, claims 8,000 Catholics killed; in Segesser, vol.

camp followers of the looted baggage train, and weigh the losses reported for individual contingents, we can arrive at a conservative estimate of 6,000 deaths during the battle and a much smaller number of wounded, for most of the wounded who could not have made their way to shelter (some of whom had been lying on the field since shortly after noon), and who along with the dead would have been stripped of their garments by the looters, must have quickly succumbed to shock in the cold of the bitter winter night.

At a review of the Protestant army held several days later, only 1,000 French and 900 Landsknechts remained (out of an original total of perhaps 8,500 infantry), and just over 700 out of 4,500 cavalry.[23] Not all the missing, of course, were casualties. Some 1,500 Landsknechts had surrendered to Guise, there were at least 200 prisoners in Catholic hands, and several hundred reiters had left the battle to escort the captive constable to Orléans.[24] Many more men had not yet struggled back to camp from their flight or their looting. The brunt of the Protestant casualties had been borne by the French infantry, who, according to one of the Spanish soldiers attacking them, "fled the field. We pursued them and inflicted a great carnage, killing them as if they had been sheep."[25] And, according to another Spaniard, "without losing more than six men, we broke them and killed three thousand of them."[26] De Thou wrote that the Huguenots admitted after the battle to 3,000 casualties not counting the captured Landsknechts.[27] This would put total losses at around 4,500 men, at least a third of their original number, including more than half of their infantry.

Casualties in the royal army may have been even heavier. Probably over a thousand Swiss were dead or wounded, including, as we have seen, their colonel and most of their officers. All but one of the cavalry commanders of the army had been killed, wounded, captured, or routed by the end of the battle, and the admission of a total loss of 800 gentlemen later reported by Throckmorton was probably not an exaggeration. Many more of the cavalry may have been wounded as they routed from the field and very few of the French *légionnaire* infantry regiment must have survived death or wounds in a mile-long chase by the Huguenot cavalry (or, according to one report, drowning from a panicked attempt to avoid pursuit by swimming across the Eure river).[28] In all, somewhere around 3,000 infantry casualties and, counting prisoners, more than a thousand cavalry casualties were probably

1, 623, Pfyffer reports 6,000 enemy dead; Hernando do Campo, one of the Spanish officers present, in Cimber and d'Anjou, vol. 5, 92, notes 4,000 enemy and 1,000 friendly dead; Layard, "Dispatches", 71, claims 10,000 total dead; and La Noue, 664, more than 7,000 total.

[23] Bèze, vol. 2, 306.
[24] *Ibid.*, 306 counts 1,400 Germans taken prisoner; Throckmorton counted 2,000, 500 of whom were retained for the king's service and the other 1,500 disarmed and sent on their way back to Germany: Throckmorton PRO/SP 70/48, fol. 26r.
[25] Hernando do Campo, Cimber and d'Anjou, vol. 5, 92.
[26] Juan de Ayala, *ibid.*, 89.
[27] Jacques-Auguste De Thou, *Histoire universelle* (16 vols., Paris, 1734), vol. 4, 485.
[28] PRO/SP 70/48, fols. 192–93.

sustained by the royal army, or somewhere between a fifth and a quarter of their total original numbers. For the battle as a whole then, some 9-10,000 of the slightly more than 30,000 soldiers who had stood in line gazing at each other that morning had become casualties of some kind by the end of the day, and probably one in five of those who had begun the battle had met their death in it.

THE LESSONS OF BATTLE

In the aftermath of the chaos of battle there was much for the new commander of the royal army to arrange, and the captive English ambassador Throckmorton has left an account of an impressively busy army headquarters, with Guise involved in constant meetings, consultations, and interviews. Besides seeing to the disposal of the dead and the care of the wounded, there was thanks to be given at a Christmas service in Dreux cathedral where the captured enemy banners were offered up before being sent on their way as trophies to the court.[29] There was also an accounting to be made and a narrative truth to be fashioned when Guise and the principal surviving noblemen and officers of the army rode to nearby Rambouillet shortly after Christmas to be received by a grateful but wary court. Castelnau, who observed the scene, is worth quoting at length.

Their majesties, with all their court, made their way to Rambouillet, where the duke was ordered to join them. He came accompanied by most of the lords, gentlemen, and captains of his army. After the royal dinner, as Guise was in the hall to pay respects to their majesties, he gave them a public account, in the form of an address, of all that had happened in this battle, beginning with the regret he had to have seen so many brave Frenchmen, princes, lords, and gentlemen oppose each other at the expense of their blood and their lives in a battle the likes of which would have been sufficient to make some fine conquest against foreign enemies. Then, he went on at length about the wisdom of the constable, leader and general of the army, as much for his having embattled the army to take advantage of all the natural features of the place, as for having so effectively urged each and every one on to combat that even the least courageous to whom he showed the way was resolved to do well there, presenting them with the example of his accustomed valor all over the field. After this, he spoke of all the charges made by the prince of Condé, to whom he gave all the praises that could be given to the commander of an army who refused to order anything that he would not courageously risk himself. He told of how, after several charges, both [the constable and Condé] were finally taken prisoner, and many brave lords, captains, and gentlemen were killed or wounded. He also praised the Swiss very fully. He then digressed to speak of the misfortune which had come to the marshal de Saint-André, commander and leader of the advance guard, who, after having been captured, was killed by a gentleman who held a grudge against him.

He did not forget the admiral, who was compelled to quit the field, and he strongly praised his own brother, the Duke d'Aumale, who had been thrown to the ground and had broken his shoulder; as well as the grand prior, his other brother, who had been extremely

[29] *Ibid.*, fol. 25v.

diligent, staying in the saddle for two or three days before the battle, always in front, on the flanks, or to the rear of the enemy, where he conducted himself as valiantly as could have been desired. He gave a similarly flattering account of Damville and Martigues, but he h   a   r   d   l   y mentioned the *Landsknechts* at all, for they had done so little on either side. He spoke modestly of himself as just a simple captain and private individual in the army, with his company and a few gentlemen friends, who had honored him by following and accompanying him on that day, where, after the capture of the said constable, and the death of the marshal de Saint-André, the rest of the army had done him the honor of requesting that he command them. And, having joined them, and taken their advice, they had done such that with the will of God, the victory and the battlefield remained to them, and it is still held until they discover what it would please the king to command them.

And after this discourse, he presented to his Majesty a large number of those who had accompanied him to Rambouillet, and the king, thanking him for the good service which he had performed that day, ordered and requested that he accept the command of the army during the absence of the constable, and thus he was made lieutenant general and great honor was rendered to him by the soldiers as well as those of the court.[30]

Missing from this account of Guise's extremely politic, generous, and yet calculating public rhetoric, however, was the fact that despite the great slaughter and valor which had characterized the battle itself, it had proved impossible to quickly follow it up and exploit the victory. The day after the battle Guise had written to Gonnor: "I wish, for the service of the King, that I could see you here for half an hour so that you might pass on to the Queen the many things I have in mind which seem to me of importance if we are to take advantage of this victory."[31] But whatever measures Guise had in mind, pursuit of the defeated enemy army was not one of them. The remnants of the Protestant army were allowed to withdraw to Orléans without opposition, where the surviving infantry provided a more than adequate garrison for the city. The Huguenot and German cavalry, while sorely tested in the battle, had incurred relatively few fatalities. Within weeks Coligny had reorganized and refreshed them and launched a raid into lower Normandy which quickly restored the most important towns of that area to Protestant control.

For the royal army the victory had proved as costly and disorganizing as a defeat. Though some components of the army had suffered few casualties, like the Spanish, or the Landsknecht regiment which never even came to blows with the enemy, others had sustained heavy damage. The Swiss had suffered terribly and the regiment of French provincial *légionnaires* had largely been annihilated. There may have also been critical losses of men, horses, and equipment from the looted trains. Most important, however, most of the higher leadership of the army was dead, wounded, or captured, and the heavy cavalry, as we have seen, so crippled with losses that Guise had to authorize the creation of seventeen new companies of

---

[30] Castelnau, vol. 1, 129–30.
[31] Guise, *Mémoires*, 500.

gendarmes, a process that could not be completed overnight. The army had to be rested, refitted, and nursed back to health before it could be again deployed for any serious operations of war. Furthermore, less than 24 hours after the victory Guise was writing letters trying to arrange for funds to pay his troops. Within weeks he was forced to undertake a reduction of the French infantry and to busy himself trying to procure basic items like stockings and shoes for them, while also trying to cope with the disorders caused by the Spanish troops, whose pay was stranded just north of the Spanish border at Bayonne.[32] To top it all off, the artillery of the train was mired on roads made impassable by winter rains. The high drama of battle, in other words, was quickly succeeded by the grinding realities of the army's normal administrative, logistical, and disciplinary problems. In all, it would take over seven weeks before the army could overcome its victory enough to begin the siege of Orléans.

But if the main direct military consequence of the victory was simply an opportunity to organize a siege of Orléans unobstructed by the now diminished and dispersed Huguenot field army, the most important long-term consequences of the battle of Dreux were to be found in the intellectual realm, that is, in the lessons contemporaries drew, or thought they could draw, from the battle. For the crown and its principal military leaders the narrow margin of victory – Dreux after all could almost as easily have been a Huguenot victory – merely strengthened the appreciation of the high and uncontrollable risks involved in committing the main defensive instrument of the realm to the chance and chaos of a pitched battle. The carnage of the battle was also disquieting, though not because the elites mourned the deaths of so many ordinary footsoldiers. It was the loss of so many great nobles and hundreds of gentlemen members of the gendarmerie that was shocking, and, as we have previously seen, fear of the possibility of the destruction of the nobility was to become a compelling and overarching component of strategic decisions and reluctance to risk them in battle as the wars continued.

Yet at the same time, on the psychological level, the mutual slaughter of Frenchmen in the first great battle of the civil wars must have swept aside any remaining hesitations to the normalization of the killing of each other by the military elite of France. Here Guise's harangue of the court at Rambouillet clearly reflects on balance the construction of a new rhetorical framework posited on the emphasis of the normalcy of heroic action by friend and foe alike, rather than the absurdity and tragedy of internecine warfare.

There were also other lesser lessons drawn from Dreux that would influence the royal army in the future. The heroic resistance of the Swiss pikemen solidified the crown's faith in its use of large numbers of such troops even though, as we have seen, their lack of firearms and extremely limited tactical uses made them increasingly less useful as the regime of siege warfare evolved. Conversely, the lamentable

---

[32] *Ibid.*, 502.

showing of the Landsknechts ("It is certain that not in fifty years had there entered into France such cowardly men as they, even though they gave the best appearance in the world," according to the *Histoire ecclésiastique*)[33] must have influenced the crown against them, for almost no Landsknechts were to be employed by the crown in the rest of the early wars despite the fact that they were, as Biron reminds us, much better suited than the Swiss for the types of duties called for from infantry during the civil wars.

Contemporaries also did not come to the conclusion of modern historians that by the mid-sixteenth century heavy cavalry had been eclipsed by the rise of firearms and mass infantry armies. In fact, heavy cavalry had ruled the field at Dreux and its mobility and shock power had been decisive for the outcome of the battle. And the chief victim of the new firearm technology had not been the cavalry but the Swiss pike phalanx, whose ranks were mown down by the pistol fusillades of the deep German reiter formations. Even the heavy lance, the weapon *par excellence* of the essentially medieval knights on both sides, had shown its mettle, enabling the Huguenot *hommes d'armes* to penetrate and ride through the block of Swiss pikemen and, when their lances were used up, preventing them from successfully breaking into the formation of veteran French infantry under Martigues near the end of the battle.[34] To contemporaries the lessons must have seemed rather obvious: to increase as much as possible the number of heavy cavalry – an effort, we have seen, wholeheartedly embarked on by the crown in the second and third civil wars – and to hire as many as possible of the mercenary German reiters, a lesson taken to heart by both sides.

The battle of Dreux, then, besides illustrating some general points about the nature of battles during the epoch – the difficulties of arranging battles, the chaos and risk of the battlefield, the terrible human carnage which even the most primitive of weapons can wreak in a very short time, the costs of victory as well as defeat, and the lack of decisive results – can also be seen to have had a not unimportant influence on the future course of the wars and on the nature of the royal army itself. It simultaneously removed the last psychological barriers to the mutual slaughter of French military elites while proving that the cost of such actions was potentially unbearable. Lessons drawn from the event, particularly about the risks involved in battle, would continue to influence the strategic decisions of the crown and the army leadership throughout the period of civil war covered by this study. And the actual performance of the various components of the army led to conclusions about the high military value of certain types of extremely expensive troops – the Swiss, the gendarmes, and the reiters – which would continue to shape the composition and therefore the strategic and tactical usefulness of the royal army, as well as its

---

[33] Bèze, vol. 2, 299.
[34] All of the Swiss casualties for which the exact cause of death is mentioned are identified as being killed by small arms fire: Segesser, vol. 1, 621, and 625–26, note 1. Bèze, vol. 2, 303, mentions the tactical effect of the exhaustion of the Protestants' lances.

8

The defense of Chartres, 1567–68

"NO MORE FAITHFUL AND BETTER SUBJECTS THAN THEY"

Sire, the leaders of this city of Chartres have been advised to send their deputies to you in order to recount to Your Majesty all that was done and all that occurred during the siege of the said city. I very much wanted to have this letter accompany the deputies to serve as testimony to the efforts they have made since I arrived here for your service, of which I will not be silent, but will declare to Your Majesty that I found them to be so faithful and devoted to all that concerned your interest that all I commanded them they promptly carried out, and I do think, Sire, that you have under your authority no more faithful and better subjects than they.[1]

So wrote Nicolas des Essars, sieur de Linières, military governor of Chartres, to Charles IX on March 30, 1568, a few days after the formal promulgation of the peace treaty which had brought the second and shortest of the civil wars to an end. Linières' effusive praise was in part self-congratulatory. He, after all, had just led the people of Chartres and a portion of the royal army in a successful two-week-long defense of the city.[2] His, and their, staunch resistance to Condé's army had served royal purposes well, for though the crown had agreed to peace terms out of fear of losing the city, the Huguenots' lack of success in the siege had been equally influential in their decision to conclude an uneasy peace. Given the importance the defense of the city had played in bringing the war to an end, Linières was therefore justified in emphasizing to the king the loyalty, obedience, dutifulness, and co-operation of the townspeople. Yet, as we shall see, the relationship between Chartres, its military governors, and the soldiers of the royal army who defended it, as well as the city's reactions to the burdens placed on it by the war, were a great deal more complicated and somewhat less thoroughgoingly amicable than Linières' missive might suggest. An analysis of the interaction of the town of Chartres with the crown's military forces during the second civil war, in fact, illuminates a number of points about the relationship of the royal army to the localities in or near which

[1] BN Mss. Fr. 15,545, fol. 106.
[2] The fundamental and indispensable source for the siege is the "Etat des depenses faites par la ville de Chartres, pendant les troubles et pendant le siège de ladite ville (1er Octobre 1567 – 18 April 1568)," ed. by Lucien Merlet, *Bulletin historique et philologique du comité des travaux historiques et scientifiques* (1840), 394–438, hereafter abbreviated as *EDC*.

it operated as well as sheds light on the types and magnitude of support typically required or demanded by royal forces in their operations of war.

The army depended heavily on regular requisitions of money, goods, and services from the towns of the areas in or near its operations. Units on their way to and from the army had to be provided for and the contingents of troops which were routinely dispatched as garrisons to towns and cities with strategic value along its line of march and communications also had to be supported. When the army as a whole passed by or stopped for a while the demand for such resources could be quite enormous. Towns near to the war zone and their officials naturally sought to escape such burdens as much as possible and the correspondence of the times is replete with complaints and pleading about the presence and expense of the soldiery and the logistical and financial demands of commanders. Of course much more than simply the financial and economic burdens of supporting military operations was at stake. What was also endangered was the independence and autonomy of municipalities, for the presence of royal military commanders and troops constituted a direct challenge to the political power of ruling groups as well as an unspoken but omnipresent threat of physical coercion, violence, and disorders. Yet as strong as the imperative was for towns to avoid as much as possible any entanglement with formal military operations and their associated demands, it must also have been clear that to be conquered by the enemy was an incalculably worse fate than the cost of supporting the royal army in its defense of localities. Town leaders had to walk a fine line between reducing or avoiding altogether the burden of defending themselves and compromising their town's ability to successfully defend itself when real danger threatened. The royal army, after all, was the chief defensive force of the realm, and if the approach of danger tended in fact to reduce resistance to its presence the actual arrival of the Huguenot army quickly removed any basis at all for opposing the ascendancy of military over civil authority. Towns therefore alternated between alert and alarm at the enemy's approach and relaxation of tension as the armies moved away, between constant maneuvering to avoid the expenditure of scarce resources on threats that might never materialize and constant calculation of the odds of possible dangerous outcomes if the costs of cooperation were not accepted. The struggle to balance the pressing needs of the army and the military authorities against local interests and welfare marked the interaction of the royal army with loyal towns and cities in each and every one of its campaigns and profoundly shaped the environment within which the wars of the period were waged.

Such considerations, however, may not have clouded the minds of the Chartrain delegation to the court, on whose behalf Linières had written to the king, for their purpose was more singleminded than simply "to recount to Your Majesty all that was done and all that occurred during the siege of the said city." The deputies of the town traveled to Paris, in fact, to complain of the financial obligations their municipality had been forced to incur during the war and especially during the recently lifted siege, and to seek the king's permission to levy a tax on the town's inhabitants to pay off these debts. As the preamble to the detailed inventory of the costs of the war to the municipality which later was to serve as the basis of the tax assessment explained:

The inhabitants of the city of Chartres, seeing the stirring of the enemies of the kingdom, began to keep themselves on alert, to maintain a watch, and to strengthen themselves from their own resources as best they could. Nevertheless, because their strength and forces were not sufficient to the task, they were forced to raise a sum of money from among themselves for the pay and maintenance of four companies of soldiers, for repairing the ramparts of the said city, and for tending to its affairs. In addition to having to endure the passage of several companies of foot and horse, to whom they were compelled to provide all sorts of food and munitions, they sustained several garrisons, and survived a violent siege in the course of which the peace treaty was signed. In all these things the said city suffered an incalculable expense; and, to cover these costs, they agreed to levy on themselves sums of money and even foodstuffs and supplies in kind, with promise of reimbursement and restitution to those who advanced them. And thus did the governors, council members, and other principal officers of the city obligate themselves to compensate these citizens, and thus are they daily pursued for the said restitution. Unable to satisfy these claims, they went back to see the king, whose good pleasure it was to grant them the authority to assess, distribute, and raise money equal to the loans they made for the above purposes, to the end that from them, reimbursement can be made either in money or in kind. To this purpose, the said lord ordered the councilors to submit a statement of expenditures to be examined and validated by the commissioner deputized for this task. Following this command, the said councilmen prepared this present statement containing the expenditures made by them.[3]

The survival of this *état* of expenditures permits us to analyze the interplay between the city of Chartres and the royal army during the second civil war in great depth and to illustrate with some precision exactly what types of burdens local communities had to bear in order to support the military forces which defended them. The *état* itself is a remarkable document. It contains thirty-four chapters and 529 individual entries of expenditures and costs, from candles used in the countermines to the provision of food and drink for the governor's table; from materials used in the defense of the breach to the money paid to messengers and spies, the townspeople who worked on, and the soldiers who manned the defenses; from the cost of erecting a new scaffold and burying the dead to that of providing more than 600,000 loaves of bread to royal troops over the course of the war. No item was too small to be included, and from the chapter titles and the descriptive information that accompanies many of the individual entries (such as the names of individuals and the identification of places and moments), it is possible to reconstruct in detail the milieu of events and decisions which generated the entries embodied in the inventory itself.[4] But before proceeding to a closer examination of the intertwined

---

[3] *EDC*, 396.
[4] Each chapter in the *EDC* is headed by a descriptive title which identifies specific events or categories of expense and sometimes the date or period over which the expenses occurred. Within chapters individual entries, which are also sometimes dated, identify the person, item, or quantity involved and

experiences of the royal army and Chartres during the second civil war, it is important to recount briefly the overall flow of principal strategic events which created and influenced the interactions of army and city.

"IN ALL THINGS ENEMIES OF SOLDIERS"

Following their failed attempt to capture the king at Meaux in late September of 1567, the Huguenot leaders decided to take advantage of the initiative they had seized to mount a blockade of Paris that was maintained for more than a month, though not very effectively, as contingents from all over the kingdom for both armies arrived in the region of the capital. On November 10 the constable led the royal army out of Paris to fight the heavily outnumbered Huguenots in the battle of Saint-Denis. This clash and the growing numerical superiority of the royal army caused the Protestants to move south, to near Melun, on the Seine, where their rear was protected by Orléans, which had fallen to them again as in the first civil war. In late November the royal army, now under Anjou's command, left Paris and marched to Nemours, from which it launched its two-week pursuit of the Huguenot army across Champagne, missing an opportunity to bring it to battle at Notre-Dame-de-L'Epine, near Châlons-sur-Marne. In mid-January, 1568, the Huguenots re-entered France with a large and formidable force of German mercenaries. As we have explained elsewhere, the crown and the army leadership decided not to risk a battle and instead to adopt a defensive posture, hoping that the enemy army would break up of its own accord from lack of pay and the winter elements. But Condé and Coligny managed to keep their force together and marched to Orléans, where in late February they joined a strong contingent from the south which had already relieved a desultory royal siege of Orléans and forced the surrender of Beaugency and Blois. With the bulk of the royal army camped in the faubourgs of Paris and obviously unwilling to fight, Condé decided to strike a damaging blow to the Catholic cause by rewarding his unpaid troops with Chartres, a rich urban prize of about 8,000 inhabitants located in the heart of the agriculturally prosperous Beauce.[5] The Huguenots reached Chartres at the end of February and while part of their army functioned as a blocking force to the east, towards Paris, the rest, about 9,000 men, surrounded the city and used their small artillery train of nine guns (only five of which were the siege-worthy cannons) to pound a breach in the northern wall near the Drouaise gate, launching a general assault on March 7.[6]

---

give it a monetary value. In aggregate the document identifies several thousand pieces of information. In addition the editor of the document, Merlet, provides several helpful identifying notes.

[5] Jean Favier, *The World of Chartres* (New York, 1990), 18, 26; Lehr, 49.

[6] For a detailed narrative of the defense of the city see Henri Lehr, "Le siège de Chartres en 1568," chapter 2 of *La Reform et les Eglises Reforméesa dans le département actuel d'Eure-et-loire (1523–1911)* (Chartres, 1912), *passim*.

But Linières, who had been appointed governor in mid-February, and who had entered the town with some 4,000 royal troops at the last moment before it was surrounded, mounted a very active defense with the aid of the townspeople which threw back the assault on the breach, and successfully sealed it off with strong inner fortifications. Though Condé changed the site of his battery, the fight was out of the Huguenots, who were being steadily weakened by mass desertions, and a truce was declared on March 13. By the 17th Linières could report to the king that the Protestants had withdrawn and on March 24 peace was proclaimed.[7]

Thanks to Linières's leadership, the troops of the royal army, and the efforts of the townspeople, Chartres had survived. But as dramatic as the two weeks of fighting may have been, the interaction of the royal army and Chartres during the second civil war had not been limited to the siege itself. For the people of Chartres, the experience of civil war was directly related primarily to the presence of troops in the city itself or in passage through the neighborhood whether or not there was any fighting, and even when the main armies were hundreds of miles away. Figure 24, which identifies the number of companies of royal troops stationed at Chartres or passing by the city on a week by week basis between October, 1567, and April, 1568, provides a history of this presence over the course of the entire second civil war.[8] It divides these forces, as the Chartrains themselves did, into three main categories of troops: the companies of French infantry raised at the expense of the city to serve as the town's local garrison under the command of the royal governor, the columns of royal troops who passed by the city on their way to or from the main army and for whom the city was required to provide *étapes*, or supplies of various kinds, and royal troops in garrison, primarily those who entered the city with Linières and served as its defenders during and immediately after the siege. As can be seen, there was both a constant presence and episodic passages of troops at Chartres throughout the war. When war broke out, besides the cavalry company of Adrien de Gallot, sieur of Fontaine-la-Guyon, who was named its governor on September 29, the city contained no regular troops, and had to depend for its security entirely on six companies of bourgeois militiamen, each of one hundred men. When word came that Orléans had fallen and that Huguenot forces were operating in the area the *échevins* concluded that their own troops were not adequate to the situation and petitioned the crown, probably at the urging and certainly with the knowledge of the governor, to be allowed to raise some companies of regular troops at their own expense. A royal letter of October 17 granted permission to support a garrison of four companies of 300 men each under the command of Fontaine-la-Guyon.[9] But here began a long-running dispute between the the town and its

---

[7] BN Mss. Fr. 15,545, fol. 178.

[8] *EDC passim*, but especially 396–402 for the garrisons and *étapes* and 403–10 for the details of the distribution of food rationing during the siege, which identify all the infantry and cavalry companies in the city.

[9] *EDC*, 396 and note 1. A guide to the chronology of much of the struggle between governor and town, and town and garrisons, is provided by the payments made to various couriers and deputies who sped

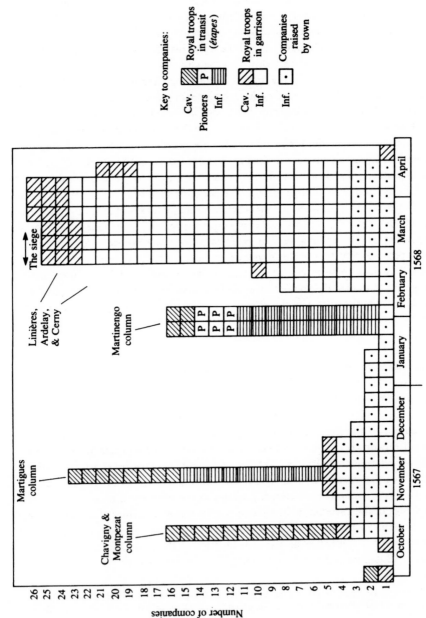

Fig. 24. Weekly tally of troops present or in transit at Chartres during the second civil war, 1567–68

governor over military affairs. Though money had been advanced to the captains who were to recruit and organize the companies, the town also had immediately asked for permission to reduce their size to 200 men each, an action which was apparently resisted by the governor, for on October 20 the town ceased to deliver the complimentary crocks of wine that Fontaine-la-Guyon had been receiving daily since his arrival in the city.[10] But the reduction in size of the companies was approved by the king on October 24, their first musters took place on October 26, and throughout November and early December, while the main armies continued to operate near Paris, only a few days' march away, the town dutifully supported the companies (though the *échevins* managed to replace the royal paymasters with officials of their own choosing), which mustered somewhere between six and seven hundred men.[11] When the main armies moved away to the east during late December the *échevins* promptly sought royal permission to disband two of the companies. The governor again opposed this and complained to the king about the meddling of the town in military affairs. In the end the royal council, while admonishing both parties to patch up their quarrel, ordered the governor to reduce the garrison, and by mid-January, with the Huguenot army in fact beyond the kingdom's eastern border, the garrison was even further reduced to a single company and a small 14-man bodyguard for the governor.[12] But in late January, as the Huguenot column from the south was approaching Orléans, and Condé's army re-entered France, a new dispute over troops erupted, this time provoked by the arrival of a regiment of French infantry under Count Sarra de Martinengo, an Italian soldier of fortune in the royal service.

Martinengo's men represented the third major contingent of troops passing by Chartres since the beginning of the war for whom the city had been ordered to organize an *étape*. Chartres sat on one of the main routes to Paris from the south and the west, and once during October and once again in November major columns of royal troops had spent several days in or near the city on their way to the capital. On October 21 the sieurs of Chavigny and Montpezat arrived with a contingent of perhaps a dozen gendarme and light cavalry companies – probably a bit more than 1,000 men. The town was ordered to provide 15,000 loaves of bread, wine, and a large quantity of oats, which necessitated hiring local bakers, teamsters, porters, guides, and royal sergeants to prepare, pack, and deliver the rations over a period of three days. Despite gifts of wine to the cavalry's officers, the *étape* was marred by "ung conflict et recontre" which resulted in the loss of a horse and a wagon belong-

---

back and forth on their supplicatory missions to the court, *ibid.*, 402–3. The *EDC*, 426–29, also identifies the payments made to various spies for intelligence reports about enemy forces and movements in the surrounding territory.

[10] *EDC*, 396–97, 436.
[11] For the musters and strengths, *EDC*, 396–97; on the replacement of the paymasters, *ibid.*, 402–3.
[12] *Ibid.*, 396–97 and note 1.

ing to one of the town teamsters, the first of many such incidents that was to plague the inhabitants.[13]

About a month later, on November 17, a second and larger contingent arrived on its way to the royal army, nine cavalry and nine infantry companies from Brittany, about 3,000 troops, led by the viscount of Martigues. The town was again ordered to mobilize its resources to deliver large quantities of bread, wine, and oats, and again there were disorders: soldiers seized oats "by force and violence from the storeroom of oats which had been made in the Tour du Roy"; the guide provided to Martigues to lead his troops on to their next stop was robbed by them as he returned to the city; and the town had to absorb the losses associated with the disposal of more than 5,000 loaves of bread which had been prepared for but not been consumed by the soldiers.[14]

By early January, 1568, however, despite its dispute with the governor, the expense of maintaining its own garrison, and the burden of having to provide *étapes* for the large contingents of passing troops, the city may well have counted itself fortunate. There had been no fighting near the city, the main armies had moved far to the east through Champagne, and the town had managed to reduce the size of its resident garrison. But with the arrival on January 25, 1568, of Martinengo's force, consisting of ten foot, three pioneer, and one cavalry company, about 2,000 men, the war began to return in earnest to the very doorsteps of the city.[15] Martinengo had orders to leave part of his force in garrison at Chartres and to send the rest of it on to Janville, a small town just to the west of Toury, on the main road from Estampes to Orléans, where they could screen the latter. The town and its governor reacted to this addition to the garrison by sending a messenger to court protesting that the extra troops were not necessary to provide an adequate defense for the town.[16] Matters were made worse when Martinengo decided to disobey his orders and keep his whole force at Chartres. He and the governor began acting menacingly towards each other, frightening the town authorities, and his men, who had not been paid in some time, were in no mood to be polite to a place which clearly resented their arrival. In a letter to the queen mother on January 27 explaining the reasons he had not proceeded (he thought splitting his force up was dangerous and was worried about being attacked by cavalry on the march across flat, open country), Martinengo complained that the protests of the townspeople "have more their private interests in mind than how they could be of service to Your Majesties," and that "the habitants are in all things enemies of soldiers," adding that he wanted to give his men some rest and that he had promised that they would receive their pay before leaving the town, otherwise he feared they would desert him on the road to

---

[13] *Ibid.*, 398–99.
[14] *Ibid.*, 399–400; Martigues' column is also described in detail in BN Mss. Fr. 3,898, fols. 227–36.
[15] *EDC*, 400–2.
[16] *Ibid.*, 401, note 1.

Janville.[17] As it turned out, Martinengo's force remained in the city for almost two weeks, living "à discretion" off the inhabitants and consuming large quantities of bread, wine, oats, and other supplies. In response to the town's protests the queen dispatched the lieutenant governor of Orléanais, the Sieur de la Trémoille, with his gendarme company to mediate the dispute. La Trémoille successfully negotiated the departure of most of the troops on February 5, but they refused to go

> unless they were provided with 6,000 loaves of bread, 20 *poinçons* of wine, and a keg of cannon powder, with horses and harnesses to transport these supplies on their way, and several other onerous conditions for the town, by reason of which, other than the transport, [which was] provided by the town, the said town settled with the Captain Langan, left by the Count of Martinengo in the town to command those who remained of his companies, for the sum of ... 450 livres.[18]

The town fathers, grateful that violence had been averted, and a heavy burden lifted from their community, voted 283 *livres* to reimburse La Trémoille for the upkeep of his cavalry company during its stay in the town, and, in all, this incursion of friend-ly troops cost the town more than 2,300 *livres*. It also probably came as no surprise when the teamster who had been engaged to transport the baggage of the departing troops returned without his wagon, having been forced to cut its traces in order to save his team from being seized.[19]

By the time Martinengo left Chartres it was clear that Condé's army was heading to Orléans, putting Chartres directly in danger, and Anjou began making alterna-tive provisions for its defense. A regiment of Gascon infantry in garrison at Villeneuve and Joigny on the Yonne river, under the command of Jehan de Monluc, the former governor of Pignerol, were ordered on February 7 to march westward to Montargis and then on to Chartres, followed by another regiment, of French infantry, under the count of Cerny.[20] On the 12th Anjou ordered Linières, who had just successfully completed a similar mission to Chaumont, to proceed with his gendarme company and an engineer to take command in Chartres.[21] Despite an effort by Fontaine-la-Guyon to block the appointment, Linières arrived at Chartres on the 24th to replace him, only to find that the arrival of the Gascons had thrown the place into an uproar.

On the same day Linières was ordered to Chartres, Monluc had received orders to leave his men and proceed immediately to Gascony to join his father, who was ill, and command of the Gascons was given to the Sieur d'Ardelay, a brother of

---

[17] BN Mss. Fr. 15,544, fol. 138r.

[18] *EDC*, 401–2.

[19] *Ibid.*, 402.

[20] Monluc's regiment had been set in motion to the west as early as February 5, 1568, and multiple, sometimes conflicting, orders for his movements were issued on February 7, 8, and 11. See, respec-tively, BN Mss. Fr. 15,544, fols. 178r, 189r-90v, 197r-98r, and 215r-16r. The February 10 order to Cerny is *ibid.*, fol. 207r.

[21] BN Mss. Fr. 15,544, fol. 22r. The actual commission was dated February 16, *Henri III*, vol. 1, 34.

Brantôme.[22] That Monluc's, now d'Ardelay's, troops were causing trouble was not surprising. Raised in Gascony by the senior Monluc, they had marched north the previous October, arriving in December to join Anjou's army after fighting a pitched battle on the way, having exhausted their powder and worn out their shoes.[23] Jehan de Monluc had proved to be a quarrelsome commander and the companies were sent to Rheims, where, unpaid, they so oppressed the townspeople that the cardinal of Lorraine wrote to Anjou in protest.[24] Finally they received one month's pay, though half of it was in cloth, and as they had passed through Montargis on their way to Chartres their pay was at least three months in arrears.[25] Money was dispatched to pay them but, as an indignant letter from the king to Monluc senior dated March 11, 1568, reveals, it never reached the regiment.

Monsieur de Monluc, some of the captains of those who had come with the sieur de Monluc, your son, after having received two months of their soldiers' pay, took themselves off to Gascony with your son without paying anything to the poor soldiers of their companies of what was due to them for their salary and places. And not being content to have carried off the pay of their companies, they took many of the soldiers with them and left the numbers of those who remained so diminished that they came to nowhere near their required strength. Because this affair displeases me so greatly, I desire that they be punished, and I ask that you seize the said captains as soon as they arrive in Gascony and punish them so severely that they be made to serve as an example to others who might be tempted to steal or carry off the poor soldiers' pay, and contrary to their oath, after having received the money, abandon their duty and service to the King.[26]

So d'Ardelay's unpaid and understandably angry Gascons had arrived at Chartres on the 19th but, according to D'Aubigné, "The insolence of his Périgourdins had so excited the wrath of the entire Chartrain region against them," that the town refused them entry and drove them off with warning shots from the walls, and Huguenot cavalry attacked the regiment's servants and baggage in their camp near the town.[27] Yet the situation at Chartres was critical, for spies sent out by the town had reported the presence of the Huguenot artillery train at Orléans.[28] A royal letter dated the 22nd ordered the citizens to admit the Gascons and: "The inhabitants, somewhat softened by the fear of the danger with which they were threatened, received ... d'Ardelay, but only after having made him swear an oath

[22] BN Mss. Fr. 15,544, fol. 221. D'Ardelay's appointment may have been determined by chance; on February 7 he was employed by Anjou to take a dispatch to the court, and he may have been the only available Gascon officer near the regiment of sufficient distinction to be given its command, *ibid.*, fol. 190v.

[23] BN Mss. Fr. 15,543, fols. 44r and 74r.

[24] BN Mss. Fr. 15,544, fol. 16r.

[25] *Ibid.*, 34r.

[26] The theft is first mentioned in a council memo of March 2, BN Mss. Fr. 15,545, fol. 5; the king's letter to Monluc senior is *ibid.*, fol. 48.

[27] D'Aubigné, vol. 2, 295–96. While camped outside the town d'Ardelay's troops apparently lived by pillaging a nearby monastery, *EDC*, 404.

[28] *EDC*, 427–29 for various spy reports on the artillery at Orléans.

that neither he nor his soldiers would seek revenge for the past, and that they would treat the bourgeois with a great deal of moderation and forbearance."[29]

On the 26th, Cerny's regiment also safely made its way into the city, the last reinforcement to enter before the Protestant army sealed off the town. The garrison which the city was now to support during the two weeks of the siege consisted of twenty-two infantry companies – the Gascon and French regiments and three of the companies which had been raised by Fontaine-la-Guyon – and three cavalry companies, altogether more than 4,000 troops. There was now one soldier present for every two Chartrains, and the requirements of these troops and of the siege itself were by far to outshadow the previous wartime demands on the town. The approach of danger and the demands of the siege were also to unite temporarily soldiers and citizens in a common endeavor under Linières' leadership. But as soon as the siege ended, city delegates were on their way to court to beg the king to order the removal of soldiers from the city. Despite their efforts the soldiers lingered on until mid-April, actually spending more time in the city after the siege than before it, at enormous expense for the town, which finally was forced to borrow more than 9,000 *livres* from a Parisian lender to make up enough of the soldiers' arrears in pay that they were willing to move on.[30] Over the course of war more than 11,000 royal troops had passed through or been stationed in the city. Once the last of the royal troops had gone the accounting of the costs to the city of its cooperation with the army could begin.

"A VIOLENT SIEGE"

Towns and cities were among the most complex social and economic organizations in early modern France. They were also repositories of the most varied types of skills and resources. As vulnerable as many of them were to determined attack, from a defending commander's point of view they also presented numerous advantages, for many of the things that armies frequently lacked in the field or had to transport with them at great trouble and expense were readily available in towns. In the specific case of Chartres, a prosperous city situated in one of the most productive agricultural regions in France, what made it a rich potential prize for the Huguenot besiegers also made it a cornucopia of resources to be utilized by its defenders: large numbers of craftsmen who could be put to work providing the equipment of war (the town's heavy and light artillery, powder, matchcord, round and grape shot, arquebus balls, incendiary devices, corselets for the soldiers at the breach, and hundreds of pikes), ample supplies of physical labor (to dig the inner trenches, construct redoubts, reinforce the walls, fill the breach, and carry supplies and the wounded), a wealth of skilled and knowledgeable administrators and professionals (to organize and manage the varied aspects of the town's own efforts and to provide

[29] EDC, 404, note 1. Quote is De Thou, vol. 5, 411.
[30] EDC, 437.

such services as medical care), virtually unlimited amounts of materials useful for stationary defenses (stone from buildings and roads, rooftiles, barrels and boxes, furniture, mattresses, beds, and cloth and lumber of all types), plentiful stores of food and the capacity to prepare and deliver them (grains and dried legumes of all kinds, full wine cellars, livestock, poultry, fish, cheeses, salt and condiments of all kinds, fodder, and an infrastructure of food preparation industries), and, finally, financial resources (the ready cash and valuables hoarded by prominent citizens or the local religious institutions, local government coffers, the town treasury itself, and fairly sure knowledge of how to tap such funds).

But as the accounts of sieges during this era make clear, a successful defense of a city depended upon more than abundant resources. Unity of command had to be established, defense plans coordinated, defenders correctly deployed, and the varied human and material resources of the city marshaled to sustain the military defense. From all the accounts of the siege it is clear that Linières, unlike the previous governor, was quickly able to establish an unquestioned authority. One of his first acts was to have a new gallows constructed, a more than symbolic hint to his soldiers and the townspeople that surrender was out of the question, though there is no evidence from the *état* itself that the gallows was ever used.[31] Accompanied by the city leaders, he conducted a swift survey of the defenses and ordered a whole series of ameliorative measures: strengthening walls, building inner works, preparing armaments and ammunition, organizing a hospital, creating a mine and counter-mine service, and setting up a security, surveillance, and signaling system centered on observers in the cathedral tower. Equally important were arrangements for the provision of food and drink for his troops, which involved requisitioning foodstuffs, establishing warehouses, organizing the bakers and butchers, and arranging for the transport and distribution of rations to the soldiers at the wall. The town's own paramilitary types, its artillery and militiamen, had to be assigned to their stations, and a large corps of pioneers mobilized from among the less well-off inhabitants and refugees.[32]

The municipality's expense account of the siege certifies in great detail not only the resources provided but also the harnessing of a significant portion of the townspeople to the defense of the city. It identifies directly or indirectly several hundreds of citizens who contributed to or were actively involved in the siege, from seamstresses to physicians and candlemakers to blacksmiths. In addition, some 600 men served in the town militia and more than a thousand people worked as pioneers. It would be difficult to imagine that any family in the city did not have one or more members involved in the defense. This meant that Linières could dispose of more

---

[31] *Ibid.*, 436.

[32] *EDC* references to food and drink for the defenders, 404–10; the cathedral watch, 406; town artillery, 411–15; bullets, 415–16; pikes and corselets, 417–18; and incendiary devices, 416–17; the corps of first 1,000, then 400 pioneers, and their tools, 420 and 425–26; miners, 420–32; and repairs to the walls and fortifications, 421–25.

than 6,000 individuals, including the garrison, in the defense of the city, or two-thirds the strength of the Huguenot attackers (a large number of whom were pinned down as a covering force miles from the city towards Paris), about two defenders to every yard of the slightly more than two-mile circumference of the city walls.[33] Such a large number of defenders meant that he could conduct a vigorous war of sorties against the attackers, first to attempt to burn down the surviving buildings of the faubourgs so as to deny their shelter and protection to the enemy, and then in harassing attacks on their outposts or counterattacks when they managed to capture some portion of the town's fortifications themselves.

The potent combination of garrison and townspeople became most important during the most critical moment of the siege. The besiegers had arrived in full force on February 28, and while the defenders worked frantically on their fortifications and mounted multiple sorties, the Huguenot army took up positions all around the city. On March 2 Condé decided to place his batteries on high ground which over-looked the town's northern wall and the Drouaise gate. Though the choice had some obvious advantages, for batteries located there could take much of the wall under flanking fire, in fact, as all subsequent commentators have pointed out, it was a singularly incompetent decision, for there were other much weaker parts to the defenses, and the northern wall, which bordered on the lower town, could easily be backed up with inner works or if it fell sealed off with relative ease from the upper town.[34]

After several days of suppressive fire against which the defenders of the ramparts could only erect curtains of cloth to mask their positions, on the morning of March 5 the Protestant artillery began a serious bombardment of the Drouaise gate and the section of wall to its east. On the afternoon of the 7th while fighting surged back and forth over a ravelin, a type of bastion which protected the gate, a large section of the wall collapsed and the Huguenots, filling the ditch with fascines and barrels, launched a general assault, which the royal soldiers were able to meet with equal or superior numbers and after some heavy fighting repulse. The breach, ravelin, bat-teries, and beginning of the assault are pictured quite realistically in one of Tortorel and Perrissin's engravings, reproduced in Figure 25.[35] The next day the battery recommenced, attempting to enlarge the breach. But Linières and the townspeople had already completed an inner series of containment works, and when the Huguenots began to mount another assault they were stymied by the fire of massive charges of scrap iron from a large cannon nicknamed "la Huguenote," mounted on an inner bastion which commanded the breach and the ditch. A reconnaissance finally led Condé to conclude that the breach was unassailable, and he began to redeploy his guns, but with the negotiation of a truce on the 13th, the crisis had passed and the siege was over.[36]

---

[33] Lehr, 48. Lehr also provides a 1575 map of the town and its defenses between pages 68 and 69.
[34] On Condé's incompetent direction of the siege, see Lehr, 49–51, 54–56.
[35] Franklin, *Les grandes scènes.*
[36] Lehr, 63, 65.

Fig. 25. The siege of Chartres, 1568, from Franklin, 1886

During the crisis there were three keys to the successful defense of the breach. The first, of course, was the fighting done by the regular soldiers and those members of the town defensive contingents, such as the artillery and the pioneers, who had to operate under constant fire. The second was the closing off of the breach and the construction of an even more formidable series of inner fortifications. Here the efforts of the townspeople were absolutely critical. The *état* provides a virtual inventory of their possessions – furniture, barrels, lumber, trees from a nearby cemetery, vast amounts of firewood, bales of wool, animal skins, hundreds of yards of cloth for screens and sandbags, and "besides those cloths an infinity of others for which they ask no compensation" and "also such a great number of beds had been put in the breach that it is impossible to estimate [their number]."[37] And the business of constructing the inner works was, with the exception of the oversight of the royal engineer, entirely the work of the citizenry, enabling the soldiers to stay at the walls on alert day and night. It was the lavish support of the latter by the town, enabling constant vigilance and sustained resistance by a well-nourished soldiery, that provided the third key to the defense. The *état* indicates that in its material support of the active defenders nothing was stinted. Soldiers and all townspeople defending or working on the walls were provided free of charge with

[37] For the quotes and all the materials used in the breach, *EDC*, 418–19.

218

firewood and candles, daily bread and wine and, when fish from the river ran out because the Huguenots turned it from its course, ample daily portions of beef and pork despite the fact that it was Lenten season. The soldiers actually at the breach received extra rations and the wounded were provided with a diet which included fruit, mutton, and a large array of pharmaceutical concoctions. Most lavishly provided for, however, was the household table of the governor himself and those of his principal commanders, who were supplied with finer quality bread and wine purchased from local hostels, fowl and game, sugar, prunes, oil, spices, raisins, and ample provision of meat of various kinds.[38] If the siege had dragged on for some time this largesse may have had to have been restricted, for the diversion of the Eure river meant that despite the full granaries flour to make bread would at some point have run out for lack of milling facilities.[39] But as was usually the case in the early wars, the Huguenot army had not planned, nor had it the means, to mount a lengthy siege. Linières must have know that, with the peace negotiations continuing, he had only to hold out for a few weeks to save the city.

"AN INCALCULABLE EXPENDITURE"

Still, the human price of victory in even this relatively short siege was high. Three to four hundred Huguenot soldiers are said to have died in the fighting, and some 250 deaths are reported for the defenders.[40] In addition, we can deduce from the bread ration accounts that there were more than 500 wounded and sick royal soldiers, several score of whom were severely wounded enough that they continued to receive special care for weeks after the siege ended.[41] Total casualties of at least 800 men meant that close to one-fifth of the royal army's troops in the city had become casualties in just two weeks of fighting. We have no idea at all of the number of civilian casualties.[42]

Besides the loss of life, the material and financial cost of the siege for Chartres was also quite high. The total cost of supporting the royal army and defending the city during the second civil war, according to the city's own calculations, was 87,801 *livres*, a sum which does not include collateral damage to private individuals or dwellings in the city, nor the cost to the villages of the surrounding countryside which were apparently terribly devastated by the Huguenots.[43] Figure 26, which

---

[38] For the food and drugs and fruits provided to the wounded and sick, and Linières' table, *EDC*, 407–10, 411, and 431–32.

[39] *EDC*, 409, mentions the disappearance of fish; a few handmills were constructed to produce flour, but they obviously would have failed to provide for some 12,000 inhabitants and defenders, *ibid.*, 422.

[40] Lehr, 67.

[41] Lehr, 67, estimates, and based on the EDC it seems a reasonable approximation, 630 sick and wounded of whom about 500 were wounded, 69 seriously enough to be continued on rations far into the month of April.

[42] See Appendix, Part D.

[43] See Victor Carrière, *Introduction aux études d'histoire ecclésiastique locale* (Paris, 1936), vol. 3, 364–71, which uses the damage inflicted by the Protestants around Chartres during the 1568 siege as an

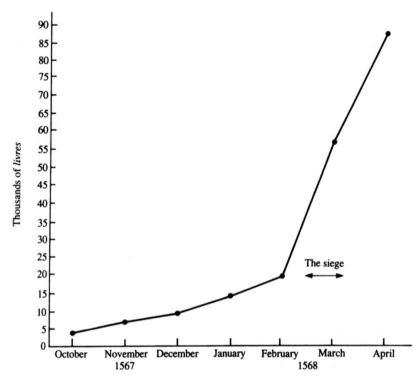

Fig. 26. Cumulative monthly costs of war incurred by the municipality of Chartres,
1567–68

traces the cumulative monthly cost of the war to the city, dramatically illustrates the
differential impact of what could be called ordinary wartime costs – increased
vigilance, a local garrison, and supplies for passing troops – with the level of expenditures required by the actual defense of the city against an enemy army. Costs
accumulated before the siege at a steady rate of from three to four thousand *livres*
per month, but jump to ten times that level during the month of the siege and
remain at seven times that level even after the peace, during April, as the royal
troops lingered on and the city began repairing its damages. In all, more than three-
quarters (77.5 percent) of the total costs of the war to the municipality were
incurred during the siege itself and its immediate aftermath. If the war had ended
when it did, at the end of March, and the siege had somehow been avoided, even if
the ordinary costs of war had continued into April, the total cost to the city would
have only been about 27,000 *livres* (though this was no mean sum) rather than
87,801 *livres*. If, on the other hand, the siege had lasted three months instead of two

example. Carrière is in part arguing against Lehr, who claims that the damage was exaggerated and
that much of it was done at the direction of Linières, Lehr, 65–67.

Table 8.1. *Expenditures by the city of Chartres during the second civil war,*
1567–1568

General category	Subcategory	Cost in livres	Category total	%
Soldiers	Pay	13,065		
	Compositions	10,503		
	Bonuses	1,695		
	Medals	882		
	Reimbursements	340		
	Funerals	691	27,176	31
Rations	Bread	13,046		
	Wine	19,392		
	Meat	2,544		
	Other Food	2,530		
	Forage	4,734		
	Handling	1,269	43,515	50
Administration	Police	254		
	Guides	74		
	Spies and diplomacy	1,321	1,649	2
Munitions	Cannoniers	295		
	Artillery guns	277		
	Ammunition	1,653		
	Other weapons	826	3,051	3
Fortifications	Walls	6,391		
	Breach	3,519		
	Mines	151	10,061	11
Heat and illumination	Firewood and candles	1,607	1,607	2
Medical	Care	713		
	Wastes	28	741	1
Total			87,801	100

weeks, the total cost would have been closer to a quarter of a million *livres*. If the city had fallen to the enemy and was sacked, the costs could have been even higher. It was within these grim and extensive parameters of possibilities of danger and expense that the city leaders of Chartres, and of all towns and cities involved in similar situations during the civil wars, had to maneuver.

What, in the end, had the expenditures on goods and labor consisted of? Table 8.1 provides a more detailed breakdown of the costs of the war for Chartres. By far the largest article of expense – in fact 50 percent of the total – was foodstuffs. Over the course of the war the town provided the equivalent of 263 wagon-loads of wheat (each containing one *muid*, or 2,880 *livres* by weight, something over a modern ton) and 145 wagon-loads of oats, 328 beasts for slaughter, and 2,301 *poincons* (approximately 10,000 gallons) of wine. From the flour made from the wheat over 624,000 ration loaves of 12 ounces each were prepared, 525,000 alone (including 43,500 loaves to townspeople) during the siege and its aftermath. But wine, representing 50 percent of food expenditures, as opposed to 33 percent for bread, was by value the most expensive food item furnished to the troops. Next in importance to food, constituting three-tenths of all expenses, was 27,177 *livres* in cash, half paid directly in salaries to soldiers, and slightly more than a third on compositions, or the sizeable bribes negotiated by troops before they would leave the city. Another 11 percent of the total cost of war came from expenditures on the walls and fortifications, including repairs after the siege, the costs associated with defending and closing the breach alone constituting a third of this sum. In fourth place, contributing 3 percent of all expenditures, were artillery and the munitions of war. None of the other categories of expenses – the provision of administrative services, heat and lighting, medical service and public hygiene (the disposal of the many corpses), accounted for more than 2 per cent each of total costs.

From these figures it can be roughly calculated that at least four-fifths of the total costs incurred by the city during the war and the siege came from the provision of food and pay to soldiers of the army and less than one fifth from direct war-related costs of administration, munitions, and fortifications. As large a contribution as the labor services and skills of the citizens were, then, it was the physical goods of the city, its cash, food, materials, and equipment, that were most required by war, even when the city was directly and desperately involved in the fighting. And most of the material goods required, like money, wheat, oats, wine, and cattle, had to be provided from the accumulated savings and material reserves of the city, they could not be created on the spot. Most of the costs of war were clearly related to its labor intensive nature: it was the cost of paying and feeding soldiers rather than capital intensive investment in the technology of war such as weapons, ammunition, and fortifications, that drove up the total. The warfare waged by the men of the royal army and the loyal townspeople of France was still recognizably and inescapably a phenomenon of the products and commercial profits of the rural capitalism which dominated all but a few of the major cities of the kingdom. Even in the zones of modestly sized detachments and garrisons, away from the maneuvering of the main armies for the advantages they needed in order to give battle, the impact of providing goods and services for war could be heavy. Even though Chartres had been visited by what was only a fraction of the royal army, the chronic burden of defensive support had still been significant, for whether or not the soldiers actually did any fighting or not, they had to be fed and they had to be paid.

The varied nature of the town's contributions to the type of war waged by the royal army during the siege also hints at a wholehearted cooperation with the military once it became clear that the approach of the Huguenot army meant that the even more severe burden of defending the city had to be borne if it was to be saved from the enemy, and it is clear that the shared dangers of the siege must have temporarily reconciled soldier and civilian. The sources are silent about troop disorders in the city, and indeed despite the danger to the troops they may have eaten better than they had at any other time in the war.[44] They would have witnessed the industry exhibited by the townspeople in their own defense and surely they would have been aware that their wounded were well taken care of as well. And while it is impossible to imagine any town bourgeoisie feeling great affection for any sizeable group of soldiers, it is clear from some of the expenditures after the siege that the town leaders were extremely thankful to the troops of the army, and especially to Linières and the other leaders, for their active and brave defense of the city.

Among the soldiers singled out for recompense or money awards after the siege were, ironically enough, given the earlier struggle over them, the men of two of the original companies raised in October of 1567 to form the town's own garrison: each man was given a bonus of a single *livre*, the equivalent of several days' pay, enough to support a good celebration. The count of Cerny was reimbursed for the loss of a horse and Captain Rancé, the sergeant-major of the Gascons, who had served as Linières' second-in-command, was given a bonus of about two weeks' pay. Others singled out were the *chevallier* Pelloys, the royal engineer, who received the very handsome sum of 780 livres "to recompense him for the services he rendered to the king in the said town, both before the siege, during it, and afterwards." The captain of mines, the royal commissioner of *vivres*, the household of the governor, a captain who escorted a load of powder into the city immediately before the siege, and two gentlemen who had risked their lives to slip through the siege lines in disguise, were also singled out for small awards.[45]

Obviously all these represented what in the eyes of the city was exceptionally loyal or critical service during the siege. But in addition, the defense of the town was commemorated by the expenditure of another relatively large sum, 882 *livres*,

for thirty-one gold medallions, made in Paris, having on one side the arms of the king and on the other side the robe of Our Lady and the arms of the town, which were presented as a sign of victory to the captains of the companies in garrison in the said town, for having sustained the assault and fulfilled their duty in the defense of the town. Two of them, those of the sieur of Linières and that of Pelloys, royal engineer, were put on gold chains and the others were threaded and hung from silken ribbons only.[46]

Besides the practical value of these gold medallions, each worth about one-half of an infantry lieutenant's monthly pay, and the special honor paid to Linières and his

---

[44] According to Lehr, 59–60, Linières did threaten with death those bourgeois who refused to appear at musters of the town units to be used in defense of the walls and, apparently in an attempt to shame them, forced them to hand over their corselets (which were never returned) to his under-armored men. *EDC*, 418.

[45] *EDC*, 429–31.

[46] *EDC*, 430.

engineer, the design, combining signifiers of monarchy, faith, and city, symbolized a state of cooperation and common cause that was and had to be extremely rare and very fragile. For, in fact, the interests of municipality and royal army almost never coincided, and at the same moment the medals were being distributed to the military leaders of the garrison the town's petitioners were speeding on their way to Paris to implore the king to rid them of the men who had just saved them and to raise a loan in order to hasten their departure.

An attempt by the crown to leave an even more lasting monument to the mutual effort of inhabitants and troops was strenuously resisted. On the day the Huguenots assaulted the breach, d'Ardelay, the colonel of the Gascon regiment, had suffered a head wound defending against a diversionary attack mounted on the opposite side of the city. He lingered on for a dozen days before dying, and, informed of his death by Linières, the duke of Anjou ordered that he and De Chaulx, Linières' cavalry lieutenant, who had also been killed, should be given a lavish funeral by the town, which was done, and that in addition d'Ardelay "be interred in the great church in the most honorable place that could be."[47] When the cathedral chapter hotly protested Anjou's desire for erection of what was in essence a military mausoleum he was promptly backed up by a direct order from the king himself.[48] The historian De Thou takes up the story.

De Linières wished to honor d'Ardelay by having him entombed in the great church. But the canons objected, arguing that, according to custom and the statutes drawn up by their predecessors, it was forbidden that anyone at all be interred in a place so specially consecrated to the Virgin, and that, moreover, the construction of their Church did not allow for digging up the earth, since it was all vaulted underneath. The king nevertheless commanded that a tomb be constructed in the church and that d'Ardelay be placed there. The chapter pretended to give their consent, in light of the great service the captain had rendered to the town, but in order to preserve the profound veneration and religious respect they had always had for this sacred place, they had the body of the deceased secretly removed one night and transferred it to a neighboring church.[49]

Should we see in this defense of sacred ground only the myopia of the cathedral chapter, or a more symbolic resistance to the threat posed to local autonomy and practice by the implantation of a permanent military presence in the city? There is some evidence that though the memory of the fact of the siege lived on in Chartrain memories, the temporary and tenuous links forged to their governor and the royal army rapidly disappeared. The town, assured with a promise it would be repaid, had advanced 450 *livres* to the men of Linières' gendarme company after the siege to enable them to head home. But the men had never been paid by the crown, and Linières himself was killed almost exactly a year later at the battle of Jarnac, "since which decease the town's habitants have not known to whom to apply," the *état*

[47] *Henri III*, vol. 1, 136; the funeral expenses are detailed in *EDC*, 432–35.
[48] *EDC*, 432, and note 1.
[49] De Thou, vol. 5, 416.

mournfully concluded.[50] And as the struggle passed into local legend the role played by the leaders and soldiers of the royal army in the defense of the city was largely repressed. The tradition that remained was that a statue of the Virgin which looked down from the Drouaise gate became bullet proof during the battle and that all the Protestants who looked upon her at once fell dead as though they had looked at the Medusa. A variant of the legend maintained that the Virgin herself had appeared on the ramparts at the breach at the decisive moment of battle to protect the city, in a clear but certainly unselfconscious parallel to the canons' defense of her ground in the cathedral from defilement by men of war.[51]

---

[50] *EDC*, 431. As Lehr, 48, points out, the irony of Linières' death at Jarnac is that he had originally fought with the Huguenots at the battle of Dreux before changing loyalties and returning to the royal army.

[51] Lehr, 69–70; H. J. L. J. Massé, *The City of Chartres* (London, 1900), 5; and Georges Monmarché, *Chartres* (Paris, 1949), 62.

9

A host of strangers: The army's presence on campaign, 1568–69

This army was raised, first for the honor of God and the preservation of the authority of our Holy Mother Church, Catholic, Apostolic and Roman, and then to maintain and conserve the crown of the King, our very honored Lord and brother, to foil the intentions of our enemies risen up in arms against us; to resist them, and restore to that Lord's subjects the peace and tranquility, of which the malice of the times has deprived them ... Our intention is to cause all persons, of whatever quality, whether they be on the payroll of the King or of some other, to live with the order, duty, and lawfulness which is right and necessary in the army of a very Christian Prince, as well as with regard for what is due to the love, fear, and honor of God, the maintenance and execution of Justice and its splendor and integrity, as well as [to uphold] order and military discipline among the soldiers in order that they be led safely on campaign, in combat with the enemy, and lodged without disorder, and the subjects of the King be guarded from the oppression and violence of the said soldiers and men of war...and thus will they be assured that they will [be able to] live without being harassed, beaten, pillaged or tormented, but will live in safety under the protection of the severity of the Justice which we intend to visit on those who transgress against this ordinance, hereafter declared, which we wish to be exactly and inviolably observed for the punishment of the grand and execrable impieties and detestable vices which ordinarily happen and are committed.[1]

So runs the preamble to an ordinance "sur le faicte de la police et règlement du camp," issued by the duke of Anjou in 1568, at the beginning of the third civil war, to the units of soldiers he had gathered at Estampes in preparation for the long march south to the Poitvin theatre of operations. Many such ordinances have survived from the period of the early civil wars, and specific rules governing troop behavior can also sometimes be found in the capitulations signed with foreign troops. The problems such codes attempted to address were hardly idiopathic. Besides the standard military concern with the responsibility of soldiers to obey orders, fulfill their duties with care, avoid quarrels, bring complaints they had of their treatment to the proper authorities, assist the camp military police, and to not desert, the codes issued by the army's commanders and the monarchy are also

[1] Ordinance of October 7, 1568, *OM* no. 123.

replete with prohibitions of certain types of undisciplined, predatory, and violent behavior towards civilians.

According to La Noue, at the beginning of the first civil war the main armies of both sides behaved rather well towards civilians. When he remarked on this to the deeply experienced Admiral Coligny, he received in response a proverb: "De jeune Hermite, vieux Diable."[2] Indeed, the good behavior did not last, and as La Noue noted in a passage that could have equally well been applied to the troops of the royal army: "And so our infantry lost its maidenhead, and from this illegitimate union ensued the procreation of Mademoiselle Plunder, who since then has grown so much in dignity, that she is now called Madame. And if the civil war continues on, I have no doubt that she will become Princess."[3] As the civil wars continued, and complaints by loyal subjects about the exactions of the royal army mounted to higher and higher levels, ever more explicit and detailed ordinances "sur le règlement et conduite des gens de guerre" were issued. In aggregate, they furnish a detailed picture of the types of troop behavior the crown wished but was obviously increasingly unable to suppress.[4]

One of the greatest areas of concern was the behavior of troops on the march. It is clear from the regulations that units often marched without permission or without notifying the authorities of their route, insisted on roundabout rather than direct routes, and threatened and mistreated the commissioners who were assigned to oversee their movements. Soldiers extorted or accepted bribes to pass by and

---

[2] La Noue, 640. Brantôme, *Oeuvres*, vol. 1, 171, recounts an apocryphal conversation between the Marquis de Pescayne and the papal legate, later Clement VII, with the French army during one of the Italian campaigns. To the legate, who had objected to various troops disorders, the marquis lectured, "Monsieur le légat, il n'y a chose plus difficile à ceux qui exercent la guerre que de servir en mesme temps et égalle discipline à Mars et à Christ, parce que l'usage de la guerre en ceste corruption de milice est du tout contraire à la justice et à la religion." It was advice that accurately summed up the attitude of most leaders on the impossibility of maintaining well-behaved troops.

[3] La Noue, 641.

[4] A number of royal ordinances from the first half of the sixteenth century formed the legal base for rules of conduct at the beginning of the wars of religion. According to A. Navereau, *Le logement et les ustensiles des gens de guerre de 1439 à 1789* (Poitiers, 1924), *passim*, the most fundamental of these codes was that issued in 1549, during the reign of Henri II. It and many other *règlements* of all kinds can be found in the appropriate volumes of the collections by Fontanon and Isambert. Coligny's pre-civil war regulations for the infantry, "Ordinances de M. De Chastillon sur la discipline militaire," which is reproduced in Cimber and d'Anjou, vol. 8, 403–6, is sometimes cited as the first example of an effective, practical code. Coligny's rules are quite simple and clear, and it is much more likely that they were actually read to the troops, like Strossi's march regulations for infantry cited below, than many of the major printed ordinances, which often were intended to provide detailed regulations aimed at the organization of musters and avoidance of fraud in the payment of troops.

What should not be lost from sight is that the behavior the crown was principally trying to regulate was that directed towards its friends and supporters! Towards the enemy almost anything was possible and the rules of war were often ignored. As La Noue, *Discours*, 651, referring to the sack of Rouen by the royal army in 1562, points out: "le sac ne dura que trois jours, ordre qu'on doit tenir aux villes qu'on veut conserver, à sçavoir, un jour entier pour butiner, un autre pour emporter, & l'autre pour composer. Mais en ces affaires-là, les superieurs abbregent ou alongent le terme, selon qui'ils veulent, & qu'ils se pourront faire obeir. Laquell obeissance se monstre bien plustost és petites places pauvres, qu'és grandes villes opulentes."

spare the communities assigned to them as campsites, ending up in unprepared rural villages which they used as bases for looting expeditions to surrounding villages, pillaging houses and damaging mills. On the march soldiers and their servants straggled and left their columns to forage without authorization or oversight by officers. They used their firearms to shoot at domesticated pigeons in coops along the road, and cut down fruit trees or removed vine-props for firewood. They confiscated livestock, especially plowhorses, to carry their sick, and never returned the animals to their owners. Besides horses, they stole mules, cattle, carts, and wagons to carry their baggage. They used violence or the threat of violence to force the people they met on their way to provide them with food and forage without repayment, and ignored the safeguards given to travelers and traders by the king or the army command.

Even when troops stopped where they were supposed to, disorders continued. They often ignored the billets assigned to them by the army's quartermasters and forced themselves onto other hosts, lodging in the theoretically off-limit dwellings of officials, the nobility, and the bourgeoisie, or, even worse, installed themselves or stabled their horses in churches and chapels. The ways in which they mistreated the people they were lodged on were numerous: they demanded bread, wine, meat, straw, hay, oats, firewood, salt, and vinegar be provided for them without payment, carried off or broke the household utensils and amenities their hosts were obliged to provide for them without reimbursement, extorted money, and stole provisions or requisitioned them at coerced below-market prices as they departed. They also used violence against the people with whom they were lodged, striking or wounding their hosts and hostesses or other "simples gens," throwing them out of their own homes, even murdering them. Pregnant women and elderly men were explicitly identified by the ordinances as the object of attacks and mistreatment. In camps of longer duration, such as at assembly points and at sieges, they robbed and mistreated the sutlers and local people who came to sell food, threatened and attacked the *munitionnaires* from whom they purchased their daily rations, and tried to force or bribe contractors to sell them their best products before they were delivered to camp.

Whether on the march or in camp, soldiers regularly conspired to prevent the execution of the summary justice, usually death by hanging, which the regulations intended to be visited on malefactors. They gave false witness, refused to hand over wrongdoers, and helped those who were arrested to escape. The behavior of the army's leaders was also roundly condemned. Officers refused to hear the complaints of victims of mistreatment, operated under false names, tolerated the presence of unenrolled vagabonds and criminals, refused to discipline or supervise their men, and granted unauthorized permission to leave the army. Not even the army's provosts escaped accusations of extortionist practices.

Even in the best of circumstances such excesses and predatory behavior were possible, but when the campaign ground on, conditions worsened, and pay was lacking, misbehavior by desperate, needy, and callous troops and mistreatment of civilians became inevitable. Yet, as the example of Chartres in the previous section suggests, beyond the actual specific behavior of troops, there were two other prime determinants of the impact war had on the areas it touched: first, the number and types of troops involved, and second, where and how long they stayed. Although the cumulative number of royal troops who were stationed at or who passed by Chartres during the second civil war was impressive, their stay was short, and they constituted only a fraction of the royal army. What was the magnitude and pattern of the army's presence on campaign in the larger areas it operated in? And what did the general pattern and framework of its operations imply for the types of predatory behavior we have been describing? To answer these questions we will first analyze the relentlessly changing human makeup of the army – its composition, overall numbers, reinforcement, and attrition patterns – in the campaigns of 1568-69 during the third civil war. Both the pauses and the pulsations of activity which marked the campaigns were closely related to the ebb and flow of the supply of the human material of war, and this, in turn, had a defining influence on the environment in which soldiers operated and on the type of impact the army had on its surroundings. We will then investigate what the army actually did during the 1568-69 campaign by analyzing how much of its time was spent fighting, in camp, or on the march, the distances it moved, and the lengths of time it typically stayed in individual localities, all of which defined, in a general sense, the framework for its interaction with the civilian world. Finally, we will discuss how these operational rhythms – the turnover of troops and the time spent in different types of action and places – may have contributed to the types of attitudes and behavior among the soldiers and their leaders, attested to by the disciplinary codes of the era, which threatened the coherence of the army and the well-being and property of the civilians among whom it operated.

PATTERNS OF REINFORCEMENT AND ATTRITION

One of the most important types of campaign rhythms governing the nature of the army's presence in its theatre of operations was the fluctuation in size and composition due to its reinforcement and attrition patterns. To determine those patterns during the third civil war, Figure 27 reconstructs the size and composition of the army at eleven different points in time, from its initial bivouac at Saumur in September, 1568, to the battle of Moncontour, at the beginning of October in 1569.[5] The first thing to note is that the army experienced a series of significant

---

[5] Based on sources cited in the Appendix, Parts A–C; chapter 5, note 23; and chapter 6, notes 15 and 17. The detailed narratives found in Gigon, and Segesser, vol. 1, 498–620, were extremely useful. Figure 27 and succeeding displays in this chapter refer to units actually with the main army, not all the military forces in the Poitvin theatre of operations in 1568–69. In reconstructing the composition and size of the army I am certain that no major contingents were missed and reasonably confident that the number of companies involved and the tracking of departures as well as arrivals is accurate.

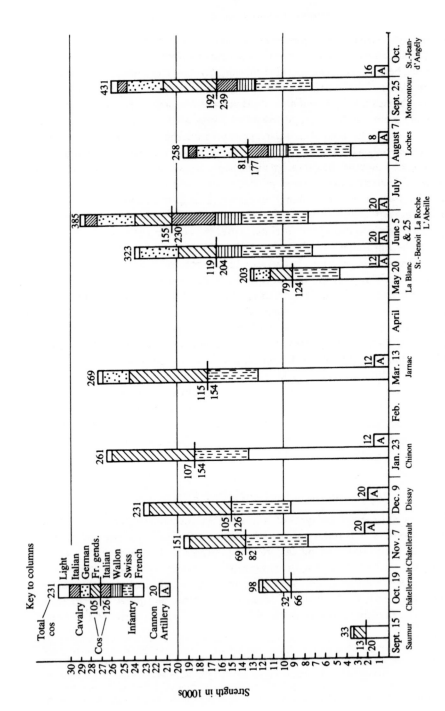

Fig. 27. Estimated strength and composition of the royal army during 1568–69

fluctuations in strength over the course of the campaign, building its numbers up and seeing them decline, only to be rebuilt and then decline again every few months, with the peak strengths attained being sustained for increasingly shorter periods of time in each successive buildup. Over the period from September to early December, 1568, while fighting an active fall campaign, the army built its strength to slightly less than 20,000 combatants (not counting the artillery). From mid-December to mid-January, a succession of reinforcements pushed its numbers to around 27,000 combatants, the strength with which it began the Jarnac campaign in the spring of 1569. By May hard campaigning had reduced the army to about half this strength, 13,000 combatants, until another round of reinforcements, including the assimilation of the remnants of Aumale's separate army, pushed its numbers to the highest point in the campaign, close to 29,000 combatants. But this high point could not be sustained after the battle of La Roche L'Abeille in June and by mid-August the army had again shrunk to less than 20,000. Another round of reinforcements in September then raised the army to a strength of about 27,000 combatants at the time of the battle of Moncontour. Though it is harder to estimate fluctuations in numbers after Moncontour, by the time Saint-Jean-d'Angély surrendered in early December, casualties, desertions, and departures had probably again reduced the army to less than 10,000 combatants.

The second noteworthy point is how buildups in the strength of the army depended almost exclusively on an increase in the total number of units – companies of infantry and cavalry – joining the army, rather than maintaining the strength of the units already with the army, and with a growing dependence on foreign troops as the campaign progressed. During the Jarnac campaign, for example, it took 269 companies (154 infantry and 115 cavalry) to reach the army's peak strength of about 27,000 combatants; at the height of its powers during the summer campaign of 1569 it took 385 companies (230 infantry and 155 cavalry), a 43 per cent increase in the number of such units, to reach a peak strength of about 29,000 combatants, a level only 7 percent higher than at Jarnac; at the time of Moncontour, despite an addition of 46 more company sized units, for a total of 431 (239 infantry and 192 cavalry), an increase of 12 percent over the summer figures, the army's peak strength, at about 26,000 combatants, had actually shrunk by 10 percent.

Obviously, over the course of the campaign it was only by continually reinforcing the army with new formations that it was able to rebuild its strength and stay in the field. To find enough units to sustain this flow of reinforcement meant drawing on units from all over the kingdom and abroad. A brief nominal listing just of the major formations which joined the army during the campaign reads like an exhaus-

Estimates of actual strengths at any one point in time, in the absence of detailed muster totals, contain a possibly sizeable degree of error, for it was often necessary to extrapolate across dates and estimate declining strengths according to a standard attrition rate of 4 percent per month, when no other figures were available. I am confident that the general ranges of total strengths to be attributed to the army at different dates does reflect the actualities of the campaign, and the fluctuations noted by all observers, accurately enough.

tive litany of the crown's military resources.[6] In September, 1568, at Saumur, Montpensier with some companies of gendarmes and a Poitvin infantry regiment under Richelieu was joined by a Breton infantry regiment and cavalry contingent under Martigues. By October, at Châtellerault, Montpensier had been reinforced by two major formations (about four regiments) of veteran French infantry under Brissac and Strossi, and two advance groups of gendarmes under Guise and Longueville. In early November, after this army had fought the battle of Messignac, Anjou arrived at Châtellerault to take command, bringing with him the Swiss infantry, a large number of cavalry units, and the artillery train. At Dissay in mid-December, after the battle of Jazeneuil, Brissac and Strossi were joined by another three French infantry regiments and large contingents of infantry and cavalry raised in Languedoc by Sarlaboz and Joyeuse. The buildup continued in the winter camp at Chinon, and by the beginning of the Jarnac campaign, in late January, 1569, more gendarme companies were added, Brissac and Strossi received more French infantry companies, and the count of Tende had arrived from Dauphiny and Provence with another infantry regiment and more cavalry. Immediately before the battle of Jarnac the army received two regiments of mercenary German reiters, the first foreign troops to reach the west, besides the Swiss, since the beginning of the war six months before. In June, at Saint-Benoit, the worn-out but still substantial elements of Aumale's eastern army added to the total two more regimental sized formations of French infantry, a Wallon infantry regiment, more gendarmes and light cavalry, a new reinforcing Swiss regiment, and two more regiments of reiters. Just a few days later and immediately before the battle of La Roche L'Abeille Jehan de Monluc joined the army with his regiment of Gascon infantry, and a large papal contingent of infantry and cavalry marched into camp. By August, in the camp at Loches, the deterioration of the French forces with the army had left it almost entirely composed of foreign troops, but in September the last desperate scrapings of the bottom of the barrel by the crown produced Marshal Cossé with a substantial French infantry reinforcement from the north and the remainder of the kingdom's gendarmes.

By the time of the siege of Saint-Jean-d'Angély, as Table 9.1 indicates, more than 500 company sized units had been sent to the army, including 254 French infantry companies (102 veteran and 152 raised for the war) and 185 French cavalry companies (including 175 old and new gendarme companies), or practically every existing or newly raised native military unit in the country. In addition, 88 companies of foreign mercenaries (66 infantry and 22 cavalry) from the Spanish Low Countries, Germany, Switzerland, and Italy, had joined the camp. As the war progressed these foreign contingents, whose companies were much larger, on average, than their French counterparts, came to form an increasingly important part of the army. Table 9.2, which calculates the relative proportion of French and foreign troops (including the artillery train) at the points in time featured in

<hr />

[6] *Ibid.*, for what follows.

Table 9.1. *Cumulative numbers of infantry and cavalry companies joining the royal army, 1568–69*

Type of troops	No. companies
Infantry	
Veteran French	102
Newly raised French	152
Foreign	66
Infantry subtotal	320
Cavalry	
French gendarmes	175
French light cavalry	10
Foreign	22
Cavalry subtotal	207
Total	527

Table 9.2. *Percentage of French and foreign troops with the royal army during 1568–69*

Date	Locality	Percentage French	Percentage Foreign
9–15–68	Saumur	100	0
10–5–68	Châtellerault	100	0
11–7–68	Châtellerault	69	31
12–8–68	Dissay	76	24
1–23–69	Chinon	81	19
3–13–69	Jarnac	73	27
5–20–69	Le Blanc	55	45
6–5–69	Saint-Benoit	46	54
6–25–69	La Roche L'Abeille	39	61
8–7–69	Loches	28	72
9–25–69	Moncontour	49	51

Figure 27, graphically demonstrates the inability of the crown to complete more than one major pulse of campaign activity and begin a second, much less support a third, from its own French resources, despite the commitment of a steadily escalating proportion of all the French units raised for war throughout the kingdom. By the summer of 1569 almost half of the army was foreign, a proportion that rose steadily until at Loches, in August, almost three-quarters, and even at Moncontour,

Table 9.3. *Estimated overall attrition in the royal army, September, 1568, to October, 1569*

Troop type	Cumulative total joining army	Remaining at Moncontour	Net attrition	% attrition
French foot	23,200	7,200	16,000	69
Foreign foot	14,900	9,000	5,900	40
French horse	11,400	5,500	5,900	52
Foreign horse	5,700	4,200	1,500	26
Total	55,200	25,900	29,300	53

after an all-out effort emptied most of the rest of the kingdom's garrisons and provinces of French units, a majority of the royal army was foreign.

The need for continual reinforcement, of course, was directly tied to the attrition rates experienced by the army. In the absence of detailed army muster records it is impossible to be very precise about attrition. But by estimating the approximate total strength of the successive major waves of reinforcements which joined the army, as in Table 9.3, we can get a rough idea of the total manpower sent to the army over the course of the campaign.[7] According to this method, between September, 1568, and early October, 1569, a total of about 55,200 men were needed to keep the army near or slightly above 20,000 effectives and on four brief occasions push its strength above 25,000 men. Of the approximately 55,200 troops who joined the army over the course of the campaign only about 25,900 remained at the time of the Moncontour campaign, a net loss of 29,300, which represents a gross attrition rate of 53 percent over thirteen months, or roughly 4 percent a month. Were we to count the results of the siege of Saint-Jean-d'Angély this overall attrition rate would probably rise to near 60 percent, for after the battle of Moncontour there were no significant additions to the army's strength and a large number of soldiers, almost all French infantry, became casualties of one type or another at the siege.[8]

Not all of the missing soldiers were combat casualties, which to the point in the campaign right after Moncontour remained in the low thousands. Some of the missing soldiers belonged to units which were detached from the army for garrison duty elsewhere in the theatre, or to units which were so worn down they were released to go home. By far the most important sources of attrition seem to have

---

[7] Excluding the artillery train, which varied from about 1,000 to 2,500 men.

[8] For the attrition of infantry and cavalry see chapters 4 and 5. According to Parker, *Military Revolution*, 46–61, ordinary attrition for the armies of the period ran from 2–4 percent per month even in the absence of major actions. When I have had to estimate attrition for individual units or formations I have used a 4 percent per month rate because all of the documents of the time speak of the extreme conditions (weather, forced marches, lack of supplies, sickness, and desertion) the army operated under throughout the campaign.

been sickness and desertions. From the point of view of maintaining the effectiveness of the army in the field, however, all soldiers who disappeared can be attributed to attrition, whatever its causes, and the calculations in Table 9.3 leave a general impression that it took the provision of two soldiers to keep a single soldier in the field over the course of the long campaign.

Table 9.3 also suggests differential attrition rates for different types of soldiers. All French troops, whether infantry or cavalry, tended to be reduced by attrition at much higher rates than all foreign troops, whether infantry or cavalry. But within both the French and foreign troop categories, cavalry suffered losses by attrition at much lower rates than did infantry. To some extent these differences between foreigners and Frenchmen reflect a time dimension: more of the foreign elements joined the army later in the campaign and therefore had less time to become as reduced in numbers. But other factors were also clearly at work that favored foreign troops in general and cavalry in particular. Foreign troops were better and more regularly paid than French troops, which would have enabled them to provide for themselves better when regular supplies ran out. Foreign troops may also have exhibited more solidarity than French troops, since it was harder for them to desert, and their wounded and sick were probably less likely to be abandoned, given the enormous baggage trains and numbers of extra mounts and servants they were usually accompanied by. Foreign troops also tended to refuse detached duties, a source of constant attrition and chances for desertion, and a luxury French units were not accorded. Finally, though it is impossible to prove, with the exception of the Swiss, who though avid for their pay were very disciplined, foreign troops had a reputation for an amazingly organized and premeditated rapaciousness – the possibility of booty which motivated all soldiers must have been of particular importance in drawing men to service in a foreign country. Descriptions of returning columns of reiters, with wagons groaning under the weight of their plunder, accompanied by vast herds of captured livestock, abound in contemporary accounts of the wars.

Cavalry in general were more likely to be dispersed over the countryside in order to maximize forage and watering opportunities, and their mobility must have given them an advantage over the infantry in gathering a minimum level of supplies, just as their extra mounts made it easier to carry extra food. Their mounts may have also made cavalry service less physically wearing than service as a footsoldier. And cavalry of the French gendarme sort tended to be made up of noblemen, who in most cases would have more resources than ordinary footsoldiers and who may also have been healthier and better nourished than ordinary soldiers. Like foreign troops in general, French cavalry units may therefore have been physically, psychologically, and socially much better equipped than the infantry for the type of predatory behavior that could maximize their survival even under the worst of circumstances.

The net result of the combination of reinforcement and attrition during the 1568–69 campaign, though the same could just as easily be said about the other civil wars, was that, quite apart from the movements of the main body of the army, the theatre of operations was the scene of constant movement by bodies of troops, both large and small, and even individual soldiers. From the beginning of the campaign, throughout its course, and after its end, columns of troops wended their way to the theatre from all points of the compass and from all over the kingdom and its immediate foreign neighbors. The requirements of the army in the third civil war, as we have seen, drew units of native troops from every part of France. A majority of those French companies were, in fact, brand new formations. Arriving at the theatre after approach marches of various distances and difficulty, often having fought actions on the way, each group of a few hundred or thousand men brought with it, like Monluc's regiment in the second civil war, its own distinctive experience of support or neglect, discipline or ill-discipline, confidence or fragility. Once they arrived at the theatre of operations they had to find the main army, often through contested or logistically exhausted territory. As far as the communities and peoples they encountered are concerned, it is hard to imagine how they could have been expected to have any sympathy towards them. Almost all the troops who arrived were complete strangers to the theatre and in the case of troops from abroad they were literally foreign. If foreign, and in many cases simply if from a different part of France, they did not even share a common language with the civilian populations of the theatre.

Arriving and departing troops were even further separated from the people they operated among by the cultural chasm which has always, and in the early modern period especially, divided soldier from civilian. The soldiery were an instrument of barely controlled violence and destructiveness and their vocation and values were based on completely different assumptions about rules of law, property rights, and the application of force and coercion that in any other context would be clearly criminal behavior. The social composition of some types of units must have resulted in even further distancing. Among French troops the gendarmerie, with its large contingent of nobles, whose behavior even in civil society was often arrogant and violent, was picked out for special condemnation by contemporaries, and it is hard to imagine that its predisposition to hard treatment of civilians was not reinforced by its class makeup. The most extreme complaints, however, were reserved for foreign troops, and a brief examination of the capitulations signed with such troops can explain why, for such contingents, organized explicitly for plundering, were treated as completely insulated and self-sufficient communities even within the army itself and reserved to themselves alone the right to regulate and judge the behavior of their own members.[9]

Against the unceasing tide of groups of men approaching the army, however, there was also the continuous undertow of men leaving it. Desertions were often numerous, and contributed knots of truly desperate and dangerous men moving across the landscape. At least as important was the flotsam and jetsam of wounded and sick

[9] See the capitulations mentioned in note 4 above.

men left behind and the many smaller groups of men who were detached from the main body as garrisons for local communities and who, as much of the correspondence about bad troop behavior makes clear, were usually completely abandoned to their own devices and forgotten as the main army moved on.[10] Even before the war ended, moreover, it was common for the army to furlough units temporarily, particularly cavalry units, when it went into one of the longer bivouac camps that punctuated the periods of marching and fighting, and the departure of such units, who were often in extremely bad shape and sometimes dismissed because they were mutinous, often left a trail of outrages. And, of course, when the war ended, and the army disbanded, the movement of contingents, units, and smaller groups of hardened and basically unsupervised men was repeated, but this time outward from the campaign region to every corner of the kingdom and across the frontiers.

THE DIVISION OF TIME: MARCHING, CAMPING, AND FIGHTING

At the center of these comings and goings of troops was the concentration of hundreds of companies of soldiers, tens of thousands of mounts and draft animals, the wagons and carriages of the artillery, baggage, and supply train, and an uncounted number of camp followers which constituted the main army itself. It was the cumulative impact of the movements and actions of this great conglomeration of violent strangers (paralleled, of course, by those of the enemy army) which established and principally defined the nature of war's presence in any theatre of operations. What were the general patterns that defined the royal army's presence during the 1568-69 campaign? A day-by-day reconstruction of the major types of activity – marching, camping, and fighting – that the army was engaged in from the establishment of its first camp at Saumur on the Loire on September 2, 1568, to the surrender and occupation of Saint-Jean on December 3, is given in Figure 28.[11] Over this period of 457 days, some contact with the enemy was made on 86 days, or 19 percent of the time. More than half of that time (11 per cent of the entire period) was invested in the campaign's single formal siege, and only 35 days (8 per cent of the whole period) in all other types of fighting. But of those 35 days on which some kind of combat besides the single major siege occurred, only about a dozen witnessed serious fight-

---

[10] For examples of troops left unpaid on the periphery of the main actions see chapter 11 below. Amboise Paré's "Apologie, et traite contenant les voyages faits en divers lieux" provides a clinically grisly account of many of the battlefields and the medical care of the period, Paré, *Oeuvres*, vol. 3, 676–734.

[11] Based primarily on Segesser, which includes an "Itinerarium des Regiments Pfyffer, 1567–1569" in Appendix V of vol. 1, 666–70, and Gigon, who used Segesser and his own detailed knowledge of the theatre of war to provide a day-by-day account of the army's movements and actions, including correct identification of placenames and mileages. I supplemented measurements, when necessary, with the distances indicated on a modern roadmap of France. Segesser's Appendix V includes two very detailed maps of the track of the Swiss, and Gigon also provides several useful maps of the campaign up to the battle of Moncontour.

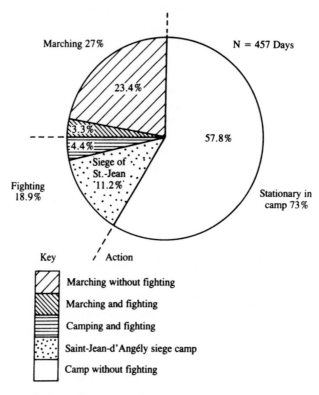

Fig. 28. Time study of the army's actions, September 2, 1568 to December 3, 1569

ing by any part of the army and only a half dozen saw all or most of the army actually literally engaged with the enemy. The rest of the non-siege contacts involved skirmishes between outposts or rearguards, or raids. The army spent 81 percent of its days, in other words, without any contact or engaged in no fighting at all with the enemy. The vast majority of the army's time was spent instead in stationary camps or on the march without engagement with the enemy. From the beginning to the end of the campaign the army remained stationary in its camp on 335 days (73 percent of all days) on only 20 of which did it see any kind of fighting besides the 51 days of the siege of Saint-Jean-d'Angély, and spent 122 days on the march (27 percent) only on 15 of which did it see any action. Another way to express this division of labor is to say that it took more than five days of feeding and supplying the army to get it in a position to have a single day on which some part of it could see action in some manner.

But although this identifies in a general way how the army spent its time over the course of a campaign that lasted more than a year, it does not, of course, address the

Table 9.4. *Daily lengths of the army's marches, 1568–69*

Length of march (miles)	No. marches	% marches
1–5	21	17
6–10	33	27
11–15	33	27
16–20	27	22
21–25	8	7

way in which such actions were sequenced within the period nor the intensity with which they were pursued. In fact, the operations of the army during the 1568-69 campaign can be divided into seven distinct periods of alternating activity and inactivity. In four of those periods the army remained in the same locality for a relatively long period of time – from 27 consecutive days in winter camp on the Loire to 51 days at Saint-Jean-d'Angély. But the 122 days of marching and all of its fighting except for the siege took place during three periods of active campaigning: the fall and winter campaign of 1568, the Jarnac and La Roche-L'Abeille campaign in the spring and summer of 1569, and the Moncontour campaign in the fall of 1569. Periods of great inactivity, then, alternated with pulsations of activity when all the hard marching and fighting was done, and the army, for logistical purposes, changed from a sitting to a moving target. But even within the periods of activity, that is, of open campaigning, the movements of the army tended to be concentrated in bursts of a number of consecutive or near consecutive days of hard marching dictated in part by the changing military situation. Though it is not possible to measure every twist and turn of these movements, over the 314 days of open and active campaigning we have just identified the army marched a total of approximately 1,400 miles. But 956 of these miles, or 68 percent, were concentrated in nine separate bursts totaling 71 days of marching, or only 23 percent of the open campaigning. During these bursts of activity the army achieved some fairly rapid rates of march through very different types of terrain and weather conditions, averaging as much as 16 miles each day and covering total distances of anywhere from 67 to 222 miles per burst. When we look, as in Table 9.4, at the length of all daily marches undertaken by the army, we can see that more than half were of at least 11 miles or more but that marches of more than 20 miles, those reaching the physical limits possible under the conditions of the time, were rare. When the army marched at all, then, it tended to cover fairly substantial distances in relatively short periods of time.

The key to assessing the impact of the army on localities, of course, is the number of times it visited and the amount of time it spent in them. When we follow the path of the army during the third civil war we discover that across the period of 457 days

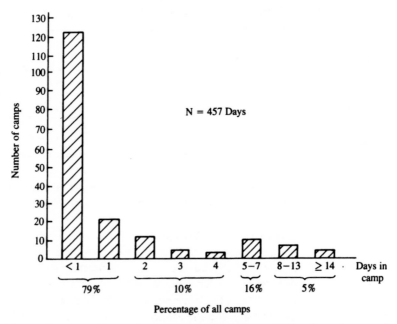

Fig. 29. Duration of the royal army's camps, September 2, 1568 to December 3, 1569

the army stayed in 181 camps whose varying lengths are illustrated by Figure 29.[12] Seventy-nine percent of all the army's camps during the war lasted one full day or less, 19 percent more than one day but less than two weeks, and only 2 percent two weeks or more. Of the camps lasting 2 weeks or more, three – the initial assembly camp at Saumur (28 days), the winter camp at Chinon (28 days), and the summer camp at Loches (37 days) – marked the major periods of inactivity for the royal army and in the latter two cases pauses to allow a thoroughly exhausted force to rest and recuperate on the fringes of the campaign area after long operations in logistically barren territory. When we factor in the camp at Saint-Jean-d'Angély (51 days), the four longest stays, representing less than 2 percent of all the camps the army made, accounted for 32 percent of all the days in the campaign. By contrast, camps lasting one day, representing 79 per cent of all the camps made, only accounted for 31 percent of all the days in the campaign. To put this another way, the royal troops spent one-third of the campaign in camps that lasted only one day, a majority of the campaign in camps lasting one week or less, and a third of the campaign in camps lasting two weeks or longer. But the total number of longer camps

---

[12] A stay of less than one day means that the army arrived partway through the day or in the night, spent the night, and then departed immediately the next morning, spending less than 24 hours in the place. The fact that the army did not actually camp in a place does not necessarily mean it went untouched as the army marched through or near it.

(only 11 percent were as long as five days) was quite small and the number of short camps quite high (89 percent lasted four days or less) which, of course, from the point of view of the time frame in which most communities interacted with the main body of the army, was highly significant.

When we plot on a map of the whole theatre of operations in the west the total number of days spent by the army in every place it established a camp over the course of the 457 days of the campaign, as in Figure 30, we find that though 181 separate and distinct camps were established during this period, only 158 localities were visited by the army. Seventeen towns were visited twice by the army and six (Loudon, Chinon, Châtellerault, Poitiers, Chavigny, and Confolens) received three separate visits, while 135 communities received only a single visit over the course of a campaign lasting more than a year. Taking into account the impact of multiple visits, however, does little to change the overall picture of the army's presence in individual communities, for 89 percent of the communities where the main army stopped to camp had to endure the immediate presence of the army for a week or less.

How are we to interpret the significance of these patterns? First, one can only conclude that direct contact between the main body of the army and local communities was usually of short, even very brief, duration. Brief stops must have been considered a godsend by places which otherwise would have had to face the prospect of supporting enormous numbers of soldiers from quite limited resources for longer periods of time. But it must also certainly have contributed to the emotional isolation of soldiers from the populations they moved among, for two-thirds of the places they stayed were never revisited and at only about one out of every ten of the localities they visited did they spend more than a week. The army's patterns of marching and camping, then, put the very populations it was theoretically there to protect in some danger of systematic mistreatment, particularly when the soldiers themselves may have been in a needy state or in the position to avoid recognition and retribution, which, moving fast and being far too numerous to be properly policed, they almost always were.

But even if most places were in direct contact with the army for only short periods of time, the fact remains that a very large number of communities had been visited by the army, and hundreds of additional places touched by it as it marched along even if it did not establish a camp in them. And as a glance at Figure 30 reveals, the royal army, not to mention the Huguenot army, had cut a very large swath through most of the theatre of operations. By the end of the campaign there must have been few communities in the area who had managed to avoid altogether the enormous hosts of armed and dangerous strangers. Furthermore, it did not take much time for a force of over 30,000 souls and perhaps 15,000 animals to strip even a moderately sized town or village of its accumulated agricultural resources. We have seen how many provisions the 4,000-man garrison of Chartres could consume in a matter of a few weeks – the main army itself could consume the same amount

The army's presence on campaign, 1568–69

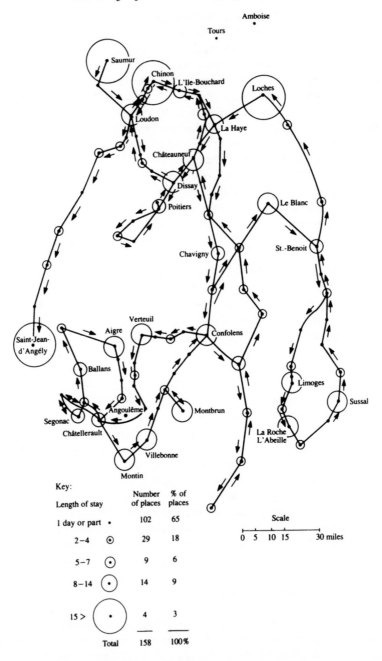

Fig. 30. The army's length of stay in communities in the western theater, 1568–69

of product (and more because of its larger number of animals) in a matter of days. So while stays of short duration were the rule, the length of those stays was dictated perhaps as much by the amount of time it took to exhaust the logistical possibilities of a place as by the military situation itself.

Although the army was organized to provide a certain minimum of rations to troops while on the march, Figure 30 confirms that the locations of its longer camps (even Saint-Jean-d'Angély) were all on the periphery of the campaign area. The meaning of this pattern is fairly transparent: nowhere in the main campaigning area touched in 1568-69 did the army spend more than a total of two weeks in one place because almost nowhere in the campaign area were there enough resources (water and forage for horses, bread, wine, meat, shelter and firewood for soldiers) to support such large numbers of men and beasts for a longer period of time, and without a great deal of advance planning the transportation net was simply inadequate to bring supplies in the needed quantities from more than a few miles away. Whenever the army camped it would exhaust local resources in a matter of days or a week, and would, whatever the military situation, have to move on to the next place that was untouched either by itself or the enemy.

The spoor revealed by Figure 30, then, resembles that of a great predator which has to stay constantly on the move in order to avoid overhunting of its territory. The army command and the crown, of course, were well aware of the impact troop movements and the presence of the army had on local communities, and some effort was expended during the civil wars to regulate and ameliorate that impact. In the mid-1560s a number of *commissaires de guerre* were created in the provinces who were supposed to oversee the establishment of *étapes*, serve as guides and overseers of troops on the march, and regulate musters. The army itself had its own military police, the various provosts and their archers, who were responsible for enforcing discipline in camp and on the march. And the logistical needs of the troops were supposed to be provided for by the *commissaire général de vivres* and his assistants, who were responsible for the establishment of depots, and the procurement, preparation, and delivery of daily rations, which often entailed the establishment of contracts with networks of merchants, the *munitionnaires*, for the timely delivery of quantities of grain, meat, and wine.[13] And, as mentioned previously, over the course of the civil wars increasingly detailed sets of rules attempted to regularize and regulate the behavior of troops in camp, on the march, and in garrison.

[13] Michaud, "Les institutions militaires," 38–42, provides a good short description of the development of the *commissaire* system. The military correspondence of the times is replete with orders for the provision of forage, food, and shelter. See especially *Henri III*, vols. 1–2, *passim*. For the operation of the *étapes* system see the example of Chartres, in 1567–68, in chapter 8 above. When the army was involved in stationary operations long-term contracts with entrepreneurs would be negotiated. A contract with merchants from Niort for the camp at La Rochelle signed in late 1572, for example, called for the *concessionnaire* to furnish *every day*, for a period of six months, 30,000 12-ounce loaves of bread, 10,800 *pintes* of wine, and 20,000 *livres* of beef: BN Mss. Fr. 4,554, fols. 102–4. Gigon, note M, 380–84, describes the administration and provisioning of the army during 1568–69. Navereau, *Le logement, passim*, traces the history of the relationship between lodging soldiers and their hosts.

All these efforts were only partially successful, and, as the civil wars dragged on, especially after 1574, apparently less and less effectual. There were never enough *commissaires de guerre* to oversee troop movements properly, and the number of provostial police was also limited. The latter had their hands full simply trying to keep order in the main army itself, and disorders or outrages by troops and their camp followers who were on detached duty or operating on the fringes of the army's operations completely escaped oversight. Despite the best efforts of the logistical service, there were times when the army went unsupplied – during the third civil war longer camps at Chinon, Le Blanc, and Loches were all dictated by the need to recuperate from operations in areas left bereft of supplies by the season or their own sterility. But while the provision of the daily bread ration to troops only rarely failed, larger logistical problems were caused by the fact that the troops, as we will see in Chapter 11, were rarely paid. Theoretically the supply system was designed to be financed by the payments made by the troops when they purchased their rations each day. In truly desperate situations unpaid soldiers would demand and the army would sometimes provide the bread ration at a discount or even free for a time.[14] But the bread ration, even though the center of the soldiers' diet, was not enough in and of itself to nourish the army, and when pay failed, and loans from their officers dried up, or even when there was pay but local conditions of shortage greatly inflated prices, troops were unable to obtain the portions of meat, wine, legumes, and other fresh products which they desperately needed, and thought they were entitled to, without extorting it from their civilian hosts, the localities they were staying in, or the areas they were passing through. The cavalry, more

[14] For example, Anjou wrote to the king on October 7, 1569, immediately after Moncontour, *Henri III*, 125–26, that it was essential to pay the troops, "lesquelz commancent a demander le pain de la munition sans payer, pour ce quilz disent quilz n'ont plus d'argent. J'ay desja este contrainct de commander que il leur fust delivre, d'autant que nous avons maintenant plus besoing d'eulx que jamais et il y eust eu craincte quilz nen s'en feussent allez. Cela causera une confusion bien grande pour ce que, quand il ne fault quilz payent le dict pain, ilz en prennent beaucoup plus, et sera bien malaise d'y pouvoir satisfaire; il en fauldra endurer, et, silz estoient payez, cela remediroit a tout." *Ibid.*, 126–27, also contains a letter sent the next day describing a scheme submitted to the military council by the *commissaires des vivres* to regularize the financing of the soldiers' rations.

In general soldiers were treated more indulgently at critical points in the campaign. An indication of the reasoning behind indulgence can be derived from a comment made by Sipierre, who had been appointed temporary commander at the siege of Orléans in 1563, after Guise's death, to the papal legate, who had objected to demands by the soldiers to break the meat fast rules in order to maintain their strength. According to Brantôme, *Oeuvres*, vol. 1, 171–73, Sipierre argued: "Monsieur, ne pensez pas regler nos gens de guerre comme vos gens d'eglise: car autre chose est de servir Dieu et servir la guerre. Voulez-vous que je vous die le vray? Ce n'est point en ce temps, ny en cest' armee, compose de plusieurs sortes de gens, que vous devez faire telz scrupules: car, quand a vostre beurre, fromage et laictage, nos soldats francois ne vous en veulent point, comme vos Italians et Espagnolz. Ils veulent manger de la chair, et de bonne viande, pour mieux sustanter. Ilz en mangeront aussi bien deca comme dela, et a ouvert et a cachette, quelque deffence qui en soit. Parquoy, faictes mieux: Ordonnez leur de'en manger, et donnez leur en une bonne dispence et absolution. Que si d'euxmesmes ilz s'en dispensent, vostre authorite en sera plus supprimee; au contraire, de plus ell'en sera eslevee si leur permettez, et chascun dira: 'M. le legat, cet homme de bien, nous a donne dispence; et cela s'en resonnera mieux par tout.'"

highly paid than the infantry and capable of ranging much further afield to gather supplies, were generally not even provided with the army's daily *pain de munition* on the march. When pay failed they had no choice but to take what they required, which included fodder and forage for their mounts.[15] Often desperate, and sometimes completely unregulated, the soldiers with the army or moving to or from it, had every incentive to forage, loot, and coerce the local populations because, moving rapidly through communities of complete strangers and rarely staying more than a day in a single place, having no basis of commonality with their hosts, they had no disincentives to the unruly and predatory behaviors which the army codes of the time sought to prevent.

[15] See Navereau, *Le logement.*

10

The destruction of an army: The siege of La Rochelle, 1573

THE STRUCTURE OF OPERATIONS

The royal army's siege of La Rochelle in 1573 was the most important and decisive military episode of the entire period of the early wars of religion. To the extent that current histories provide any explanations for the army's failure in four months of sustained assault to take the prime bastion of Protestantism in France they tend to focus on the well-organized and fanatical resistance of the town's Huguenot citizens and their refugee allies or to stress disunity in the Catholic camp. What is never examined in any detail is the actual course that the besiegers' efforts took, the significant military obstacles the army faced but ultimately failed to overcome, and the destructive impact of those events on the army itself.

In abstract terms, of course, a siege is a fairly easy military operation to understand. Besiegers simply physically blow a hole in the town's defenses large enough to enable assaulting troops to penetrate into the place and overwhelm the defenders. If the assault fails, it is renewed until the exhausted defenders are overcome or surrender on terms. If the defenses ultimately prove too strong to be taken by storm, the besiegers rely on a tight blockade to starve the place into submission. But in the actuality of sixteenth-century siege operations, each of these stages was fraught with problems and dangers for the besieging army. For though unprepared urban places were often taken with comparative ease (or were betrayed) during the first civil war, as time went on even relatively vulnerable places like Chartres, Poitiers, or Saint-Jean-d'Angély could, as we have noted, be turned with relatively few resources into formidable military obstacles capable of lengthy resistance to besiegers. Sixteenth-century siege warfare, moreover, was far from the science it was later to become in the hands of a Vauban. Since each target presented unique and unpredictable problems, to accurately discern a place's principal strengths or weaknesses in order to besiege it, wrote Monluc, "C'est la chose la plus difficile et importante en la guerre."[1] In his advice to the duke of Anjou on the conduct of the siege of La Rochelle Monluc also reminds us of the importance of speed in the approach to the city's ditch and walls, for every delay gave an energetic defender

---

[1] Monluc, *Commentaires*, vol. 2, 572.

opportunities to repair the damage the attackers had inflicted and to improve his defensive works at the point of attack.[2] The assault on the breach itself was the most dangerous of all military operations (and would remain so well into the nineteenth century), for at the narrow and physically difficult point of attack the defenders could enjoy parity or even superiority of numbers and from both frontal and flanking positions deploy a variety of crude but murderously effective anti-personnel weapons, from rocks and burning pitch to grenades, massed arquebus fire, and cannons firing massive charges of jagged pieces of metal and stones against the uncovered attackers. Furthermore, if the assaults failed or had to be repeated, then the attackers, just as much as the defenders, found themselves involved in a race for time against the entropic forces that were intrinsic to siege warfare: exhaustion of local supplies, disease, mounting casualties and fatigue from constant, boring, and dangerous duties, plummeting morale, and widespread desertions.

As we have seen, after the first two civil wars the army's principal theatres of operation shifted to the south and west of the kingdom, far from its principal sources of strength and support in the Paris region and the north of the country. After the battle of Moncontour in 1569, the royal army fought almost no open field actions and instead conducted a series of bitter sieges beginning with Saint-Jean-d'Angély and continuing through the next three civil wars which, we have argued, were increasingly more costly and difficult for the army and the crown to sustain. Of all those operations, the siege of La Rochelle was by far the most important, and failure to strike a third and potentially decisive military blow against the Huguenots (the destruction of their field army in 1569 and massacre of most of their army's leaders in Paris in 1572 being the first two) by reducing that city to obedience provides most dramatic evidence of the crown's growing military difficulties. It would only be after another seven decades of struggle and a second great siege of that bastion that the crown would finally eliminate the Huguenots as a serious military threat. Besides representing a missed opportunity, however, the 1573 siege also contributed, in conjunction with the other military trends we have been tracing, to a dramatic lowering of the royal army's fighting qualities and military effectiveness from the mid-1570s onward.

The first chapter of this book has already presented a brief overview of the course of the siege. This chapter in contrast develops a much more finely detailed and nuanced analysis of the royal army's experience at the siege. Though they differ somewhat in the details they provide and are sometimes in disagreement on minor points, a number of contemporary accounts and histories of the siege, from both points of view, do exist, and the information they contain makes it possible to identify and then trace sequentially the principal types of military operations which were undertaken during the period of the siege. From the point of view of the royal

---

[2] Larroque, *Receuil des travaux*, 322–31, which contains a detailed discussion by Monluc of measures he thought Anjou should take to insure the efficient operation of the siege.

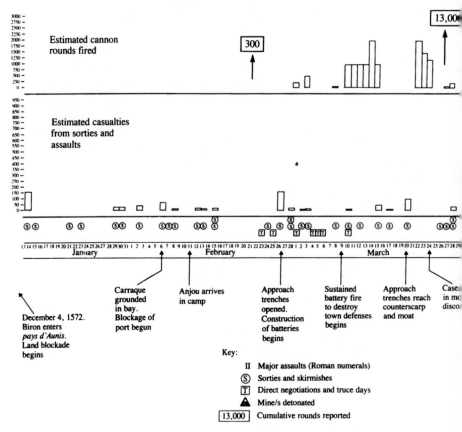

Fig. 31. Siege of La Rochelle. Chart of daily operations, January–June, 1573

army's experience, three sources which are particularly valuable and informative should be mentioned. The first is a series of letters written by Biron from his arrival near La Rochelle in late 1572 until Anjou's arrival to take over command in early February, 1573, which outline in detail the problems the army encountered in its preliminary operations. The second is the daily journal, or *aide-mémoire* book, kept by the duke of Nevers, one of the most prominent noble leaders at the siege and the principal director of the primary siege operation against the bastion of the Evangile and the northern wall of the city. The third is a lengthy after-action report written by the duke of Anjou for Charles IX which recapitulated the decisions and operations of the siege in a blow-by-blow manner while attempting to justify his actions and explain the difficulties which led to the siege's failure.[3]

[3] For sources on the siege see chapter 1, note 17 and the Appendix, Part F. Also see chapter 6, *passim*, for much of the artillery operations at the siege. Brantôme, who was eyewitness to most of the siege's

The structure of operations

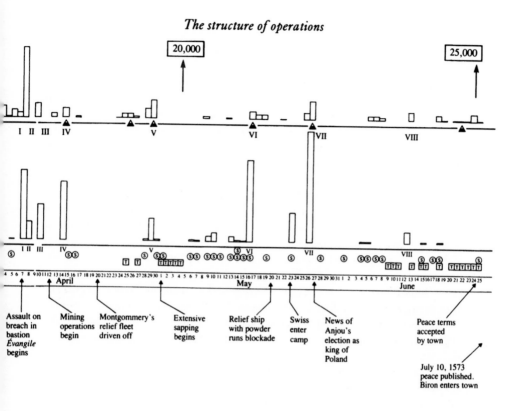

Taken collectively, these documents enable us to follow the army's day-to-day operations during the siege in great detail and analyze its experience on three different but interrelated levels: that of the structure and flow of operational events; that of the expectations, decisions, and frustrations of the leadership; and that of the experience of the officers and soldiers who endured its hardships, fought its actions, and in the end were broken as an effective military instrument.

A chart of the daily operations of the army at the siege of La Rochelle from mid-January to late June 1573 is presented in Figure 31. The individual components of this chart were identified by an exhaustive combing and comparison of the sources that involved a great deal of triangulation of data, making choices between discrepant dates and claims, and translating verbal descriptions (such as "many killed

dramatic moments, recorded a number of impressions: *Discours*, 75, 78–79, 80–84, 91, 156–58, 160–61, 165–66, 203, 220, and 223.

249

and wounded") into numerical estimates that have a degree of arbitrariness to them. It is important for the reader to understand that despite its appearance, Figure 31 does not pretend to great quantitative precision, for it is rooted in contemporary claims and estimates that though essentially quantitative in nature, were also fairly imprecise. It is possible, however, to be fairly confident that the chronological relationships to one another of the different categories of plotted events, their relative incidences, and their relative magnitudes, are reasonably accurate. By simultaneously displaying several disaggregated series of information the chart allows us to study the interactions of the various types of military activities and to identify with some certainty the overall structure of the army's siege operations as well.

The major types of events tracked by Figure 31 are the estimated number of rounds fired each day by the army's artillery batteries, the dates and numbers of sorties and major assaults, the estimated daily number of the army's casualties from fighting in the sorties and assaults, detonations of the besieger's mines against the fortifications, and the number of days on which negotiations and/or truces took place. Indications of the army's own estimates of the cumulative number of artillery rounds fired by various dates are also shown. Finally, the chart annotates the operational series by identifying the chronological situation of a number of discrete events which help to mark different stages or important moments in the course of the siege.[4]

Perhaps the first thing to be noted is the length of the siege. Although Biron entered the *pays d'Aunis* in December 1572 to begin the investment of the city, supplies continued to flow into La Rochelle until early February 1573, and it was only in mid-February, after Anjou's arrival on the spot, that the port was sealed off and the city fully surrounded on land. Construction of the approach trenches and batteries themselves did not begin until the night of February 26–27. So by June 25, the date on which the town agreed to peace terms and ended the siege, though some of the royal army had been in place for seven months, the actual formal siege operations had lasted for about four months. That the siege of La Rochelle was one of the longest of the period should alert us to the fact that an effort of more than three to four months of such warfare would in any case have been almost impossible for the army to sustain. But, of course, the siege was never intended to last as long as it did.

An examination of the artillery work at the siege shows that more than half of the total rounds fired were used over a 2-week period between March 9 and 26 to obliterate the defenders' fortifications and pound a breach at the intended point of attack on the bastion of the Evangile. Over the next twelve days another 6,000 rounds were used to selectively soften the defenses, further prepare the breach, attempt to silence the casemates discovered in the ditch and, in a final paroxysm of firing on April 7, support the first great assault. By the morning of April 8 the royal

⁴ See Appendix, Part F.

artillery had already expended almost 80 percent of the rounds it was to fire during the entire siege, and, as can be seen, substantial bombardments later in the siege were on a far smaller scale and were used almost entirely to accompany the infantry assaults. Though problems with ammunition supply plagued the besiegers throughout the rest of the siege, by the end of the second week in April the artillery had completed its most essential job of suppressing the defenses and pounding a reasonable initial breach, but the attack was stalled at the ditch, where it would remain, despite great efforts, for the rest of the siege. The limit on the use of artillery once the actual assault stage had been reached is underlined by the adoption of alternative means of defeating the fortifications. Mining operations which were both dangerous and unpredictable in their effects were begun immediately after the failure of the first three assaults, and explosions of mines beneath the walls would lead off all but the last of the later major assaults. But disappointment over the effects of the mines also led to the initiation of extensive sapping (whose slow but sure methods had changed but little since ancient times) in early May in an attempt to bring down larger sections of the walls and bastion.

From April 7 onwards, then, fighting concentrated on the control of the town's ditch and the base of the wall and the bastion, in a total area perhaps 40 yards deep and 400 yards long, from which new assaults could be mounted. Bombardment gave way as the main form of attack to repeated major assaults by the army's infantry, eight in all, each costing several hundred casualties. While the first four of these assaults were all mounted over the course of seven days, later assaults could only be mounted after intervals of about two weeks or longer, as the army became increasingly exhausted. The four assaults during the second week in April, then, mark in retrospect both the climax of the army's attack and its almost complete stalemate. Despite the employment of mines and sapping, prospects for a successful assault worsened rather than increased, and the two major assaults mounted in May, the sixth and seventh of the series, which represented the army's last gasp, led to higher rather than lower casualties from the fighting.

The dramatic spikes of casualties sustained during the major assaults have to be set against a generally lower but chronic level of casualties from other kinds of fighting. The defenders were well armed with light artillery and *arquebuses à croc*, and even after their major counter-batteries were destroyed, their continual harassing fire and sniping made it extremely dangerous for soldiers and pioneers to be exposed in the trenches or the ditch. But forming an even more continuous and costly background to the army's operations were the constant skirmishes and sorties fought between anywhere from a handful to hundreds of soldiers on both sides near the walls and in the ditch and approach trenches. Almost all of these combats were initiated by the defending garrison, and were intended to destroy the attackers' works, delay their approaches and assaults, and force them to keep a constant, anxious, and fatiguing watch. More than sixty sorties are identified by the sources and many more took place which were not specifically recorded. Hardly a day went by without some type of such fighting, which from the beginning of digging of the approach trenches and particularly after the struggle for control of the ditch began, involved the most brutal of hand-to-hand fighting and plentiful use by the defenders of hand grenades and incendiary devices. As we shall see below, the town suffered a less favorable ratio of casualties versus the army in these operations than when it defended the breach during major assaults, but the alternative was to cede the initiative entirely to the army and allow it to continue its works unimpeded. For the army, the total number of casualties caused by the chronic sorties was much less overall than those inflicted during the great assaults. But they were a constant drain on its strength and were capable on occasion of inflicting considerable damage. During a surprise attack on the trenches on May 27, the day the crown's Swiss reinforcements arrived at camp, for example, the army suffered more combat casualties than in three of its major assaults. The relentless nature of the sortie warfare is a tribute to the active and determined nature of the city garrison, but it was also very effective, contributing eventually, as we will see, to an almost complete intimidation of the royal troops as the siege dragged on.

Against the background of constant sorties and sniping, then, two great contrasting rhythms or stages of the siege played themselves out for the royal army. The first was essentially an artillery duel to suppress the defenses and establish the conditions for assaulting the breach. The second was a grim succession of costly infantry assaults, renewed at longer and longer intervals, assisted by the artillery but also prepared by explosive mines and traditional sapping methods. But as the gaps and interruptions within the series of events, as well as the presence of a number of truce days reminds us, many days at the siege saw little or no fighting. During the period of 117 days that encompassed the heart of the siege, from the beginning of the bombardment on February 28 to the last rounds fired by the army's cannons on June 24, 66 days, or 56 percent of the total saw no firing by the royal artillery at all. Furthermore, from February 23 through June 25, a period of 123 days, there were 27 days, or 22 percent of all days, the whole or part of which were used for negotiations, or truces, though some of those days were marred by violations. These 27 truce days were concentrated in three clusters. The first, in late February, represented the final attempts to persuade the town to yield as the approach trenches were being opened but before the bombardment began in earnest. The second, in late April and early May, represented a renewed attempt to talk the town into accepting terms after the failure of the first four major assaults in the second week in April and the turning back of Montgommery's effort to relieve the siege by sea, while the third, from mid-June to the actual end of the siege, after the failure of the two great assaults in May, marked the end of the army as an effective fighting force and the abandonment of any serious effort to take the city while peace negotiations were finally concluded.

Despite these interruptions, what is impressive is the sustainment of the various kinds of fighting at daily and weekly intervals over a period of several months. Even a day without barrages, or sorties, or assaults was not necessarily a day without danger or travail, for sniping continued, mines collapsed or blew up by mistake, pioneers continued their work, and guard duty had to be performed. The longer the siege went on, moreover, the more wretched conditions became for the army. A day passing without dramatic fighting became simply another day on which operations did not advance, supplies became scarcer, the number of wounded needing care mounted, and, as we will see, the soldiers' willingness to obey orders and fight, even if only in self-defense, continued to erode. It is to a more detailed analysis of this process of deterioration that we now turn.

"I WAS EMBARKED WITHOUT BISCUIT"

"Ils m'embarquerent sans bisquit," wrote Anjou of his departure from Paris on January 3, 1573, referring to the delays which had plagued preparations for the siege since the previous fall, including a postponement of the siege to the following spring and a decision to defer a levy of 6,000 Swiss troops to aid in the siege.[5] As he rode south accompanied by a small train and little money, Anjou began to collect disquieting information that the city's garrison was larger than had previously been thought, its situation difficult to completely invest without a larger force than the approximately 10,000 French infantry who had initially been assigned to the operation, and that the preparations at the site of the siege remained incomplete. A succession of letters from Biron kept him informed about the local difficulties, but he pushed on despite misgivings that he "risked shame," arriving at the besiegers' camp on February 11.[6] What he found was not encouraging.

Though Biron had been operating near La Rochelle since early December, his efforts had been handicapped from the beginning by the fact that there were not enough local materials to make the many fascines and gabions which would be essential to protect the pioneers and soldiers in their works, and a shortage of artillery horses meant multiple wearing trips to Châtellerault were necessary to bring the army's munitions to the magazine it constructed near the city. There was also a shortage of soldiers. Biron could count only twenty-six companies of French infantry in camp at a muster held on January 5, which "provides the occasion to all to resolve themselves to serve Your Majesty and to conduct themselves in a regular, orderly, and soldierly fashion. I promise, Sire, without this everything would have unraveled and threatened to have caused great prejudice to your service."[7]

Work was also delayed by a series of skirmishes with the city's garrison which, because of the soldiers' lack of familiarity with the ground, often did not go to the army's advantage. Soon enough, though, more soldiers began arriving at camp, but they brought with them new problems and Biron was forced to write that the

[5] BN Mss. Fr. 4,765, fol. 57v.
[6] *Ibid.*, fols. 57r-58v, quote from 58v.
[7] Biron, *AHG*, 62.

dissension and non-cooperation he had feared had begun to raise its head. Complaints about the behavior of the French troops in the region had already been numerous, and a regiment of Poitvin troops under Lude had initiated "ung grande querymonie," refusing to muster because of a dispute over how much pay they were owed.[8] A "grande compagnie desbordée" led by a Captain Saint-Martin arrived, causing havoc by its ill-discipline, leading Biron to complain that "Having been sent to besiege La Rochelle, I am besieged by the said Saint-Martin and his men. Because there is not a single sutler, nor any man who leaves the camp who is not robbed...I am more fearful of him than of those of La Rochelle."[9] The gendarmes assigned to the operation, who were essential for picket duty and skirmishing over open ground, soon began to desert in droves for lack of pay. Some of them had been on duty in the area for more than four months, yet they had not been paid in over a year.[10]

Despite these difficulties, by early January, as the landward blockade was tightened, Biron's active leadership had led the defenders to decide to forego sorties temporarily because of mounting casualties. But a mixed squadron of ships and galleys under Baron de la Garde which had been on station since mid-December was still unable to prevent boats from entering the city harbor, and Biron did not have enough troops both to successfully blockade the city by land and provide guards for the construction of forts on either side of the bay leading to the city. In a series of letters written in early January, Biron argued that even when the 57 infantry companies assigned to the operation were all in camp, sickness and attrition would quickly reduce them to half strength. This would be an entirely inadequate number, given the strength of the city's defenses, which could only be approached on the north side due to extensive marshes and the sea, the need to protect the artillery, man the trenches and guardposts, and provide a rotation for relieving units.[11] Yet, as Biron reminded Anjou:

Monseigneur, the important thing is where you are and what you attack, because capturing La Rochelle, no one will be able to resist you. Failing there, all will attempt to resist you, for all the rest is nothing more than a diversion, especially in that in the other provinces there is hardly the means to take fortified places.[12]

More letters followed, stressing the same themes and reporting difficulties encountered in assembling the artillery – part of the train remained at Châtellerault and 100 *milliers* of powder were stranded at Orléans – and more delays in beginning the bay forts.[13] Anjou, by now fully alarmed, reported to the king from La Guerche on January 18 that he had ordered Admiral Villars to send forty companies of

---

[8] *Ibid.*
[9] *Ibid.*, 62–63, 67.
[10] *Ibid.*, 64, 71.
[11] *Ibid.*, 62–71, also 72–73, 74, and 75–76.
[12] *Ibid.*, 70.
[13] *Ibid.*, 65, 70, 71–96; BN Mss. Fr. 4,765, fol. 58v.

Gascon infantry operating near Montauban to camp, and reminded the king that there was still a shortfall of 300,000 *livres* in the money he had been sent to hold a general muster with upon his arrival at camp.[14] On the 25th Anjou again wrote to his brother to stress the necessity of a muster if they hoped to "tenir en office les soldats," and avoid desertions.[15] By the 26th, Biron could report to Anjou that most of the original units ordered to camp had arrived or were about to arrive and that he expected all the artillery to be in camp by the time Anjou arrived.[16] In further letters he reported that the work on blocking the harbor remained incomplete despite the sinking of a number of hulks in the channel, but he assured Anjou that once he had arrived it would take only two days to situate the cannon and begin the approach to the walls.[17] In his final letter to Anjou on February 9, two days before the duke's arrival, he again had to report on a lack of progress in closing the harbor and on the fact that the infantry were clamoring for their pay. Their monthly term had passed without payment nine days before, and though food was still abundant at the site, it was very expensive, and without pay he thought it would be very difficult to retain the soldiers in obedience.[18]

When Anjou and his retinue arrived at camp on February 11 he discovered that much of what had been promised was not ready. Instead of the two days promised by Biron to get the batteries in position, two weeks had to be devoted to completing the bay forts and sinking enough additional hulks to block the harbor. There was much disagreement among the army's leaders on how to approach the defenses, and an air of unreality hung over the camp as the soldiers of each side called out to one another across the wall, killed and wounded one another in sharp skirmishes, and then intermingled and talked during truces. The English ambassador, Walsingham, passed along reports that there was such confusion and discontent in camp that many troops had already deserted, and the humanist Cauriana, who was present, wrote that it was difficult to get the soldiers to obey orders because they had not been paid.[19] Perhaps in an attempt to restore discipline, one of Anjou's first acts was to have a Captain Cadet executed for robbery, over the protests and pleas of the other captains.[20]

Anjou remained certain, however, about the importance of the operation for, as he wrote Villars in reference to the diversion of troops from other areas to the siege, "You know that the place before which I presently find myself, being at once the source and the root, requires that the cure be first employed here in the assurance that, once cut off and uprooted, the rest of its branches will wither and die by them-

---

[14] *Henri III*, vol. 1, 219–20.

[15] *Ibid.*, 224–25.

[16] Biron, *AHG*, 80–83.

[17] *Ibid.*, 83–87, 88, 89, 90–94.

[18] *Ibid.*, 94–96.

[19] Cauriana, 45, 47, 49; *CSPF/E*, vol. 10, no. 800.

[20] Simon Goulart, *Mémoires de l'éstat de France sous Charles neufièsme* (3 vols., Meiderbourg, 1578), vol. 2, fol. 143v.

selves."[21] But his continuing apprehension that his force was inadequate also led him to remind the king of the need for the Swiss, for without them, "Having a large artillery train, and little infantry, against a well-protected natural fortress of the first order, defended by men resolved to make the ultimate sacrifice, he would have to leave the artillery unprotected during assaults."[22]

Meanwhile, on the night of February 26, while the massed drummers of the army tried to mask the noise, work was begun on the parallel trench. It would eventually run from the northeast corner of the town, near the Coignes gate, across the northern face of the city, to link up with an earlier constructed fort to the west of the bastion of the Evangile (see Figure 32 for a diagram of the fortifications and the siege works).[23] From about midway along its length the approach trenches began to creep southwards towards the bastion and the town wall, both of which were partially protected from bombardment by the town's ditch and high counterscarp. It would take over three weeks to reach the counterscarp, for the approach was slowed by bad weather and a lack of gabions to protect the pioneers and soldiers from fire from the city walls. To the heavy casualties from this fire were added those from constant sorties on the trenches by the garrison, taking advantage of careless sentinels, wet powder, and negligent officers. Finally, on March 23, a trench was begun along the counterscarp parallel to the defenses. Guard posts were established and batteries overlooking the ditch and the fortifications positioned for point-blank fire, but the lack of gabions kept the attackers constantly exposed to fire and attacks by grenades and incendiaries. In order to assault the breach in the bastion, the counterscarp itself first had to be cut to allow the attackers to descend into the ditch before mounting the opposite side. But rainy weather and a growing shortage of pioneers, whose numbers had already been reduced to less than a thousand, two hundred of whom were needed to work the guns, slowed the work, even though Nevers tried to encourage the workers by providing them with extra wine rations.[24] Tempers also grew short. Nevers and Biron constantly quarreled and Puygaillard, one of the main infantry commanders, threatened to kill the pioneers if they did not work faster, an action which Nevers found very bizarre.[25] Even worse, their arrival on the counterscarp led the attackers to discover heretofore unexpected difficulties.

---

[21] *Henri III*, vol. 1, 232.

[22] *Ibid.*, 238.

[23] Sources for Figure 32 include, from Cauriana, a copy of a contemporary sketch map annotated in Latin and a very detailed plan of the city and its defenses in 1573 (both maps from the establishment J. Muller of La Rochelle); from Genet, part 1 (February, 1848), very useful maps of the entire area of operations, and a detailed reconstruction of the city's defenses and the siegeworks, on which I have relied heavily for the positions of batteries and the location of the approach trenches. Vaucheret, in Brantôme, *Discours*, 159, provides a copy of a drawing showing a bird's-eye view of the city's defenses from the perspective of the attackers.

[24] BN Mss. Fr. 4,765, fols. 20v and 60r. Nevers' account, *ibid.*, fols. 16r-28v is especially good on the operations up to the first great assault and for indications of the quarrels between him and Biron over the direction of the works.

[25] *Ibid.*, fol. 24r.

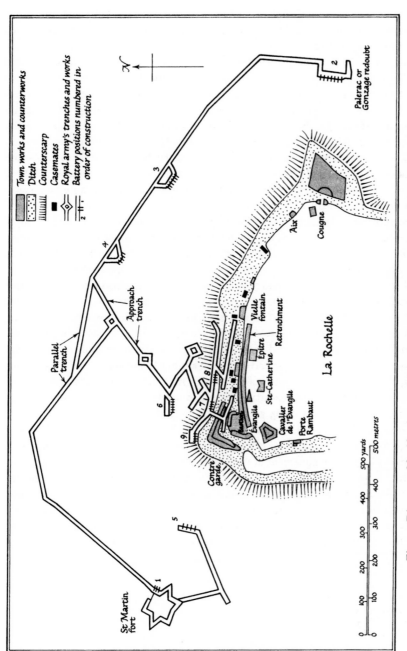

Fig. 32. Diagram of fortifications and siege works on the northern side of La Rochelle, 1573

On March 24 casemates sunk in the bottom of the ditch to the level of their firing apertures were discovered from which a murderous flanking fire could be delivered on anyone trying to operate in the ditch itself.[26]

By the end of March the artillery commissioners reported that almost 15,000 artillery rounds had been fired.[27] But there were difficulties in moving the big guns onto the counterscarp because though 1,500 pioneers were required to drag them to their new positions, only 600 were now left.[28] Although most of the city's rampart defenses had been razed by the bombardments and a large breach created in the bastion of the Evangile, the defenders, aided by the slowness of the approach and sure now where the assault would come, constructed inner works to cut off the neck of the bastion and elevated positions from which to overlook possible points of attack. Despite these difficulties the batteries on the counterscarp were soon ready to support the assault. But when Anjou visited the works at sunrise on the 29th, expecting the pre-assault bombardment to begin, he concluded that the path from the counterscarp to the ditch was too small and steep to allow proper reinforcement of the attack and it was also discovered that the rains had filled the ditch – which was normally dry – with waist-deep water, and so the attack had to be postponed.[29]

The slowness of the work and growing casualties had also begun to affect the discipline and morale of the troops, a state of affairs that was not improved by the arrival of the companies of Gascons sent by Villars. The Protestant historian Goulart described these troops as an "armée ramassée de rafiens & brigandeaux pour la pluspart," and according to D'Aubigné they were so undisciplined that Villars had been forced to suspend operation around Montauban, "realizing he was incapable of any military operation because his men, recruited for the most part in the towns which had experienced massacres, accustomed to killing without putting themselves in danger of being killed, sought only abandoned houses, merchants, peasants, women and children for their prey."[30] The nobility in camp, hardly disciplined themselves but eager for glory, concerned with deteriorating conditions, and dismayed by the postponement of the attack, clamored for an assault, arguing that without improvement in camp discipline the army would desert, for the soldiers were already suffering from hunger, the cavalry could not feed their horses, and sickness had begun to spread through the tightly packed and insanitary camps. They predicted that if the army had to stay before the city for more than two more months conditions would be so bad that the siege would have to be lifted.[31]

---

[26] *Ibid.*, fols. 21r, 60r; Genet, part 2 (March, 1848), 719–20.

[27] D'Aubigné, vol. 4, 16.

[28] BN Mss. Fr. 4,765, fol. 24r.

[29] *Ibid.*, fols. 28r, 61r.

[30] Goulart, vol. 2, fol. 179r; D'Aubigné, vol. 4, 57.

[31] Goulart, vol. 2, fol. 284r. See Holt, *The Duke of Anjou*, 28–34, for a summary of the dissension and conspiring among the greater nobility at the siege.

"WELL ASSAULTED, BETTER DEFENDED"

The time for the assault on the bastion finally arrived on April 7, some two months after Anjou's arrival. At 6 a.m. the most furious bombardment of the siege began, lasting until late afternoon and expending some 3,000 rounds.[32] The bastion was blown down almost to ground level and remaining exposed parts of the curtain wall toppled. About 4 or 5 p.m., as the sun was setting, the infantry assault went in. From the beginning it was a disaster. To about 200 of the nobility, armed with cuirasses and small shields, had been assigned the task of scaling the breach, while to the infantry had fallen the task of nullifying the nearby pillboxes and reinforcing the attack on the breach. The undisciplined nobility, eager "for your service," as Anjou later wrote the king, crowded too rapidly forward and blocked the infantry from entering the ditch, so that the attacks on the bastion went in at first without the supporting attack on the casemates, from which the defenders kept up a deadly flanking fire.[33] From the bastion and the walls the defenders rained incendiary devices and grenades on the attackers on the breach and in the ditch, burning many of them in their armor so horribly that, according to La Popelinière, the other soldiers turned their heads away so as not to have to witness the terrible sight.[34] Among the defenders the ministers and women of the town particularly distinguished themselves in operating small cranes which could be swung over the parapets to drop incendiaries on the troops in the ditch.[35] After a combat lasting about two hours, in which for the loss of perhaps sixty dead the defenders had inflicted more than 300 casualties on the attackers, Anjou called the assault off. All that the royal soldiers had managed to achieve was to gain a small foothold at the base of the bastion. During the night both sides hurried to repair damage to their positions and in the case of the attackers to strengthen a covered assault bridge running down the counterscarp and across the ditch to their toehold at the base of the bastion, which was protected with banks of earth thrown up by the pioneers.

Anjou was displeased by the day's action and later remarked on the significance of this first rebuff on the soldiers,

This day greatly cooled the ardor of our soldiers, even though there had not till then been many deaths. And to that hour, they had been in good spirit, which then began to cool, as also happened with part of the nobility, who excused themselves from going to the bastion or accomplished nothing for the poor order they kept and the confusion which ensued.[36]

He was determined to renew the assault the next day but was shocked to learn that only 100 cannon balls remained to be fired.[37] Several hundred were hurriedly trans-

[32] BN Mss. Fr. 4,765, fols. 29r, 66v.
[33] *Ibid.*, fols. 29r, 65v.
[34] La Popelinière, vol. 1, fol. 142v.
[35] *Ibid.*, and Goulart, vol. 2, fols. 232v-33r, and 284r-v.
[36] BN Mss. Fr. 4,765, fol. 65v.
[37] *Ibid.*, fols. 29r-v and 65v.

ported from the fleet and rewards of one *teston* per ball were offered to those of the remaining pioneers brave enough to venture into the ditch to retrieve expended balls.[38] The night passed in the eerie light of the flares hung by the defenders so they could not be surprised, and as the sun rose on the morning of April 8 the town laid down a smokescreen so thick "you would have thought it was a pit of Hell," covering the wall and the ditch and concealing from sight the defenders and their attempts to repair their positions.[39] After a slight bombardment at 9 a.m. another assault on the breach was launched but not really pressed home. After its failure the remaining pioneers, wearing planks covered with metal sheets for protection, and suffering heavily from the continuous rain of anti-personnel weapons, began work to improve the lodgement at the base of the bastion.[40]

On the 10th Anjou changed tactics somewhat, launching a surprise escalade attack on the southeastern corner of the city at the same time that the attack on the bastion was renewed. The escalade failed and the assault on the breach was again turned back in confusion primarily because of the flanking fire from the casemates, and altogether more than 300 casualties were again suffered. In Anjou's opinion of the repulse, "The shame was greater than the damage."[41] But in a conference with Nevers later in the day it was decided to construct works in the ditch itself to mask the casemates and to enlarge the breach by exploding a mine underneath it. Work was immediately begun on both projects, but Anjou was now beginning to question the fighting spirit of his men. The soldiers, he thought,

took everything with ill temper, constrained as they were to purchase food instead of simply pillaging everything and paying nothing. It angered them even more to see things go exactly the opposite of how they wished. And, to tell the truth, some tried to discourage others from serving in some of the places, fearing that they might be constrained to go there themselves.[42]

They began to resist being ordered into positions near or in the ditch where they feared they were likely to be attacked. One of the casemates which had been briefly occupied during the assault was promptly abandoned by nervous troops, "who began to frighten themselves and be greatly vexed, and even to openly disband, such that I expected in the end to find myself someday left all alone."[43] The work necessary to erect protective barriers for the soldiers and to improve the positions in the ditch and at the bastion was hardly advancing at all, for of several thousand pioneers available at the beginning of the siege, now only 400 survived, half of whom were still needed to work the guns.[44]

By midday of the 14th, however, the miners reported that the explosive charge was in a proper position to detonate.[45] A short but furious bombardment attempt-

[38] *Ibid.*
[39] Goulart, vol. 2, fol. 284v.
[40] *Ibid.*
[41] BN Mss. Fr. 4,765, fol. 66r.
[42] *Ibid.*, fol. 66r.
[43] *Ibid.*, fol. 66r-v.
[44] *Ibid.*, fol. 66v.
[45] *Ibid.*, fols. 30v, 66v.

ed to topple the defenders' repairs to their works and suppress their fire while the attacking soldiers crowded into the ditch to be ready to spring into action after the mine was blown. About 4 p.m. the mine exploded, bringing down a great part of the bastion and killing a number of its defenders. But the terrible effect of this imperfect technology on the attackers was unfortunately even greater. Brantôme, who was present, takes up the story.

The day the mine exploded, backfiring against us and killing more than three hundred men, I had urged Monsieur Strossi to stay in the place where this great carnage would occur, so that once the mine blew, we would be ready and in good position to go to the assault. And in fact, Monsieur Strossi was persuaded, and we would have stayed had not Monsieur de Cosseins [commander of the regiment of the king's guards], a valiant, wise and experienced captain, sensing the danger that the mine might turn against us as it indeed did, led us away, dragging me by the arm, saying I was a madman and that I would not want to taste of such a fricassee as that one. He led us to the trench in the ditch in order to be under cover. No sooner did we get there than the mine unloaded its violent mysteries against our side. It was the most pitiful thing I ever saw, our poor soldiers dismembered, mutilated, crippled. There is no heart so hard it would not weep with compassion for them. The advice of Monsieur de Cosseins served us well, for without it, we would have been fricasseed along with the others.[46]

The explosion had blown tons of rock and earth onto the pioneers, miners, and soldiers waiting in the ditch, killing, mutilating, or burying alive hundreds of them and destroying the bridge which crossed from the counterscarp to the bastion. The disaster stunned the survivors, who at first refused to go to the assault and blocked the men trying to descend into the ditch to reinforce the attack and to remove the dead and wounded. Although the attack eventually got underway and was renewed several times, faced with a hail of deadly small-arms fire from a retrenchment within the bastion, few of the attackers actually tried to climb very high on the breach, and the attack was finally called off. Anjou, who fatalistically refused to blame the miners for the tragedy since many of them had also perished in the blast, nevertheless thought that the bastion could have been taken if the soldiers had gone up the breach in good order.[47]

None of this bothered me as much as it discouraged the soldiers who were starting to say that they were being butchered and that they were badly treated and that nevertheless we were not yet surfeited by these losses. I could do nothing about any of this because I could not exercise the remedy I would have wanted; the soldiers were supported by some of the masters-of-camp, and in imposing Justice, I would have had to execute so many of them that I would have found myself afterwards all alone.[48]

---

[46] Brantôme, *Discours*, 83–84; BN Mss. Fr. 4,765, fols. 31r, 66v-67r.
[47] *Ibid.*, fols. 66v-67r.
[48] *Ibid.*, fol. 67r.

The first four major assaults, at the cost of more than 2,000 casualties, had accomplished little more than to effect a lodging in the ditch and at the base of the bastion of the Evangile. The way up the breach was now quite open, but the internal entrenchments of the defenders made it impossible to approach or remain at the top. Another tactic had to be tried, and it was decided to take the casemates, increase the number of mines, and bring down more of the walls from which the defenders continued to fire on the attackers. Before this work could get underway, however, news came that the count of Montgommery's relief fleet was nearing the coast, and several thousand troops and some of the army's guns had to be transferred to the forts on the bay and an entire regiment of Gascons loaded onto the royal fleet.[49] Montgommery arrived on April 19, but after a brief skirmish revealed he was outgunned and, faced with a superior force, he sailed away on the night of the 20th. The maritime crisis averted, Anjou could return to the siege, but the delay had been expensive in several ways. According to Cauriana, "all the works that our soldiers had constructed in the ditch and at the foot of the bastion were set on fire by the incendiaries the enemy hurled onto them, and everything we were able to destroy by cannon, shovel, and mine, was restored by the skillful activity with which they had thwarted our plans."[50] The duke of Bouillon reported that only a handful of pioneers could be found to work in the trenches or the mines each day.[51] Valentine Dale, the English agent, wrote to Burghley that the news was that "The poorer sort of the camp are much distressed for victuals," and "that the king's camp is much annoyed by dysenteries and other languishing diseases."[52] Cauriana confirmed that "Our soldiers, weakened by hunger, were dying in great numbers, or filthy and covered with rags, appeared more the beseiged than the besiegers. They had allowed a great fear of the enemy to overtake them and no longer executed the orders of their leaders."[53] There were even incidences of soldiers deserting to the city.[54] Anjou summed up the dismal state of affairs as "This is the state in which I found myself: without cannon balls, without pioneers and with half-hearted soldiers."[55]

But he was still determined to take the bastion, and more mines were planted at its tip. To mount the bastion itself was not difficult, but it had proved impossible for his forces to maintain themselves at the top. At about 11 a.m. on April 29 the mines were blown, to greater effect than expected, destroying half the bastion, but raining material on the soldiers on the counterscarp on the marsh side of the bastion. An

[49] *Ibid.*, fols. 31v–32r, 67r–68r; Cauriana, 101–13.
[50] Cauriana, 113.
[51] BN Mss. Fr. 4,765, fol. 68r.
[52] *CSPF/E*, vol. 10, nos. 911, 948.
[53] Cauriana, 113.
[54] Throughout the siege there had been deserters from the town to the camp and vice versa. Some of these travelers were obviously spies, but it would be interesting to know more about the motivation for such changes of side.
[55] BN Mss. Fr. 4,765, fol. 68r.

assault force of 600 men began the attack. But the soldiers indeed went very reluctantly, and nothing their officers could do could make them advance against the artifices, light cannon, and musketry fire coming from the retrenchment. Though the officers tried to renew the attack several times, they were not, according to Nevers, supported by their soldiers, "who did nothing more than put their noses over the parapet."[56] The part of the bastion gained, however, was suitable for building a subterranean gallery from which future attacks could be launched and the inner defenses mined or sapped. The part of the assault which had been directed at the nearest casemate, still untaken after more than three weeks of trying, proceeded better, but the soldiers who nervously occupied it cowardly abandoned it again the next day to a false alarm that it was about to be counterattacked.[57]

By the end of the first week in May, then, conditions in the camp had reached a new low. Montgommery's fleet had interrupted the supply of food from Brittany, and the contract with the merchants who were supplying the army with food, which called for the delivery every day of 30,000 loaves of bread, 10,800 *pintes* of wine, and 20,000 *livres* of beef, was also about to expire. The *concessionnaires* were reluctant to renew it without a 20 percent increase in their fee.[58] The gendarmes in camp were in such bad shape due to the lack of affordable feed for their horses that Anjou simply dismissed them and ordered fresh companies to camp.[59] By now only 200 pioneers were left and calls for volunteers for day labor from the surrounding areas went unanswered.[60] According to D'Aubigné, "Here began the dysenteries in the army and the soldiers without pay were no longer being attended to; they lay in wait for the lords to pass so they could show them the maggots in their sores."[61] The French infantry units on which the main burden of the assaults had fallen were below half strength (on May 7, for example, Cosseins' royal guard regiment could only muster 840 men out of an authorized strength of 2,000).[62] The lack of troops made it difficult to mount a sufficient guard, and those who remained made constant excuses not to enter the trenches. Some of the troops, especially the Gascons, fled every time the enemy launched a sortie. Having by now expended more than 20,000 rounds, a lack of powder left the artillery without the means to harass the defenders, who promptly stepped up their sorties.[63]

The tactical dilemma of the army was succinctly summed up by Valentine Dale:

---

[56] *Ibid.*, fols. 34v, 68v.
[57] *Ibid.*, fol. 68v.
[58] *Ibid.*, fol. 35v. The contract for supplies is BN Mss. Fr. 4,554, fols. 102–4. From the beginning there had been problems with the provision of bread, wine, and beef for the siege. As early as January, 1573, Biron, *AHG*, 63–64, was writing: "les entrepreneurs sont des trompeurs, car ce qui leur est ordonne et commande le soir, le lendemain appres ilz ne le tiennent."
[59] BN Mss. Fr. 4,765, fol. 76r–v; *OM* no. 171, for the May 11, 1573, replacement order.
[60] BN Mss. Fr. 4,765, fol. 35v.
[61] D'Aubigné, vol. 4, 27.
[62] BN Mss. Fr. 4,765, fol. 36r.
[63] *Ibid.*, fols. 35v, 44r–v, 47v, 48r, 69r.

"Monsieur lies in the dike under the courtine yet the rampart is theirs of the town and what trenches and fosses are within are not known but there are divers gabions and platforms which command the rampart at the place of the breach."[64]

Finally, on May 16, a sixth assault on the bastion was attempted, but, "well assaulted, better defended," it was repulsed as before with great loss, especially among the officers. Anjou himself had now lost faith in those around him, whom he accused of always promising great feats but accomplishing little.[65] To complete the camp's discomfiture, on May 20 occurred a "très grand dommage": a relief ship carrying powder managed to evade the fleet and enter the harbor just when the defenders' supplies had run so low after the last assault that they had to suspend sniping at exposed soldiers in the royal army's trenches.[66]

But the imminent arrival of 6,000 Swiss reinforcements continued to give Anjou hope that a final supreme effort could take the city. The Swiss marched into camp on the morning of May 23, very raw and inexperienced, according to one observer, and armed only with pikes.[67] Their arrival, breaking the boredom of the siege, was an event of great interest, and many soldiers and officers abandoned their posts and flocked to see them. The Rochellais, who, according to Anjou, were alerted of the arrival by traitors, took advantage of the confusion of the moment to launch an attack on the trenches. Taking the besiegers who had remained completely by surprise, the enemy raced through the trenches, spiking four cannons, capturing a number of standards, and killing and wounding several hundred soldiers without resistance.[68] A Catholic account of the siege concluded that: "According to the old captains, they executed as beautiful a sortie as was ever made by a besieged city: they carried off the plate of the Count of Retz, and of Monsieur Strossi, and some of the baggage."[69] This was also Nevers' opinion, who added that the captains of the army were utterly dismayed by the disorder.[70] A counterattack managed only to kill a score or so of the attackers who had lingered in their looting of the camp. Anjou was appalled: "I can assure you...that our soldiers fled rather than fight, which gave me quite a bad opinion of the day of the assault. I had prisoners made of the captains and ensigns in order to have them hung, but seeing the assault so near, I thought it would be better to have them killed while performing some good service."[71]

And so, despite the disaster, preparations continued for another assault. The arrival of the Swiss meant that a proper guard could again be mounted in the trenches and some of the newcomers were also willing to work as laborers in the

---

[64] *CSPF/E*, vol. 10, no. 1000.
[65] BN Mss. Fr. 4,765, fol. 70r.
[66] *Ibid.*
[67] Cauriana, 125.
[68] BN Mss. Fr. 4,765, fols. 39v–40r, 70v; *Henri III*, vol. 1, 263.
[69] Goulart, vol. 2, fol. 288r.
[70] BN Mss. Fr. 4,765, fol. 40r.
[71] *Ibid.*, fol. 70v.

ditch.[72] Biron reported that the three mines which were being dug would soon be ready for detonation, and shortly after midnight, on the morning of May 26, the soldiers were awakened to begin readying themselves for a dawn assault. At dawn a tremendous bombardment of the defenses, which the defenders had again obscured by a thick smoke, began, and the mines were lit. But only two of them exploded, and several hours passed during which the defenders were able to repair the damage before the third mine went off, creating a climbable breach. "Around ten in the morning, all the French regiments began to march forward to the trenches in good order, the soldiers crying out, with tears in their eyes, to God, to take pity on them, to their friends, forgiving each other for their offenses against one another, seeing the danger they were about to confront."[73] The plan was to assault the bastion with French infantry followed by the nobility and then a thousand or so Swiss who were willing to volunteer for the storming of the breach. The first attack by the French infantry went up the breach led by the officers who had been arrested and condemned for the debacle on the 23rd. According to Nevers, the officers and sergeants led well but the soldiers fought non-energetically, "leaving their captains alone."[74] Just as it was time for the nobility to go in, one of the masters-of-camp reported that the breach was too difficult to assault successfully and Anjou, "fearing that by taking the city, the nobility would be lost," tried to persuade the Swiss to precede them into the ditch.[75] But the Swiss, sensing that they were about to be sacrificed, refused to go before the nobility.[76] Though the assault was renewed several times over the course of the afternoon, at the cost of many more casualties, despite the efforts of their leaders the ordinary soldiers could not be made to press it home. Anjou, unwilling to risk his nobility, balked by the Swiss, and confronted by the unwillingness of his French soldiers to press the assault, finally called off the attack in the late afternoon. A surprise attack launched at the same time on the other side of town had also failed.

Anjou was beside himself with frustration. He wrote the king: "I am so extremely angry that nothing more could be done on the occasion of this failed assault, for the wickedness of the soldiers' hearts...Having seen what I saw this day, I am almost ashamed to be French."[77] Later, looking back at the failed assault, he concluded:

That day was the crown of all our misfortunes, and made me lose all hope of doing anything of value, because I had lost Cosseins, Guoaz, and Paulliac [masters-of-camp] and the best part of the captains and even more all the good soldiers without whom it was very difficult to take any city, even if the breach was large from one end to the other.[78]

[72] *Ibid.*, fol. 71r.
[73] Goulart, vol. 2, 288r.
[74] BN Mss. Fr. 4,765, fol. 42r.
[75] *Ibid.*, fols. 71r-v.
[76] *Ibid.*, fol. 71v.
[77] *Henri III*, vol. 1, 264.
[78] BN Mss. Fr. 4,765, fol. 71v.

But his trials for the day were not yet over. Late in the afternoon, after the attack had been called off and the survivors had returned to their trenches, a bizarre occurrence took place. Without any provocation from the city or any apparent cause, a panic swept through the army. Brantôme many years later recalled:

And just as it [the assault] was halted, transpired the most extraordinary event which had occurred for a long time in the army, and without any cause: suddenly alarm swept all the trenches, that the enemy was sortying and that they were already upon us, all of which was untrue: so that a great terror and dread took hold of our infantry, and nearly all the nobility wavered and did not know what to do. And even worse, some were so afraid that they took it into their heads to save themselves in the marshes, and many fled there, but were afterwards recognized by their mud-caked stockings...Nevertheless, no one knew what was going on, except that all was in alarm and in such uproar and disorder as had never before been seen. We were in the King of Poland's tent at that time, as I have said, and tried to exit from it into the greatest press and mob I ever saw...Finally, we made it out and ran to the ditch. Monsieur Strossi, with me always at his side, discovered then that it had been nothing and that the enemy had not even shown his head above the rampart nor sortied from any gate, because he was busy enough elsewhere seeing to his assaults, escalades and surprises. Afterwards, everyone wanted to know the origin of this alarm and uproar. Some said that it was some tumult that traitors among us had invented and circulated; others were saying that we had frightened and terrorized ourselves without cause. Yet others said that it had been sent from heaven as some divine punishment, or that it had all occurred *divinitus aut fato*.[79]

The following morning, a bleak and depressing scene awaited the army's leaders. Anjou, whose tent had been trampled in the panic, described himself as "half dead," and Nevers was so exhausted and depressed by the previous day's failure that he was unable to leave his quarters.[80] I thought I would find only myself, reported Anjou, being "sans munitions, sans pionnieers, sans soldats, capitaines et noblesse."[81] The trenches were almost completely empty of French soldiers and he was forced to order the greater nobility at the camp to take turns mounting guard.[82] To add insult to injury, the Rochellais mounted a derisive demonstration on the walls, displaying the flags captured the previous day as well as playing cards and dice to indicate that their opponents only played at war.[83]

Over the next few days Anjou worked hard to restore the army's spirit and discipline. Rewards were distributed to wounded officers for having performed well in the assault even if their men had not.[84] There was a need to reorganize the infantry:

There were no masters-of-camp nor hardly any captains, and few soldiers...Seeing that the companies had been so weakened, I decided to reduce them to the smallest possible number in order to spare you the expense, and broke more than a third to fill out the others, because

---

[79] *Ibid.*, fol. 42v; Brantôme, *Discours*, 157–58.
[80] BN Mss. Fr. 4,765, 43v, 72r.
[81] *Ibid.*, fol. 72r.
[82] *Ibid.*
[83] *CSPF/E*, vol. 10, no. 1027; Brantôme, *Discours*, 79.
[84] BN Mss. Fr. 4,765, fol. 43v.

such companies for the most part were only of twenty-five or thirty men. I leave to you to imagine what a good appearance it made to see the flags enter in guard followed by such numbers of soldiers.[85]

But it was clear to everyone that the army had completely lost its effectiveness as a fighting force. Soldiers refused to go into the ditch, complaining loudly that the descent into it was too difficult because it was four times deeper and wider than the one they had fought in at Rouen in 1562. Anjou had the entrances improved, "But if the peace had not followed, and it had been necessary to go again to the assault, I think that they would have found some new excuse."[86] Battery positions were begun on the opposite side of the town in an attempt to develop a more favorable approach, but there were no pioneers in camp, and a few *goujats*, some Swiss, and peasant volunteers had to do the work.[87] The preparation of additional mines was delayed by a lack of powder.[88] According to an English report, only 2,000 French troops were left, and, as Anjou later admitted, without the presence of the Swiss the siege would have had to have been immediately lifted.[89]

A few die-hard nobles attempted to persuade Anjou to try a surprise escalade of the walls, but word got out and the remaining nobles, ill-disciplined as usual, crowded so noisily to the attack that it had to be called off.[90] A final surprise daylight scaling of the walls on June 12 was more successful, gaining some of the towers and the original wall, only to be confronted by an even more formidable series of internal fortifications which the length of the siege had allowed the defenders time to construct. Anjou thought that the town could have been taken in the surprise attack if the soldiers had not cowardly refused to follow the assault party of nobles on top of the wall, and "for several days, these shameful defeats threw such terror into the souls of the soldiers, that at the least noise, at the least suspicion, they abandoned their standards, turned away, and threw down their weapons."[91]

Anjou, who had known for weeks that he had recently been elected king of Poland, was eager, despite the protests of Biron, to end the conflict. Seeing "Moreover...that I had no hopes of taking the city by force, nor the means to undertake another assault, which I did not want to hazard, since such an effort would fall on the Princes and the nobles of your army, which could lead to an even greater loss for you than if we were to take the town,"[92] he agreed to a truce which continued to be renewed until negotiations culminated on June 25 in the acceptance of peace terms. Outside the town the soldiers of both sides intermingled, exchanged greetings,

---

[85] *Ibid.*, fol. 72r.
[86] *Ibid.*
[87] *Ibid.*, fol. 75v.
[88] *Ibid.*, fols. 44r-v, 47v, 48r, 72v.
[89] *CSPF/E*, vol. 10, no. 1041.
[90] BN Mss. Fr. 4,765, fols. 45r, 73r.
[91] *Ibid.*, fol. 73r; Cauriana, 139.
[92] BN Mss. Fr. 4,765, fol. 74r.

traded wine for fresh beef, drank together, and talked over the events of the siege.[93] On July 10, after approval by Charles IX, the peace was published, and Biron made a brief ceremonial entry to the town.[94] But the army's camps had already been rapidly emptying as the nobility left for home and the leadership began to oversee the demobilization or transfer of the infantry and the removal of the artillery to provincial depots and Paris.[95] Anjou himself soon left by galley, "to avoid the murmuring and mutiny of the soldiers, for that they were unpaid," according to the English.[96]

THE COST AND MEANING OF DEFEAT

In his report to the king Anjou had no lack of targets to blame the defeat on. There was dissension in the army itself, even treason, and incompetence in the operation of the sea blockade. He had been forced to "embark without biscuits," and had lacked munitions, soldiers, and supplies. There were never enough pioneers or materials for the siegeworks. There were critical shortages of cannon balls, and later, powder.[97] But in the end, the simple fact was that the French infantry was unable to successfully storm the breach despite repeated attempts. In the face of repeated failures, the soldiers lost their will to fight, "saying that they were sent to die for no purpose and without accomplishing anything," and in this they were supported by some of their officers, who "cooled the ardor of the soldiers when they should have warmed it..."[98] But when forced to explain the reasons for this failure of morale, Anjou, who had little sympathy in any case for the common soldiers, went right to the vulnerable heart of the French military system.

Also, it must be kept in mind that the soldiers one is constrained to employ at a siege are dissolute, accustomed to living unrestrained and pillaging everyone without paying for anything. They are forced to live off the ration they must purchase, which infinitely vexes them. And, if they lose hope of quickly looting the city, they desert. This is especially so, for they are suffering hardships they never before experienced, so much that sometimes I thought to see myself all alone, an extremity that I was reduced to in the end.[99]

Yet Anjou was also aware that the siege had been an unusually hard fought one: "I will say to you truthfully that according to some old captains, there has never been a more beautiful siege as this one here, and at which such beautiful things were done but all to no avail."[100] In the elder Monluc's opinion as well, "This siege was

[93] Goulart, vol. 2, fols. 279r, 291r.
[94] *Ibid.*, fols. 279v, 280r.
[95] BN Mss. Fr. 4,765, fols. 52v–53r; *Henri III*, vol. 1, 279–81.
[96] *CSPF/E*, vol. 10, no. 1100.
[97] BN Mss. Fr. 4,765, fols. 75r–77r.
[98] *Ibid.*, fols. 75v–76r.
[99] *Ibid.*, fol. 76r.
[100] *Ibid.*, fol. 75r.

grand, long, and beautiful, but as well assailed, better defended," though he thought "A great error was made risking so many men in the assaults."[101] There remained those who thought the siege was prematurely abandoned for purely political reasons. As the son of Marshal Tavannes later wrote:

Whatever information the King had, La Rochelle was reduced to necessity without a ship that entered there since there was no more powder. We had attacked at the strongest point and on the same side the Rochellais might have chosen to show us themselves: a great ditch cut precipitously in rock, a bastion with a platform, a great rampart eighty paces wide. We triumphed over the treachery, the fortifications, and the weather; 3,000 men were dead inside those walls. They would have surrendered twenty times without the intelligence from the outside. The ditch was penetrated in four places; three great breaches made within twenty feet of the rampart, all three covered with mantelets and gallery. We were lodged in one tower, fifty paces of curtain wall on piles ready to bring down, two or three mines ready to fire, three-quarters of the bastion of the Evangile was ours. Their defeat was unavoidable. At that moment, a general peace was proposed. The King wanted this peace in order to chase his brother to Poland, not wishing him to have the honor of finishing the war; on the contrary, he hoped that his reputation would be lost.[102]

From the distance of several centuries, however, and not wishing to take anything away from the brilliant defense of the city by its inhabitants, it is hard to see what more the army could have done. It had, after all, mounted eight major assaults under the most brutal of conditions. Brantôme claimed that the army suffered 22,000 casualties at the siege.[103] According to Cauriana:

Deadly fevers and other maladies had reduced our army to such a state that out of ten combatants it would be hard to find one who was not suffering from wounds or from hideous sores. The strength of the execution, the nobility, in particular, had suffered. The harsh weather encountered during the siege had weakened our bodies, and far from being able to fight the enemy, we could hardly draw a breath. Most sustained themselves far more by their courage than their meager physical strength, and recovered only with great difficulty after their return. It was therefore not possible to remain there any longer.[104]

In the absence of any official record of casualties, it is difficult to be too precise about what the siege in the end had cost the army. But all the evidence, direct and indirect, points to a conclusion only slightly less severe than that of Brantôme and Cauriana. When we add up the estimated losses from the eight major assaults and the sixty-one sorties identified in Figure 31, we get a cumulative total of almost 4,700 dead and wounded, and this figure does not include losses from counter battery fire and sniping, which were also severe.[105] A very conservative guess would be that the army suffered at least 6,000 combat casualties over the course of the siege. Sickness and desertion would surely have doubled this figure.

---

[101] Monluc, *Commentaires*, vol. 3, 434.
[102] Tavannes, *Mémoires*, vol. 25, 404.
[103] Brantôme, *Oeuvres*, vol. 4, 90.
[104] Cauriana, 147.
[105] See note 4 above.

In all, 93 companies of French infantry, about 18,000 men at initial strengths, a couple of thousand cavalry, 3–4,000 pioneers, and several hundred artillery personnel had taken part in the siege, perhaps 22,000 men in all (including the nobility, but excluding the Swiss and the sailors of the fleet).[106] Near the end of the siege many infantry companies could muster no more than twenty-five men for duty and the few companies of cavalry at the siege were a shadow of their former selves.[107] The English claimed that at the very end of the siege only 900 French soldiers remained.[108] This was an exaggeration, but when we analyze the assignments and strengths of the remaining infantry companies after the siege, including those that were disbanded, it seems fairly certain that at a maximum no more than about 7,400 French troops remained, or less than half of the original strength.[109] According to all witnesses only a handful of pioneers had survived, and as we have seen previously, the artillery personnel had been reduced to 27 percent of its original strength by the middle of May.[110] Overall, then, it seems fairly certain that more than half of the army had become casualties in the four months of fighting, and it is entirely possible that as many as two-thirds of the French effectives had been put out of action.

The casualty rate among the officers of the army may have been even higher. We have previously seen, in the case of Rouen in 1562, how casualties among the cadre could climb to high levels even in a short, and compared to La Rochelle, relatively easy siege. Brantôme claimed to have seen at La Rochelle a casualty list kept by Philippe Strossi, the colonel general of French infantry, which listed 266 officers killed.[111] This may have been an exaggeration, but perhaps not by much. A Catholic account published immediately after the peace identified by regiment and by name 132 officers down to the rank of enseign who had been killed in the siege.[112] Eighty of those slain officers came from the three most veteran French infantry regiments at the siege – those commanded by Cosseins, Gohas, and Guas – which in their original strength included a total of about 100 officers, which meant that over the course of the siege the equivalent of every officer in those three regiments was killed in action, and this total, of course, does not include the wounded.

Another indication of the casualty rate among the army's cadre can be gleaned from a list of prominent persons killed or wounded at the siege which ended up in English hands, and that is analyzed in Table 10.1. The list contained the names of 155 French leaders at the siege – great noblemen, regimental officers, and company captains. As the fighting progressed, when officers on the list were wounded or killed, the anonymous compiler noted that fact next to their names.[113] By the end of

[106] See chapter 2, Table 2.9, and chapter 3, Figure 10 and Table 3.1.
[107] BN Mss. Fr. 4,765, fols. 72r, 76v.
[108] *CSPF/E*, vol. 10, no. 1089.
[109] Calculated from *Henri III*, vol. 1, 279–81.
[110] See BN Mss. Fr. 3,240, fols. 86–88, 100–6; and p. 181.
[111] Brantôme, *Oeuvres*, vol. 4, 90.
[112] Goulart, vol. 2, fols. 291r–93v.
[113] PRO/SP 70/125, fols. 122–45. See also *ibid.*, 70/127, fols. 225–26.

Table 10.1. *Leader casualties at the siege of La Rochelle, 1573*

Individual outcome	No.	%
Unharmed	42	27
Wounded	47	30
Killed or died of wounds	66	43
Total	155	100

the siege, of the 155 men on the list, only 42, or 27 percent, had received no entry by their names – that is, had escaped injury (though three had been captured in sorties). Sixty-six men, or 43 percent of the total, were noted as killed in action, and 47 men, or 30 percent, were wounded, a total casualty rate within the leadership at the siege of 73 percent.

Few armies in history could continue to sustain such enormous casualty rates and still remain a useful fighting force. It is also hard to imagine what more could have been expected of an army when more than half of its men had become casualties of one kind or another and up to three-quarters of its officers killed or wounded in combat. Indeed, as we have noted several times before, after La Rochelle a number of trends began converging to reduce the royal army's military effectiveness. France was a demographically robust country and in the overall scheme of things casualties could always be replaced. But, not even counting those men drained off into the Protestant armies, the number of nobles who were willing and economically able to go on campaigns and even the number of adventuresome or desperate common men who were temperamentally and physically suited for the ordeals of war must have been limited. There must also have been a limit to the number of suitable or talented leaders that a class-rigid society like France could produce every generation. Areas which had repeatedly been asked to contribute from their resources for the artillery train must have been reaching the end of their patience, and La Rochelle showed that a single siege could empty the kingdom of guns and munitions faster than they could be stockpiled over the course of several years. Finally, as we will see in the next chapter, the royal treasury was so depleted and the costs of war so high that from the mid-1570s onward the crown was increasingly able to mount only very modest military ventures and to maintain its unpaid, desperate, and undisciplined forces in the field for increasingly shorter periods of time.

But if the country as a whole, particularly those areas in which campaigning on a large scale had taken place, was to find it increasingly more difficult to sustain the burdens of war, the changing nature of the war itself after the mid-1570s also made it more difficult for the army to endure and survive its rigors. Open-field battles faded from memory and sieges fought by an increasingly inadequate and poorly supported military establishment became the rule. In this process the resistance of La Rochelle was more than a beacon of hope and a sign from the heavens for the

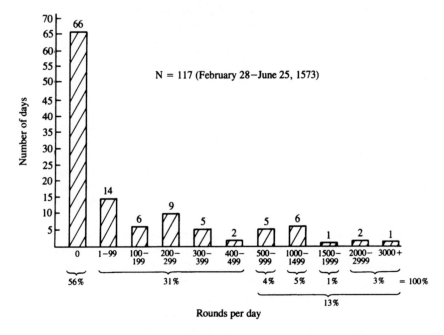

Fig. 33. Analysis of royal artillery's daily rate of fire at La Rochelle, 1573

Protestants who had survived the great massacre. It was a harbinger of the type of military stalemate that was to characterize the final decade and a half of the civil wars, a future that can best be illustrated in its military elements by a simple analysis of the rates of artillery fire at the siege and a comparison of the ratio of casualties inflicted on each other by the defenders and attackers.

As Figure 33 shows, the number of days on which the defenders of La Rochelle had to sustain major bombardments was quite limited. On only 15 out of the 117 days between February 28 and June 24, 1573, did the royal army's artillery fire more than 500 cannon rounds and only on four occasions 1,500 or more rounds. Despite the concentration of most of the kingdom's available artillery assets at La Rochelle, the 25,000 total rounds fired turned out to be inadequate, given the extensive area that had to be prepared and the strength and depth of the fortifications, though enough to exhaust the kingdom's reserves. The lesson here was not only that, in the absence of effective high explosive shells, the moderately up-to-date defensive works of a single medium-sized city could resist even the most determined bombardment that royal forces were capable of, but that a town only had to be able to withstand up to two weeks of heavy bombardment in order to exhaust the attackers' resources while simultaneously utilizing its relatively large labor force to repair

Table 10.2. *Comparison of attacker's and defender's combat casualties at the siege of La Rochelle, 1573*

| Type of combat | Estimated casualties to | | Ratio army : town |
	Royal army	Town	
Sorties	1,186	372	3.2 : 1
Major assaults	3,480	327	10.6 : 1
Total	4,666	699	6.7 : 1

damage and build internal works so strong that even if the targets of the primary bombardment were lost it did not doom the city.[114]

Since, unlike more modern times, artillery fire in and of itself could not reduce defenses to impotence, unless the army was capable of mounting a very long blockade without destroying itself, cities had to be taken in the end by infantry assault. But the introduction of gunpowder weapons which had led to the easy conquest of old-style fortifications by mobile artillery had also led to the development of the close range firearms, crude canister charges, grenades, and incendiaries which gave a disciplined and determined defender every advantage against exposed infantry attacks. The magnitude of this advantage can be demonstrated by comparing the ratio of estimated casualties inflicted by the defenders and attackers during the eight major assaults and sixty-one identified sorties fought during the siege. These figures, for which no great claims to precision are made, yet which are nonetheless striking, are presented in Table 10.2.[115] In the sorties, where the Rochellais almost always had the advantage of surprise and superior knowledge of the ground, the town enjoyed a 3:1 advantage in casualties. But even this favorable ratio would have quickly turned against them given that the royal army's effectives outnumbered the active defenders by a ratio of at least ten to one. What made the defense viable was that the defenders, protected by their works and deploying extremely lethal close-range antipersonnel weapons, were consistently able to inflict ten casualties on the exposed royal troops coming to the attack during the major assaults for every single casualty they themselves suffered. At the point of attack, then, the defenders, many of them without previous military experience, were able to create a killing ground that the royal troops, despite repeated attempts, were never, finally, able to cross. Though the defenders suffered very heavy casualties relative to their numbers – and the figures do not include such sources as sickness, or casualties from other bombardments or during work on the walls – on the

[114] The information on the bombardment of Sancerre recorded by Géralde Nakam, *Au lendemain de la Saint-Barthélemy* (Paris, 1975), Lery, in 346–48, demonstrates an almost identical pattern. From mid-February to mid-August, 1573, the besiegers fired a total of 5,915 rounds. Only on seven days were more than 100 rounds fired, but those 4,992 rounds (an average of 713 rounds per day, about one-fifth of the maximum daily bombard at La Rochelle) represented 84 percent of all rounds fired. From April through August only 923 rounds were fired, an average of just 11 rounds per day.

[115] Appendix, Part F.

killing ground itself the inhabitants of La Rochelle and the royal army were evenly matched. Not all towns, of course, could have mounted such a defense, which depended not just on works and weapons, but also on the fanatical discipline and motivation of a ruthless religious minority faced with possible extermination. But the lesson surely must have been that in the presence of a suitably motivating ideology, a relatively small number of urban defenders could fight an entire royal army on equal terms and even in defeat, as the bitter siege of Sancerre during the same civil war showed, inflict terrible damage on it.[116]

Given the convergence of so many cumulatively negative trends in the army after more than a dozen years of warfare, not even the conventional remedies proposed by Anjou after the fact in his report to the king could have solved the intrinsic military problems the siege posed. Anjou complained that he lacked enough soldiers to encircle the city securely and to mount simultaneous attacks on several breaches.[117] But where would the cannon and munitions to pound several breaches have come from when it exhausted the crown's reserves to make a single assailable breach in the city's fairly modern but by no means state-of-the-art fortifications? And how could the presence of ten or even twenty thousand extra troops have helped those who had to cross the killing grounds? Where would those troops have come from? More troops would have only led to even worse pay problems and disorders, increased supply problems, and added to the insanitary concentration of men and animals in which sickness quickly bred. Given the increasing inability of the crown to support the army financially after even a few months in the field, it is also hard to see how a longer blockade to starve the city into submission could have guaranteed success without the disintegration, as happened at La Rochelle, of the increasingly more hungry, desperate, and unruly troops. Conventional military solutions, then, which called for more of every type of resource, either quickly would have met the limits the realities of the era set on their procurement, or even if they could somehow have been assembled, could not be expected, given the technical difficulties the fortifications posed and the determination religious fanaticism produced, to have changed the essential parameters of the situation, or to have significantly limited the prohibitively expensive and ruinous nature of the operation.

So, in the mid-1570s, as the reign changed and the wars continued, the army, increasingly a shadow of its former self, faced the prospect of fighting dozens of potential La Rochelles, though it would turn out in the future that Catholic religious exaltation would join Protestant as a key ideological cement in the defense of towns against the royal army. To consistently get its men across those killing grounds would have required either a much more determined application of discipline than the army was capable of employing, or the introduction of the kind of ideological preparation that can cause troops to overcome such obstacles by ignoring casualties, exactly the ingredients that the royal army was most lacking.

[116] On a smaller scale Sancerre seems to have produced similar casualty ratios. See Appendix, Part F.
[117] BN Mss. Fr. 4,765, fol. 77r.

Paying for war

"WITHOUT MONEY ONE CAN DO NOTHING"

Within days of the departure from Paris in late November 1567 of the "bien belle et grande armée" which her son the duke of Anjou was to lead in the fruitless pursuit of the Huguenots across Champagne during the second civil war, the queen mother, Catherine de Medici, wrote indignantly to Anjou's principal military advisor, Marshal Cossé,

I would be very distressed if you or others believed that I would want to risk the lives of so many good men, such good servants of this crown as you all are, and the life of my son, which I cherish more than my own, by a reluctance to find the money to pay those who are in the camp and the good subjects of my son the King. Because, God's Mercy, he sent his brother with his army paid for one month, and on the tenth of this month begins the payment of another. I hope to send him what will be necessary to pay the sum that falls due at that time, and on the twentieth, the payment for the remainder of the army, which is not due so soon. I am certain that I will have the money to pay it and to shame all those whom you say will abandon my son for lack of payment, for I cannot believe, having left their homes and come with such affection, for the most part without having been ordered to the aid of the King my son, and having proved their good will in this last battle, as you witnessed, such men would ever want to forsake my son for such a flimsy reason, in such a just and reasonable cause.[1]

Her maternal bluster and protestations notwithstanding, lack of money to pay the army's soldiers plagued the campaign almost from the beginning. As late as February 1568 a third of the gendarme companies which had begun the campaign had not yet received their wages since the first quarter of the preceding year and though two-thirds had received a pay for the second quarter at the beginning of the campaign, their wages for the rest of 1567 were more than half a year in arrears.[2] As the campaign wore on many infantry units were also unpaid. As the armies moved back to the west the crown frantically disbanded companies left behind as garrisons in an attempt to conserve costs, and even the front line infantry involved in what was to be the climactic event of the campaign, the defense of Chartres, remained unpaid, as the examples of Martinengo's and Ardelay's regiments show: both were three to four months in arrears and many of the latter's officers had absconded with

---

[1] *CDM*, vol. 3, 84.
[2] BN Mss. Fr. 4,552, fols. 108–10.

Jehan de Monluc to Gascony after stealing the funds intended for the payment of their men.[3] As the crown's own German mercenaries arrived near the end of the war there was no money to pay them. Apparently the only troops who got regular pay, besides the Swiss, were the Flemish gendarmes commanded by the count of Arembourg, who according to Brantôme, "Even though his troops refreshed themselves a bit on the countryside, they nevertheless lived very modestly, because the King of Spain paid them quite well."[4] Those who had questioned the ability of the king and the queen mother to maintain financially the finest army of the early civil wars for more than a short period of time, then, were quite accurate in their assessment of the situation, despite Catherine's indignant reaction.

The inability to continue to pay for the army during the second civil war was by no stretch of the imagination a unique event for the period of the religious wars. Money matters, particularly the lack of pay for their troops, dominate the command correspondence of the times. The example of the first civil war, before the accumulation of crippling financial weaknesses from later wars, is telling. Signs of financial difficulties surfaced as early as June of 1562, when the queen mother wrote to Gonnor, later Marshal Cossé, the superintendent of finances, who was in charge of military expenditures, that the only veteran infantry company left in garrison at Calais had not been paid in more than three months, and she feared that its men were about to endanger the place by deserting.[5] In July Bourdillon, the commander of French Piedmont, reported that his soldiers had not been paid for six months, and the governor of Brittany, the duke of Estampes, who had been ordered to disband some recently raised troops as an economy measure, protested to Lieutenant General Navarre:

Remonstrate also that, if the said Duke of Estampes releases his men, there is great danger that he will weaken himself and strengthen his enemies, because such men follow the *éscu* ... There is also great need to pay some regard to the poor *mortepayes* of places, to whom is due more than three years of service, only half of which has been authorized.[6]

At the end of the same month Cardinal Bourbon wrote the queen that the garrisons of Picardy were due six months' pay, and in such necessity that local merchants had cut off their credit and refused to accept their captains' promises for repayment. He was afraid they would out of desperation disband or even betray their places to the enemy.[7]

---

[3] See BN Mss. Fr. 15,545, fols. 4, 5, and 17–18 for an example of the shifting, reduction, and disbanding of units in March of 1568, near the end of the second civil war. On Martinengo's and Monluc/Ardelay's regiments' pay arrears see chapter 7.

[4] Brantôme, *Oeuvres*, vol. 2, 180.

[5] *CDM*, vol. 1, 343.

[6] *Ibid.*, 359, note 1. Lublinskaya, *Documents*, 97; a postscript to Estampes' letter notes that the *mortepayes* of Brittany were due three years' wages, *ibid.*, 98.

[7] *Ibid.*, 120.

By mid-August Catherine was reporting to the duke of Estampes that even in the camp of the main army, which had been in the field only a bit more than two months, there were delays in paying the troops on time, though a letter to Gonnor in late August from Treasurer Moreau, who was with the army at the siege of Bourges, reported that there was enough money on hand to pay the August musters.[8] After the fall of that city, however, the governor, Monterud, wrote to the governor of the province of Berry that the two infantry companies ordered to join the garrison from Moulins were owed four months' pay and without a personal loan from him would have starved, for the price of food in the wake of the passage of the main army through the province was very high.[9] By late September the army was kept in being by hopes of a sack of Rouen, an event which the queen mother desperately tried to avert by promising an extra two months' pay if the soldiers spared the city. The soldiers ignored the promise and sacked the city while some of their captains, according to Moreau, stole the 400 *marcs* of silver which had been delivered to the local mint to be made into *testons* to pay part of their men's arrears.[10]

After the sack of Rouen much of the French component of the army disbanded with their loot, and it was only with great difficulty and further reinforcement from the outer provinces of the kingdom that Guise and the constable managed to rally enough force to preserve Paris and then pursue Condé to the battle of Dreux in December. But the great victory at Dreux did nothing to improve the army's financial plight. Secretary Robertet reported to the duke of Nemours at Lyon in January 1563, "You must understand, Monseigneur, that we are today so short and deprived of money, that not a penny can be found for the army of Monseigneur de Guise, where, for this reason, everyone is nearly dying of hunger."[11] And Guise's correspondence in early 1563 is filled with references to efforts to collect bits and pieces of funds from various provincial *recettes* and towns to pay his men. The Spanish troops with the army, whose pay was stranded at Bayonne, were in particularly bad shape, but even the Swiss' pay was almost two months in arrears, a fact that drove Guise to despair, since as long as they remained unpaid the wages owed them were calculated on the old muster rolls, that is, those before the carnage at Dreux.[12] Asked to submit a detailed account of the army's expenses, Guise agreed, but added that it might serve little purpose, "for such a statement is of no use without money."[13] During the same period Marshal Brissac, who had been put in charge of the occupation of Rouen and the blockade of the English army at Le Havre, wrote continually to Gonnor (who was also his brother) of his lack of funds: the twenty-three companies of French foot in the area, for example, were from three to four and

---

[8] *CDM*, vol. 1, 377–78; Ruble, "Guerre civile de 1562 en Berry," 159–60.
[9] *Ibid.*, 163.
[10] Layard, "Dispatches", 53, 55; *CDM*, vol. 1, 430, note 1.
[11] *Ibid.*, 477, note 1.
[12] Guise, *Mémoires*, 500–6; for the Spanish, 502; the Swiss, 503, 505. There were still the same concerns about the Swiss in March, 1563, see *CDM*, vol. 1, 529–31.
[13] Guise, *Mémoires*, 503.

a half months behind in their pay.[14] Outside the main area of operations the situation was even worse, and early in 1563 Catherine had to remind Gonnor that the garrison at Montreuil in Picardy was now owed eight months' backpay.[15]

By March the queen mother was complaining from the camp at the siege of Orléans that not a single *sou* was left to meet the army's needs and that the soldiers were in great want. She pleaded with Gonnor to send 400,000 *livres*, "This army, being in a state of such want that, without that, it will ruin everything, and be of no service," and this financial distress played a critical role in the decision to negotiate an end to the war with Condé.[16] Even after peace had been made with the Huguenots, and funds had been found to pay off most of the German mercenaries of both armies, financial distress continued to haunt the operations to oust the English from Le Havre. During the preliminary skirmishes at the siege master-of-camp Richelieu, commander of one of the veteran French regiments (who was killed in action later at the siege), wrote to the queen of one of the consequences for his regiment of the lack of money.

Madame, I appeal to you, for there is only one surgeon in my regiment who has followed me, and no apothecary, physician, nor tents to shelter the sick. The receiver, David, who remains in Paris in charge of the money which is due from our collection of alms, is not yet here. Please order him to retire to this place to provide for his wounded and sick. Please order the treasurer who collected the alms from this muster, to remit them into the hands of someone who follows our bands in order to distribute them where I know they will be needed for the sick and wounded and the support of the surgeons, who do not wish to serve any longer, as much as it has been four months that nothing has been received.[17]

A few days later the count Rhingrave, writing to the queen to complain about the high price of food at the siege and the lack of pay for his Landsknechts, warned of possible desertions, "because the soldier cannot live on air, and arrange for our payment. Because where there is hunger and necessity, there will arise disorder, [and] the damage will fall on the service of the King and of you, Madame."[18] Four days later Marshal Brissac reported desertions among the French troops,

complaining that even though they have been paid for a month in the last fifteen or sixteen days, they are nevertheless in such need because of the four or five months they have been left in arrears and the debts that they have therefore been forced to take on. It will thus be impossible for them to maintain themselves on campaign, if an order is not promptly given for their payment.[19]

Examples of the entropic effect of exhausted finances on the army, and the pleading and admonitions this evoked, could easily be multiplied for each of the suc-

---

[14] Louis J.H. Delaborde, *Gaspard de Coligny, Amiral de France* (3 vols., Paris, 1879–82), 508 and note 1; Charles Marchand, *Le maréchal François de Scepeaux de Vieilleville* (Paris, 1893), 222–23.

[15] *CDM*, vol. 1, 467.

[16] *Ibid.*, 520, 522.

[17] Lublinskaya, *Documents*, 246.

[18] *Ibid.*, 264.

[19] *Ibid.*, 265–66.

ceeding civil wars. At the beginning of the Jarnac campaign in 1569, for example, an anonymous letter to the Protestant Cardinal Châtillon claimed:

There is owing to the Gendarmerie 12,000,000 *livres* for six quarters; to the 6,000 Swiss with Monsieur 300,000; to those with Aumale 100,000; besides what is owed to the infantry with M. D'Anjou. The cost of the two armies amounts to 900,000 *livres* per month besides the Gendarmerie and artillery which is short 2,000,000 each quarter.[20]

Châtillon's informant may not have been too far off in his estimates. At the nadir of the army's fortunes during the third civil war, in August 1569, Tavannes wrote, in a long report to the king explaining and defending the army's actions during the previous months:

Finally, I must speak of the patience and incommodity endured by the captains as well as the soldiers, for a year, and throughout the harsh winter, with no end of sickness and mortality. This is a considerable and great achievement, to be praised, given that the cavalry only had one muster and the infantry one other. There had been some loans to the infantry, which amounted to little, as you can see by the attached *état*, which shows that three-quarters of the payments [to the army] were lacking. It could thus be said that if ever an army suffered, this one was of that number ... Moreover, may it please his Majesty to order that henceforth the finances arrive on time so that the commander be able to honor the promise he makes based on the statements which are sent to him, and that his credit and authority be upheld among the soldiers. Until now, the power to order and to instill discipline has been impaired, for lack of it. With your intervention in this matter, we may thus be able to prevent the soldiers, both infantry and cavalry, from abandoning the army, which is the sole means for abbreviating the war.[21]

But in September, two weeks before the battle of Moncontour, Ambassador Norris was reporting to Cecil that the king's Swiss were still owed three months' pay and his German reiters five months', and, as we know, these were the troops to whom priority of payment was given.[22]

That individual or detached units went unpaid for long periods of time or that campaigns were always hampered by a lack of funds should come as no surprise: it was the normal state of affairs for all European armies during the sixteenth century.[23] What is remarkable about the French wars of religion, however, is that though a lack of money may have helped to bring each individual civil war to a halt, during the second half of Charles IX's reign it never prevented them from almost immediately breaking out again and becoming a chronic and almost continuous phenomenon. In a sense, the problem was not that wars were too expensive, but that they were not expensive enough. The crown could always scrape up enough money to pay its active troops for a few months at the beginning of each war, but it could

[20] *CSPF/E*, vol. 9, no. 155.
[21] For Tavannes' very detailed analysis of the campaign, see BN Mss. Fr. 18,587, fols. 470–80; quote from fols. 478–79.
[22] *CSPF/E*, vol. 9, no. 440.
[23] See, in particular, Parker, *Flanders*, 127–206, for the problem of financing the Army of Flanders and soldiers' responses.

never consistently maintain them financially beyond the first two or three months. Too cheap to start, wars were then too expensive to finish, and once penury set in, a brutal triage of forces developed. Those units out of the main area of operations were abandoned to their own devices first. Then portions of the field army were neglected, usually the French infantry and light cavalry, followed by the gendarmerie, in favor of the foreign mercenaries – primarily the Swiss and the reiters – on whom the survival of the army in battle was thought to depend heavily and whose solidarity and organization allowed them to successfully protest arrears by a unified refusal to fight.

But soon even the foreigners went unpaid as well, though this actually could work to their advantage, as the authorities were quick to point out to them. When some Swiss units left the army of the Duke d'Uzès in Languedoc in 1575 because they had not been paid, Henry III directed his agents: "It will be necessary to remonstrate to them that the delay in their payment, because of momentary difficulties, will turn in fact to their advantage because they will be paid what is due them according to the old muster rolls."[24] A practice, according to Castelnau,

to which the Reiters and Landsknechts have since become accustomed as much as the Swiss. Of course, it is only the Colonels and Captains who profit, and it is something that a Prince who makes use of these Nations should beware, for in the end, there are in effect only half the soldiers, and the others are on paper, and it is necessary to pay those who are returning from the time of the first muster in Germany or Switzerland.[25]

The singlemost concern of commanders, of course, was that without money the troops could not support themselves, their morale tumbled, disorders and disobedience grew, and operations became impossible as the army began to disintegrate. Tavannes spoke for scores of commanders when he wrote to the king during the first war, "Your Majesty might also contemplate how to help me with some money, because you know that without it, one can neither attack nor defend."[26] And, on another occasion: "I fear that since they are so poorly paid, I am raising brigands instead of soldiers ... "[27] During the fourth civil war Admiral Villars wrote to inform the queen mother of the forces and money he had been forced to raise to defend Guyenne, noting that: "Your Majesty knows that without money one can do nothing ... When I pay the soldiers, I can endeavor to discipline them and to prevent them from going plundering; otherwise they will cause six times more damage than had been done before they arrived."[28] As Biron wrote in his advice to the king before the sixth civil war,

---

[24] *Henri III*, vol. 2, 175.
[25] Castelnau, *Mémoires*, vol. 1, 114.
[26] L. Pingaud, ed., *Correspondence des Saulx-Tavannes* (Paris, 1877), 89.
[27] *Ibid.*, 50.
[28] Jean Loutchitzki, "Documents inédits et originaux," *Bulletin de la Société de l'histoire du Protestantisme français*, 22 (June–Sept. 1873), 263.

The most important and chief point is finances, because without these, everything is stayed and nothing can be executed, it being the sinews of war ... And for the execution of your commands to organize the forces and armies and all the rest, it is necessary to seek out the necessary means and to foresee what is required and what might be necessary if something out of the ordinary should occur. Above all, it is imperative to see that there be no lack of pay, because more service will be gotten out of ten thousand men who have been paid than from eighteen thousand who have not been paid; it is thus that order and discipline are established. Otherwise, if pay lacks, the soldiers will leave the ranks and make excuses for their fondness for plundering. There are a great number of examples of this, but the best is the one of the beautiful and grand army that Your Majesty had in Limousin [in 1569], which totally vanished due to lack of pay and supplies and could not be reassembled for three months afterwards.[29]

But, of course, the crown was never willing or able to follow this advice, and as the wars dragged on not only did the number of troops it was able to put in the field for any length of time steadily decline, but those smaller numbers of troops were also increasingly less well maintained when they were in the field. The behavior of troops towards the civilian population, whether friend or foe, as we have seen, was predatory and destructive, and all contemporaries were in agreement that the behavior of soldiers continued to worsen over time, deteriorating even more rapidly after 1576, the terminal date for this study.

At the root of both the growing destructiveness and lack of operational effectiveness was the financial plight of the army and its troops. Brantôme, writing from the vantage point of a slightly later date, made a comparison that summed up the corrosive effect of chronic financial disarray on the French infantry well, and which could without much modification be extended to all of the soldiers serving in the royal army.

I have nevertheless at other times observed the soldiers of our bands stay in camp for two or three months without a muster. The Devil take it if they had dared to steal anything at all. Of course it is true that they did not lack the daily ration; and what is worse, if they were owed four or five or six months, one most often caused them to lose the greatest part of it. But nowadays, our infantry is so thoroughly corrupted and very different from that which it was. Also, it is said that there are no longer any *soldats d'assaut*, not that I would say that there are no longer any good soldiers at all. There might be some as good as ever, but they are more interested in pillaging, stealing, thieving, and seeing to their profit, than to pursuing honor. And the cause of this is that they are no longer obedient; and, responding to this, they claim that they are no longer being paid by the King.[30]

THE PRICE OF WAR

What exactly was the cost to the crown of maintaining the royal army? Let us begin to answer this question by examining what could be considered the crown's

[29] Biron, *LD*, vol. 1, 61, 64.
[30] Brantôme, *Oeuvres*, vol. 5, 377.

Table 11.1. *The army in peacetime: annual cost of the royal army, ca. 1560–74*

Type of expense	Amount (*livres*)	%
Gendarmes	2,300,000	48
Infantry	1,247,000	26
Artillery	152,000	3
Subtotal	3,699,000	77
Royal Guards	279,000	6
Mortepayes	93,000	2
Fortifications	350,000	7
Galleys and *marine de Ponant*	200,000	4
Swiss pension	200,000	4
Subtotal	1,122,000	23
Total	4,821,000	100

"normal" military expenditures during the period of the early wars. Budgetary information on royal finances during the early wars of religion is scarce as well as fragmentary. But Table 11.1, drawn from a number of different sources, attempts to calculate the normal yearly military budget during peacetime during the 1560s and early 1570s.[31] Total annual costs were in the range of some 4.8 million livres, about three-quarters of which was spent on the peacetime gendarmerie and infantry companies. The artillery, including procurement of munitions, salaries, and expenditures on the Arsenal in Paris, accounted for a minuscule percent of normal spending. Other major items were fortifications and the royal guard, which together accounted for 13 percent of the total. *Mortepayes*, the navy, and an annual pension for the Swiss cantons accounted for another 10 percent. Even in peacetime, therefore, around 90 percent of the military budget was spent on salaries rather than capital improvements, equipment, or supplies.

---

[31] Two state budgets from the period were used: that of 1567, in Roger Doucet, *L'état de finances de 1567* (Paris, 1929), and that of 1574, BN Mss. Fr. 17,870, fols. 278–82. Philip Dur, "Constitutional Rights and Taxation in the Reign of Henry III" (Ph.D. diss., Harvard University, 1941), also contains some useful *états*. Wherever possible summary amounts in the state budgets were compared to individual department budgets, and in some cases the department budgets themselves were used: for example, for the infantry in 1572, the *états* in BN Mss. Fr. 3,193, fols. 203–10 (for the south), 211–25 (for the north); for the *marine de Ponant* in 1574, BN Mss. Fr. 17,870, fols. 287–89; for *mortepayes* in 1571, ibid., fols. 284–85; for galleys in 1560, BN Mss. Fr. 3,898, fols. 237–38. For examples of *gendarmerie* budgets see, for 1559, BN Mss. Fr. 3,150, fols. 39–50; for 1560, BN Mss. Fr. 21,543, fols. 28–47; for 1567, BN Mss. Fr. 4,552, fols. 18–26; for 1574, BN Mss. Fr. 3,193, fols. 184–93. From year to year there were small fluctuations in the categories of expenses, but over the whole period, as far as I have been able to determine, annual "normal" military expenses fluctuated by only about 5 percent from the yearly total given here.

During this same period the gross annual revenues of the crown fluctuated between 10 and 14 million *livres*.[32] An *état* of 1567 analyzed by Roger Doucet, for example, showed revenues of 10,216,194 *livres* and military expenditures of 4,341,093 *livres*.[33] Around 40 percent, then, of yearly revenues were normally devoted to current military expenses. This was the basic cost of maintaining the peacetime army. Not represented in this total, of course, was the burden on royal finances from the monarchy's previous wars. In 1560 the royal debt, an inheritance of the Hapsburg–Valois wars, was estimated to be in the neighborhood of 40 million *livres*, despite the fact that some substantial portion of royal property and income had been alienated for various lengths of time in order to pay for them. By 1576, the royal debt had climbed to 100 million *livres*, and the difference was almost entirely the legacy of the first five wars of religion.[34] So throughout our period, even in a "normal" year, much of the crown's yearly income of 10–14 million livres had to be spent on interest and principal repayments of loans specifically floated to finance earlier wars or to try to reduce accumulated arrears in normal military expenditures. The effect that accumulating deficits and the measures taken to circumvent them were to have on the short-term financing of military operations will be explored in the third, and the long-term deterioration of royal finances due to the civil wars, in the fourth section of this chapter.

The key to comprehending the magnitude of the cost to the crown of maintaining its forces in wartime is to be found, as the peacetime budget hints, in the overwhelmingly labor-intensive, rather than technical or material, requirements of the expanded force that went with the royal army on campaign. As we have noted before, the peacetime army was too small to constitute a single proper field army, much less provide units for an entire area of operations, or, in the context of widespread rebellion, the entire kingdom. Therefore, adequate preparation of the army for war was primarily a matter of a drastic expansion of personnel, from domestic or foreign sources, doubling or tripling peacetime numbers. Large formations of troops were required, and such large formations entailed a tremendously expanded scale of expenditures. A single 10-company regiment of French infantry, and there were normally at least six in the main field army, cost about 20,000 *livres* per month in salaries. The army's standard Swiss contingent, comprised of twenty companies totaling 6,000 men, cost 73,000 *livres* per month. The regiment of 5,250 Landsknechts led to the aid of the crown by the Rhingrave in 1562 were to receive monthly wages of 67,000 *livres*. The cost of a single month's service by a tactical regiment of gendarmes of nine companies and 750 men came to about 24,000 *livres*, and the main army usually contained anywhere from five to nine such groups. A regiment of German reiters containing ten *cornettes* and 3,600 effectives cost close to 130,000 *livres* per month. And the standard 12–20-gun field artillery train

[32] Martin Wolfe, *The Fiscal System of Renaissance France* (New Haven, 1972), 106, 205–6.
[33] Doucet, *L'état de finances*, 3–6.
[34] *Ibid.*, 8, 10; Wolfe, *Fiscal System*, 113, 159.

Table 11.2. *The army at war: monthly costs of the royal army, December 1567 and January 1568*

Type of expense	Amount (*livres*)
December	
Gendarmes	(337,396)
French light cavalry	76,794
French infantry	302,517
Foreign infantry	142,265
Artillery train	42,843
États and guard	28,454
Vivres	26,610
Miscellaneous	14,913
Treasury costs	10,000
December total	981,792
Additions in January	
German cavalry	314,000
Foreign light cavalry	32,500
Added January expenses:	346,500
January total	1,328,292

consumed another 30–40,000 *livres* every month it was in the field.[35]

One of the most ubiquitous types of staffing or administrative documents to survive the period are the *états* which endlessly compute the monthly costs of every possible type of unit and the actual or hypothetical cost of entire armies. Such paper exercises were hardly theoretical, and a uniquely complete set from the second civil war can be used to estimate the total monthly cost of the royal army during December, 1567, and January, 1568. This army, it should be recalled, represented perhaps the largest force put in the field at one time during the early civil wars, and questions about the crown's ability to provide for it financially had provoked the irritation expressed by the queen mother to Marshal Cossé quoted at the beginning of this chapter.

The estimate of the cost of Anjou's army, presented in Table 11.2, provides striking evidence of why the crown found it impossible to maintain its military effort against the Huguenots for very long.[36] Total charges for the army during the month

[35] Derived from sources already extensively cited in chapters 4–6. But for some additional statements of unit costs see BN Mss. Fr. 17,870, fols. 295–96.

[36] See especially the *état abregé* of December, 1567, BN Mss. Fr. 4,553, fol. 101. Other *états* in *ibid.* are artillery, fols. 95–100, *vivres*, fol. 102, and staff, fols. 112–14. Nevers and Aumale are included with Anjou's *états*. There is a separate *état* for Martigues' Bretons, who were paid through January by the Estates of Brittany, BN Mss. Fr. 3,898, fols. 227–36. Monluc's Gascons were paid by the province for their first month but were then on the king's payroll. The Flemish gendarmes, who were being paid

of December came to almost 1 million *livres*, or almost triple the monthly cost of the ordinary military budget. These expenses were increased by more than an additional 300,000 *livres* in January 1568, when pay for German mercenary cavalry and Savoyard light cavalry were added. The army's cost in January therefore was running around 1,328,000 *livres* per month, or an annual rate of almost 16 million *livres*. Even this enormous sum does not represent total military expenses during the war: the cost of the remaining garrisons in Picardy, Metz, Lyon, and Piedmont, and all infantry and light cavalry companies raised for operations outside the northeast are not included (a guess of at least another 100,000 *livres* per month for those expenses would probably be conservative), nor are such regular items as the royal guards, the normal artillery budget, fortifications, and the galleys, and the Swiss pension, which would have represented additional monthly obligations of about 92,000 *livres*.[37]

The level to which royal military expenditures had climbed in January 1568, then, implied an annual spending level of about 18 million *livres*, or much more than the whole of annual royal revenues (more than half of which were normally committed to non-military expenses). Revenues could never be raised high enough (especially since much of the country escaped from taxes during civil disorder) even to begin to cover such large wartime obligations. As a short-term measure, of course, the government could adopt all kinds of fiscal expedients and borrow money from anyone it could persuade or coerce to provide it, often at ruinous interest rates. During the second civil war, as we have seen, enough was raised or borrowed to pay most of the main army for the first two or three months in the field – that is, enough to get it assembled and on campaign. But by February, 1568, bankruptcy stared the government in the face. Thus financial problems dictated military policy, and this, the shortest of the wars, was brought to a negotiated end in March of the same year.

Such ruinous levels of expenditure were the norm rather than the exception during the religious wars. In early 1569 the combined formations of Anjou's and Aumale's armies would also have cost more than a million *livres* per month. During the fourth civil war the armies (and fleet) assembled for the sieges of La Rochelle and Sancerre, and other places were well on their way to monthly expenditures of near this magnitude.[38] Even smaller field forces were tremendously expensive. The army scraped together for Marshal Cossé in 1570, exclusive of any gendarmes, had a monthly price tag of over 300,000 *livres*, or almost as much on an annual basis as the entire royal military budget in peacetime.[39] Such financial burdens could only be sustained for a few months or, in the third civil war, heroically, for half a year. But

by Spain, are not counted. The expense of the French gendarmerie, which was paid by the quarter, is estimated for a force level of 143 companies prorated for one month. For the January figures for the army, see the *abregé*, BN Mss. Fr. 17,870, fol. 294; and PRO/SP 70/96, fols. 114–15, 119–20.

[37] See Table 11.1.

[38] See the preliminary financial *états* for the siege of La Rochelle, BN Mss. Fr. 4,554, fols. 92, 98–100 and for an estimate of troop costs at the siege of Sancerre, BN Mss. Fr. 15,556, fols. 1–2.

[39] BN Mss. Fr. 4,554, fols. 21–22.

in all the wars the crown ran out of money before it could achieve any type of permanent and decisive military victory over the Huguenots. Once the money ran out, it was only a short time before the royal armies lost their effectiveness and began to disintegrate. At that point the crown had no choice but to enter into premature, and usually unfavorable, peace negotiations. The cost of fighting had outrun both the ability and the will of the monarchy to sustain its military effort.

The scale of expenses incurred also meant that the crown could not even afford to pay its troops in order to demobilize them in an orderly fashion, and so the immediate aftermath of war was usually an unregulated and chaotic event. French troops who had not been paid in some time were often simply dismissed to make their way home however they could. The gendarme companies would be promised a general muster within a few months as they were sent back to their home provinces, still unpaid. All need for suppliers, pioneers, and horses for the artillery train ended immediately with the peace. Demobilized soldiers, hardened by their wartime experiences, caused disorders, and looted and pillaged their way home, often in bands too strong for local officials to handle. The small number of commissars and military police (who also more than likely had not been paid) were, of course, helpless once the army had broken into a number of smaller bands.

Foreign mercenaries posed special problems because the enormous sums of money that they were frequently owed were impossible to raise quickly. Because they were both numerous and unified – the German reiters were considered especially dangerous – priority had to be given to getting them out of the country as soon as possible. Usually some combination of a cash downpayment and letters of credit drawn on foreign financial centers persuaded them to leave, but it was always a scramble to pay them at the end of each war because their contracts specified that they continued to draw their pay until they had returned home, and in the meantime they plundered and ravaged the provinces near the border where they awaited their mustering out.[40]

The chaos of demobilization, then, was principally a product of the financial problems caused by the enormous costs of maintaining military forces in the field for long periods of time. And the same problems repeated themselves at the end of each civil war. The financial circumstances of demobilization, however, are perhaps less important than its result for our understanding of the cycle of events that underlay all the civil wars. Wars were so expensive that at their end the crown had to demobilize right back to the *status quo ante bellum* – the military unpreparedness that marked its armed forces before each war – while desperately trying to find some means to meet yet another wave of unpaid obligations.

---

[40] See especially the voluminous correspondence in BN Mss. Fr. 15,608.

THE SOURCES OF PAYMENT

The gap between the cost of waging war, and the portion of the crown revenues actually or directly available for war, provides a good idea of the main reason – a lack of sufficient resources – why military operations rested on such a precarious financial base. But there were also other, more specific obstacles and problems involved in the financing of the army. A basic weakness was the cumbersome structure of the royal fiscal system: funds were geographically dispersed and of uneven magnitudes, vulnerable to disruption, often uncollectable, and dependent on increasingly dubious sources. The first of these problems can be illustrated by the geographical pattern of funding the crown relied on in September 1566, for a general muster to be held the following December to pay the preceding April quarter's wages of its ninety-one peacetime gendarme companies, which is illustrated by Figure 34.[41] The relative degree of reliance on the different tax *généralités* of the kingdom reflected the influence of the intertwined confluence of three factors: the number of companies stationed in their regions, the fiscal resources of particular *recettes*, and the strategic and political importance of the areas the *recette* covered. The predominance of the *généralité* of Paris in the provision of wages to the gendarmerie is striking: 45 percent of the companies and 46 percent of the total gendarme bill depended on the Paris *recette*. Lyon with 19 percent of the companies and 18 percent of the salaries was a distant second, and Tours, with 15 percent of both, third. A similar pattern held true for the peacetime infantry, two-thirds of which was stationed in the north of the country, mostly on the frontier, who were almost entirely paid with funds drawn from the *généralité* of Paris, or if across the Alps in Piedmont, from the Lyon *recette*. As the loci of the campaigns moved to provinces far to the south and west of Paris after 1567, the army had to operate in regions that were simply not capable, even if there had been no difficulties encountered in collecting money, of providing financial resources of a large enough magnitude to sustain the large numbers of companies required by the main field army. Not only were the more distant *généralités* less able to provide financial resources on the scale of Paris and the north, there were often the political sensibilities of more independent provinces and cities to be negotiated, and the limited regular resources available in those areas were inevitably disrupted by the depredations of campaigning. As in the case of artillery resources, then, the strategic direction the war took removed the army from the core area of north and northeastern France that had been almost completely reconquered in the first and then successfully defended from major defections in the second civil war. The Paris region had the most secure royal revenues and, perhaps rivaling Lyon itself, the largest concentration of municipal and international financial agents upon which royal credit operations depended. This is not to say that the peripheral *généralités* were unimportant, but that it was only in the Paris region that the crown could quickly or easily put its

[41] BN Mss. Fr. 3,194, fols. 99–101.

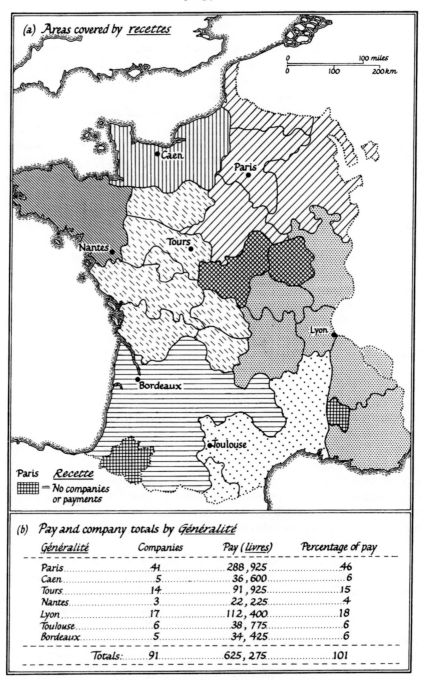

(a) *Areas covered by* *recettes*

Caen

Paris

Nantes

Tours

Lyon

Bordeaux

Toulouse

Paris   *Recette*

▦ = *No companies
or payments*

(b) *Pay and company totals by* *Généralité*

Généralité	Companies	Pay (*livres*)	Percentage of pay
Paris	41	288,925	46
Caen	5	36,600	6
Tours	14	91,925	15
Nantes	3	22,225	4
Lyon	17	112,400	18
Toulouse	6	38,775	6
Bordeaux	5	34,425	6
Totals:	91	625,275	101

Fig. 34. Distribution of gendarme pay by *généralité*, April quarter, 1566

hands on the massive sums of money (from taxes or borrowing) needed to pay its expanded military forces when war came. Funds assigned on the theoretically regular tax revenues of the other *généralités* were likely to be unavailable, or to involve sometimes insurmountable obstacles of transportation halfway across the kingdom to where they were needed during the midst of hostilities.

When regular revenues were or became unavailable, as always happened, extraordinary and sometimes extremely unreliable sources had to be relied on. The implications of this situation for the paymasters of the army can be well illustrated by three examples drawn from the third civil war. In October of 1568, the king issued an *état* specifying the payment of the 152 companies of gendarmes he had ordered mobilized at the beginning of the war.[42] From the start the funds assigned to get the campaign underway were in deficit. The total cost of paying all 152 companies so they could take the field (since most had not been paid at all since the end of the previous war) was 1,575,000 *livres*, some 50,000 of which had already been disbursed. The crown was able to assign another 974,000 *livres* from various sources to finish the pay of 107 companies, who were collectively owed 1,047,000 *livres*, leaving a starting deficit of 74,000 *livres* for them. To the 45 remaining companies, 29 of which were already with or on their way to the main army under Anjou, no funds had been assigned, leaving a total shortfall of 551,000 *livres* and no ready source of money to provide for it. At the very beginning of the campaign, in other words, only two-thirds of the money needed to pay the principal shock cavalry arm of the army (for no foreign cavalry would reach Anjou's army until the spring of 1569), was available.

The origin and nature of the 974,000 *livres* allocated to the gendarmerie, detailed in Table 11.3, is also revelatory. Fifty-two percent of the total came from Paris, but only 58,500 *livres* from existing treasury funds. Another 31 percent was to come from Toulouse and Languedoc, none of which was from regular tax sources. Altogether, 72 percent of the assigned funds were to be provided from three extraordinary, one could even say emergency, sources: contributions from the clergy and the city of Paris, and the 300,000 *livres* loan from Languedoc. An additional 10 percent appears to have come from private sources. Only about one-fifth of the money assigned was provided from what could be considered regular treasury sources, and 60,000 *livres* of that total were actually derived from funds that had been set aside to help complete the pay owed to Casimir's German mercenaries for their service in the Huguenot army during the second civil war. Only 5 percent of the allotment was based on sources in the province of Poitou, which was intended to be the main theatre of operations.

Having started with enormous lump sum expenses which could only be partially met by funds assigned from essentially emergency sources – gifts and loans – the army, especially its French components, staggered forward over the course of the

---

[42] BN Mss. Fr. 3,193, fols. 195–201.

Table 11.3. *Identity of funds assigned to the gendarmerie, October, 1568*

Location and type	Amount (*livres*)	%
Paris region		
Gift of the clergy	218,357	22
Treasurer of war	58,500	6
Gift of the city of Paris	180,000	19
Privately raised	45,000	5
Subtotal	501,857	52
Elsewhere		
Tours *recette*	17,500	2
Bordeaux *recette*	44,500	5
Poitiers, privately raised	50,000	5
Lyon *recette*, reiters' pay	60,000	6
Languedoc/Toulouse, loan	300,000	31
Subtotal	472,000	49
Total	973,857	101

next year's campaign essentially without pay. According to Tavannes, writing in August, 1569, the gendarmes had received only one quarter's and the infantry two months' wages since the start of the war a year earlier. The troops had been kept going by occasional advances or loans from their officers and fairly consistent provision of their daily rations, but at a cost, as we have previously noted and Tavannes specifically mentions, of a loss of discipline, widespread disorders, and the practical disintegration of the combined armies of Anjou and Aumale in the summer of 1569.[43] The battle of Moncontour was to restore the army's military fortunes, but the continued wear of the lengthening campaign and the debacle of the concluding siege of Saint-Jean-d'Angély utterly exhausted the crown's financial fortunes. It was not until the following year, 1570, that the crown managed to field an army at Orléans under Marshal Cossé whose task it was to prevent Coligny's peripatetic Huguenot column from advancing on Paris. Just how desperate the financial situation had become can be graphically illustrated by an analysis of the royal *état* providing authorization to Adrien Petrenel, the *trésorier extraordinaire des guerres*, for the initial payment of Cossé's force.[44]

The *état* specified that Cossé's force was to be composed of 3,000 reiters, 8,000 Swiss, and 8,200 French infantry, plus artillery and French gendarmes, slightly over 20,000 combatants. The gendarmerie and artillery were to be paid from different sources than those specified in the *état*. To provide for the first month of pay for the Swiss and the French and the first two months for the reiters, as well as

[43] See p. 279 above.
[44] BN Mss. Fr. 4,554, fols. 21–22.

advance money for collecting a stockpile of rations, start-up money for the artillery train until its own funds came in, and two months of command and staff position salaries for the marshal and the other major leaders of the army, required an initial 435,250 *livres*. Petrenel was said to have on hand or expected to receive within days some 301,758 *livres*, or 69 percent of the army's first month's requirements, leaving a deficit of 133,492 *livres*, 96,000 of which, or 22 percent of the total month's bill, had been assigned from various sources but still had to be collected. There was no source of funds, real or theoretical, specified for the remaining 37,492 *livres*, or 9 percent of the first month's charges.

If Marshal Cossé had managed to lead his army into the field with only a 9 percent deficit he would have commanded one of the most solvent military operations of the epoch. But, in fact, the sure provision of 69 percent of the first month's costs is evidence of the exhaustion of the short-term finances of the crown rather than the ability, in this case, to go beyond a single month's financial requirements. A breakdown of the elements of Petrenel's budget, presented in Table 11.4, shows the manner in which the crown was scraping the bottom of the fiscal barrel in 1570. Sources in Paris and Lyon were together supposed to supply 50 percent of this relatively small monthly amount. Thirty-one percent was to be provided by the cities in or near the staging area of the army and its proposed area of operations: Orléans, Bourges, and Chalon-sur-Sâone. Nine percent of the expected total and 12 percent of what was actually on hand came from loans from private individuals.

In all, twenty-four different sources of funds had to be tapped to provide one month's pay for the army. Only 26 percent of the expected total came or was designated to come from standard taxes actually designed for support of the army: the *taillon* and the *crue* of four *sous*. Twenty-nine percent was supposed to be provided by funds from the sale of offices (*parties casuelles*) or the royal domain. Cash payments by royal officials (Parlement, the *Grand Conseil*, and various financial officers) and private individuals contributed another 10 percent. Finally, almost one-third of the first month's funding for Cossé's army came from loans obtained from the city of Orléans, more Parisian officials, and five prominent members of the court and military nobility. The reliability of the funds yet to be received was dubious, particularly the hoped for proceeds from the sale of royal domain in Brittany, and almost exactly half of the money from regular sources of taxation and sales of offices or crown property had yet to be received by Petrenel; a note in the manuscript expresses skepticism about their arrival.[45] To put this starkly, what should have been the most stable and regular of normal revenues were the least reliable of the lot. The army treasury was instead forced to rely on cash contributions, chiefly from the crown's own bureaucratic servants, or loans from those same officials, private individuals, and what was essentially an occupation tax levied on the city of Orléans. The trend towards auto-financing and private rather than

---

[45] *Ibid.*, fol. 22v.

Table 11.4. *Identity of initial month's funding of Marshal Cossé's army, at Orléans, spring, 1570*

A. Origins of assigned funds			
Origins	Funds received	Total expected	%
Paris	118,866	140,866	35
Lyon	24,000	58,000	15
Orléans	60,000	60,000	15
Bourges	45,892	45,892	12
Brittany	–	40,000	10
Individuals	37,000	37,000	9
Chalon-sur-Sâone	16,000	16,000	4
Total	301,758	397,758	100

B. Types of funds assigned				
Type of fund	On hand	Missing	Total	%
Taxes				
Miscellaneous cash	13,000	–	13,000	3
Creu of 4 *sous* and taillon	68,055	34,000	102,055	26
Sales				
Parties casuelles	54,466	22,000	76,466	19
Royal domain	–	40,000	40,000	10
Cash advances				
Royal officials	31,337	–	31,337	8
Individuals	8,900	–	8,900	2
Loans				
City of Orléans	60,000	–	60,000	15
Royal officials	30,000	–	30,000	8
Individuals	36,000	–	36,000	9
Total	301,758	96,000	397,758	100

tax-derived funding is underlined by the identity of the private lenders. If the crown was able to squeeze its officials, it depended for private loans from nobles closely associated with the world of the court and the army itself: the individuals who provided 36,000 *livres* (some of which they had borrowed on their own credit) included the Alsatian mercenary Bassompierre (2,000 *livres*), the colonel general of infantry Strossi (9,500), the duke of Anjou himself (10,000), and the widow of Marshal Brissac, whose son, the other colonel general of infantry, had been killed in action in the previous year. The terms upon which some of the borrowing rested also testifies to the end of royal credit: the *état* notes mournfully that 42,000 of the 66,000 *livres* loaned by royal officials and private individuals had been advanced to the crown for a term of only fifteen days.[46] So, inaugurated with a built-in deficit, a quarter of its funds uncollected and assigned to dubious because exhausted or distant regular sources, its most reliable funding that squeezed from royal officials or provided by the world of the greater military nobility, its credit in some cases reduced to two-week terms, the last major army fielded by the crown during the third civil war found itself in greater danger from royal bankruptcy than from the enemy army itself.

Conditions were even more desperate for garrisons and units on the periphery of the main areas of operations. Garrisons of the fortified places of French Piedmont, along with those of Calais and Metz, were among the most important components of the frontier defenses of the kingdom. Even during civil war the crown was reluctant to reduce their size, though their most veteran companies were often ordered to the main army and replaced by newly raised native units or sometimes, in the case of Metz or the Piedmont, by foreign troops. In July 1570, near the end of the third civil war, Petrenel summarized, in another *état*, the fiscal status of royal garrisons in Piedmont, Languedoc, and Dauphiny for the preceding year, 1569.[47] These figures, which are presented in Table 11.5, show that the troops in those garrisons had received only 26 percent of their pay in 1569. But those in Dauphiny and Languedoc had fared much better than the troops in Piedmont, having received six months' pay, so that in July 1570 they were only a year behind on their wages. Those in Piedmont had received 60,000 *livres* of the 249,424 *livres* owed them for 1569, but 24,000 of the latter had gone to pay the salaries of officers with staff positions who had left at the beginning of the war to serve with the main army in France. The companies stationed in Piedmont had in fact only received 14 percent of their 1569 wages.

Treasurer Petrenel's concern, of course, was not simply how much was still owed these troops, but also how much money he had on hand to pay them and from where the funds not yet received were to come, and what he noted speaks volumes about the deepening financial disaster within which the army had to make its way. According to Petrenel's calculations he actually had received or been assigned more – 216,980 *livres* – than was needed to pay the 200,768 *livres* in 1569 wages still owed the troops. But of the money allocated to pay them, only 13,080 *livres* had actually come into Petrenel's coffers. Ninety-four percent of the money he was supposed to use to pay the arrears, in other words, was missing, and a look at the supposed sources of those funds reveals why. Eighty-seven percent of the money assigned to Petrenel was dependent on the sale of property: 30 percent from rebel property in Bourges and Lyon, 39 percent from the sale of church lands, and 18 percent from the sale of royal domain in Dauphiny. With the exception of 28,000 *livres* assigned

[46] *Ibid.*
[47] BN Mss. Fr. 4,554, fol. 25.

Table 11.5. *Identity of funds assigned to pay 1569 troop arrears in Languedoc, Dauphiny, and Piedmont, July, 1570*

Source of funds	Nominal amount	On hand	Uncollected
Sale of:			
Rebel property at Bourges	30,000	–	30,000
Rebel property at Lyon	35,000	6,000	29,000
Church domain	84,380	–	84,380
Royal domain in Dauphiny	39,600	–	39,600
Other:			
Restes of 1569 at Lyon *recette*	28,000	7,080	20,920
Total	216,980	13,080	203,900
Percentage	100	6	94

from the surpluses of the 1569 fiscal year at the Lyon *recette* (and given the circumstances it is hard to imagine the surplus was that large – only 7,080 *livres* of it had actually been delivered to Petrenel), no regular, predictable, or easily collectible tax revenues were assigned. Having been paid almost nothing in a year and a half, the Piedmont garrison was dependent for its deliverance on funds that, in a sense, might as well have been on the moon.

The lack of financial support for the army in the third civil war was not for lack of trying. The evils attendant upon penury were well known and the crown and its treasury officials resorted, as they had in the first two wars and would continue after the third war, to ever more extraordinary and desperate expedients to find money to wage war against the Huguenots. The preliminary financial orders at the beginning of the fourth war, for the siege of La Rochelle, exhibit the same patterns. According to the treasurer's *états*, some 162,000 *livres* were required in November and December of 1572 for preparations of men and materials for the siege. All but 7,500 *livres* of that sum had been borrowed from Parisian money lenders, and the rest was assigned to the dubious proceeds from sale of some vacant offices in Brittany. Through the first month of 1573 the cumulative expenses for preparations were around 534,000 *livres*, of which, the treasurers reported, only 287,600 had actually been paid, leaving a deficit of 246,000 *livres*. That deficit, and continuing expenses of around half a million *livres* each month thereafter, they hoped to finance by the forced sale of 100,000 *livres* of *rente*, yielding 1.2 million *livres* of principal, levied on forty-two cities throughout the kingdom, and more loans from private individuals.[48] The fourth civil war, like all its predecessors, was to be financed on short-term expedients. But the long-term result of both the high cost of waging war and the drastic, though ultimately self-defeating expedients adopted to payroll the army's operations, had set in train a

[48] BN Mss. Fr. 4,554, fols. 92, 98–100.

relentless and ultimately self-defeating process which by the beginning of the fifth civil war in 1574 was well on its way, as we will see in the concluding section, to systematic impoverishment and even destruction of the monarchy's finances, with all the attendant effects on military operations that this entailed.

A "SHORTFALL" OF 16 MILLION *LIVRES*

If the failed siege of La Rochelle represented a crucial turning point in the military fortunes of the crown in its campaign against the Huguenots, and the lowest point to that time of the deterioration of capacity of the royal army itself, the conclusion of the fourth civil war also marked a closely connected milestone: the almost irredeemable degradation of royal finances themselves caused by the cumulative impact of fighting four major civil wars within a single decade. Royal finances, which had come out of the crucible of the Hapsburg–Valois wars heavily encumbered by unpayable short-term obligations and a crushing burden of long-term indebtedness, had little time to recover, despite draconian economy measures, before the outbreak of the religious wars in 1562. During that first civil war the crown had suffered from the ignominious seizure of several of the most important provincial tax *recettes* by the Protestants: Tours and Caen, for example, and Lyon, which was lost for the duration of the war. After the chaos and expense of the first civil war, including the reduction of Le Havre in the summer of 1563, the crown was only granted four years of peace to put its military and financial house in order before the outbreak of the second civil war. From late 1567 to mid-1573 the royal army was engaged almost continuously in three major civil wars. At the end of this massive effort there are clear signs of a significant degradation of finances and resources just at the moment when the fifth, longest, most complicated, and most frustrating of the early civil wars began.

What exactly was the state of royal finances which formed the framework for the operations of the royal army after La Rochelle? It is possible to answer this question with some certainty because we are fortunate to possess for that moment in time one of the few prospective royal budgets, drawn up at the commencement of each fiscal year, to survive the era. The document, an "Estat par estimation de l'entière valleur des finances ordinaires du roy pour ceste présente année 1574," was drafted sometime before the Huguenots' Mardi Gras revolt in February 1574 pushed the kingdom into the fifth and final civil war of Charles IX's reign.[49] The *état* is divided into two parts: an estimation of the revenues which could be expected from all sources during 1574 and the expenditures the crown wished or needed to make over the same period. Within those two broad accounting categories detailed estimates and statements of income and liabilities are given, but the overall purpose of the document was to identify the amount of additional funds which would be needed to

---

[49] BN Mss. Fr. 17,870, fols. 278–82.

meet the expenses of the coming year once all the anticipated income had been expended. The document therefore enables us to reconstruct the anticipated state of royal finances for 1574 before any new or extraordinary measures were proposed to deal with the grim findings which by this stage in the wars of religion the royal council would only too certainly have to confront.

Figure 35 summarizes the crown's estimated revenue picture for 1574.[50] Nominal gross receipts were predicted to be in the neighborhood of 14.8 million of *livres*. The most important source of revenue was the 8 million in taxes to be collected by the general *recettes*, most of which – the *taille*, the *creus* of 3 and 4 *sous*, the frontier fortification tax, and the *taillon* – had been imposed on the kingdom specifically for military purposes at various times since the Hundred Years War. Nominal gross income from the royal domain properly speaking, mostly various *aides*, *gabelles*, and tariffs, was estimated at 5 million. Miscellaneous sources of extraordinary revenues, such as the gift of the clergy, receipts from the sale of wood, the *parties casuelles*, and *franc fiefs et nouveaux requêtes*, as well as some recovered unexpended assignations from 1573, were to be another 1.8 million. But the 14.8 million of nominal royal income was not, according to the document, what the crown's treasury officials actually expected to be able to collect during 1574. The regular tax revenues of the *recettes* were predicted to produce only 6.7 million, or 83 percent of their nominal value, primarily because the *creu* of 4 *sous*, considered uncollectible, had been forgiven taxpayers. Of the 5 million book value of the royal domain revenues almost four million, or 79 percent, had been alienated for varying periods of time. Even the category of extraordinary income was only expected to produce 86 percent of its nominal value, principally because the major custom tariff at Lyon had also been alienated and almost half of the money intended to come from *rentes* constituted on the gift of the clergy had already been consumed by the siege of La Rochelle.

Collectible gross receipts, then, were anticipated to be only 9.2 million in 1574, or 63 percent of nominal gross revenues: more than one-third of the crown's income was alienated, forgiven, or considered uncollectible. But only about half of even this relatively sure 9.2 million was actually available to meet expenses, for the general *recettes* themselves carried fixed charges for collection expenses, salaries, and local commitments of funds which amounted to 4.2 million *livres*, and which had to be deducted before any surpluses started their journey in the accounting books or on the bad roads of the kingdom to the central treasury. Furthermore, the officials who compiled the budget, and we can assume that this was probably an optimistic estimate given continued unrest in most of the south and southeast of the country, predicted an additional 500,000 *livres* in *non-valeurs*, that is, revenues that would turn out for various unanticipated reasons to be non-productive during the fiscal year. When these local charges and *non-valeurs* were subtracted the crown was left with estimated expendable revenues for 1574 of only 4.5 million, that is, only 32

---

[50] *Ibid.*, fols. 278–80r for revenues.

Fig. 35. Anticipated royal revenues for fiscal 1574

A. Performance status of nominal gross revenues

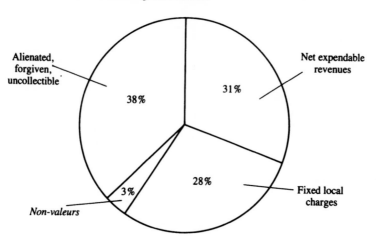

B. Net anticipated receipts (*livres*), 1574

Source of revenue	Nominal gross revenue	Predicted yield	% yield
Recettes Généralés	8,010,539	6,686,738	83
Domaine	5,000,000	1,028,249	21
Other Extraordinary	1,780,000	1,530,000	86
Gross Revenue Total:	14,790,539	9,244,987	63
Adjustments to yield			
Fixed local charges		(4,200,000)	
Non-valeurs		(500,000)	
Net receipts total:	4,544,987		
Percentage of nominal gross revenue:	31%		

percent of nominal gross revenues of 14.8 million *livres*. Under any circumstances, such an anticipated shortfall would have pointed to an extremely precarious financial situation, but the true scale of fiscal disaster is only revealed by comparing the reduced capability of the royal treasury to pay, to the liabilities and expenses the crown anticipated facing during the same period.

Fig. 36. Anticipated royal expenses for fiscal 1574

A. Total expenses by category

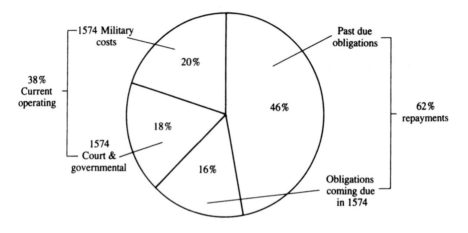

B. Status of total anticipated expenses (*livres*)

Category of expense	New in 1574	From past years	Total	% of total
Military	4,038,068	–	4,038,068	20
Court and governmental	3,528,469	–	3,528,469	18
Military arrears, 1573	–	376,778	376,778	2
Obligation repayments	3,185,689	8,744,703	11,930,392	60
Total	10,752,226	9,121,481	19,873,707	100
Percent	54	46	100	

Those costs are summarized in Figure 36, which shows that the crown anticipated expenses during fiscal 1574 of 19.9 million *livres*.[51] Current operating
expenses were expected to account for 10.8 million, or 54 percent, and unpaid and
overdue financial obligations from preceding years for 9.1 million, or 46 percent. As
far as direct military expenditures during 1574 are concerned the crown planned to
spend 4.4 million, including 377,000 *livres* for pay arrears left over from 1573 and
the end of the fourth civil war. This was a bare-bones figure, in which the appro-
priation for the gendarmerie had been slashed by almost half what was really
needed, the costs of the royal guards, Arsenal, and *marine de Ponant* were included
under the court budget, and the salaries for *mortepayes* and a significant portion of

[51] *Ibid.*, fols. 280r–82v, for expenses.

Table 11.6. *Origins of royal obligations due or past due in 1574 (in livres)*

Origin	Due in 1574	Past due	Total	%
Italian bankers	724,160	25,000	749,160	6
Italian states	–	1,908,333	1,908,333	16
Imperial cities	2,211,676	–	2,211,676	19
Owed to German mercenaries	–	5,859,454	5,859,454	49
Swiss	–	400,000	400,000	3
Royal officials	60,000	333,500	393,500	3
Bad assignations	–	215,566	215,566	2
Miscellaneous	189,853	2,850	192,703	2
Total	3,185,689	8,744,703	11,930,392	100

artillery costs were excluded as expenditures by including them under the category of fixed charges in the income portion of the document. Governmental and court expenses, which included the royal household, pensions, and diplomatic and administrative costs, were anticipated to be about 3.5 million while another 3.2 million was needed for loan repayments falling due for the first time during the new fiscal year. When the repayments coming due in 1574 are added to those due from previous years (including the 1573 arrears in military salaries), we find that 11.9 million *livres*, or 60 percent of all the anticipated expenses of the fiscal year, consisted of loan repayments or other overdue financial obligations.

It is not without interest to review, as in Table 11.6, the origin of the many obligations coming due or overdue for payment in 1574. They represent, in fact, the detritus of a decade of civil war and reflect the mosaic of obligations and expedients to which the crown had been driven, quite beyond the alienation of revenue and the sale of offices and property, in order to wage war against its own subjects. Almost every single *livre* owed by the crown had its origin in the wars of religion. The 41 percent of the total owed due to loans from Italian bankers and states and the Imperial cities reflect sums which had been explicitly raised in order to pay troops, while 49 percent of the total represented overdue obligations to German mercenary troops, mostly the reiters, who had served in both the royal and Protestant armies during the civil wars. To these obligations could be added a Swiss debt of 400,000 *livres* (which would have more than doubled to 844,000 *livres* if the 1573 troops' arrears and the 1574 subsidy to the cantons were counted). Even the sums owed to crown officials represented for the most part back pay or compensation for suppressed offices which had been diverted to military purposes (that owed to officials in Rouen, for example, had been used to pay the Picardy garrison in 1573), while bad assignations from the previous year were the result of non-producing revenues against which some of the crown's obligations had been assigned during the fourth civil war. The bottom line of royal finances for 1574, when net anticipated expendable revenues of 4.5 million *livres* were applied to anticipated costs and obligations of 19.9 million, was a working deficit of 15.3 million (a "faulte de fonds de 16,238,643 *livres*" according to the *état*, which included an arithmetic error of one million *livres*).[52] This in a year in which it was planned to maintain the lowest level of peacetime military forces since the era following the treaty of Cateau-Cambrésis fifteen years before. With more than a third of royal revenues alienated or uncollectible, and another third consumed by fixed local charges, the crown had barely enough money to pay a skeleton peacetime force, and no money at all to pay additional anticipated obligations of three times that magnitude. And in this provisional budget for the 1574 fiscal year no provision at all had been made for war should it be renewed, as in fact it would be for the next two and a half years, adding at least another 500,000 *livres* to the deficit every month. After the conclusion of the fifth civil war in 1576, at what would turn out to be the midpoint of three decades of religious wars, the convergence of military and financial exhaustion would be even more advanced than in 1574, completing the destruction of the effectiveness of the royal army and setting the stage for the almost complete collapse of the power and authority of the monarchy in the succeeding period.

[52] *Ibid.*, fol 282v.

Conclusion: The limits to action

The surviving administrative documents, correspondence, and memoirs from the reign of Charles IX suggest many different images of the royal army – as an institution, in action, and as a specialized type of human community – images that are reflected through the various historical prisms that have been used to construct the chapters of this book. One such image is the grand review, the public inspection of the army's various contingents ranged for battle, such as Henry II's review of the royal army at Pierrepont in 1557, which was earlier used to portray the army on the eve of the civil wars.[1]

Such staged and orderly events continued to be held, periodically, at important campaign junctures throughout the wars of religion. The units of the army, horse, foot, and artillery were led out of camp and arranged *en bataille*, that is, each individual contingent according to its tactical fighting formation, and all the units collectively as a continuous battle line of the type into which the leaders planned to deploy them when combat was in the offing. Part ritual, part psychology, part calculated public relations, the reviews also had a practical side. Marching the units to the reviewing ground and ordering them into their tactical formations gave the marshals-of-camp and the sergeant-majors an opportunity to verify visually the army's strength and to study the spatial and temporal dimensions of its full deployment, and sometimes to try out different formations.

Though the details varied a bit, what then followed at reviews generally conformed to a common pattern. Contingents would be put through their tactical evolutions, which were quite simple, such as raising and lowering their pikes in unison, firing a volley into the air, or simulating a cavalry charge, and sometimes a sham battle would be arranged in honor of the commanders, mercenary leaders, and grandees who led the army, or, if they were present, the king himself or the queen mother. The potentates would then inspect the units, proffering their hands for the kisses of the captains, who would swear to do them good service; noting fine martial displays (principally associated with good quality horseflesh and gilded armor and weapons); disbursing gifts and rewards; and encouraging the men with a brief harangue in which promises of prompt pay often played a prominent part. The inspection finished, a final collective salvo from the entire battle line was

[1] See pp. 38–40.

301

discharged as the soldiers, prompted by their officers, shouted such slogans as "Vive le Roy!" or "France! France! Bataille! Bataille!".[2]

The image produced and surely intended to be conveyed by such occasions was of an orderly, organized, disciplined, and obedient soldiery and of great power and force under strict and regimented control. We can be allowed to doubt, however, whether the tangible expressions of unity, solidarity, and identification with the just cause of the king symbolized by the review had more than a tenuous and temporary impact on the ordinary soldiers who made up the overwhelming proportion of the army's membership. As Rabutin's description of the Pierrepont review reminds us, for the ordinary soldiers of the army such occasions meant heat, dust, and thirst, and the discomfort of standing fully equipped in formation for hours at a time.[3] Furthermore, the contrast of the army's orderly participation in the review with the disorder and disobedience which marked so much of its activities on campaign is striking.

The sources often throw up a counter-image of a soldiery out of control, as at the sack of Rouen in 1562. According to Castelnau:

And so this great city full of all sorts of wealth was pillaged over the course of eight days, without regard to either religion, even though the day after the capture, it had been proclaimed that, on pain of death, each company and ensign, of whatever nation, was to return to camp and leave the city. Very few obeyed, excepting the Swiss, who have always maintained, and still maintain, great discipline and obedience, and who carried off no other loot than a bit of bread and things to eat, and kettles, pots, and utensils, and vessels to use in the army. But the French would rather let themselves be killed than leave, as long as there was anything left to take.[4]

Appalled at the flight of some of the gendarmerie before a Protestant probe of the defenses of the faubourgs of Paris in 1562, the duke of Guise bellowed out in rage: "Ah! gen-darmes de France, prenez la quenouille et laissez la lance."[5] After the surrender of Saint-Jean-d'Angély, in 1569, royal troops violated the safeguards contained in the surrender terms by attacking the defenders as they marched off in column. Brantôme described the scene:

At the time Saint-Jean was taken by honorable composition, as M. de Pilles and his men were returning, M. de Biron was at the head, conducting the column. Someone informed him that

---

[2] Based on a number of references to major reviews and receptions of troops; for the first war, Brantôme, *Oeuvres*, vol. 6, 221; *CSPF/E*, vol. 5, no. 387; Jules de La Brosse, *Histoire d'un capitaine bourbonnais au XVIe siècle* (Paris, 1929), 301; Lublinskaya, *Documents*, 117; and Paschal, *1562*, 70, 79, 82, 109–10; for the second war, Arigo Davila, *The History of the Civil Wars of France* (Dublin, 1760), 112; Castelnau, *Mémoires*, vol. 1, 210; Brantôme, *Oeuvres*, vol. 6, 79; Tavannes, *Mémoires*, vol. 25, 18; BN Mss. Fr. 15,544, fol. 62r; *CSPF/E*, vol. 8, no. 1981; for the third war, Frank Delage, *La troisième guerre de religion en Limousin* (Limoges, 1950), 70–71, from which comes the quoted slogans; Gigon, 244–45; BN Mss. Fr. 17,528, fols. 15v–16r; La Popelinière, vol. 1, fol. 150v; Castelnau, *Mémoires*, vol. 1, 243, *CSPF/E*, vol. 9, nos. 300 and 430; for the fourth war, BN Mss. Fr. 4,765, fol. 59r; and for the fifth war, D'Aubigné, vol. 4, 206, 260; and *Henri III*, vol. 2, 408.

[3] See p. 39.

[4] Castelnau, *Mémoires*, vol. 1, 108.

[5] Brantôme, *Oeuvres*, vol. 6, 46.

some of our men were robbing those towards the rear. He turned quickly and took his sword in hand and tried to kill all those troops which were in line here and there, in order to deliver the others, and crippled a great many of them. "Ha! Scoundrels!" he exclaimed to them. "It was not two days ago that you would not dare look them in the face nor would you attack them. As soon as they had surrendered themselves and were without force and resistance, you want to run them through! I'll kill all of you and teach you to dishonor your king so that it will be claimed that he broke his vow."[6]

And King Charles himself wrote to Matignon in 1574, "I am extremely angry with the cowardliness of these scoundrels of soldiers who performed so badly during the assault on the Château of Domfront." And he ordered different units to the siege "so that their soldiers will redeem the disgrace of the others."[7]

But the kind of imprecations hurled by the king or great nobles like Guise or Biron also carried proof of their own irrelevance for the soldiers. Biron's claim that the violation of the conditions of surrender at Saint-Jean-d'Angély would dishonor the king was obviously not a consideration which the soldiers, angered at the long resistance of the garrison and deprived of a chance to loot the surrendered town, would have respected. Guise's imputation of lack of soldierly – and noble – qualities to the gendarmerie ("take up the distaff" must have been for him a powerful insult) and Charles IX's concern that the honor which had been lost by one group of soldiers should be redeemed by others rested on aristocratic notions of honor and duty not shared by the majority of their troops.

The unmediated voices of the common soldiers during the wars of religion are largely mute. But the army leadership firmly believed that material gain was the prime motivation of its soldiers. "Such men follow the *éscu*," explained the duke of Estampes in 1562.[8] And Anjou in 1573, it will be recalled, attributed the failure of the assaults at La Rochelle to soldiers who were "dissolute, accustomed to living unrestrained and to pillaging everyone without paying for anything. They are forced to live off the ration they must purchase, which infinitely vexes them. And, if they lose hope of quickly looting the city, they desert."[9]

Almost all contemporary observers thought the behavior of soldiers increasingly degenerated into sheer brigandage as the wars continued. Brantôme even reported that the soldiers invented euphemisms for their own behavior: "il faut parrossier" meant that they planned to go looting from parish to parish, and "nous allons nous raffraischer" that their regiment had been detached from the main army and assigned a province to pillage, though he added, "What I have said on this is not to restrain the plunder, nor the grub; because it is necessary that they live and that they profit."[10]

---

[6] Brantôme, *Oeuvres*, vol. 5, 154.
[7] *CDM*, vol. 4, 304–5, note 1.
[8] Lublinskaya, *Documents*, 97.
[9] BN Mss. Fr. 4,765, fol. 76r.
[10] Brantôme, *Oeuvres*, vol. 5, 381.

The phrase, "il faut qu'ilz vivent et gaignent" goes, I believe, directly to the heart of what it meant to be a soldier during the civil wars and helps to explain the widespread disorder of the times. Anjou noted in 1573 that without pay it was difficult to hold the troops to what he called "l'office de soldat".[11] The "office" of soldier, of course, included the willingness to march and fight and obey commands, that is, operate obediently so that the army could fulfill its military function in a timely, disciplined, and effective manner. But, in return, there was an implicit contract that soldiers would be regularly supplied, fed, and paid, that they would not be wantonly or stupidly sacrificed, and that if they survived, they would receive some portion of the spoils of war. But the contract also assumed that the men would be able to live the "vie militaire," that is, a life that while not exactly carefree was more extravagant and of looser moral tone than more conventional roles.[12] Because the military occupation, with its dangers, fighting, and handling of weapons, was not considered base or derogating, even ordinary soldiers could claim privileges that in some important ways entitled them to a simulacrum of the life of a highly skilled master craftsman or even a nobleman. Ordinary French infantry, not to mention the gendarmerie, for example, were not required to perform most manual tasks. They did not dig trenches, prepare camps, or build fortifications: all of that was the task of the pioneers. Nor did many of them prepare their own food or even carry their own weapons, armor, and baggage on the march. These tasks were performed for them by the numerous pages, *goujats*, campwomen, children, and other assorted followers of the army or devolved, usually quite brutally, upon the hapless civilians they were quartered on. And though they might be hanged for an offense against army regulations, they were not whipped (not a single one of Brissac's or Montluc's men were reported to have lash scars), though their camp followers might be.[13]

Without attempting to minimize the fatiguing nature and essential grimness of much of a soldier's life on campaign, the fact of the matter is that the conditions of service in the royal armies of the wars of religion were a long way from the incessant drilling and fatigues as well as the systematic coercion and brutality that characterized later seventeenth- and eighteenth-century armies. No matter the letter of army regulations, infantrymen and cavalrymen, not to mention the artillery personnel, operated more like skilled and somewhat independent contract workers, and the army as a whole as a cross between a warrior society and a specialized labor force, than the cowed and obedient soldiers of the leviathan machines spawned by the Military Revolution and later military reforms.[14] As the wars dragged on, campaigns lengthened, and the difficulty of its tasks grew, the army and its operations also began to suffer increasingly from the long-term effects of a systematic,

---

[11] *Henri III*, vol. 1, 224.
[12] On this theme see especially Hale, *Artists and Warfare.*
[13] See for example the range of punishments set forth by Anjou's camp regulations for the army at the siege of La Rochelle in 1573, *OM* no. 169.
[14] McNeill, *The Pursuit of Power*, 117–43.

and fatal, lack of financial support. The soldiery, denied those positive aspects of the "vie militaire" which the crown had provided more regularly in the past, increasingly acted out – with widespread disobedience, desertion, and pillage – their conclusion that the contract obligating them to, as Admiral Villars put it, "vivre et contenir selon l'art militaire" had been dissolved.[15]

A strange and grisly incident at the end of the third civil war, in 1570, and recounted by Brantôme, may be interpreted to reflect the increasing resentment and anger felt by the higher command at their growing lack of control over the troops:

After the third war and the third peace, the King retired to Angers, and it was necessary that M. D'Estrosse repass the troops who were in Guyenne over the Loire River. Seeing his companies encumbered by too many of the soldiers' trollops and whores, and having issued several bans to drive them off, and seeing that they had no effect, as they were passing over the bridge at Ce, he had more than eight hundred of these poor creatures of a sudden pushed off, who pitifully crying for help, were all with great cruelty drowned...and it might have happened that many soldiers, friends of their trollops, would have mutinied, if order had not been restored.[16]

Unable to enforce discipline or good order on their troops, equally unable to punish directly such a large group of hard-bitten and dangerously armed men, the colonel general of infantry, who was not known as a particularly cruel man, took out his deep-seated frustration on their camp followers, a group closely identified with the unfettered "vie militaire" that had become the bane of the kingdom.

It would be a mistake, however, to attribute the royal army's failure to defeat the Huguenots between 1562 and 1576 principally to its undisciplined and predatory soldiers, for their behavior was much more a symptom than a cause of the difficulties facing the army. These had much deeper roots. What I have sought to do in this book is to make clear the reasons for this military failure and why that failure produced three decades of chronic, indecisive, and destructive civil war. The royal army's failure, I have argued, was deeply rooted in an intractable set of military problems that hampered its operations in all the civil wars: the small size and awkward disposition of its peacetime forces; difficulties and slowness of mobilization; the demands of fighting a large-scale and unrelenting internal war in the greatest kingdom in Europe; the unavoidable entropic impact on its armed forces of primitive conditions, faulty organization, and poor communications; the impossibility in any case of maintaining expensive forces in the field for long because of financial problems; and unplanned and chaotic demobilizations. During each war these problems manifested themselves in an unchanging cycle of interconnected events that radically reduced the chances of achieving clear and favorable military decisions against an enemy that, though much weaker, was nevertheless able to

---

[15] Loutchitzki, "Documents," 259.
[16] Brantôme, *Oeuvres*, vol. 6, 132.

organize from its own or foreign resources sizeable and dangerous conventional field armies and to rely on the fanatical defense of a small number of nearly impregnable fortified places. As a result, despite the deployment of massive resources in each war, the royal army's operational, logistical, and financial problems rapidly multiplied in the face of sustained resistance, leading to military exhaustion, breakdown of discipline, disintegration, and premature, insincere peace settlements that returned the royal army to the *status quo ante bellum* – the original state of unpreparedness in which it would again have to face the next outbreak of hostilities.

This cycle of military insufficiency was not, of course, unique to the French civil wars. The scale, technical problems, and expense associated with the new type of gunpowder warfare had all been prefigured in the long series of Hapsburg–Valois wars, and every army of the period had to struggle with them. And when religion merged with civil war elsewhere, as in the Low Countries, a variant of this cycle of military insufficiency soon manifested itself. Military and financial exhaustion, however, were not enough to bring such large-scale civil wars to a quick end when religious hostility, intense mutual suspicion, and absolutist ideological goals combined to guarantee the continual renewal of war.

In the French case, the cycle of military insufficiency became entangled with two other developments that over time increased the royal army's problems, prolonged the course of the civil wars, and further magnified their destructiveness. The first of these was the shift of the strategical and operational focus of the royal army away from its most secure resource base in Paris and the north of the kingdom. After the outbreak of the second civil war in 1567, the army was in the field in nine of the next ten years, either chasing the main Huguenot armies or conducting difficult and often unsuccessful sieges of Protestant strongholds south of the Loire river. As has been shown in previous chapters, these operations escalated operational difficulties and steadily eroded the effectiveness of all of the army's main technical branches at a time when the human and material resources available for waging war had begun to diminish. There is abundant evidence that by 1576 the survivors of the constant campaigning were affected by increasing war weariness, and while we will never know the precise total of army casualties we do know that officers of all grades, because they led from the front and shared the risks of action with their men, suffered extremely high casualties, especially at sieges. These critical losses steadily diminished the effectiveness of the army's leadership, as the original generation of officers was replaced by new leaders whose only military experience was of interminable and ferocious civil war. It was this depleted and thoroughly debased officer corps that would provide the leadership for the increasingly fragile and undisciplined royal forces that would continue to fight the civil wars for two more decades after 1576.

The second crucial development that negatively affected the chances of military victory was the profound failure of royal finances traced in the preceding chapter. Mobilizing and keeping afoot the sizeable forces needed to fight campaigns was an extremely expensive proposition, and even under the best of conditions total state income was not enough to finance protracted war. Over time the development of chronic political and social disorder further reduced revenues, while the short intervals between the wars never allowed the royal treasury sufficient time to recover. The desperate expedients adopted to finance the wars – principally whole-sale alienations and borrowing at ruinous terms – rapidly led to increasing indebt-edness, unmanageable deficits, and by 1576 more or less permanent financial paralysis.

The collapse of royal finances and the more difficult operational situation that developed after 1567 deepened and accentuated the serious problems the crown already faced in attempting to bring the protracted civil war in France to a clear conclusion. Though the crown always managed to raise enough money to begin each war, from about 1570 onwards the forces that its diminishing financial resources could support became steadily smaller and less effective. Penury and disorder prevented the most basic military maintenance tasks in peacetime. Commanders were forced to postpone campaigns or to keep their troops inactive because of the difficulty of assembling adequate forces or supplies or because they simply were unable to pay their men. The small permanent cadre of the army could no longer count on being retained between wars or even regularly recalled during wartime itself. Bereft of official support, governors and commanders were left to their own devices, constructing satrapies that were often as independent and hostile to royal directives as the enclaves of their Huguenot counterparts. Common soldiers, released from the "office" of soldier by the inability of the crown and their commanders to provide for an adequate "vie militaire," acted up and acted out, turning for survival, whether under recognized military authority or not, to the brigandage that became an ever more ubiquitous part of French life after 1576.

There is a story that when, in early 1575, the repatriated new king, Henry III, the former duke of Anjou, arrived at the camp of the royal army near the end of the unsuccessful siege of Livron, he was so appalled by its disastrous condition that he shouted at the city's walls "Oh! miserable town! How you have cost me good men and delayed other good affairs! Let us remove ourselves from here, comrades. We go, we go to France, because there is more to gain there than here!"[17] Though possibly apocryphal, Henry's dramatic verdict applies very well to the military situation the royal army had generally found itself in from the siege of Saint-Jean-d'Angély onwards. The new king's suggestion that a more favorable or significant decision was somehow to be obtained elsewhere in the kingdom, however, contained a sizeable dose of self-deception. For though it is tempting to think that a different outcome to the early wars might have occurred had Orléans actually been taken in 1563, the siege of Saint-Jean-d'Angély avoided in 1569, or La Rochelle captured in 1573, the ability of the crown and its army to complete its

---

[17] Arnaud, *Dauphiné*, vol. 1, 316.

conquest of the remaining Protestant strongholds that dominated so much of southern and western France would not have improved significantly. Indeed, the army that returned to the north of France with Henry III was further away from victory in 1576 than it had been in 1562.

Under Henry III, then, the basic pattern of military deadlock, disorder, and destruction would not change. *Faute de mieux*, the crown renewed the campaign against the Huguenots in 1577–78, only to see its inadequate and unpaid army melt away at sieges which, even when successful, were more notable for the widespread atrocities committed by its troops than for any notable shift in the overall balance of power between the weakened monarchy and its desperate and determined opponents. Even when, in the 1580s, the strategic focus of the main royal army shifted back to the north, the same obstacles to obtaining a military decision remained. Financial exhaustion crippled operations; and the breakdown of law and order and of government itself became ever more widespread, leaving brigandage and popular uprisings in its wake.

The struggle against the Huguenots was dramatically changed politically – if not militarily – by the assassination of the duke of Guise in 1588. Much of the country defected from the royal cause as the Catholic League mounted an independent attempt to destroy Henry III, deny the succession to Henry of Navarre, and restore ultra-Catholic direction both to local and national affairs. During these later years, major battles regained some of their importance, but, as before, decisive victory proved elusive. After the death of Henry III, Henry of Navarre, who succeeded in holding the remaining loyalists and most of the Huguenot movement together, led the counteroffensive against the League. But his royal army found itself, as had the army of Charles IX, engaged in lengthy and ultimately unsuccessful sieges of major cities, like Paris and Rouen. In addition, Henry IV's military road to victory was frustrated by the same foreign intervention that had plagued the royal army throughout the religious wars (though now it was the leaders of the Catholic League who called on Philip II of Spain to send the duke of Parma and his Army of Flanders against the royal army). In the end, political manipulation and compromise as well as continued fighting was needed to bring the civil wars to a close. Exhausted after thirty-six years of civil war, the political and religious sources of opposition had finally dried up. Henry's conversion to Catholicism removed the main reason for the opposition of most Catholics, while his personal ties to his former comrades-in-arms in the Huguenot movement neutralized all but the most reflexive Protestant opposition to the crown. Massive bribery of the grandees who led the forces of the Catholic League allowed the royal army to move with eventual success to eliminate the remaining remnants of military resistance as well as to suppress the brigandage and popular unrest spawned by the wars.

Given a respite from civil war, France was quick to recover, and, before his assassination in 1610, Henry IV had managed to rebuild the country's military infrastructure as well as to amass the *sine qua non* of early modern warfare, a substantial warchest. But one should not overestimate the degree of military security created by Henry IV, even with the help of more than a decade of peace. The crown and its royal army were still far from having uncontested control of French affairs, for, among other factors, the Huguenots had emerged from the peace negotiations with considerable military power intact. The royal bureaucracy was still too underdeveloped and the royal army too weak in peacetime and too fragile in wartime either to guarantee internal peace or allow France to deploy her considerable but latent military strength effectively abroad. The final, and this time, decisive military victory over the Huguenots would be delayed until the middle years of the seventeenth century.

The grim political and religious stalemate that characterized France in 1576, and continued to do so until the end of the century, simply cannot be understood if the military dimension of the five civil wars of Charles IX's reign is glossed over or ignored. What should be clear from this study is how the nature of the royal army, its strategic disposition, and the largely unprecedented military situation itself put enormous constraints on the application of force by the crown against its Protestant subjects during the period 1562–76, and how the failure of the royal army to achieve a decisive military victory over the Huguenots during the early wars of religion created a constellation of military factors that would enable potentially rebellious groups to continue to pose significant military dangers to the peace of the kingdom long after the formal ending of the wars in 1598.

Military factors, then, and especially the failure of the royal army to deal a knock-out blow to the Huguenots during the reign of Charles IX, were crucial in determining the course and conduct of the inconclusive and destructive nature of the wars of religion that afflicted France from 1562 on. While the intense religious hostility of the rival confessional groups provided ample *casus belli*, the incomplete nature of the Military Revolution meant that the royal army was not capable of completely overcoming Huguenot military resistance before exhausting itself to such an extent that each war was brought to a premature end. Even in the face of increasingly serious political breakdown, material destruction, and human suffering, however, mutual suspicion, increasingly bitter memories, and absolutist ideological goals precluded any genuine or workable peace settlement while providing both sides with sufficient justification to repeatedly renew the struggle.

Solutions had to be found to the inadequacies of the existing standing army and to the fiscal and financial problems which so often immobilized it, before the royal army could effectively wage long-term, large-scale wars. But military and political innovations of some magnitude would be required to turn fighters into soldiers and polyglot and episodic armies into the permanent and uniform leviathans of the old regime. As long as warfare was not the technical and financial monopoly of the state, internal military conflict had the effect of postponing the changes that were needed to solve the problems created by the beginnings of the Military Revolution. Ultimately the triumph of that revolution would require internal peace, and such peace would not be found in France until after the Fronde. Only then would the seemingly chronic cycle of military insufficiency finally be broken in a manner that simultaneously enabled France to dominate Europe militarily and made successful armed defiance of the French monarchy by its own subjects an impossibility – at least until 1789.[18]

---

[18] On the continuing search in Europe for decisiveness in war from the seventeenth century to the age of Napoleon, see Weigley, *The Age of Battles.*

Appendix
The royal army during the Wars of Religion

A Sources for a general narrative of the early wars, 1562–76

Besides the original manuscripts from the *Bibliothèque nationale* and the *Ordonnances militaires* series of the *Dépôt de la Guerre (Service Historique de l'Armée de Terre, Château de Vincennes)*, many of which are identified in sections B–D below or in chapter footnotes, two indispensable collections of correspondence are Hector de la Ferrière-Percy and Gustave Baguenault de Puchesse, eds., *Lettres de Catherine de Médicis* (Paris, 1880–1909), 11 vols., and *Index*, by André Lescort (1943), and Michel François, ed., *Lettres de Henri III, roy de France* (Paris, 1959), 6 vols. *The Calendar of State Papers, Foreign Series, of the Reign of Elizabeth* (London, 1901–50), 23 vols. and the documents to which it refers in the State Paper Foreign series of the PRO contain a wealth of information on events in France. Also useful are Abel Desjardins, ed., *Négociations diplomatiques de la France avec la Toscane* (Paris, 1865), vol. 3, and M.N. Tommaseo, ed., *Relations des Ambassadeurs Venitiens sur les Affaires de France au XVIe siècle* (Paris, 1838), vols. 1–2. Other useful collections of documents and correspondence are Sidney H. E. Ehrman and James W. Thompson, eds., *The Letters and Documents of Armand de Gontaut, Baron de Biron, Marshal of France (1524–1592)* (Berkeley, 1936), 2 vols.; L. Pingaud, ed., *Correspondence des Saulx-Tavannes au XVIe siècle* (Paris, 1877); M. Belisaire Ledain, ed., *Lettres adressées à Jean et Guy de Daillon, Comtes du Lude, Gouverneurs de Poitou de 1543 à 1557 et de 1557 à 1585*, vol. 12, *Archives historiques du Poitou* (1882); Alphonse de Ruble, ed., *Commentaires et Lettres de Blaise de Monluc, Maréchal de France* (Paris, 1870), vols. 4–5; A. Lublinskaya, *Documents pour servir à l'histoire des guerres civiles en France (1561–65)* (Moscow, 1962); C. Douais, "Les guerres de religion en Languedoc d'après les papiers du Baron de Fourquevaux (1572–1574)," *Annales du Midi*, vol. 4 (1892), 25–67, 331–61, 475–509, and vol. 5 (1893), 71–102, 170–218, 332–73; and the *Archives historiques du département de la Gironde* (Bordeaux, 1859–1903), 38 vols.

The most important memoirs and early histories are: Gaspard de Saulx, *Mémoires de Gaspard de Saulx, Seigneur de Tavannes*, in M. Petitot, ed., *Collection complète des mémoires relatifs a l'histoire de France*, vols. 23–25 (Paris, 1822); Blaise de Monluc, *Commentaires de Blaise de Monluc, Maréchal de France*, ed. Paul Courteault (Paris, 1911), 3 vols.; Michel de Castelnau, *Les mémoires de Messire Michel de Castelnau, seigneur de Mauvissière*, 3rd. ed. by Jean Godefroy (Brussels, 1731), 3 vols.; François de la Noue, *Discours politiques et militaires*, ed. F. E. Sutcliffe (Geneva, 1967); Theodore de Bèze, *Histoire ecclésiastique des églises réformées au royaume de France*, eds. G. Baum and E. Cunitz, (Nieuwkoop, 1974), 3 vols., reprint of Paris edition (1883–89); Simon Goulart, *Mémoires de l'estat de France sous Charles neufiesme*, 2nd ed. by Heinrich Wolf (Meidelbourg, 1578), 3 vols.; Jean de Serres, *Mémoires de la troisième guerre civile*, is included in vol. 3 of Goulart, *Mémoires*; Henri Lancelot-Voisin de la

Popelinière, *L'Histoire de France* (La Rochelle, 1581), 2 vols.; Agrippa d'Aubigné, *Histoire universelle*, ed. André Thierry (Paris, 1981–93), vols. 1–7; Pierre de Bourdeille, *Oeuvres complètes de Pierre de Bourdeille, seigneur de Brantôme*, ed. Ludovic Lalanne (Paris, 1864–82), 11 vols., and the excellent modern edition of the *Discours sur les colonels de l'infanterie de France*, ed. Etienne Vaucheret (Paris, 1973); Jacques-Auguste De Thou, *Histoire universelle* (Paris, 1734), 16 vols.; and Arrigo Caterino Davila, *The History of the Civil Wars of France* (Dublin, 1760). There is a scattering of interesting pieces in M. L. Cimber and F. d'Anjou, *Archives curieuses de l'histoire de France depuis Louis XI jusqu'à Louis XVIII* (Paris, 1834–41), 30 vols.

In addition to the works cited in notes 1–3 of the introduction, general secondary works which were helpful in framing the political and military situation of the early civil wars are: Lucien Romier, *Les origines politiques des guerres de religion* (Paris, 1913), 2 vols.; N. M. Sutherland, *The Massacre of St. Bartholomew and the European Conflict, 1559–1572* (New York, 1973); Henry M. Baird, *History of the Rise of the Huguenots of France* (New York, 1879), 2 vols.; Bernard Vogler, "Le rôle des Électeurs palatins dans les guerres de religion en France (1559–1592)," *Cahiers d'histoire*, 10 (1965), 51–85; Pierre Champion, *Catherine de Médicis présente à Charles IX son Royaume (1564–1566)* (Paris, 1937); and Nancy L. Roelker, *Queen of Navarre. Jeanne d'Albret (1528–1572)* (Cambridge, 1968).

There are also a number of mostly older, but still serviceable studies of many of the important military leaders of the time, some of which contain copies of correspondence and documents. The most valuable of these are: A. Ph. v. Segesser, *Ludwig Pfyffer und Seine Zeit. Die Schweizer in den drei ersten französichen Religionskrieges* (Bern, 1880–81), 2 vols.; Franklin C. Palm, *Politics and Religion in Sixteenth-Century France: A Study of the Career of Henry of Montmorency-Damville, Uncrowned King of the South* (Gloucester, Mass., 1927); Alphonse de Ruble, *Antoine de Bourbon et Jeanne d'Albret* (Paris, 1881–86), 4 vols.; Henri d'Orléans, Duc d'Aumale, *Histoire des Princes de Condé pendant les XVIe et XVIIe siècles* (Paris, 1863–96), 7 vols.; Louis J. H. Delaborde, *Gaspard de Coligny, Amiral de France* (Paris 1879–82) 3 vols.; Charles Marchand, *Le maréchal François de Scepeaux de Vieilleville et ses Mémoires* (Paris, 1893) and *Charles Ier de Cossé, Comte de Brissac et Maréchal de France (1507–1563)* (Paris, 1889); Francis Decrue, *Anne duc de Montmorency, Connétable et Pair de France sous les rois Henri II, François II, et Charles IX* (Paris, 1889); Jules de la Brosse, *Histoire d'un capitaine bourbonnais au XVIe siècle: Jacques de la Brosse (1485–1562)* (Paris, 1929). See also Paul Courteault, *Blaise de Monluc historien. Etude critique sur le texte et la valeur historique des Commentaires* (Paris, 1907); R. de Bouille, *Histoire des ducs de Guise* (Paris, 1849–50), 4 vols.; Pierre de Vaissière, *Le baron des Adrets* (Paris, 1930); Alphonse de Ruble, "François de Montmorency, Gouverneur de Paris et de l'Ile-de-France," *Mémoires de la société de l'histoire de Paris*, vol. 6 (1879), 200–89; Léon Marlet, *Le Comte de Montgomery* (Paris, 1890); and L. Pingaud, *Les Saulx-Tavannes* (Paris, 1876).

Finally, there are a number of older, regionally or locally focused studies which provide information on the wars. Those I found most helpful in keeping track of the principal military events outside the path of the main royal armies during the early wars were: Claude Devic and J. Vaissete, *Histoire générale de Languedoc avec des notes et les pièces justificatives* (Toulouse, 1889), vols. 11 and 12; Louise Guiraud, *Etudes sur la Réforme à Montpellier* (Montpellier, 1918), 2 vols.; Le Vicomte de Brimont, *Le XVIe siècle et les guerres de la Réforme en Berry* (Paris, 1905), 2 vols.; Guillaume Daval and Jean Daval, *Histoire de la Réformation à Dieppe, 1557–1657*, ed. Emile Lesens (Rouen, 1878), 2 vols.; Eugène Arnaud,

Sources for individual wars

Histoire des Protestants du Dauphiné aux XVIe, XVIIe, et XVIIIe siècles (Geneva, 1970), reprint of 1875–76 edition, vol. 1, *Histoire des Protestants de Provence, du Comtat Vénaissin, et de la principauté d'Orange* (Paris, 1884), 2 vols., and *Histoire des Protestants du Vivarais et du Velay, pays de Languedoc* (Paris, 1888), vol. 1; Pierre Cavard, *La Réforme et les guerres de religion à Vienne* (Vienne, 1950); Maurice Pallasse, *La sénéchaussée et siège présidial de Lyon pendant les Guerres de Religion* (Lyon, 1943); Paul Viard and Roger Galmiche, *Etudes sur la Réforme et les guerres de religion en Bourgogne*, vol. 15, no. 4 (Dijon, 1905) of *Revue bourguignonne*; Edmond Belle, *La Réforme à Dijon des origines à la fin de la lieutenance générale de Gaspard de Saulx-Tavanes (1530–1570)*, vol. 21, no. 1 (Dijon, 1911) of *Revue bourguignonne*; Edmond Cabié, *Guerres de religion dans le sud-ouest de la France* (Geneva, 1975), reprint of 1906 edition; G. Tholin, "La ville d'Agen pendant les guerres de religion du XVIe siècle," *Revue de l'Agenais*, 14 (1887), 97–113, 201–17, 430–50, 489–515, 15 (1888), 193–218, 322–48, 409–34, 16 (1889), 27–43, 197–222, 385–98, 17 (1890), 97–120, 281–301, 488–510, 18 (1891), 57–70, 225–41, 19 (1892), 22–39, 118–33, 20 (1893), 52–67, 177–200; Nicolas de Bordenave, *Histoire de Béarn et Navarre*, Paul Raymond, ed. (Paris, 1873); and A. Communay, *Les Huguenots dans le Béarn et la Navarre* (Paris, 1885).

B Sources for individual wars

1st war, 1562–63

In addition to BN Mss. Fr. 15,876 and 15,877, the *mémoires-journaux* of the duke of Guise provide an important additional source for the administration and operations of the army during the first civil war: *Mémoires de François de Lorraine, duc d'Aumale et de Guise*, in J.-F. Michaud and J.-J.-F. Poujoulat, eds., *Nouvelle collection des mémoires pour servir à l'histoire de France depuis le XIIIe siècle jusqu'à la fin du XVIIIe* (Paris 1839), vol. 6, esp. 496–506. See also Pierre de Paschal, *Journal de ce qui s'est passé en France durant l'année 1562 principalement dans Paris et à la cour*, ed. Michel François (Paris, 1950); Alphonse de Ruble, "Documents inédits sur la guerre civile de 1562 en Berry," *Société des Antiquaires du Centre Bourges*, 15 (1887–88), 127–66; "Lettres anecdotes qui furent écrites au Cardinal Borromée, par le Cardinal de Ste. Croix, nonce du Pape Pie IV auprès de la reine Catherine de Médicis (1561–1565)," in Jean Aymon, ed., *Actes ecclésiastiques et civiles de tous les synodes nationaux des églises réformées de France* (La Haye, 1710), vol. 1, 1–285; A. H. Layard, ed., "Dispatches of Michele Suriano and of Marc' Antonio Barbaro, Venetian Ambassadors at the Court of France," *The Publications of the Huguenot Society of London*, vol. 6 (1891), x–xii, 1–107; "Discours abbregé et mémoires d'aulcunes choses advenues tant en Normandye que en France depuis le commencement de l'an 1559, et principalement en la ville de Rouen," in A. Heron, ed., *Deux Chroniques de Rouen* (Rouen, 1900), vii–xxv, 173–366; and Edouard Forestié, *Un capitaine gascon du XVIe siècle: Corbeyran de Cardaillac-Sarlabous, mestre de camp, gouverneur de Dunbar (Ecosse) et du Havre-de-Grace* (Paris, 1897). The best study of the campaign and battle of Dreux is Le Commandant Raymond de Coynart, *L'Année 1562 et la bataille de Dreux. Etude historique et militaire* (Paris, 1894). Among the general sources cited above, the *CSPF/E* is particularly rich because of the extensive English operations in Upper Normandy; but Bèze, Segesser, Lublinskaya, and De la Brosse, *opera cit.*, and Ruble, *Antoine et Jeanne* also all contain useful documents.

313

Appendix

2nd war, 1567–68

Besides the daybook of Anjou's headquarters in BN Mss. Fr. 15,543, 15,544, and 15,545, and the administrative documents in BN Mss. Fr. 4,553, 4,554, and 15,608, *CDM*, *Henri III*, and Segesser are also important. For the battle of Saint-Denis see the excellent study by Anne Lombard-Jourdan, "La bataille de Saint-Denis (10 Novembre, 1567). Tradition, propaganda, et iconographie," *Paris et Ile-de-France*, 28 (1978), 7–54. Claude de Haton, *Mémoires de Claude de Haton*, ed. Felix Bourquelot (Paris, 1857), vol. 1, contains some interesting information on the rival armies in Champagne. None of the early histories or memoirs, curiously, contain detailed accounts of the siege of Chartres, the pivotal event which ended the second war. The fundamental source for the siege is "Etat des dépenses faites par la ville de Chartres, pendant les troubles et pendant le siège de ladite ville (1er Octobre 1567–18 April 1568)," ed. Lucien Merlet, *Bulletin historique et philologique du comité des travaux historiques et scientifiques* (1840), 394–438; the best modern account is Henri Lehr, "Le siège de Chartres en 1568," chapter 2 of *La Réforme et les Églises Réformées dans le département actuel d'Eure-et-Loir (1523–1911)* (Chartres, 1912), 40–70.

3rd war, 1568–69

Besides Villeroy's log in BN Mss. Fr. 17,528 and the documents in BN Mss. Fr. 15,549, 15,550, 4,554, 17,870, and 18,587, a very interesting day-by-day account of the Italian contingent with the army in 1569 is the anonymous *Narratione della guerra in Francia* (1569), Vatican Library, *Fonds Barberini*, Mss. 5040. Of the previously cited works, Tavannes, *Henri III*, Segesser, and the *CSPF/E* are the most helpful. The third war is very competently covered by S.-C. Gigon, *La troisième guerre de religion. Jarnac-Moncontour (1568–69)* (Paris, 1909), see especially his *Notes* and *Pièces justificatives*, and Franck Delage, *La troisième guerre de religion en Limousin, Combat de la Roche-l'Abeille, 1569* (Limoges, 1950). See also Jean Pablo, "La bataille de la Roche-l'Abeille," *Bulletin de la Société de l'histoire du Protestantisme français*, 101 (January–March, 1955), 1–25, and "La troisième guerre de religion," *ibid.*, 102 (January–March 1956), 57–91.

4th war, 1572–73

Besides BN Mss. Fr. 3,240 and 4,554, and Nevers' and Anjou's accounts in BN Mss. Fr. 4,765, Biron's letters to Anjou and the king and queen mother from November, 1572, to February, 1573, in *Archives historiques du département de la Gironde*, 14 (1873), documents xxxv–lxii, 60–96, detail the preliminaries to the siege. Of the histories, Goulart, *Mémoires*, is a key, especially his detailed account of the siege of La Rochelle: vol. 2, 97r–156r, 167r–176r, 232v–239r, 269r–280r. Goulart, *ibid.*, 280r–294r, also reproduces a Catholic account, "Le Discours et Recueil du siege de la Rochelle, en l'année 1573" (Lyon, 1573). See also Philippe Cauriana, *Histoire du siège de la Rochelle en 1573*, trans. from the Latin by La société littéraire de la Rochelle (La Rochelle, 1856) (which has a very useful discussion of sources on the history of the siege, ix–xliii); Amos Barbot, *Histoire de la Rochelle depuis l'an 1199 jusques en 1575*, vol. 3, in *Archives historiques de la Saintonge et de l'Aunis*, xviii (1889), 19–197; Guillaume le Riche, *Journal de Guillaume et de Michel Le Riche, avocats du roi à Saint-Maixent (de 1534 à 1586)* (Geneva, 1971), reprint of 1846 edition, 104–45. Among previously cited sources, *Henri III*, *CSPF/E*, Lude, Douais, and Brantôme, *Discours*, are all valuable, to which can be added Jean Loutchitzki, "Documents inédits et originaux.

Quatrième guerre de religion, 1572–1573," *Bulletin de la Société de l'histoire du Protestantisme français*, 22 (June–Sept. 1873), 252–68, 299–311, 352–74, 401–13. Though old, the best, and still very useful, secondary account of the siege is A. Genet, "Relation du siège de la Rochelle par le duc d'Anjou, en 1573," *Le Spectateur Militaire*, 44 (Feb., 1848), 513–49, (March, 1848), 697–735 and 45 (July, 1848), 403–28, (August, 1848), 510–32. For the naval operations during the siege see Charles Bourel de la Roncière, *Histoire de la marine français* (Paris, 1904–32), vol. 4, 138–54.

5th war, 1574–76

Besides the army documents in BN Mss. Fr. 3,256 and 4,555, the most useful of previously mentioned sources are *Henri III*, the *CDM*, and the *CSPF/E*. Goulart, Haton, and Le Riche, *opera cit.*, should also be consulted. Arnaud, *Dauphiné*, vol. 1, contains a good account of the siege of Livron, and Bouille, *Ducs de Guise*, vol. 3, is helpful for operations in Champagne and Burgundy. For a lucid analysis of the role of the new duke of Anjou (the former duke of Alençon) in the political anarchy of the time see Mack P. Holt, *The Duke of Anjou* (Cambridge, 1986).

C *Sources for the composition and strength of the army*

1st war, 1562–63

Information on the forces of the royal army during the first civil war is scattered and incomplete. Many bits of information can be gleaned from the chronicles and early histories, but the most important documentary evidence comes from the following sources. For the period April to August, 1562, that is, from the assembly of the army at Paris to its positioning on the Loire preparatory to the move against Bourges, Navarre's strategic memo of early July, discussed above, pages 55–57, provides a good overview of the forces in hand or expected to be in hand by August. For the initial assembly at Paris, Paschal, *1562*, *passim*, provides numerous reports of units entering the city, the formation of the king's camp, and the movement of the artillery to the ramparts and the army's initial cantonment at Longjumeau. BN Mss. Fr. 15,876, fol. 130 contains a list of the captains of infantry companies with the army in May or early June. Ambassador Sainte Croix's 23rd dispatch, Aymon, *Actes ecclésiastiques*, vol. 1, 168, reports the number and types of units with the army as it marched from Paris and Middlemore, after a visit to the army's camp in mid-June, reported on its composition and strength to Throckmorton, *CSPF/E*, vol. 5, no. 238. Navarre's July 11 report on the near battle of Talcy and the seizure of Beaugency identifies the major subdivisions of the army, BN Mss. Fr. 15,876, fols. 237–39, also published by Ruble, *Antoine et Jeanne*, vol. 4, 414–19. Segesser, vol. 1, 237–347, provides detailed descriptions of the Swiss contingents throughout the war, and the German troops brought to France by the Count Rhingrave are detailed in the capitulations, BN Mss. Fr. 4,552, fols. 83–85, and 4,553, fols. 35–36.

In mid-August the army moved on to Bourges, and then to the siege of Rouen, returning to Paris in late November and early December. For royal forces at the siege of Bourges, PRO/SP 70/41, fols. 20–23, 39–40. There are several undated (August–October, 1562) and intermixed documents in BN Mss. Fr. 15,877, fols. 132–36, which list units on the march from Bourges, in the Orléannais–Berry region, and on the march to Rouen, as well as those sent to Champagne with Saint-André to attempt to prevent the Protestants' German mercenaries from entering the country. *Ibid.*, fol. 135 provides a strategic overview of forces in the kingdom in October 1562. There are additional lists of the gendarmes sent with Saint-André in *ibid.*, fols. 30 and 337. A staffing memo sent by La Brosse to the king and three subsequent royal replies, *ibid.*, fols. 144, 267–68, 327–28, and 329, and published in La Brosse, 350–55, specify the forces left behind in the Orléannais in September which later rejoined Guise at Paris in December. The major subdivisions of the army at the siege of Rouen are clearly shown in the diagram of the siege which appears in chapter 3, Figure 12, and many of the French infantry companies at the siege are identified in BN Mss. Fr. 15,877, fols. 347–49. The units left behind in Normandy after the siege can be tracked in Castelnau, vol. 1, 108–10, 132, and 136–145; Marchand, *Vieilleville*, 216–30 and *Brissac*, 499–512. For royal troops under the command of Tavannes, and later Nemours, at the siege of Lyon, see Tavannes, *Mémoires*, vol. 24, 337–46, and his dispatches in Pingaud, *Correspondence*, 96–147, as well as the Sieur de Vauguyon's September dispatch from Lyon, BN Mss. Fr. 15,877, fol. 64. Lot published several lists of troops involved in those operations, 256–61, especially the muster roll of troops brought by Maugiron from Dauphiny, 258–61; and documents on the artillery at the siege are in BN Mss. Fr. 3,213, fol. 42 and 3,085, fols. 74–77. The units ordered to France from the Piedmont garrisons are identified in *CDM*, vol. 1, 392.

The fundamental documents for the army from December 1562 onward are Guise's detailed report on the battle of Dreux, *Mémoires*, 496–500, and his correspondence on army matters after the battle, *ibid.*, 500–6. The printed version of the report on Dreux is included in Cimber and d'Anjou, vol. 5, 103–14. For a list of the Breton units which joined the army before Dreux see BN Mss. Fr. 22,310, fols. 165–66. The Spanish and Gascon contingents sent to Paris before Dreux are enumerated in Monluc, *Commentaires*, vol. 2, 565; Paschal, *1562*, 110; *CSPF/E*, vol. 5, nos. 1197 and 1205; and the "Lettres de deux espagnols contenans des relations de la bataille de Dreux," in Cimber and d'Anjou, vol. 5, 85–93, esp. 87 and 91. *CDM*, vol. 1, 501 and note 1 describe royal forces expected at the siege of Orléans in March, 1563. No *état* of the main army's artillery train has survived, but from scores of accounts it is clear that the train varied from 20 to more than 40 guns at various times in the campaign. The estimate of artillery train effectives is based on similar sized trains in 1567 and 1568, which are documented below.

Finally, though no single inclusive listing of the gendarmerie has survived, it is possible to identify its units by comparing the following: a general *département* of 1561, BN Mss. Fr. 3,243, fols. 45–46; a general *département* from early 1562, in Communay, "Gascons," vol. 21, 384–86, which appears authentic but which I have not been able to find in the archives; a partial list from early 1562, BN Mss. Fr. 3,185, fol. 15. Information on promotions of captains, *creues*, and creations of new companies after the battle of Dreux in PRO/SP 70/48, fols. 184–87, can be compared with La Popelinière's description of promotions and creations of gendarmes after the battle, vol. 1, fol. 349r. There is a partial *département* for February, 1563, BN Mss Fr. 3,185, fol. 15, and the first general postwar *département* in May, 1563, *OM* no. 48, also published in Susane, *Cavalerie*, 60–63.

2nd war, 1567–68

For the second civil war there is more complete and detailed documentation on the royal army than for any of the other early wars. One reason for this is the survival of the "Journal des occurences principalles et Resultat du Conseil du duc d'Anjou sur icelles," which covers the period from November, 1567, through February, 1568. The journal entries, which contain an enormous amount of information helpful for identifying major formations and individual units, run interspaced with other documents and correspondence throughout BN Mss. Fr. 15,543 and 15,544. To this may be added an uniquely full collection of *états* detailing the organization, strength, and financial costs of the army during December–January 1567/68. The most important of these *états* for the forces with Anjou, Aumale, and Nevers are: for December 1567, BN Mss. Fr. 4,553, fols. 95–100 (artillery), 101 and 104–7 (summaries of all categories), 112–14 (staff and specialists); for January 1568, BN Mss. Fr. 17,870, fol. 294, and PRO/SP 70/96, fols. 114–15, 119–20. There are additional artillery *états* for November 1567 and February 1568, BN Mss. Fr. 4,554, fols. 1–3, 10–14. There are separate *états* for Martigues' Bretons for November through January, BN Mss. Fr. 3,898, fols. 227–36, and for the forces with Nevers, BN Mss. Fr. 3,240, fols. 70–71, and 4,553, fols. 89–90. A preliminary list of Savoyard cavalry is PRO/SP 70/94, fol. 77. There are marching and lodging orders for the main army for 6 December in BN Mss. Fr. 15,543, fols. 60–61, and for an undated time (though clearly sometime in January, 1568) in PRO/SP 70/96, fol. 31. See also Blaise de Monluc's description of the mobilization of the Gascon forces who joined the army in *Commentaires*, vol. 3, 39–47. For the gendarmerie at the beginning of the war, see the general *assignation* for 1567, BN 4,552, fols. 18–26, and two later *départements*, BN Mss. Fr. 3,187, fols. 38–39, and 3,194, fols. 105–9. For mobilization, creations, and assignments during the war the fundamental document is the summary of payments to companies, BN Mss. Fr. 4,552, fols. 108–10. Additional companies can be identified from: royal instructions to Monluc to conduct a siege of La Rochelle, BN Mss. Fr. 15,544, fols. 187–88; the order of march for Anjou's army, PRO/SP 70/96, fols. 231–32, which identifies companies within the tactical regiments into which the army's cavalry was organized; and the *état* of Martigues' Bretons mentioned above. There is no single demobilization document, but royal instructions from February and April, 1568 differentiating old from new companies and ordering their payment can be found in *OM* nos. 10, 15, and 117.

All of these documents for the second war can also profitably be supplemented by: for the prewar mobilization at the time of Alba's march, BN Mss. Fr. 4,553, fols. 38–39, an *état* of infantry companies in the north of the kingdom with strengths and estimates on what was needed to bring them up to strength (this document is undated but can be placed chronologically by examining the names of individual captains); 4,552, fol. 123, troops raised in the south and southeast for service in Piedmont; and, for the Swiss, Segesser, vol. 1, 474–97, and *OM* no. 96, the July, 1567, capitulation contract for the 6,000 Swiss hired to flank Alba. *CSPF/E*, vol. 8, nos. 1804, 1833, and 1845, specifies many of the forces pouring into Paris at the beginning of the war. For a more detailed look at the forces Nevers brought from Piedmont and Brissac's infantry command at Paris in October, 1567, see chapter 4, pp. 97–100; for forces passing through or garrisoning Chartres, chapter 8, pp. 209–15; and for forces available to Monluc in the west and southwest the royal instructions for the siege of La Rochelle mentioned above. There is also a very important series of letters from Anjou's camp at Chartreux, near Paris, in early March, BN Mss. Fr. 15,545, fols. 4, 5, and 17–18, which confirms the presence of more than 200 infantry and light cavalry units serving in the campaign area from Normandy to Champagne. To the latter can be added BN Mss. Fr. 3,220, fol. 85 which identifies the infantry units delegated to return to Piedmont after the war, and a mass of correspondence, including some capitulation documents, on the effort to rid the kingdom of the reiters of both sides in the spring and summer of 1568, in BN Mss. Fr. 15,608.

3rd war, 1568–70

Documentation on the third war is also scattered and somewhat incomplete. But a good starting point in reconstructing organization, units, and strengths, is Gigon, old but still very useful, including the special notes and *pièces justificatives*, 356–403, especially notes D, E, J, and K, which are studies of the army's composition in November, 1568, and January, June, and September, 1569, respectively. The *pièces justificatives*, 384–403, include several informative letters from Anjou taken from BN N. Acq. 6,003. *CSPF/E*, vols. 8 and 9; Lude; *CDM*, vol. 3; and *Henri III*, vol. 1, 45–154, all contain useful references. There is much useful information in BN Mss. Fr. 17,528, fols. 3–113, which contains Villeroy's court logbook from October, 1568, to June, 1569, and most of the official war-related correspondence for 1569 is in BN Mss. Fr. 15,549 and 15,550.

The fundamental document for the army in late 1568 is an "Estat des Regiments des companyes tant de Gerndarmerye que infanterye. Estans en larmee du roy...le 8 December, 1568," in BN Mss. Fr. 17,528, fols. 119–124r, which details the subdivisions, companies, and forces with Anjou at the beginning of December, 1568 (the document is misdated 1569, but internal evidence makes it clear it is from 1568), including forces expected but not yet arrived. An important addition to the latter, fols. 124–25, "Sommaire des forces et gens de guerre levez & entretenuz tant pour larmee du roy que celle de Monseigneur le duc d'Anjou son frere que pour les provinces de son Roy*me* soubz les lieutenans gnraulx de sa Majeste," gives an essential global account of all the forces (except the gendarmerie) maintained throughout the kingdom, including garrisons – almost 300 companies of infantry, light cavalry and reiters, reckoned to be more than 70,000 troops without the gendarmerie. Another valuable document for mid-1569 is the "Estat du pain de munition ordonner pour la nourriture des gens de guerre de l'armee du Roy conduicte par monseigneur Estans a Limoges le XIIIIme jour de juing MVcLXIX," which identifies the major subdivisions of the army, number of companies, and bread ration strengths for all but the gendarmerie after the merger of Aumale's force with the main army, BN Mss. Fr. 4,554, fol. 14. Other useful documents are lists of the units with Nemours around Lyon early in the war, BN Mss. Fr. 3,213, fols. 60–1 and 3,222, fol. 18, and with Cossé in Picardy, BN Mss. Fr., 3,216, fols. 17–18 (dated from internal evidence); capitulations with two different levies of Swiss, *OM* no. 125 (October, 1568), and *OM* no.139 (February, 1570), and two different contingents of German reiters (in late 1568), *OM* no. 128 and BN Mss. Fr. 15,608, fols. 30–33. A list of the staff and specialists with the army in November, 1569, is in BN Mss. Fr. 4,554, fols. 19–20, while *ibid.*, fols. 21–22 identifies the units of Cossé's army in the summer of 1570 for whom payment had to be arranged.

The artillery train with the army in late 1568 is the best documented of any that accompanied the main army during the first five civil wars. The basic documents include BN Mss. Fr. 17,870, fols. 298–300, two planning memos compiled at the beginning of hostilities; an initial *état* for September 1568, BN 4,553, fols. 118–19; and the actual *assignations* of funds for September and October/November, BN Mss. Fr. 4,554, fols. 5–7 and 4,533, fols. 122–24, respectively, all of which collectively describe the equipment, animals, and personnel of the train in great detail. For the gendarmerie, besides the "Estat des Regiments" cited above, which gives the composition of the tactical regiments with the army in December/January 1568/69, there are initial mobilization orders for September in *OM* nos. 120 and 122; the fundamental *état* for the fall campaign is BN Mss. Fr. 3,193, fols. 195–201, which identifies both old and new companies and their distribution across the kingdom. For 1569, *OM* no. 129 is the general *département* for the gendarmerie at the height of its expansion in February, while PRO/SP 70/107, fols. 172–73 is the general *département* for July. The scaled down gendarmerie after the reductions at the end of the war can be identified by an October 1570 *état* of pay officials, BN Mss. Fr. 21,543, fols. 69–75.

4th war, 1572–73

Reconstruction of the royal army during the fourth civil war is simplified somewhat by the fact that almost the whole of royal resources were invested in the sieges of La Rochelle and to a lesser extent Sancerre. The 1572 peacetime infantry authorizations referred to in chapter 2 provide a good starting point for identifying regiments and companies and they can be supplemented by two late August and October 1572 *états* which detail the bringing up to strength of most of the veteran companies stationed on the northern frontier who would come to be involved in the sieges: BN Mss. Fr. 29,508, fols. 221–23 and 224–34. The fundamental planning documents are the financial *états* for December 1572 and January 1573, BN Mss. Fr. 4,554, fols. 92 and 98–100, from which the basic force structures planned for the two sieges can be derived; there is also a more detailed description of the forces intended for Sancerre, BN Mss. Fr. 15,556, fols. 1–2, which can profitably be supplemented by Géralde Nakam's outstanding work, *Au lendemain de la Saint-Barthélemy. Guerre civile et famine. Histoire mémorable du Siege de Sancerre (1573) de Jean de Lery* (Paris, 1975). Before the main sieges began Admiral Villars mounted sizeable operations in Gascony, but most of his infantry was transferred early in 1573 to La Rochelle. For Villars see his October–December dispatches to the court and Anjou in Loutchitzki, vol. 22, 254–68 and 299–311; the order to transfer his forces is noted in BN Mss. Fr. 3,312, fol. 1, and the arrival of his Gascon regiments at the siege by 15,557, fol. 39. There were also important operations by Damville in Languedoc which I did not attempt to follow in detail, but a general idea of the forces involved can be derived from the *Histoire générale de Languedoc*, vol. 11, 557–63. The most important documents on the preparations for the siege are Biron's letters to the court and to Anjou, in *AHG*, 60–96, which provide a wealth of information; they should be supplemented by a number of letters from the king to Lude, Lude, 230–83. Also fundamental to a reconstruction of the forces involved in the siege are Anjou's dispatches in *Henri III*, vol. 1, 192–283. For the siege itself, besides the contemporary accounts and histories, Genet's provides a useful secondary account, firmly grounded on the documents, which helps to identify forces. Anjou's after action report, BN Mss. Fr. 4,765, fols. 57–77, and Nevers' daybook, *ibid.*, fols. 15–53, also provide bits of information throughout on formations; for the late-arriving Swiss contingent, the only significant foreign troops raised for the war, see Segesser, vol. 2, 202–25. The units which took part in the siege can also be identified by working back from the demobilization orders in Nevers' daybook, fols. 52–53, an Anjou dispatch to the king, *Henri III*, vol. 1, 279–81, as well as from the casualty lists of officers at the siege: Goulart, vol. 1, 291–93; PRO/SP 70/125, fols. 122–45; and PRO/SP 70/127, fols. 225–26. For the artillery train there is a detailed list of the Arsenal personnel serving at La Rochelle, BN 3,240, fols. 100–8; and a great deal of information on the pioneers and transport of the train in Le Riche, 111–45. During the war the crown supported more than eighty gendarme companies, some 40 percent of which served at some time during the war near La Rochelle. For the gendarmes see the post-Saint-Bartholomew August 1572 call-up, *OM* no. 165; the basic 1573 *état*, BN Mss. Fr., fols. 77–93; initial assignments and reliefs for La Rochelle, BN

4,554, fol. 106 and *OM* no. 171; and the first post-war accounting for service during the war, *OM* no. 173.

5th war, 1574–76

Reconstructing royal forces during the long and confused fifth civil war is hampered by an almost complete lack of surviving central documents, especially for the first year or so of operations, but also by the increasing political and military anarchy of the last year of the war, the change of regime, and the defection of leaders like Alençon and Damville. Holt, *The Duke of Anjou*, 45–69, is an excellent modern treatment of the twists and turns of the fifth war. But in tracing the operations and composition of the royal armies put on foot during the war I have had to rely more heavily than for the previous wars on collation and comparison of the main contemporary memoirs and histories of the period, notably Goulart, La Popelinière, and D'Aubigné. Offsetting this to a certain extent are fairly full correspondences in *CDM*, vols. 4–5, *Henri III*, vol. 2, and especially the *CPSF/E*, vols. 10–11. PRO/SP 70/130, fol. 160, identifies the new infantry regiments raised to fight the early campaign in Normandy; Le Riche, 150–265 and Haton, vol. 2, 775–861 are helpful in identifying units and formations operating in Poitou and Champagne. Arnaud, *Dauphiné*, vol. 1, 283–346, esp. 297–320, gives a good account of the siege of Livron in the winter of 1574/75; Segesser, vol. 2, 226–349 details the Swiss involvement in the wars. For the confused events in Languedoc, which I made no attempt to reconstruct, see the *Histoire générale de Languedoc*, vol. 11, 589–620.

For the armies maintained around Paris and in Champagne in late 1575 and in 1576 two basic *états* have survived: one from August, 1575, "Estats de la depense de larmee conduicte par Monsieur le duc de Guise lieut general pour le roy," BN Mss. Fr. 4,555, fols. 5–6; and for October, 1575, "Etat gnal des forces tant de cheval que de pied que le Roy a ordonnee pres de luy pour son camp et armee et en champagne pres Monsieur de Guise," BN Mss. Fr. 3,256, fols. 17–20, from which it is possible to reconstruct royal forces in the winter of 1575/76. Bouille, vol. 3, is also helpful, carrying the story of the northern operations under Guise and then Mayenne well into 1576. The major French infantry formations in the army can be verified by tracking back from the September 2, 1576, "Estat des Regimens de pied francois Ensemble des mes de Camp y compagnies que le Roy a ordonne estre entretenues a son service suivant la derniere reduction quil en a faicte ou est semblablement comprins le departement dicelles,", BN Mss. Fr. 3,256, fols. 23–24.

I was unable to find artillery *états* from the fifth war, but the gendarmerie is fairly well represented in the documents. For 1574 see the basic general *état*, BN Mss. Fr. 3,193, fols. 184–93 and the March call to arms, *OM* no. 178. For 1575 see a series of announcements of general musters which help to clarify the distribution of companies: *OM* no. 199 (August), no. 205 (October), no. 206 (October), and no. 208 (December). There is an additional order to report for February, 1576, *OM* no. 212, and all companies in the gendarmerie after the Peace of Beaulieu are listed in BN Mss. Fr. 3,256, fols. 21–22 (from internal evidence probably June 1576).

Finally it should be mentioned that BN Mss. Fr. 4,555 contains a number of documents on the army from the period of the sixth civil war.

The battle of Dreux and the siege of Chartres

Dreux

The battle of Dreux was an event of great interest to contemporaries, combining as it did the novelty of being the first great ranged battle of the civil wars, a dramatic ebb and flow of action with chance favoring first one and then the other side, the presence of so many *grands*, a number of peculiar or unusual occurrences, notable feats of arms, and an extremely sanguinary outcome. There are about a dozen eyewitness accounts of the campaign and the battle that have survived, some of which almost immediately found their way into print in the pamphlet war of words which accompanied the military struggle during the first war.

On the Catholic side the duke of Guise's December 20, 1562, after action report, *Mémoires*, 496–500, and Castelnau, vol. 1, 119–31, are fundamental, both for their attention to the strategic context as well as the details of the battle. There are three eyewitness accounts by Swiss participants in Segesser, vol. 1, 621–25 and note 1, 625–26, and two useful reports on the campaign and the battle by Spanish soldiers in "Lettres de deux espagnols," Cimber and d'Anjou, vol. 5, 85–93. On the Protestant side Bèze's vol. 2, 274–317, is most complete, but Coligny's after action dispatch, PRO/SP 70/47, fols. 18–21, and several casualty reports in French, *ibid.*, fols. 30–32 are also central. Coligny's post-action report was published in Cimber and d'Anjou, vol. 5, 76–79, and it and later letters also appear in Delaborde, vol. 2, 170–85. Reports by English agents, especially Throckmorton's January 3, 1563, eyewitness account, PRO/SP 70/48, fols. 25–30, and two January 13 dispatches by Throckmorton and Smith, *ibid.*, fols. 192–95r, provide further information. La Noue, 660–67, is useful, and Jean de Mergey, *Mémoires*, in J.-F. Michaud and T.-J.-F. Poujoulat, eds. *Nouvelle collection des mémoires pour servir à l'histoire de France* (Paris, 1848), vol. 9, 567–71, provides an interesting recounting from the point of view of an individual cavalryman. Accounts of the reception of the initial news of the battle and the first official claims for its outcome, besides those by Coligny and Guise mentioned above, are Vieilleville, *Mémoires*, Michaud and Poujoulat, vol. 9, 321–25, to be controlled by Marchand, *De Vieilleville*; CDM, vol. 1, 453–56, including a letter by the king, note 1, 453–54; and Layard, "Dispatches," 69–71. Other contemporary or near-contemporary accounts which add useful details are La Popelinière, vol. 1, fols. 342v–50r; D'Aubigné, *Histoire universelle*, vol. 2, 106–26, and De Thou, vol. 4, 473–86. There are also a number of vignettes scattered throughout Brantôme, *Oeuvres*. Aumale, *Condé*, vol. 1, 184–213, and Oman, *Art of War*, 410–23, provide decent accounts, but the most useful secondary accounts of the campaign and battle are, from the Swiss point of view, Segesser, vol. 1, 256–307, and, above all, the reconstruction by De Coynart.

On the subject of military pictures and drawings see Sir Charles Oman, "Early Military Pictures," *The Archaeological Journal*, 45 (1939), 337–55; Olle Cederlof, "The Battle Painting as a Historical Source," *Revue internationale d'histoire militaire*, 26 (1967), 119–44; J. R. Hale, "A Humanistic Visual Aid. The military diagram in the Renaissance," *Renaissance Studies*, 2, no. 2 (1988), 280–98; and Lombard-Jourdan, "La bataille de Saint-Denis," 7–54.

Chartres

Perhaps because only a fraction of the royal army was involved, and very few notables fought on the Catholic side, accounts of the siege of Chartres in 1568 in contemporary histories and memoirs are few and their treatment of the event slight. On the Protestant side, Aubigné, vol. 2, 295–300, devotes only six pages to the action and La Noue, 704–6, only three pages. On the Catholic side De Thou, vol. 5, 409–16, provides a succinct account, but Davila, 132, spends only three paragraphs on the siege. As noted above, I found most useful the good modern account, based on detailed familiarity with local sources, by Henri Lehr, "Le siege de Chartres en 1568."

There are civilian casualties listed in the *EDC*, but only those persons who were injured or killed in the actual defense of the town. What is now referred to as "collateral damage" is not reported, probably because it would have been at the expense of private persons rather than the municipality itself. There is a grisly reminder of the problem the disposal of seven hundred or so corpses would have posed for a town of Chartres' size: the *EDC*, 424, refers to payments "Pour avoir faict les vidanges des hommes mortz, chiens, chevaulx et autres charongnes qui estoient dedans la riviere et aux fossez de ladicte ville et nettoye la riviere, ensemble pour avoir vuyde les yssues des bestes, vaches, moutons et autres infections estans au-dessus Saint-Morice, Saint-Jullien et derrire les Filles-Dieu, et le tout enterre pour eviter aux mauvaises vapeurs et dangers de peste." Lehr, 60, mentions the 1908 discovery of a number of the Huguenot cadavers buried near the ditch.

E *The royal ordinances*

The royal ordinances

For the period of the wars of religion covered by this study, the number of *ordonnances* regulating the conduct of the army and its troops starts to multiply from about the end of the second civil war in 1568. Those on which the argument in chapter 9 are built are, in chronological order: d'Anjou's camp and march regulations (October 7, 1568), *OM* no. 123, cited in chapter 9, note 1; an order prohibiting misuse and profaning of religious places (October 7, 1568), *OM* no. 124; Colonel General Strossi's *ordonnance* regulating the behavior of infantry on the march (1570), *OM* no. 137; a royal *ordonnance* concerning the punishment of soldiers committing crimes and disorders (December, 1570), *OM* no. 145; a royal edict on the gendarmerie, infantry, and royal guard (December 29, 1570), *OM* no. 146; d'Anjou's *ordonnance* on the conduct and discipline of the army and the camp at the siege of La Rochelle, *OM* no. 169 (February 15, 1573), which is also reproduced by Genet; the royal *ordonnance* regulating the gendarmerie in all its aspects (February 1, 1574), *OM* no. 177; the *ordonnance* of the queen mother, as regent, on the behavior of infantry and cavalry on the march and in lodgings (July 5, 1574), *OM* no. 180; a similar general royal edict issued by the recently crowned Henri III (July 1, 1575), *OM* no 196; a royal *ordonnance* regulating troop behavior issued in response to widespread depredations by soldiers (March 21, 1577), *OM* no. 227; and the rules issued by the new duke of Anjou (formerly Alençon) to the royal army at the siege of La Charité (April, 1577), BN Mss. Fr. 3,193, fols. 180–83. A July 9, 1567 capitulation with some of Pfyffer's Swiss regiment also contains a few indications of the kind of abuses the crown wished to avoid, *OM* no. 95; but the Swiss were universally considered the most disciplined of troops, and were subject to their own extended code of military justice, administered by their own provostial officials. Capitulations with reiters, on the other hand, despite the fact that they too had their own military justice apparatus, go into great detail on the kinds of misbehavior that were forbidden: see, for example, the capitulation with Lunebourg (April, 1568), BN Mss. Fr. 15,608, fols. 30–33, and especially with Bassompierre (fall of 1568), *OM* no. 128. A comparison can be made with the regulations issued by Condé to the Huguenot army in the fall of 1568, which appear in Jean de Serres, *Mémoires de la troisième guerre civile*, in Goulart, vol. 3, 158–72. For a more extended discussion of the laws of war during this epoch, see André Gardot, *Le droit de la guerre dans l'oeuvre des capitaines français du XVIe siècle*, (Paris, 1949).

F *The siege of La Rochelle*

In addition to Biron, Nevers, and d'Anjou, Goulart (for both his own account, from the perspective of the city, and the Catholic account he included) and Cauriana were the most useful contemporary accounts. For the most part the sources are agreed on the number and dating of the major assaults and most of the skirmishes and sorties. Some of the minor sorties and skirmishes are reported by only one side or the other, but in either case they have been included in the figure. Truce days indicated by either or both sides are included. There is some discrepancy in the sources on the number of mines exploded – understandably since the defenders were not always aware of the besiegers' efforts and when several mines were ignited simultaneously it was difficult for the defenders to know exactly what had transpired. Here I relied almost entirely on Catholic sources, especially Nevers, who was in overall command of the siege operations after the death of Aumale on March 3, 1573. The number of rounds fired per day was recorded in Goulart's account of the siege and was compared to Catholic accounts, for the days of major assaults, where possible. It was common practice for the defenders in a siege to count the number of rounds fired against them, probably because it enabled them to estimate with some precision how much of the besieger's powder reserves remained. The rounded off cumulative number of rounds fired by the royal army is based on Genet, part 2 (March, 1848), 722, and note 1, 722–23 (February 1573 cumulative total of 13,000 rounds); BN Mss. Fr. 4,765, fols. 35v and 75v (May cumulative total of 20,000, and June, 25,000 rounds); and D'Aubigné, vol. 4, 16 (March cumulative figure of 15,000 rounds). The royal army's casualties from assaults and sorties and skirmishes are drawn from all the sources and where there were significant discrepancies I tried to use the numbers provided by observers who were in a position to make a more direct estimate. Discrepancies often arise from some accounts stating the number killed in action while others report killed and wounded, and yet others simply give a single total for "losses". Where only one source recorded casualties I attempted to compare the magnitude and type of event which caused the casualties to similar events for which there was more complete information. Such juggling of conflicting and imprecise claims is not an exact science, and it is the aspect of the series presented in Figure 31 in which I have the least confidence. But the indications of casualties in Figure 31 do allow, at the least, an accurate enough comparison of the magnitudes of losses caused by different categories of events. Not included in Figure 31 are the losses of the defenders, which appear in comparison in Chapter 10, Table 10.2.

A similar casualty ratio emerges from the bombardment of Sancerre, though on a smaller scale. Lery, in Nakam, 349–61, lists all the defenders killed in the fighting and also gives a count of the wounded in action. *Ibid.*, 233–34, lists the defenders' strength at the beginning of the siege, and 59–60 estimates the besieging army at 7,000 men. According to an analysis of this information, from an original frontline fighting strength of 800 men, 76 (9.5 percent) were killed and 116 (14.5 percent) wounded in action, for a total loss of 192, or 24 percent. By contrast, about 1,250 besiegers are said to have died at the siege, and total casualties may have been twice that. This implies a ratio of casualties in favor of the fighting defenders of 16:1 in deaths, and 13:1 in total losses. Lery also notes the way in which those defenders who died were killed: 28 percent by cannon fire, 61 percent from arquebus fire, and 8 percent from hand-to-hand combat in the sorties (the remaining 3 percent suffered accidental deaths).

Bibliography

MANUSCRIPTS

A *Bibliothèque Nationale*
Fonds français 2,068, 3,085, 3,150, 3,178, 3,182, 3,185, 3,187, 3,191, 3,193–94, 3,197, 3,202, 3,207, 3,212–13, 3,216–17, 3,220, 3,222, 3,224, 3,240, 3,243, 3,249, 3,255–56, 3,312, 3,629, 3,898, 4,522, 4,553–55, 4,557, 4,765, 15,543–45, 15,547–50, 15,554, 15,556–57, 15,560, 15,608, 15,876–77, 17,528, 17,870, 18,587, 20,508, 20,624, 21,522, 21,524–25, 21,541, 21,543–44, 22,310.

B *Dépôt de la Guerre (Service Historique de l'Armée de Terre, Château de Vincennes)*
Ordonnances militaires, vol. 10 (1558–77)

C *Public Record Office*
State Papers 70 (Foreign)/22 to 145 (1562–77)

D *Vatican Library*
Fonds Barberini, Mss. 5040

PRINTED PRIMARY SOURCES

Aubigné, Agripa d'. *Histoire universelle*, ed. André Thierry (7 vols., Paris, 1981–93).

Aymon, Jean, ed. *Actes ecclésiastiques et civiles de tous les synodes nationaux des églises réformées de France* (2 vols., La Haye, 1710).

Barbot, Amos. *Histoire de la Rochelle depuis l'an 1199 jusques en 1575* (3 vols., Paris-Saintes, 1886–90).

Bèze, Theodore de. *Histoire ecclésiastique des églises réformées au royaume de France*, eds. G. Baum and E. Cunitz (3 vols., Nieuwkoop, 1974).

Biron, Armand de Gontaut, baron de. "Correspondence inédite du maréchal Armand de Gontaut-Biron." *Archives historiques du département de la Gironde*, 14 (1873), 1–271.

 The Letters and Documents of Armand de Gontaut, Baron de Biron, Marshal of France (1524–92), eds. Sidney H. E. Ehrman and James W. Thompson (2 vols., Berkeley, 1936).

Bordenave, Nicolas de. *Histoire de Béarn et Navarre*, ed. Paul Raymond (Paris, 1873).

Bourbon, Louis de, Prince de Condé. *Mémoires*. J.-F. Michaud and J.-J.-F. Poujoulat, eds. *Nouvelle collection des mémoires pour servir à l'histoire de France depuis le XIIIe siècle jusqu'à la fin du XVIIIe*, 6 (Paris, 1939).

Bibliography

Bourdeille, Pierre de, seigneur de Brantôme. *Discours sur les colonels de l'infanterie de France*, ed. Etienne Vaucheret (Paris, 1973).

Oeuvres complètes de Pierre de Bourdeille, seigneur de Brantôme, ed. Ludovic Lalanne (11 vols., Paris, 1864–82).

Cabié, Edmond. *Guerres de religion dans le sud-ouest de la France, et principalement dans le Quercy, d'après les papiers des seigneurs de Saint-Sulpice de 1561 à 1590* (Geneva, 1975).

Calendar of State Papers, Foreign Series, of the reign of Elizabeth. Preserved in the Public Record Office (23 vols., London, 1901–50).

Castelnau, Michel de. *Les mémoires de Messire Michel de Castelnau, seigneur de Mauvissière*, 3rd. ed. by Jean Godefroy (3 vols., Brussels, 1731).

Cauriana, Philippe. *Histoire du siège de la Rochelle en 1573*, trans. from the Latin by La société littéraire de la Rochelle (La Rochelle, 1856).

Cimber, M. L. and F. d'Anjou. *Archives curieuses de l'histoire de France depuis Louis XI jusqu'à Louis XVIII* (30 vols., Paris, 1834–41).

Communay, A. "Les Gascons dans les armées françaises." *Revue de l'Agenais*, 21 (1894), 379–91, 492–510, and 22 (1895), 165–76, 229–39, 392–406.

Les Huguenots dans le Béarn et la Navarre. Documents inédits publiés par la société historique de Gascogne (Paris, 1885).

Daval, Guillaume and Jean Daval, *Histoire de la Réformation à Dieppe, 1557–1657*, ed. Emile Lesens (2 vols., Rouen, 1878).

Davila, Arrigo Caterino, *The History of the Civil Wars of France* (Dublin, 1760).

Desjardins, Abel and Giuseppe Canestrini, eds. *Négociations diplomatiques de la France avec la Toscane* (6 vols., Paris, 1859–86).

De Thou, Jacques-Auguste. *Histoire universelle* (16 vols., Paris, 1734).

Douais, C. "Les guerres de religion en Languedoc d'après les papiers du Baron de Fourquevaux (1572–74)." *Annales du Midi*, 4 (1892), 25–67, 331–61, 475–509, and 5 (1893), 71–102, 170–218, 332–73.

Du Bellay, G. *Instructions sur le faict de la guerre* (Paris, 1548).

Estienne, Charles. *La guide des chemins de France de 1553*, ed. Jean Bonnerot (Geneva, 1978).

Franklin, Alfred. *Les grandes scènes historiques du XVIe siècle. Reproduction en fac-similé du recueil de J. Tortorel et J. Perrissin publié sous la direction de M. Alfred Franklin* (Paris, 1886).

Froumenteau, Nicolas. *Le secret des finances de France* (n.p., 1581).

Gaches, Jacques. *Mémoires de Jacques Gaches sur les guerres de religion à Castres et dans le Languedoc, 1555–1610*, ed. Charles Pradel (Paris, 1879).

Goulart, Simon. *Mémoires de l'éstat de France sous Charles neufièsme*, 2nd ed. by Heinrich Wolf (3 vols., Meidelbourg, 1578).

Haton, Claude de. *Mémoires de Claude de Haton*, ed. Felix Bourquelot (2 vols. Paris, 1857).

Henry III. *Lettres de Henri III, roy de France*, ed. Michel François (6 vols., Paris, 1959).

Heron, A., ed. *Deux chroniques de Rouen* (Rouen, 1900).

La Ferrière-Percy, Hector de, ed. *La Normandie à l'étranger: Documents inédits relatifs à l'histoire de Normandie tirés des archives étrangères: XVIe–XVIIe siècles* (Paris, 1873).

La Noue, François de, *Discours politiques et militaires*, ed. F. E. Sutcliffe (Geneva, 1967).

La Popelinière, Henri Lancelot-Voisin de. *L'histoire de France enrichie de plus notable occurrences ... depuis l'an 1550 jusques à ces temps* (2 vols., La Rochelle, 1581).

Bibliography

Larroque, Philippe Tamisay de. "Quelques pages inédites de Blaise de Monluc." *Receuil des travaux de la société d'agriculture, sciences et arts d'Agen* (1863), 322–31.

Layard, A. H., ed. "Dispatches of Michele Suriano and of Marc' Antonio Barbaro, Venetian Ambassadors at the Court of France." *The Publications of the Huguenot Society of London*, 6 (Lymington, 1891).

Ledain, M. Belisaire, ed. *Lettres adressées à Jean et Guy de Daillon, Comtes du Lude, Gouverneurs de Poitou de 1543 à 1557 et de 1557 à 1585. Archives historiques du Poitou*, 12 (1882).

Le Riche, Guillaume and Michel Le Riche. *Journal de Guillaume et de Michel Le Riche, avocats du roi à Saint-Maixent (de 1534 à 1586)*, ed. A. D. de la Fontenelle (Geneva, 1971).

Lorraine, François de. *Mémoires de François de Lorraine, duc d'Aumale et de Guise*. J.-F. Michaud and J.-J.-F. Poujoulat, eds. *Nouvelle collection des mémoires pour servir à l'histoire de France depuis le XIIIe siècle jusqu'à la fin du XVIIIe*, 6 (Paris, 1839).

Loutchitzki, Jean. "Documents inédits et originaux. Quatrième guerre de religion, 1572–73." *Bulletin de la Société de l'histoire du Protestantisme français*, 22 (June–Sept. 1873), 252–68, 299–311, 352–74, 401–13.

Lublinskaya, A. *Documents pour servir à l'histoire des guerres civiles en France (1561–65)* (Moscow, 1962).

Medici, Catherine de. *Lettres de Catherine de Médicis*, eds. Hector de la Ferrière-Percy and Gustave Baguenault de Puchesse (11 vols., Paris, 1880–1909).

Mergey, Jean de. *Mémoires.* J.-F. Michaud and J.-J.-F. Poujoulat, eds. *Nouvelle collection des mémoires pour servir à l'histoire de France depuis le XIIIe siècle jusqu'à la fin du XVIIIe*, 9 (Paris, 1848).

Merlet, Lucien, ed. "Etat des dépenses faites par la ville de Chartres, pendant les troubles et pendant le siège de ladite ville (1er Octobre 1567–18 Avril 1568)." *Bulletin historique et philologique du comité des travaux historiques et scientifiques* (1840), 394–438.

Monluc, Blaise de. *Commentaires de Blaise de Monluc, Maréchal de France*, ed. Paul Courteault (3 vols., Paris, 1911).

Commentaires et Lettres de Blaise de Monluc, Maréchal de France, ed. Alphonse de Ruble (5 vols., Paris, 1864–67, 1870–72).

Montgommery, Louis de, sieur de. *La Milice françoise* (Paris, 1636).

Nakam, Géralde. *Au lendemain de la Saint-Barthélemy. Guerre civile et famine. Histoire mémorable du Siège de Sancerre (1573) de Jean de Lery* (Paris, 1975).

Paré, Ambroise. *Oeuvres complètes* (3 vols., Geneva, 1970).

Paschal, Pierre de. *Journal de ce qui s'est passé en France durant l'année 1562 principalement dans Paris et à la cour*, ed. Michel François (Paris, 1950).

Pingaud, L., ed. *Correspondence des Saulx-Tavannes au XVIe siècle* (Paris, 1877).

Ruble, Alphonse, Baron de. "Documents inédits sur la guerre civile de 1562 en Berry." *Société des Antiquaires du Centre Bourges*, 15 (1887–88), 127–66.

Saulx, Gaspard de. *Mémoires de Gaspard de Saulx, Seigneur de Tavannes*. M. Petitot., ed. *Collection complète des mémoires relatifs à l'histoire de France*, 23–25 (Paris, 1822).

Serres, Jean de. *Mémoires de la troisième guerre civile.* Vol. 3 of Goulart, *Mémoires*.

Tommaseo, M. N., ed. *Relations des ambassadeurs venitiens sur les affaires de France au XVIe siècle* (2 vols., Paris, 1838).

Bibliography

Turenne, Henri de la Tour d'Auvergne, Vicomte de. *Mémoires du vicomte de Turenne*, ed. Baguenault de Puchesse (Paris, 1901).

SECONDARY SOURCES: BOOKS

Anderson, Fred. *A People's Army. Massachusetts Soldiers and Society in the Seven Years' War* (New York, 1985).

Arnaud, Eugène. *Histoire des Protestants du Dauphiné aux XVIe, XVIIe, et XVIIIe siècles* (3 vols., Geneva, 1970).

   Histoire des Protestants de Provence, du Comtat Vénaissin, et de la principauté d'Orange (2 vols., Paris, 1884).

   Histoire des Protestants du Vivarais et du Velay, pays de Languedoc (2 vols., Paris, 1888).

Babelon, Jean-Pierre. *Nouvelle histoire de Paris. Le XVIe siècle* (Paris, 1986).

Baird, Henry M. *History of the Rise of the Huguenots of France* (2 vols., New York, 1879).

Belle, Edmond. *La Réforme à Dijon des origines à la fin de la lieutenance générale de Gaspard de Saulx-Tavannes (1530–70). Revue bourguignonne*, 21 (Dijon, 1911).

Benedict, Philip. *Rouen During the Wars of Religion* (New York, 1981).

Biraben, J. N. *Les hommes et la peste en France* (2 vols., Paris, 1975).

Black, Jeremy, *European Warfare 1660–1875* (New Haven, 1994).

Bonney, Richard. *The European Dynastic States, 1494–1660* (New York, 1991).

Bory, Jean-René. *La Suisse à la rencontre de l'Europe. L'épopée du service étranger* (Lausanne, 1978).

Bouille, R. de. *Histoire des ducs de Guise* (4 vols., Paris, 1849–50).

Boutaric, Edgard. *Institutions militaires de la France avant les armées permanentes* (Paris, 1863).

Braudel, Fernand. *The Mediterranean and the Mediterranean World in the Age of Philip II*, trans. Sian Reynolds (2 vols., New York, 1972).

Brimont, Marie-Camille, Vicomte Thierry de. *Le XVIe siècle et les guerres de la Réforme en Berry* (2 vols., Paris, 1905).

Cardaillac, F. de. *Deux capitaines gascons au XVIe siècle, les frères Sarlabous* (Paris, 1908).

Carriére, Victor. *Introduction aux études d'histoire ecclésiastique locale* (3 vols., Paris, 1936).

Cavard, Pierre. *La Réforme et les guerres de religion à Vienne* (Vienne, 1950).

Champion, Pierre. *Catherine de Médicis présente à Charles IX son Royaume (1564–66)* (Paris, 1937).

Clamageran, J.-J. *Histoire de l'impôt en France* (3 vols., Paris, 1868).

Contamine, Philippe. *Guerre, état et société à la fin du moyen âge. Etudes sur les armées des rois de France, 1337–1494* (Paris, 1972).

   ed. *Histoire militaire de la France*, vol. 1, *Des origines à 1715* (Paris, 1992).

Corvisier, André. *Armies and Societies in Europe, 1494–1789*, trans. Abigail T. Siddall (Bloomington, 1979).

   L'armée française de la fin du XVIIe siècle au ministère de Choiseul: Le soldat (2 vols., Paris, 1964).

Courteault, Paul. *Blaise de Monluc historien. Etude critique sur le texte et la valeur historique des Commentaires* (Paris, 1907).

Coynart, Raymond de (Le Commandant de Coynart). *L'Année 1562 et la bataille de Dreux. Etude historique et militaire* (Paris, 1894).

Croix, Alain. *Nantes et le pays Nantais au XVIe siècle – étude démographique* (Paris, 1974).

Bibliography

Crouzet, Denis. *Les guerriers de Dieu: la violence au temps des troubles de religion, vers 1525–vers 1610* (2 vols., Seyssel, 1990).

Davis, Natalie Z. *Society and Culture in Early Modern France: Eight Essays* (Stanford, 1975).

Decrue, Francis. *Anne duc de Montmorency, Connétable et Pair de France sous les rois Henri II, François II, et Charles IX* (Paris, 1889).

Delaborde, Louis J. H. *Gaspard de Coligny, Amiral de France* (3 vols., Paris 1879–82).

Delage, Franck. *La troisième guerre de religion en Limousin, Combat de la Roche-l'Abeille, 1569* (Limoges, 1950).

Devic, Claude and J. Vaissete. *Histoire générale de Languedoc avec des notes et les pièces justificatives* (12 vols., Toulouse, 1889).

Dickerman, Edmund. *Bellièvre and Villeroy* (Providence, 1971).

Diefendorf, Barbara B. *Beneath the Cross. Catholics and Huguenots in Sixteenth Century Paris* (Oxford, 1991).

Doucet, Roger. *Les institutions de la France au XVIe siècle* (2 vols., Paris, 1948).
L'état de finances de 1567 (Paris, 1929).

Downing, Brian M. *The Military Revolution and Political Change. Origins of Democracy and Autocracy in Early Modern Europe* (Princeton, 1992).

Dur, Philip. "Constitutional Rights and Taxation in the Reign of Henry III" (Ph.D. diss., Harvard University, 1941).

Erlanger, Philippe. *Le massacre de la Saint-Barthélemy* (Paris, 1960).

Estèbe, Janine. *Tocsin pour un massacre: le saison de Saint-Barthélemy* (Paris, 1975).

Favier, Jean. *The World of Chartres* (New York, 1990).

Forestié, Edouard. *Un capitaine gascon du XVIe siècle: Corbeyran de Cardaillac-Sarlabous, mestre de camp, gouverneur de Dunbar (Ecosse) et du Havre-de-Grace* (Paris, 1897).

Friedrichs, Christopher R. *Urban Society in an Age of War: Nördlingen, 1580–1720* (Princeton, 1979).

Gaix, Blay de. *Histoire militaire de Bayonne* (2 vols., Bayonne, 1899–1900).

Galpern, A. N. *The Religions of the People in Sixteenth-Century Champagne* (Cambridge, Mass., 1976).

Gardot, André. *Le droit de la guerre dans l'oeuvre des capitaines français du XVIe siècle* (Paris, 1949).

Gigon, Claude. *La révolte de la Gabelle en Guyenne, 1548–49* (Paris, 1906).

Gigon, S.-C. *La troisième guerre de religion. Jarnac–Moncontour (1568–69)* (Paris, 1909).

Guilmartin, John F. *Gunpowder and Galleys: Changing Technology and Mediterranean Warfare at Sea in the Sixteenth Century* (New York, 1974).

Guiraud, Louise. *Etudes sur la Réforme à Montpellier* (2 vols., Montpellier, 1918).

Gutmann, Myron P. *War and Rural Life in the Early Modern Low Countries* (Princeton, 1980).

Hale, J. R. *Artists and Warfare in Renaissance Europe* (New Haven, 1990).
War and Society in Renaissance Europe, 1450–1620 (New York, 1985).

Harding, Robert R. *Anatomy of a Power Elite: The Provincial Governors of Early Modern France* (New Haven, 1978).

Hardy, E. *Origines de la tactique française (de Louis XI à Henri IV)* (Paris, 1881).

Hauser, Henri. *Les sources de l'histoire de France* (4 vols., Paris, 1906–15).

Heller, Henry. *Iron and Blood: Civil Wars in Sixteenth-Century France* (Montreal, 1991).

Bibliography

Holt, Mack P. *The Duke of Anjou and the Politique Struggle During the Wars of Religion* (Cambridge, 1986).

The French Wars of Religion (Cambridge, 1995).

ed. *Society and Institutions in Early Modern France. Essays presented to J. Russell Major* (Athens, 1991).

Howard, Michael. *War in European History* (Oxford, 1976).

Jablonski, L. *L'armée française à travers les âges* (5 vols., 1890–94).

Jacquart, Jean. *La crise rurale en Ile-de-France, 1550–1670* (Paris, 1974).

Jensen, De Lamar. *Diplomacy and Dogmatism: Bernardino de Mendoza and the French Catholic League* (Cambridge, Mass., 1964).

Kaiser, David. *Politics and War. European Conflict from Philip II to Hitler* (Harvard, 1990).

Keegan, John. *The Face of Battle* (New York, 1976).

A History of Warfare (New York, 1993).

Kennedy, Paul. *The Rise and Fall of the Great Powers. Economic Change and Military Conflict from 1500 to 2000* (New York, 1987).

Kierstead, Raymond F. *Pomponne de Bellièvre* (Evanston, 1968).

Kingdon, Robert M. *Geneva and the Coming of the Wars of Religion in France, 1555–63* (Geneva, 1956).

Geneva and the Consolidation of the French Protestant Movement 1564–72 (Geneva, 1967).

Labatut, Jean-Pierre. *Les ducs et pairs de France au XVIIe siècle* (Paris, 1972).

La Brosse, Jules de. *Histoire d'un capitaine bourbonnais au XVIe siècle: Jacques de la Brosse (1485–1562)* (Paris, 1929).

Lacombe, Bernard de. *Les débuts des guerres de religion (Orleans, 1559–64): Catherine de Médici entre Guise et Condé* (Paris, 1899).

Ladurie, E. Le Roy. *Le carnaval en Romans* (Paris, 1979).

Les paysans de Languedoc (2 vols., Paris, 1966).

La Roncière, Charles Bourel de. *Histoire de la marine français* (4 vols., Paris, 1904–32).

Lehr, Henri. *La Rèforme et les Eglises Réformées dans le département actuel d'Eure-et-Loir (1523–1911)* (Chartres, 1912).

Livet, Georges. *Les guerres de religion* (Paris, 1962).

Lloyd, Howell. *The Rouen Campaign, 1590–92. Politics, Warfare, and the Early Modern State* (Oxford, 1973).

Lot, Ferdinand. *Recherches sur les effectifs des armées françaises des Guerres d'Italie aux Guerres de Religion, 1494–1562* (Paris, 1962).

Lynn, John A., ed. *Feeding Wars. Logistics in Western Warfare from the Middle Ages to the Present* (Boulder, 1993).

Tools of War. Instruments, Ideas, and Institutions of Warfare, 1445–1871 (Urbana, 1990).

Major, J. Russell. *From Renaissance Monarchy to Absolute Monarchy: French Kings, Nobles and States* (Baltimore, 1994).

Mallet, M. E. and J. R. Hale. *The Military Organization of a Renaissance State: Venice, c. 1400 to 1617* (New Haven, 1984).

Mandrou, Robert. *Introduction à la France moderne: essai de psychologie historique, 1500–1640* (Paris, 1961).

Marchand, Charles. *Charles Ier de Cossé, Comte de Brissac et maréchal de France (1507–63)* (Paris, 1889).

Le maréchal François de Scepeaux de Vieilleville et ses mémoires (Paris, 1893).

Bibliography

Mariéjol, J.-H. *Charles-Emmanuel de Savoye duc de Nemours* (Paris, n.d.).

Marlet, Léon. *Le Comte de Montgomery* (Paris, 1890).

Massé, H. J. L. J. *The City of Chartres* (London, 1900).

McNeill, William H. *The Pursuit of Power. Technology, Armed Force, and Society, since A.D. 1000* (Chicago, 1982).

Michaud, Helène. *La Grande Chancellerie et les écritures royales au seizième siècle (1515–89)* (Paris, 1967).

Monmarché, Georges. *Chartres* (Paris, 1949).

Naef, Henri. *La conjuration d'Amboise et Genève* (Geneva, 1922).

Navereau, A. *Le logement et les ustensiles des gens de guerre de 1439 à 1789* (Poitiers, 1924).

Nef, John U. *War and Human Progress* (New York, 1950).

Neuschel, Kristen B. *Word of Honor. Interpreting Noble Culture in Sixteenth Century France* (Cornell, 1989).

Oman, Sir Charles. *A History of the Art of War in the Sixteenth Century.* Reprint of 1937 ed. (New York, 1979).

Orléans, Henri d', Duc d'Aumale. *Histoire des Princes de Condé pendant les XVIe et XVIIe siècles* (7 vols., Paris, 1863–96).

Pallasse, Maurice. *La sénéchaussée et siège présidial de Lyon pendant les Guerres de Religion* (Lyon, 1943).

Palm, Franklin C. *Politics and Religion in Sixteenth-Century France: A Study of the Career of Henry of Montmorency-Damville, Uncrowned King of the South* (Gloucester, Mass., 1927).

Parker, Geoffrey. *The Army of Flanders and the Spanish Road, 1567–1659* (Cambridge, 1972).
   The Military Revolution. Military Innovation and the Rise of the West, 1500–1800 (Cambridge, 1988).

Pepper, Simon, and Nicholas Adams. *Firearms and Fortifications. Military Architecture and Siege Warfare in Sixteenth Century Siena* (Chicago, 1986).

Pernot, Michel. *Les guerres de religion en France, 1559–98* (Paris, 1987).

Picot, Emile. *Les Français italianisants au seizième siècle* (Paris, 1906).
   Les Italiens en France au seizième siècle (Bordeaux, 1902).

Pingaud, L. *Les Saulx-Tavannes* (Paris, 1876).

Pontbriant, A. de. *Le capitaine Merle* (Paris, 1886).

Potter, David. *War and Government in the French Provinces. Picardy, 1470–1560* (Cambridge, 1993).

Redlich, F. *De Praeda Militari. Looting and Booty, 1500–1815* (Wiesbaden, 1956).
   The German Military Enterpriser and His Work Force (2 vols., Wiesbaden, 1964).

Roberts, Michael. *The Military Revolution, 1560–1660* (Belfast, 1956).

Rocquain, Felix. *La France et Rome pendant les guerres de religion* (Paris, 1924).

Roelker, Nancy L. *Queen of Navarre. Jeanne d'Albret. (1528–72)* (Cambridge, 1968).

Rogers, Clifford J. *The Military Revolution. Readings on the Military Transformation of Early Modern Europe* (Boulder, 1995).

Romier, Lucien. *Catholiques et Huguenots à la cour de Charles de IX...(1560–62)* (Paris, 1924).
   Les origines politiques des guerres de religion (2 vols., Paris, 1913).
   Le Royaume de Catherine de Médicis; la France à la veille des guerres de religion (2 vols., Paris, 1925).

Rott, Edouard. *Histoire de la réprésentation diplomatique de la France auprès des cantons suisses,*

Bibliography

de leurs alliés et de leurs confédérés (2 vols., Berne, 1900–2).

Roziers, Marcel Burin des. *Les capitulations militaires entre la Suisse et la France* (Paris, 1902).

Ruble, Alphonse, Baron de. *Antoine de Bourbon et Jeanne d'Albret* (4 vols. Paris, 1881–86).

Jeanne d'Albret et la guerre civile (Paris, 1897).

Salmon, J. H. M. *The French Religious Wars in English Political Thought* (Oxford, 1959).

Society in Crisis: France in the Sixteenth Century (New York, 1975).

Schalk, Ellery. *From Valor to Pedigree* (Princeton, 1986).

Segesser, A. Ph. v. *Ludwig Pfyffer und Seine Zeit. Die Schweizer in den drei ersten französichen Religionskrieges* (2 vols., Bern, 1880–81).

Soman, Alfred, ed. *The Massacre of St. Bartholomew: Reappraisals and Documents* (The Hague, 1974).

Susane, Louis-Auguste. *Histoire de l'artillerie français* (Paris, 1874).

Histoire de la cavalerie françoise (3 vols., Paris, 1874).

Histoire de l'infanterie française (5 vols., Paris, 1876).

Sutherland, N. M. *The French Secretaries of State in the Age of Catherine de Medici* (London, 1962).

The Huguenot Struggle for Recognition (New Haven, 1980).

The Massacre of St. Batholomew and the European Conflict, 1559–72 (London, 1973).

Tilly, C., ed. *The Formation of National States in Europe* (Princeton, 1975).

Thompson, I. A. A. *War and Government in Hapsburg Spain, 1560–1620* (London, 1976).

Thompson, James Westfall. *The Wars of Religion in France, 1559–76* (New York, 1909).

Vaissière, Pierre de. *Le baron des Adrets* (Paris, 1930).

Viard, Paul, and Roger Galmiche, *Etudes sur la Réforme et les guerres de religion en Bourgogne* 15, *Revue bourguignonnne* 15 (Dijon, 1905).

Vindry, Fleury. *Dictionnaire de l'état-major français au XVIe siècle* (1 vol. plus *Atlas*, Paris, 1901).

Weigley, Russell F. *The Age of Battles. The Quest for Decisive Warfare from Breitenfeld to Waterloo* (Bloomington, 1991).

Winter, J. M. *War and Economic Development* (Cambridge, 1975).

Wolfe, Martin. *The Fiscal System of Renaissance France* (New Haven, 1972).

Wood, James B. *The Nobility of the Election of Bayeux, 1463–1666. Continuity Through Change* (Princeton, 1980).

Yardeni, Myriam. *La conscience nationale en France pendant les guerres de religion (1559–98)* (Paris, 1971).

Zupko, Ronald E. *French Weights and Measures Before the Revolution* (Bloomington, 1978).

SECONDARY SOURCES: ARTICLES

Babelon, Jean-Pierre. "Le palais de l'arsenal à Paris." *Bulletin Monumental*, 128 (1970), 267–310.

Benedict, Philip. "The Saint Bartholomew's Massacres in the Provinces." *The Historical Journal*, 21 (1978), 205–25.

Berenger, J. "Les armées françaises et les guerres de religion." *Revue internationale d'histoire militaire*, no. 55 (1983), 11–28.

Bonnerot, Jean. "Esquisse de la vie des routes au XVIe siècle." *Revue des questions historiques*, 65 (July, 1931), 5–88.

Cederlof, Olle. "The Battle Painting as a Historical Source." *Revue internationale d'histoire militaire*, 26 (1967), 119–44.

Clouas, Ivan. "Les aliénations du temporel ecclésiastique sous Charles IX et Henri III, 1563–87." *Revue d'histoire de l'Eglise de France*, 44 (1958), 5–56.

Contamine, Philippe. "L'Artillerie royale française à la veille des guerres d'Italie." *Annales de Bretagne*, 76, no. 2 (June, 1964), 221–61.

"Les industries de guerre dans la France de la Renaissance: L'exemple de l'artillerie." *Revue historique*, 172 (1984), 249–80.

Corvisier, André. "Le mort de soldat, depuis la fin du moyen âge." *Revue historique*, 254 (1975), 3–30.

Genet, A. "Relation du siège de la Rochelle par le duc d'Anjou, en 1573." *Le Spectateur Militaire*, 44 (Feb., 1848), 513–49, (March, 1848), 697–735, and 45 (July, 1848), 403–28, (August, 1848), 510–32.

Hale, J. R. "A Humanistic Visual Aid. The Military Diagram in the Renaissance." *Renaissance Studies*, 2, no. 2 (1988), 280–98.

"The Early Development of the Bastion: an Italian Chronology, c. 1450–c. 1534." J. R. Hale, J. R. L. Highfield, and B. Smalley, eds. *Europe in the Later Middle Ages* (London, 1965), 466–94.

Iung, J.-E. "Le poids des guerres de religion en basse Auvergne, la nourriture des troupes royales de 1567–88." *Mélanges Pierre Fournier* (Clermont-Ferrand, 1985), 83–111.

"L'organisation du service des vivres aux armées de 1550 à 1650." *Bibliothèque de l'Ecole des Chartres* (1983), 269–306.

Kelly, Donald R. "Martyrs, Myths, and the Massacre: The Background of St. Bartholomew." *American Historical Review*, 77 (1972), 1339–40.

Kiernan, V. G. "Foreign Mercenaries and Absolute Monarchy." Trevor Aston, ed. *Crisis in Europe, 1560–1660* (London, 1965), 117–40.

Knecht, Robert J. "Military Autobiographies in Sixteenth-Century France." J. R. Mulryne and Margaret Shewring, eds. *War, Literature and the Arts in Sixteenth Century Europe* (New York, 1989), 3–21.

Koenigsberger, H. G. "The Organization of Revolutionary Parties in France and the Netherlands during the Sixteenth Century." *Journal of Modern History*, 27 (1955), 335–51.

La Barre-Duparcq, E. de. "L'art militaire pendant les guerres de religion, 1562–98." *Séances et travaux de l'academie des sciences morales et politiques* (1863, pt. 2), 275–315, (1864, pt. 1), 247–70, (pt. 2), 89–110, 263–83.

La Ferrière, Comte Hector de. "La seconde guerre civile." *La revue des questions historiques*, 37 (1895), 116–67.

Lecestre, Paul. "Notice sur l'arsenal royal de Paris jusqu'à la mort de Henri IV." *Société de l'histoire de Paris et l'Ile-de-France*, 42 (1915), 185–281, and 43 (1916), 1–82.

Livet, Georges. "La route royale et la civilization française de la fin du XVe au milieu du XVIIIe siècle." Guy Michaud, ed. *Les Routes de France depuis les origines jusqu'à nos jours* (Paris, 1961), 57–100.

Lombard-Jourdan, Anne. "La bataille de Saint-Denis (10 Novembre, 1567). Tradition, propaganda, et iconographie." *Paris et Ile-de-France*, 28 (1978), 7–54.

Lynn, John A. "How War Fed War: The Tax of Violence and Contributions during the Grand Siècle." *The Journal of Modern History*, 65 (June, 1993), 286–310.

Bibliography

"Tactical Evolution in the French Army, 1560–1660." *French Historical Studies*, 14 (1985), 176–91.

"The *trace italienne* and the Growth of Armies: The French Case." *The Journal of Military History*, 55, no. 3 (1991), 297–330.

Major, J. Russell. "Noble Income, Inflation, and the Wars of Religion in France." *The American Historical Review*, 86 (1981), 21–48.

Michaud, C. "Finances et guerres de religion en France." *Revue d'histoire moderne et contemporaire*, 28 (1981), 572–96.

Michaud, Helène. "Les institutions militaires des guerres d'Italie aux guerres de religion." *Revue historique*, 258, no. 1 (1977), 29–43.

Oman, Sir Charles. "Early Military Pictures." *The Archaeological Journal*, 45 (1939), 337–55.

Pablo, Jean de. "Contribution à l'étude de l'histoire des institutions militaires huguenotes, ii, L'armée huguenote entre 1562 et 1573." *Archiv für Reformationsgeschichte*, 48, no. 2 (1957), 192–216.

"La bataille de la Roche-l'Abeille." *Bulletin de la Société de l'histoire du Protestantisme français*, 101 (January–March, 1955), 1–25.

"La troisième guerre de religion." *Bulletin de la Société de l'histoire du Protestantisme français*, 102 (January–March 1956), 57–91.

Potter, David. "The Duc de Guise and the Fall of Calais, 1557–58." *The English Historical Review*, 388 (July, 1983), 481–512.

Radonant, R. "L'Éloquence militaire au XVIe siècle." *Revue d'histoire littéraire de la France*, 18 (1911), 503–52.

Ruble, Alphonse de. "François de Montmorency, Gouverneur de Paris et de l'Ile-de-France." *Mémoires de la société de l'histoire de Paris*, 6 (1879), 200–89.

Salmon, J. H. M. "Peasant Revolt in Vivarais, 1575–80." *French Historical Studies*, 11 (1979), 1–28.

Stewart, David. "Sickness and Mortality Rates of the English Army in the Sixteenth Century." *Journal of the Royal Army Medical Corps*, 41 (1948), 23–35.

Tholin, G. "La ville d'Agen pendant les guerres de religion du XVIe siècle." *Revue de l'Agenais*, 14 (1887), 97–113, 201–17, 430–50, 489–515, 15 (1888), 193–218, 322–48, 409–34, 16 (1889), 27–43, 197–222, 385–98, 17 (1890), 97–120, 281–301, 488–510, 18 (1891), 57–70, 225–41, 19 (1892), 22–39, 118–33, 20 (1893), 52–67, 177–200.

Van Doren, Llewain Scott. "Civil War Taxation and the Foundations of Fiscal Absolutism: The Royal Taille in Dauphine, 1560–1610." *Proceedings of the Western Society for French History*, 3 (1975), 35–53.

"War Taxation, Institutional Change, and Social Conflict in Provincial France – The Royal Taille in Dauphine, 1494–1559." *Proceedings of the American Philosophical Society*, 121 (1977), 70–96.

Vogler, Bernard. "Le rôle des Electeurs palatins dans les guerres de religion en France (1559–92)." *Cahiers d'histoire*, 10 (1965), 51–85.

Wood, James B. "The Impact of the Wars of Religion: A View of France in 1581." *Sixteenth Century Journal*, 15, no. 2 (1984), 131–68.

"The Royal Army During the Early Wars of Religion, 1559–76." Mack P. Holt, ed. *Society and Institutions in Early Modern France. Essays Presented to J. Russell Major* (Athens, 1991), 1–35.

Index

CAMBRIDGE STUDIES IN EARLY MODERN HISTORY

From Madrid to Purgatory: The Art and Craft of Dying in Sixteenth-Century Spain
CARLOS M. N. EIRE
The Reformation and Rural Society: The Parishes of Brandenburg-Ansbach-Kulmbach, 1528–1603
C. SCOTT DIXON
Labour, Science and Technology in France, 1500–1620
HENRY HELLER
The King's Army: Warfare, Soldiers, and Society during the Wars of Religion in France, 1562–1576
JAMES B. WOOD

Titles available in paperback marked with an asterisk*

The following titles are now out of print:
French Finances, 1770–1795: From Business to Bureaucracy
J. F. BOSHER
Chronicle into History: An Essay in the Interpretation of History in Florentine Fourteenth-Century Chronicles
LOUIS GREEN
France and the Estates General of 1614
J. MICHAEL HAYDEN
Reform and Revolution in Mainz, 1743–1803
T. C. W. BLANNING
Altopascio: A Study in Tuscan Society 1587–1784
FRANK MCARDLE
Gunpowder and Galleys: Changing Technology and Mediterranean Warfare at Sea in the Sixteenth Century
JOHN FRANCIS GUILMARTIN JR
The State, War and Peace: Spanish Political Thought in the Renaissance 1516–1559
J. A. FERNÁNDEZ-SANTAMARIA
Calvinist Preaching and Iconoclasm in the Netherlands, 1544–1569
PHYLLIS MACK CREW
The Kingdom of Valencia in the Seventeenth Century
JAMES CASEY
Filippo Strozzi and the Medici: Favor and Finance in Sixteenth-Century Florence and Rome
MELISSA MERIAM BULLARD
Rouen during the Wars of Religion
PHILIP BENEDICT
The Emperor and his Chancellor: A Study of the Imperial Chancellery under Gattinara
JOHN M. HEADLEY
The Military Organisation of a Renaissance State: Venice c. 1400–1617
M. E. MALLETT AND J. R. HALE
Neostoicism and the Early Modern State
GERHARD OESTREICH

349